BETWEEN EDEN AND ARMAGEDDON

BETWEEN EDEN AND ARMAGEDDON

The Future of World Religions, Violence, and Peacemaking

MARC GOPIN

OXFORD
UNIVERSITY PRESS

OXFORD
UNIVERSITY PRESS

Oxford   New York
Auckland   Bangkok   Buenos Aires   Cape Town   Chennai
Dar es Salaam   Delhi   Hong Kong   Istanbul   Karachi   Kolkata
Kuala Lumpur   Madrid   Melbourne   Mexico City   Mumbai   Nairobi
São Paulo   Shanghai   Singapore   Taipei   Tokyo   Toronto

Copyright © 2000 by Marc Gopin

First published in 2000 by Oxford University Press, Inc.
198 Madison Avenue, New York, New York 10016

First issued as an Oxford University Press paperback, 2002

www.oup.com

Oxford is a registered trademark of Oxford University Press, Inc.

Library of Congress Cataloging-in-Publication Data
Gopin, Marc.
    Between Eden and Armageddon : the future of world religions,
violence, and peacemaking / Marc Gopin.
        p.   cm.
    Includes bibliographical references and index.
    ISBN 0–19–513432-X; 0-19-515725-7 (pbk.)
        1. Violence—Religious aspects—Christianity.   2. Conflict
management—Religious aspects—Christianity.   I. Title.
BL65.V55G67   2000
291.1'7873—dc21   99–37478

9 8 7 6 5 4 3 2 1

Printed in the United States of America
on acid-free paper

Acknowledgments

An earlier, smaller version of chapter 2 was published as "Religion, Violence and Conflict Resolution," *Peace and Change* 22, no. 1 (Jan. 1997), and as "Religion, Violence and Conflict Resolution," Issue Paper No. 1, *Institute for Conflict Analysis and Resolution* (Oct. 1998).

An earlier, smaller version of chapter 5 was published as "An Orthodox Embrace of Gentiles? Interfaith Tolerance in the Thought of S. D. Luzzatto and Rabbi E. Benamozegh," *Modern Judaism* 18 (Spring 1998).

An earlier, smaller version of chapter 6 was published in Hebrew as "Confronting the Secular/Religious Conflict in Israel: Suggested Solutions," in *Religious Secular Relations in Israel: Social and Political Implications*, ed. Ephraim Ya'ar and Tamar Herman (Tel Aviv: Steinmetz Center for Peace Research, Tel Aviv University, and the Konrad Adenauer Foundation, 1998).

An earlier, smaller version of chapter 7 will be published in *From the Ground Up: Mennonite Contributions to International Peacebuilding*, ed. Cynthia Sampson and John Paul Lederach (New York: Oxford University Press, forthcoming). The research for the latter book was supported in part by the U.S. Institute of Peace.

I would like to gratefully acknowledge the support that I received from Nancy Robson, whose faith in my work allowed me the time to do the research and activism upon which this book is based. I would also like to especially acknowledge the faith in me and support of my work that has been exhibited by Joseph Montville, one of the pioneers of the field of conflict resolution, who I am privileged to call a friend and a mentor.

The following colleagues have provided crucial support and valuable teaching to me on this journey: Mohammed Abu-Nimer, Scott Appleby, Kevin Avruch, Aviva Bock, Robert Eisen, Gordon Fellman, Wayne Froman, Ray Gingrich, Gershon Greenberg, Bryan Hamlin, Ron Kraybill, Louis Kriesberg, John Paul Lederach, Julia Lieblich, David Little, Marc Ross, Jay Rothman, Richard Rubenstein, Cynthia Sampson, Michael Sells, Laurence Simon, and Barbra Wien.

I want to acknowledge the vital role that the following student/friends and assistants have played in supporting me: Larissa Fast, Dena Hawes, Lynn Kunkle, Erin Mcandles, Patrick McNamara, Heidi Paulson, and Sarah Rosenberg.

My deepest gratitude to Rissa Leigh, my sister, and Jack Lewis for encouraging my path as a writer throughout many years.

My wife, Robyn, has taken this journey with me, with all its hazards and risks. She has exhibited enormous patience, provided strong encouragement, and displayed a willingness to sacrifice a secure life for the work that is the subject of this book. Together with my daughter, Ruthy, we formed a bond that allowed this book to be created. "Two are better than one. . . . For should they fall, one can raise the other, but woe to him who is alone and falls with no companion to raise him. . . . And a three-fold chord is not easily broken" (Eccles. 4:9d–12). "You have captured my heart, my sister, my bride, you have captured my heart" (Song of Songs 4:9).

I dedicate this book to my parents, Sidney Jack Gopin, of blessed memory, and Pauline Gopin. Despite the difficult path that I have chosen for my life, they have supported me and respected me and my dreams since I was a small boy. I only hope that I have honored them and aided them a small amount in return. They have come, not unscathed, through the arduous odyssey of the children of Jewish immigrants in a century that has left permanent scars on the Jewish family. I dedicate this book to the healing of all the suffering and all the conflict and anger that they and their parents—and millions of others like them around the world in many civilizations—have had to endure in this century and in this millennium.

Call to Me, and I will answer you, and I will tell you about extraordinary things, secrets that you have not known. For thus says the Eternal Being, the God of Israel, concerning the houses in the city and the palaces of the kings of Judah that were torn down. . . . I am going to bring her relief and healing. I will heal them, and I will reveal to them an abundance of peace and truth. (Jer. 33:3–6)

Brookline, Massachusetts   M. G.
October 1999

Contents

IV Conclusion

I

Introduction

ONE

Alternative Global Futures in the Balance

An unprecedented level of paradoxical religious movement characterizes the contemporary era. On the one hand, there are a greater number of people than ever before who are expressing either secular perspectives on life or views of their own religions that are completely independent of traditional religious authority, dogma and law. There is more and more experimentation in some quarters on the basic meaning systems of traditional religion. This is due both to the unprecedented level of involvement of women in public religious life and to the interesting interaction of the liberal state and free religious inquiry and experimentation. Furthermore, the unprecedented mixture of people of all faiths in many parts of the globe, especially in large cosmopolitan centers, has also given birth to great creativity in religious life.

At the same time, we are witnessing an unparalleled invigoration of extreme enthusiasm for old patterns of belief and practice on the part of many others. Whereas the former depends on the liberal state, the latter is often expressed in active opposition to state authorities, secular authorities, and the basic institutions of global secular culture.

This has set many religious people on a collision course with the rest of society and, in some cases, is creating serious levels of destructive conflict and violence. On the other hand, this religious revivalism is shaking up complacent cultural institutions of the modern state, and it is forcing most people to rethink their moral and political assumptions as citizens of their state, as well as citizens of a global society.

This extraordinary level of religious activity takes place in the post–Cold War era, which is also characterized by two countervailing trends. One trend is unprecedented economic integration and cultural homogenization, especially at the hands of the materialist culture associated with the Western forms of investment, media, advertising and entertainment. But the other trend is unprecedented cultural/religious fractionalization. People the world over are rebelling against this materialist homogenization, searching out the roots of their identities, exploring the uniqueness of their backgrounds and their original systems of meaning.

The pattern of intense integration is also felt in the liberal religious sphere in terms of multifaith communication and cooperation that has never seen its equal in human history. This, too, is transforming modern life and creating a common global culture. Thus, while the fractionating character of religious revivalism is more noticeable, and sometimes more violent, there is a quiet revolution of integration taking place as well.

It is not an age of a new world order but an age of great social, cultural, and psychological uncertainty in the context of an overwhelming and almost overpowering economic integration of the world. It is in eras of great uncertainty that we see some human beings gravitating toward traditional religious systems in search of stability and identity. But how this search is undertaken, and how it integrates or dis-integrates with the world at large, depends very much on the socioeconomic, psychological, and political situation of the individual and the individual group.

The most important implication of this is that we see very different possible futures emerging from the human interaction with traditional religion at this point in time. There are patterns at work that indicate that religion is one of the most salient phenomena that will cause massive violence in the next century. But there are other indicators from our current experience that suggest that religion will play a critical role in constructing a global community of shared moral commitments and vision. Religion's visionary capacity and its inculcation of altruistic values has already given birth to extraordinary leaders, such as Gandhi, King, the Dalai Lama, and Bishop Tutu, who, in turn, have had dramatic effects, pushing the global community toward ever-greater commitments to human rights and compassion for nonhuman and human life, regardless of race or citizenship.[1] Religion has helped set the stage for a fully functioning global moral community, which may take a long time to fully materialize but which is unquestionably closer to fruition than a century ago. There have always been exclusive religious visions of a peaceful world. Never before in history, however, have so many leaders and adherents been inspired to work for a truly inclusive vision that is multicultural and multireligious.

The contraindications to this trend are painfully apparent in the murders, the tortures, and the religious financial support for brutal regimes, all of which have been abundant in recent history. At the same time, there is an unmistakable level of global commitment to shared values that is being upheld and defended every day by literally hundreds of government and nongovernment agencies that adhere to the international agreements of the United Nations. There is no doubt that, difficult as it is to imagine, the brutal abuses in places such as Bosnia, Kosovo, Tibet, and Burma would be even worse if it were not for this global consensus. Admittedly, this consensus still lacks the teeth of enforcement, and we stand deeply frustrated at the tragic failures. But from the long view of history, there is a remarkable shift toward moral consensus. Religious leaders, visionaries, and activists have played no small role in this, especially since World War II.

As with all scientific predictions in the postmodern era, we now have to acknowledge that what we say and do—and how we decide to respond to these trends—are fundamental parts of the formation of the future. By virtue of our reactions to the patterns of the present, we steer the future in one direction or another. If, for example, we as a culture act as if religious violence will simply disappear on its own, perhaps believing that good jobs will solve all social unrest, then the future of religion will be set on one course. If, however, we see the problem of religion and conflict in all its complexity, as something that is a permanent fixture of modern life until it is addressed in a new way, then it is likely that religious history will move in another direction. How we see reality determines the future of that reality.

It is the argument of this book that religions have always interacted in highly dynamic and complex ways with the world around them. If, then, the traditional forms of analysis of religions and of social conflict insist that religions must continue to do violence to democratic culture and to the pursuit of a peaceful, civil society, then that is what the scholars will find and what some theologians will create. If, however, the world of thoughtful people is open to the infinite hermeneutic variability of religious traditions, one may discover, in the most surprising places of the religious world, the basis for a future that allows for coexistence between religious and secular people globally and even for a shared vision of civil society.[2]

Another way to look at the alternative futures is to look at these two coun-tervailing trends as expressions of two human needs.[3] One is the human need for integration. This need to merge with the larger world has always motivated human beings to search out new parts of the world around them, to meet new people, and to look for the underlying causes and origins of things, which give an overarching unity to existence. Certainly, numerous religious mythologies, as well as scientific enterprises, typify this human need. Both mystical and scientific drives to account for or merge in one's mind with the whole universe are typical of this need. The mystic meditates on the ends of the universe, while the physicist works hard on subatomic formulas that should in principle apply to the ends of the galaxy as much as they apply to her own backyard.

On the other hand, there is a clear human need for uniqueness, for being different from others. This expresses itself through the infinite ways in which human beings make themselves different, from dress and habits to various formal expressions of allegiance to small, special groups. The latter, paradoxically, often involves a complete submergence of the individual character into the larger whole of the subgroup. But the price for many of us is worth it because joining a group—even one in which we must submerge our individuality—fulfills our need for some distinctive identity and meaning system in the context of the mass of humanity and the indifferent character of the universe. The enormous universe that captivates the mind and heart of the mystic and the physicist is also so overwhelming in its physical and chronological magnitude as to make individu-ated human life feel meaningless. Unless human beings discover a meaning system that makes them unique and important, they feel the weight of an indifferent universe that has no interest in their past, present, or future, in neither their lives nor their deaths.

What happens often, and what is the central problem of religious militancy and violence (and, I would argue, many other forms of cultural and political totalitarianism), is the confusion or melding of these two human needs. Instead of developing a psychological and moral self capable of dealing with these two needs—the need for integration and the need for uniqueness—and balancing them with the help of one's will, many people are tempted to do something much more violent. They create or submit to structures that give their own subgroup a strong sense of uniqueness and then couple that with the need for integration with the world. But they do not integrate by visiting the world nonviolently but rather by trying to make it in their own image, by consuming all of it, or by developing fantasies of doing this. This becomes an insatiable drive to conquer in the hands of many ideological systems, including religious systems.

There are many unmet human needs that are active elements in causing religious conflict, including basic issues of material resources, issues of psychological trauma, issues of humiliation and shame, and issues of empowerment, to name a few; we will address these varied needs and their complex interactions. But the need to integrate warring with the need to be unique seems to be among the most fundamental causes of conflict at the level of basic identity.[4] Furthermore, it seems to be the case that those religious people who discover a balance between the two needs, the need for integration or merging and the need for distinctive identity, are the ones who negotiate their religiosity in the most peaceful ways.

To have a clear sense of one's uniqueness and to combine that with a willingness to explore and visit other worlds of meaning, without destroying them, are central ingredients in religiosity that is oriented to peacemaking and conflict resolution. In a lecture that I delivered in Belfast, I introduced to the combined Catholic and Protestant audience the biblical idea of *ger*, the stranger, who is different than the majority group addressed by biblical law but who is also a person who must be included at Jewish celebrations, cared for, and even loved. He is the quintessential outsider, who is also a litmus test of the ethical conduct of the majority group.[5] In fact, it is the loving care of strangers that is stated by the Bible as the essential lesson of Jewish enslavement in Egypt. The Exodus and its accompanying freedom are meant to give the Jewish people the opportunity to treat outsiders in a fundamentally new way than they were treated in other societies. Furthermore, and equally important, the religious law is meant to counteract the natural tendency of an abused group to pass that abuse onto others.

In a move of exquisitely brilliant irony, this special care for the outsider is supposed to take place every time that the religious group gathers for its most special and unique times of identity, the holiday cycle. Thus, the need for distinctive identity and for celebration in one's own land must not overshadow the requirement of respecting the boundaries of others—and the others' need for those boundaries in order to maintain their own identities. The *ger* is a part of one's moral universe but is not consumed by one's universe. The *ger* is included but not overwhelmed, loved but not consumed. Thus, there is integration and uniqueness, sameness and difference, which coexist in a creative set of moral and ritual practices and obligations.

I was amazed that this Belfast crowd was so receptive to this model of interreligious interaction, many of them expressing profound gratitude to me. My prejudices, based on my own history of injuries, had led me to expect that a Christian audience would not accept what I presented: a *ger* theology that celebrates particularity and boundaries. I was expressing a not-so-subtle critique of universalist religious systems that assume everyone must be under one banner. It would seem, however, that both groups in Belfast feel vulnerable and excluded and, at the same time, keen to maintain the borders of their own identities. Yet, as Christians, they cannot help but long for integration and love among all human beings, especially fellow brothers and sisters in Christ; they know this is missing from the Irish context, and it causes pain and shame. The *ger* law and metaphor gave them a profound but simple way to embrace the deepest prosocial values of Christianity, most notably love, or *agape*, without this devolving into a destruction of each group's unique identity.

The *ger* concept moves well beyond a legal category of obligation to become a metaphor of the human condition. It reifies the human situation of simultaneous sameness and difference, of the need for integration, love, and acceptance coupled with the need to have boundaries of the separated self or group.

This is a central theme of this book, and I will return to it often as a possible solution to seemingly intractable religious militancy. It also may help us address some fundamental questions of human community in the modern world and how we can negotiate integration, disintegration, and the building of community despite our deep differences.

This book will explore the question of how we can understand the violent actions of people motivated by religious zeal and will also explore the ways in which world religions have contributed to peacemaking. It is the argument of this book that organized religions can, with the aid of certain interventions, become major assets in the construction of a global civilization that manages to limit conflict to its nonviolent, constructive variety.

There are a series of reasons why the relationships among religion, conflict, and peacemaking have been misunderstood until now. It is partly due to mistakes of students of religion and partly due to mistakes of students of human conflict. Mostly it is due to the unusually complicated set of influences on religious belief and practice, which makes predicting and understanding religious behavior difficult; this sends most analysts running for cover. Furthermore, there has been a natural tendency for religiously motivated actors to distrust theoreticians and practitioners of conflict resolution, and vice versa.

But we cannot run away from this problem, because it is plainly apparent that the standard mechanisms of conflict management that have been developed by global civic institutions, as well as those of the modern state, are failing to address adequately the needs and problems of religious militants. Until they do, we face the possibility of a large section of humanity becoming increasingly alienated from the entire experiment with the modern state, as well as from the modern international system of cooperation on the civic issues of health, human rights, social justice, and basic freedoms.

Chapter 2 outlines the need for and the parameters of a new field of study—religion and peacemaking—and examines the challenges and complexity of mastering so large a phenomenon.

The second part of this book examines what has prevented the students of conflict from understanding religious conflict and why religious studies scholars have tended to overlook the prosocial elements of religion, which are critical to constructing conflict resolution and peacemaking ethics in each tradition. I also analyze two historical models of conservative religious philosophies, looking at how they could form the basis for peacemaking and what their limitations are. The conservative expression of most religious traditions presents the deepest challenge in terms of peace and conflict, and thus I direct my energies to exploring how one constructs conservative paradigms that are nevertheless committed to peacemaking on a deep level. In particular, the challenge is always to move beyond the righteous rhetoric of peace and to explore the prosocial basis and the antisocial problems of a religious paradigm, as these would interact with contemporary constructs of the liberal state or the global community.

The next section is dedicated to paradigms in the present of confronting deep social crises involving religious people and utilizing indigenous religions and cultures to heal those conflicts. At the same time, it is an investigation of how to integrate the best available techniques of analyzing and resolving conflicts with a deeper understanding and utilization of religious resources in the various world religions. This is a complicated task that involves an engagement with the field of conflict analysis as well as an in-depth look at religious systems of meaning and ethics. This section is mainly meant as a paradigm for further work in all the world's religious traditions and as a challenge to the various schools of conflict resolution to adjust their insights and practices to the world of religious human beings. It also involves a deliberate process of synthetic construction of religious institutions, myths, and values, specifically geared to the art of conflict resolution in the modern context.

Chapter 8, in particular, engages in a constructive analysis of Judaism, providing a paradigm of how one can honestly investigate the antisocial and prosocial elements of a tradition, or the conflict-resolving and conflict-generating elements of a tradition, and utilize this analysis to hermeneutically construct a conflict resolution philosophy and practice. The aim is to produce a practice of peacemaking that could appeal to even the most militant of religious revivalists in the present period.

This is by no means a final model of peacemaking but an evolving set of explorations, nor do I ever recommend applying these models blindly and haphazardly to the field. It is a paradigm of what we may be able to encourage and engender in future relations among and between religious and secular members of a given society or culture. I do not want to preempt or underestimate the importance of models of peacemaking being developed indigenously by the parties to a conflict. It is also meant to demonstrate at a basic level just how far policymakers, diplomats, and peace activists need to move from their present rigid paradigms of peacemaking. If they want to truly engage the world's religious people as authentic partners in constructing the future of civilization, they must fundamentally reconstruct their present interventions in conflicts.

This analysis is directed toward a wide range of actors, including policymakers, diplomats, conflict resolution theoreticians and activists, theologians concerned with building practical paradigms of ethics for their fellow believers, and scholars of religion who would like to analyze religious institutions through the prism of conflict theory. In particular, I focus on the fascinating confluence of religious meaning systems, rituals, laws and myths, which can only be understood in their relationship to peace and conflict through the prism of psychodyamic approaches to conflict. The relationship between personal and collective trauma, for example, and religious story, myth, and practice, is critical to understanding the compelling nature of religious violence but also to understanding the indigenous ways to heal those injuries and curtail that violence.

This brings me to the title of this book and the importance of violence to sacred stories. Eden and Armageddon are terms that emanate from Western religions, and, while Eastern religions receive a decent amount of attention, this book is heavily weighted toward Western religions. This is in part due to the stage of my research at the present time, but it is also due to the overwhelming sources of religious violence in world history that emanate out of Western religions or the Abrahamic monotheistic faiths.[6]

Eden refers to the Garden of Eden, the idyllic original place of birth of the human male and female as recorded in the beginning of Genesis. Mythically, Eden was a place of limitless vegetarian food, no toil, no suffering, no death, simple natural beauty, perfect weather, and no need for any clothing, as there was only one man and one woman. But there was one simple condition, namely, that the fruit of just one tree of the garden would not be consumed. The Eden story is about the tragedy of the human inability to accept limitations or boundaries and the need to consume everything.

As I said earlier, regarding the biblical concept of *ger*, a basic motif of this story involves the question of the need to merge with all and thus consume everything, versus the ability to make space for the Other in the world. There are many other themes that underlie this timeless myth, but it is clear that the inability to set boundaries, the failure to recognize a separate space for that which one cannot have, is a central theme. Eden is lost because of this inability, when the snake entices Eve, who entices Adam, to eat from the one forbidden tree. Then they are expelled.

While Eden is a mythical, supernatural place, it has always excited the religious dreams of devotees of the Bible, and it has stimulated the belief that Earth can be a more blessed place than it is currently. It is the protean place of mythic home and imagined homecoming. Thus, as we think of how religion can contribute to or thwart our attempts to make the earth and the global community of humankind better than it has been, especially in the twentieth century, I thought it appropriate to place Eden as one of the polar antipodes of the religious contribution to the future. This seemed especially apt because the ideal of Eden entails the ability to exult in an integrated environment of ultimate beauty, spiritual fulfillment and deep meaning for the individual. But it also expresses a perpetual warning against the excesses of the human need to merge with the whole, to consume everything, and thus to destroy the beauty that one has been given.

Armageddon refers to a place of final, cosmic battle between good and evil, between those who follow God and those who are less than human, "the beast," who will be utterly destroyed in the most horrible ways imaginable. It too is a place that is dreamt of with great imagination but imagination that is by definition sadistic. This is a vision of extreme violence, the roots of which are found in the New Testament book of Revelation, chapter 16. In addition, this is part of a much larger history of predictions of terrible cosmic battles that permeate Middle Eastern religious traditions, including the Day of the Lord predictions that are to be found in the Hebrew biblical prophets.[7] All of these apocalyptic visions utilize the human capacity to fantasize about the most horrific forms of retribution. All three monotheisms contain apocalyptic visions that generally involve violent destruction of those who are "enemies of the Lord" or "enemies of God's people" or "infidels," with parallel visions of the salvation of the few who are true to the one God, whichever name that God goes by.

There are some important versions of the apocalyptic myths that include an uncanny level of violence but also include critical references to the deep injuries of those who have suffered for God and the way in which this final act of violence is retribution for those injuries.[8] This is an important clue to why and when Western religions, in particular, turn to solutions of extreme violence to resolve the problems and tragedies of life. We will pay special attention to the collective injuries of religious people and to how religious institutions both offer comfort for those injuries and magnify their reality, perpetuating their damaging effects and fixing the hurts as permanent features of life. This is what makes processes of reconciliation so hard in religious cultures. The natural resistance to reconciliation by those who have experienced terrible injury, unrecoverable personal loss, and humiliation couples with religious rituals, which turn this reaction into a permanent fixture of the cosmos, the way the world must be until some great act of revenge is perpetrated.

As will be shown, world religions have a reservoir of prosocial values of profound subtlety and effectiveness that, if utilized well, could form the basis of an alternative to violence in coping with conflict or coping with devastating injury. But this will take a conscious effort on the part of peacemakers, theologians, and average people to engage the world of religious institutions with an eye to creating a nonviolent future. In particular, it will involve an effort to dismiss no group, give up on no subculture, as we attempt to build a peaceful future. That is not to say that one cannot condemn certain acts and achieve important consensus on delegitimizing various forms of destructive conflict. But it does mean that, in principle, we develop the courage and the skill to engage all religious communities in the belief that all communities are capable of prosocial practices and peaceful paths to future dreams. In particular, it will involve the ability to share space with secular communities and to envision a future of coexistence with them, even if a religious person's ultimate, private dreams include a hope that such communities find "the truth" of one particular religious vision.

There is an infinite set of possibilities associated with religious institutions and their behavior in terms of peace and violence. I never cease to be amazed by how the seemingly most violent religious institutions or texts in history give way over time to the most exalted values and moral practices. At the same time, the most pacifist foundations of a tradition can be turned toward the service of the most barbaric aims. It all seems to depend on the complex ways in which the psychological and sociological circumstances and the economic and cultural constructs of a particular group interact with the ceaseless human drive to hermeneutically develop religious meaning systems, texts, rituals, symbols, and laws.

This is a deeply dynamic process, no matter how rigid religious institutions may appear to the unskilled eye or to the unsympathetic or fearful critic. What we do, how we all address this vital issue in the coming years will directly affect the course of this great interpretive enterprise. We must find the way to engage this period of religious history with intelligence, with skill, with compassion, and with an eye to creating a more peaceful twenty-first century in which religion is integrally involved in creating the good global community.

To believe that we can create a perfect global community, given the serious divisions of religion and the exclusive claims to truth, is somewhat naive. But the evidence of history and the hermeneutics of religious traditions strongly indicate that we have, over time, done both better and worse at this task, and that, with the development of better skills and deeper understanding, we do have the capacity to move the world community in a far better direction, in terms of peace and conflict resolution for religious communities, than has been attempted until now.

Two points should be emphasized about the structure and thrust of this book before proceeding.

There is an overall argument that I make about world religions, violence, and peacemaking, but the case studies are not exhaustive, and they are heavily focused on Judaism and the Abrahamic faiths. Each religion is unique in terms of its approach to peace and conflict, and, as I will show, has multiple voices within the tradition as well. At the same time, there are lessons to be learned that cut across religions, both East and West. It is true, for example, that Judaism is heavily focused on worldly ethical concerns, whereas much of Buddhist discipline is geared toward the inner life and the attainment of nirvana. At the same time, elements of Judaism have always been distinctly otherworldly, and there are central aspects of Buddhism that are distinctly practical and political. No major religion that is thousands of years old, with millions of adherents, has not had broad experience with ethics, politics, and the psychology of war, peace, and interpersonal relations. Thus, all of them have lessons to both learn from and teach to each other. Therefore, although this volume's case studies have a certain emphasis, I hope that they will be instructive by way of contrast and comparison for numerous religious traditions, which we will investigate in other studies.

The second point is that my emphasis in this volume tends to be on the more conservative, strident—fundamentalist, if you will—expressions of modern religion. The reason for this is that these expressions generally have been the ones to evoke the most conflict and violence in the modern world. My recommendations for ways that these expressions of religion can be engaged more productively and ways in which civil society can proceed in better relationship with them in no way implies a disparagement of the liberal or modern expression of these same religions, the latter being far more ready to engage in peaceful coexistence with modern states and cultures. It is true, however, that I call upon liberal streams of secular and religious cultures to rethink the dichotomy between themselves and these religious enthusiasts. There is a need for both the interpreters of traditional religion and the interpreters and proponents of liberal secular or religious culture to confront the Othering and demonizing of their counterparts or adversaries. This has been painfully apparent, for example, in Jewish Israel as a major component of its culture wars and the corresponding or derivative lack of Jewish consensus on transforming the relationship with Palestinians. Thus, progressive and liberal wings of a society, sometimes especially the so-called peace camp, can be rather destructive in their indulging of their own sets of fears and hatreds. This only makes religiously sanctioned violence even more extreme.

There is a need to work on all sides to construct hermeneutics of religious traditions, as well as hermeneutics of modern culture and the modern state, that work together to prevent a descent into the kind of religious warfare that plagued the Middle Ages, the last time that religion came to dominate the lives and psychologies of millions of monotheists. There will also be a need to plumb the depths of human psychology in these matters of conflict and deep injury, to understand the nature and complexity of human conflict, and to apply this learning in new and constructive ways to religious adversaries and the conflicts in which they are engaged.

Between Religion and Conflict Resolution

Mapping a New Field of Study

Every major religion of the world has expressed at some point, through its leaders and thinkers, a commitment to the value of peace, both in classical texts and modern reformulations.[1] Furthermore, religious actors are playing an increasingly important and valuable role in resolving international conflicts. These include Mennonites, Quakers, and Catholics, who have successfully intervened in and mediated African, Asian, and Latin American conflicts, and key Buddhist leaders, such as Maha Gosananda from Cambodia, Thich Nhat Hanh from Vietnam.[2] But a faith-based commitment to peace is a complex phenomenon. While some believers creatively integrate their spiritual tradition and peacemaking, many others engage in some of the most destabilizing violence confronting the global community today. The purpose of this chapter is to outline what will be necessary for a new course of study of religion that will examine its relationship to conflict and conflict resolution methodologies.

Through our long human history, religion has been a major contributor to war, bloodshed, hatred, and intolerance. Yet religion has also developed laws and ideas that have provided civilization with cultural commitments to critical peace-related values, including empathy, an openness to and even love for strangers, the suppression of unbridled ego and acquisitiveness, human rights, unilateral gestures of forgiveness and humility, interpersonal repentance and the acceptance of responsibility for past errors as a means of reconciliation, and the drive for social justice.

There are two essential benefits to exploring a relationship between religion and conflict resolution theory. First, there is a vast reservoir of information in sacred texts on peacemaking and conflict and on prosocial and antisocial values that affect conflict. This literature contains a long history of individual struggles with the inner life, which have either led toward or away from a violent disposition. What has worked and failed to work in the past and why? What can these stories teach us about the relationship between violence and the religious person in a particular culture? The replicability of past methods of conflict resolution or methods of deterring a violent disposition should be of critical concern.

Second, religion plays the central role in the inner life and social behavior of millions of human beings, many of whom are currently actively engaged in violent struggle. Diplomats and conflict resolution experts could benefit from an in-depth understanding of the motives for either violence or coexistence. With this understanding, there might be more productive interaction between religious communities and conflict resolution strategies.

The Nature of Religious Decisionmaking Regarding Peace and Violence

It is certainly often the case that motives other than religion, such as the desperation of economically disenfranchised people, are central to conflict. However, religious language and symbolism are critical ways in which human beings interpret reality,[3] expressing the full range of emotions in religious terminology. It is essential to be schooled in how the myths, laws, or metaphysical assumptions express in the minds of believers their deepest feelings. This enables the negotiator to empathize with the forces on both sides of the conflict and to dynamically interact with the spiritual language of frustration and anger that leads to violence. Thus, even if the roots of the conflict are economic disenfranchisement, the revolt against the status quo may in fact express itself in religious terms.[4] This necessitates an intervention strategy that can acknowledge and utilize the role of religion.

It is important to understand not only the relevant texts of a religious system but also the actual practitioners themselves. What, for example, is the inner life of a Gandhian Hindu today in India who is dedicated to peace, as opposed to another Hindu who is prepared to destroy a mosque and die in the effort? What are the metaphysical priorities of each, and why do they attach themselves to differing visions of Hinduism? Clearly there is a complex array of contributing influences beyond religious instruction or orientation, and it would be valuable to examine several overtly identifiable aspects of such choices. For example, which sacred phenomena—texts, rituals, or images of God or gods—emerge most often in the minds of believers who are prone to violence, as opposed to those who are prone to conciliatory approaches? These questions raise the need for empirical studies that combine an intimate knowledge of the lived religious traditions engaged in conflict with a social scientific understanding of why particular texts and symbols are clues to both the deep motives of conflict and the possible hermeneutic ways to move religious adherents to a less violent place.

Let us illustrate with an example. Many violent trends are initiated in India with various radical Hindu parties' use (or abuse) of sacred mythic tales of the gods, using the dramas of defeat and victory to stir up rage against foreigners and, specifically, Muslims. The standard, rational, Western approach to this, which many middle-class and academic Hindus have embraced, is to fight for the strengthening of the typical components of a civil society—civil rights for all, a free press, honest courts, integrated police enforcement, and so on—and that effort is to be lauded.

I have a good friendship with Dr. Rajmohan Gandhi, one of Mahatma Gandhi's most active grandchildren, who has dedicated his life to peacemaking, to the spiritual improvement of Indian society, and to Hindu-Muslim reconciliation. Dr. Gandhi asked my opinion a couple of years ago about writing an expansion, or modern fictional continuation, of the *Mahabharatha*, one of the most central mythic epics of Hinduism, whose various episodes and characters are known by most Hindus and are retold repeatedly in literary creations, at celebrations, and on television. One of his close associates thought this to be ill-advised, considering how much else he needed to write about the urgent needs of Indian peace and conflict. Gandhi asked my opinion, and I did not know quite what to say, trying to be respectful. After I read a while later that Shiv Sena, the most radical Hindu party, had caused an immense amount of conflict by dressing up a car as a mythic god, driving it through the country, and stirring riots against Muslims, I realized what Gandhi was up to. He wants to engage the deepest myths of Hindu reality and evoke from them the ideas of nonviolence, bringing out what he believes to be their ultimate spiritual truths, which he, his grandfather, and many others see as expressing the highest virtues, including *ahimsa*, nonviolence.

I realized much later, after years of training students and researching, that Gandhi was exactly right, that our solutions must speak to the average person's mythic sense of the true and the untrue. And that if we understand exactly how fomenters of violence appeal to otherwise decent people, we may stand a chance of moving society in the opposite direction.

A close study of the sacred texts, traditions, symbols, and myths that emerge in conflict situations may contribute to several theoretical approaches of conflict analysis theory. For example, close analysis may indicate to what degree perceptions of empowerment or lack thereof are at work in a particular crisis. Psychodynamic models of conflict resolution that analyze the relationship between enemy and self or the role of deep injuries could be enriched by examining such materials. One could also examine what human needs are fulfilled by the texts or imagery involved. Finally, these phenomena may also provide a useful frame of reference for conflict resolution workshops. They could create a bridge to the unique cultural expression of a particular conflict, although more experimentation in the field will tell us how this might work well.[5] For example, in a recent training workshop for Christian peacemakers, I used Matthew 7:1 and the concept of suspension of judgment of others both as a bridge to other monotheistic traditions with similar moral values and as the theoretical frame of a conflict workshop for Christians where the parties would have extra religious motivation to humanize the Other and to suspend stereotypes during the course of their meetings.

Theories of peacemaking and conflict resolution need to analyze the nature of the leaders in society who have the courage to advocate peace with an enemy, even when they are subject to ridicule. What, for example, are the laws, prophetic texts, and rabbinic stories that passed through the mind of an Orthodox Jewish woman who was a member of a group called Women in Black, which protested the West Bank occupation on a weekly basis on the streets of Jerusalem? Why was she willing to suffer insults for what she believed? What sustains that degree of courage?[6] What, by contrast, is in the mind and heart of the West Bank settler who will die to defend his piece of sacred, ancient Israel? One may know by heart selections from the book of Joshua in which the Israelites are commanded to occupy all of Canaan, while the other dreams of the moment between God and Abraham in Genesis 18:19 where the gift of the land is based on a commitment to justice and righteousness. These textual foundations of religious positions can offer crucial insight into what creates, sustains, or, alternatively, prevents violence in Israeli life. We are beginning to understand now that both parties may see their texts through the lens of deep fears and concerns and that the actions that they see implicit in these texts and symbols may in both cases be motivated by high ideals.

Let us illustrate this. Acting like King David and conquering the land by whatever means necessary may be seen as conforming to the finest tradition of Jewish idealism, helping the Jewish people flourish militarily for the first time in two thousand years, and, in fact, being militarily stronger than even in the heyday of the ancient Jewish monarchy (the latter possibly intimates the potential arrival of the long-awaited Messiah). To think that one may be empowered to be a part of this process is astonishing enough, but to do it in the shadow of the Holocaust, the greatest destruction ever wreaked on the Jewish people, in the wake of the final showdown with a gentile world that many Jews feel has always despised them, is to be literally immersed in a divine plan.

Within this cognitive, emotive, spiritual construct, one will tend to focus on the physical, land-based markers of ownership of the land of Israel as outer manifestations of a divine spiritual program. Thus, gravesites and ancient ruins become the banners of identity and, even more important, the markers of divine intention unfolding. In this context, singing "David, King of Israel, Lives and Survives" becomes significant, while old Eastern European songs that celebrate humility and relatively quietistic moral virtues, such as right speech or judging all people favorably, tend to fade into the background. I grew up hearing all the time a song, derived from Psalms 34:13, that went, "Which man desires life, and loves the days [on earth] to see the good? [What should he do?] Guard your tongue from speaking evil things, shun evil and do the good, chase after peace and pursue it." It was a popular liturgical song in the first half of the twentieth century and one of the most magnificent songs in my family's repertoire. I do not hear that song anymore. Many peacemakers in Israel and the Jewish community, with some notable exceptions, do not know or remember such songs, and they, from their cultural construct, prefer to think of peace emanating from Jews by *lessening* the power of Jewish spirituality not increasing it. Of course, this leaves religious enthusiasts in the hands of a conflict-generating theology.

In the religious Zionist context that has come to dominate modern Orthodoxy, there has developed a fundamental disagreement over the relative sacredness of land, human life, and morality itself. For most of the history of rabbinic Judaism, when forced to choose, the priority of sacredness has been given to human life and morality over land.[7] In the twentieth century, there has been a minor but steadily growing trend to attach supreme sacredness to land and to sanction violence in order to protect it.[8] But there is still a great degree of inner confusion about these matters. This confusion is important because it implies that the choices being made for violence may be negotiable if it becomes clear that attaching too much sacredness to land is endangering human life. Fear and insecurity in the face of terrorism and war are more important in the minds of many religious people than is the sacredness of land. That means that confidence-building measures regarding the protection of Jewish life could be effective not only in the secular community but also in a large portion of the religious and fundamentalist community if it became clear that giving up land would truly lead to this protection. The vast majority of religious Jews in Israel are not affiliated with Gush Emunim or Kach, two radical religious groups that represent some settler Jews who have placed a premium on land.[9] Rather, the primary religious opposition to the peace movement is simple fear of loss of life, which has explicit *halakhic* (religious/legal) ramifications in terms of obligatory defense. Knowing this should profoundly modify the goals and tactics of conflict resolution strategies involving religious Jews.

There are a variety of possible explanations as to why people choose one religious response to conflict over another. Certainly, one cannot dismiss the cognitive or emotional needs that may be met by a particular text, idea, or spiritual image. Further, it is often true that there are powerful social motivations for affiliating with a particular group that espouses a certain approach to religious experience, an affiliation that, in turn, enmeshes the person in a particular moral, social, and political universe. The violent or politically coercive aspects of that response may be less important to the person than the other benefits received from this association. How deep is the commitment to violence? Can it be separated from the rest of the spiritual commitment? For example, the Islamic Brotherhood in Egypt, along with other religious groups, seems to enjoy great popularity for its humanitarian and postdisaster work among the poorest people of Egypt. When people vote for the Islamic Brotherhood in the polls, are they voting for caring humanitarians who fulfill the demands of the Qur'an to redistribute wealth, or are they voting for a group that works to violently overthrow the government? Clearly, we cannot know without better research, but we are certainly failing to comprehend the appeal of extremism or to adequately address the violence if we do not understand this complex interplay of religious values and institutions.

It is only partially true that what causes a person to focus on one text or another is due to one's emotional nature, family upbringing, or socioeconomic status. This is too easy a dismissal of the powerful impact of ideas and texts on human minds or hearts in the search for guidance in ambiguous ethical and political circumstances. It is the ambiguity of many human situations that is crucial here. No one would assume, at least on the individual level, that an arbitrary poverty line, for example, can predict who will become violent or anti-social. Some disenfranchised people, often in the worst of circumstances, become saints, while others become rebels, revolutionaries, and terrorists.[10] To take another example, a loving family structure will not necessarily provide a guide as to how someone will behave in complex violent or confrontational circumstances. Certainly it is helpful to have been reared in a nurturing environment, and it has been persuasively argued that the family environment has a critical impact on which personalities are more prone to either violence or altruism.[11] Yet the ambiguity remains, especially over an extended span of time, where the stress of protracted periods of fear greatly affects a person's judgment. More investigation is required into the effect of one's most deeply held beliefs on violent behavior. For many people, those deeply held beliefs and habitual actions are religious in character. The values and texts that spring to mind first in radical circumstances of societal upheaval or personal crisis are critical.

Universal Codes of Conduct and Religious Subcultures

Among people of secular, liberal religious, or cosmopolitan orientations, there is broad-based support for the notion that the best way to move society away from religious intolerance and toward more pluralism is the development of a universal set of political guidelines, such as those expressed in U.N. documents regarding political and civil institutions and individual rights. However, many religious people around the world do not share this universal, "secular" moral discourse. It is fine to wish that they did, but in moments of crisis what is needed are methods of dealing with religious actors *as they currently define themselves.* A nuanced approach will identify those actors who are prepared to engage in a more universal discourse but will also prepare us to work as well with religious actors who span the spectrum of attitudes toward modernity.

Analysis of religious peace organizations is instructive in this regard. Take, for example, Oz Ve-Shalom, the Orthodox Zionist peace organization in Israel. It has, over the course of the last twenty years, provoked a national conversation in Israel on the nature of Jewish values, writing essays and citing numerous legal and nonlegal Judaic sources that justify a peaceful solution to the Arab/Israeli wars. Its publications are dedicated for the most part to justifying this position from the vantage point of premodern *halakhic* and *midrashic* (biblical exegetical) texts, as well as by citing contemporary rabbinic authorities.[12] Many of the Oz Ve-Shalom writers happen to be quite committed to Enlightenment conceptions of human rights and civil liberties. But it is vital to their arguments that they justify their positions independently of the modern universal discourse, mostly due to the kind of people they are trying to convince. A conflict resolution expert who enters into such a universe needs to understand these subtleties in order to know how religion can be used to resolve rather than exacerbate social and political conflict. The mistake of the Israeli Left has been that it often undermines these potential allies by promoting itself politically as the group that will fight religion in Israel, rather than as the group that will fight *hateful expressions* of religion. The left fails to recognize that in lumping together all religious people it generates more conflict in Israel rather than less, and that instead of true reconciliation work, it is merely transferring enmity from Palestinians onto religious Jews.

Tracking Trends in Religious Subcultures

There are a number of ways in which religious texts and traditions can contribute to conflict resolution studies. For example, in a somewhat negative sense, the study of religious traditions and laws will reveal the dangers that lie ahead for dealing with a particular group whose leadership is buoyed by violent traditions. Subtle theological changes in a particular culture might provide an early warning system of the nascent growth of religious intolerance and the justification of violence. This would be an invaluable tool, enabling one to respond to conflict before it breaks out or reaches a stage beyond which it cannot be controlled. Tracing the full range of benign and violent interpretations of *jihad* in the Arab world, for example, would provide an important set of clues as to the state of a particular society.

Familiarity with classical sources might make it possible to distinguish where and when a leader is expressing real traditions and when he is using the religion to gain political power through the use of violence. Even if he is expressing an authentic violent source, exploration is required to see if there is room for theological deliberation, a new look at the sources, or alternative sources that might countermand the desire for violence or conflict that is implied in the tradition. Religious traditions are dynamic and can change profoundly through discussion and the influence of leadership.

In a more positive sense, conflict resolution studies should examine ways of coexistence *within* the ideal community, as it is expressed in the sacred texts and history. Leaders of most religious traditions have expressed rhetorical commitment to peace, but a serious analysis of the texts and cultures in question will yield far more than this. There have been many theologies created over the centuries that are replete with ethical precepts and inspirational literature designed to create coexistence in spiritual communities. This has something crucial to contribute to the contemporary discussion of strategies of communal conflict resolution and negotiation.

One example is the spiritual process of transformation of character through reflection and ethical improvement of one's behavior. Several theories of conflict resolution suggest the importance of personal transformation for the resolution of deep conflicts.[13] Spiritual programs of personal transformation might be combined with this kind of conflict resolution methodology in religious settings. For example, a unilateral gesture of forgiveness is encouraged in many traditions, and much has been written over the centuries on this one self-evident but extremely complex gesture. A related but different value is the requirement to confess to past wrongs, to repent, and to apologize to the victim. What are the inner spiritual/psychological dynamics of unilateral acts of forgiveness or repentance? Could such phenomena be incorporated into conflict resolution strategies among religious peoples, or even more generally?[14] It seems to me that the answer is "yes" *if* the challenge is presented equally to both sides of a conflict,[15] and if it speaks to profound cultural and religious metaphors of both adversaries.

Another aspect of religious literature that pertains here involves the critical importance of authoritative leaders. These leaders can be either living or dead, human or deified. The critical role of such leaders in the inner life of religious adherents cannot be overestimated. The role of charismatic leadership in conflict resolution theory and political psychology has received some attention.[16] How can the role of the religious leader be analyzed in this regard? In many societies, emulation of an ideal figure, including a deity, is the foundation of all prosocial values.[17] This makes the analysis of leadership critical and might suggest unique strategies of coping with violence. Gandhi understood this well and therefore undertook to study and interpret the *Bhagavad-Gita*, one of the most widely recounted books, and to reinterpret the role of battle, in order to make princes and gods into teachers of a peaceful path in life.[18] Furthermore, leaders play a crucial role in the process of injury and healing mentioned above; their smallest gestures, for better or for worse, take on mythic significance in relation to these injuries. This is a liability when one is saddled with callous leaders and a boon when a leader understands the healing power of symbolic behavior.

Religious Values, East and West, and Conflict Resolution Strategies

Many values around the globe need to be identified in terms of their importance for conflict resolution theory. Here are just a few of them.

Empathy

The critical importance of empathy in Western religious and secular traditions cannot be overestimated.[19] The concept or experience of empathy could be used in religious contexts either in terms of advocacy and long-term education or, more directly, in the conflict workshop setting. The advantages of its use as a basis for devising workshop strategies is that there would be a built-in spiritual motivation to engage in exercises emanating out of a familiar value.[20] As an example, hearing the public testimony of parties to a conflict at Moral Re-Armament's Caux retreat center is critical to its conflict resolution process.[21] Empathy is evoked by the painful story of the other party, and, in this religious setting, both parties refer to God's role in their lives. This, in turn, generates a common bond between enemies that has often led, with subtle, careful guidance, to more honest discussion and relationship building.

The religious adherent must see that her way of looking at reality is being directly addressed by the content and method of conflict resolution. If, for example, relational empathy is a key concept that informs the conflict resolution methodologies at work, one could explore a means to view that concept in positive spiritual terms, an easy leap for many religious value systems.[22] For example, in a dialogue or conflict resolution workshop involving devout Christians and Muslims, one might frame the discussion in terms of emulation of God's empathy as a vehicle to understand each others' needs and aspirations. Allah is referred to throughout the Qur'an as "the Compassionate and the Merciful," and Jesus' empathy with others in their suffering is well illustrated throughout the New Testament. Clearly, the details of how to operationalize this in a culturally sensitive fashion would have to be adjusted to each situation.

Nonviolence and Pacifism

A critical concept for the inner life in the Eastern traditions of Jainism, Buddhism, and Hinduism is *ahimsa*, nonviolence, made famous in the West by Mohandas Gandhi.[23] Certainly, in an Asian context, the elaboration and use of this principle could be a critical cultural tool to traverse ethnic and social boundaries.

Pacifism is a related, though different, concept that has had a profound impact on the early Christian church and many sectarian interpretations of Christianity.[24] Even for those Christians who do not subscribe to a purely pacifist view of Christianity, the pacifist writings, primary and secondary, are a powerful basis of discussion and debate.[25]

Sanctity of Life

Another central value in religion, often a source of controversy, could also be a source of reconciliation or joint commitments. The sanctity of life is a core value of Christian society, however one feels about the way it has been interpreted or the uses to which it has been put regarding abortion. What has been less obvious is that this value of the sanctity of life is shared across many cultures.[26] This, too, could become the basis for interreligious conflict resolution.

Interiority

Another important aspect of religious experience that will condition the nature of conflict resolution strategies is interiority. What I mean by this is that disciplines, even in societies that are quite communally oriented, are especially focused on the inner life of the individual. Prayer, meditation, the experience of divine love, ecstasy, guilt, and repentance all reflect the central importance of the inner life.[27] This means that conflict resolution techniques applied to religious groups or workshops might consider, where deemed appropriate to both sides, the usefulness of focusing on this aspect of human experience. For example, I was witness to the work of Maha Gosananda, a Cambodian Buddhist monk who is quite prominent in the efforts at Cambodian reconciliation, when he moved a large room of religious people of many faiths practically to tears, simply by recreating with them, in a matter of ten minutes, the kind of meditational practices that help generate in him a perpetual state of *metta*, loving kindness for others. *Metta* forms the basis of his work on reconciliation between enemies. Many of the people in that room were very conservative Christians, but the monk touched something quite deep in their inner lives that circumvented the cultural divide and enabled a transformative moment to take place.[28]

Buddhist Compassion

The Four Sublime Moods of compassion (*karuna*), equanimity (*upekkha*), joy in others' joy (*mudita*), and loving kindness (*metta*)[29] are an important tool of conflict resolution available in the Buddhist context. They also have important pedagogic value for the general understanding of the changes necessary in internal perceptions of the Other, who is an enemy. The focuses of the Four Noble Truths and the Eightfold Path have been mostly on restraint.[30] For example, Right Action, one path of the Eightfold Path, expresses itself in five precepts of restraint: murder, theft, adultery, intoxication, and lying. But there is a proactive character of the Four Sublime Moods,[31] at least by implication, that makes them potentially a critical tool of conflict resolution for Buddhist societies. The Moods suggest a disposition of peacefulness and compassion, which creates the groundwork for effective engagement in peacemaking.[32] On the one hand, Buddhist traditional texts on this matter place most of the emphasis on one's state of mind, and this would seem to be missing, or in need of, a proactive hermeneutic that contemporary activists and interpreters are providing. On the other hand, these Buddhist texts have much to contribute to Western approaches to conflict resolution, which systematically ignore the inner states of peacemakers and conflict resolvers. This blindness often leads to failed processes due to unexamined motives, anger, and mixed emotions that have not been dealt with internally either by the parties to the conflict or by the interveners and mediators, whose own inner states affect the intervention and therefore need to be examined.

Religious Disciplines and Conflict Resolution

Related to the experience of interiority in religious traditions is the great emphasis placed on discipline of the body. Experimentation with limiting personal violence has involved this aspect of religious experience, and it seems clear that, for Gandhi, his *brahmacharya* experiments with discipline of the body were critical to his commitment to *satyagraha* (holding on to truth) and the attaining of *ahimsa*. Self-restraint of the senses was central to his conception of self-restraint in violent situations. The multiplication of wants that is inherent in Western civilization was a key for him to the understanding of political violence, repression, and imperialism.[33]

The following is an example of how Gandhi combined religious discipline, pluralism, and conflict resolution. Religious fasting and dietary restrictions were experienced on Gandhi's Tolstoy Farm as means of promoting mutual respect and tolerance, as each religious community member—be he Parsi, Hindu, Christian, Jewish, or Muslim—would aid the others in the observance of the discipline of their respective traditions. Consider the effect on the participants or the witnesses to Gandhi's encouragement of Christians and Parsis to help a young Muslim to fast the whole day during Ramadan and to provide food at night for him. The fast itself is beyond reproach in its commitment to ancient Islamic tradition. Yet it is transformed, in Gandhi's hands, into a moment of interreligious discovery of immense power that leads the participants to nonviolence. Gandhi's concern was to provide a model for religious observance that simultaneously creates tolerance. There are very few models that have been generated by the world's religions that are simultaneously authentic to a religious tradition and simultaneously accepting of other traditions. In a certain sense, it is India's unique contribution to inter-religious peace, which Gandhi elicited from his cultural matrix. Gandhi's concept of lived religiosity that is both authentic and pluralistic needs to be examined as a model for contemporary societies that mix people of many faiths. Contemporary American examples of this include the Jewish community's organizing of volunteers for soup kitchens and homeless shelters across the country on Christmas Eve, so that Christian workers can spend the night with their families. The key is not the blurring of religious distinctions or categories but the peacemaking quality that is inherent in enabling someone else to practice her religion.

Messianism and Imagination

All three monotheisms have crucial contributions to make to conflict resolution studies in the areas of social criticism, envisioning of more just social constructions, and new possibilities of the human social order. The phenomena of religious messianic dreaming and envisioning new realities should be studied in terms of how to combine the dreaming and visioning with the imaginative element that is necessary for conflict resolution. The prophetic imagination, as it expresses itself in biblical literature, may provide a critical precedent for this use of creativity.[34]

Stages of Interfaith Dialogue and Conflict Resolution Theory

Interfaith dialogue is another important avenue of research. What models have worked better over the years, and what models have failed? Many of the considerations of conflict resolution theory regarding states or other large entities need to be applied to religious institutions. Strategies such as confidence-building measures and unilateral gestures have all been used at one time or another in inter-faith work, but little has been done to document the successes and failures of these methods in religious settings.

There are discernible patterns of progression in interfaith conflict resolution that, if properly identified, may provide a framework of analysis and activism not currently available. For example, in the past decade there has been a remarkable development in the Catholic church's attitude toward Jews and Judaism that has progressed from papal pronouncements to changes in catechisms and educational materials.[35] This is of profound importance because it represents not only a theological shift but also a commitment to change the attitudes of more than 800 million believers. The confidence-building character of this development, especially for those who have felt deeply injured by the long history of repression of Jews and Judaism, is remarkable.

There are still, however, some serious disagreements. Most of the disagreements involve acknowledging past wrongs of the church, and conflict resolution theory and practice would be useful in both analyzing this conflict and moving it toward resolution. There needs to be greater attention paid to the differences in perspective of both parties. For example, many members of the Jewish community point out past actions of the church, especially during the Holocaust and especially regarding Pope Pius XII's actions or lack thereof. But members of the Jewish community tend to underemphasize the heroism of other catholics who were particularly committed to the Jews during the Holocaust. For some Jews, this is the expression of a need to be angry at a long history of mistreatment, but for others it expresses a desire for apology from the highest sources.

We have here an interesting combination of social/psychological elements of conflict scenarios and communication difficulties informed by theological differences. Jewish tradition emphasizes that even Moses, the greatest Jewish leader and prophet of all time, must be criticized and found to have committed at least one sin, in order to make the clear distinction between a supreme God and imperfect human beings. The church, however, has a hard time criticizing a pope without undermining its own essential theological legitimacy.[36] It can, however, issue bold new statements and make substantial changes, such as Pope John Paul II's interest in investigating and repudiating the horrors of the Inquisition, *without* necessarily naming the names of the popes who obviously, by implication, were responsible for what happened. Many Jews, however, are expressing a need, it seems to me, for the Catholic church *as such* to apologize. A good conflict resolution process would delve deeply into the subtle needs of each tradition, both psychodynamically and theologically, in order to arrive at compromises and novel gestures that would satisfy the needs of both communities. Good people on both sides are doing excellent work on this, but I still hope to see greater attention to filtering this process down to the millions of adherents on both sides. It is in and through the masses of religious people that history has a nasty habit of repeating itself, unless there is a profound, broad-based transformation of relationship.

By contrast, the Christian/Jewish relationship in Russia is still at the primitive stage of trying to get the higher echelons of the Russian Orthodox church to condemn anti-Semitic beliefs, some of which are still occasionally promulgated by prominent members of its own hierarchy.[37] Such cases illustrate the fact that religious dialogue has stages of development and that there could be a fruitful interplay of conflict analysis, resolution strategies, and interfaith religious discourse.

The Protestant/Jewish relationship has also improved remarkably since World War II. The fascism of so many Europeans in the war and the results of genocide led to profound levels of soul searching, and extensive Protestant/Jewish dialogue has been quite fruitful. A worrisome trend, however, is the commitment of some conservative denominations to pour hundreds of millions of dollars into active programs of proselytizing Jewish people, particularly the vulnerable, those who are lonely in college, and senior citizens. This return to the medieval assaults on the integrity of the Jewish community is creating a backlash of hatred that is diffuse in its anti-Christian expression, certainly among the Orthodox. At present, this is still a relatively minor problem, but, depending on how the war over Christian culture goes in the United States, this could lead to serious interreligious conflict.

A telling sign of a worsening relationship is Jerry Falwell's recent assertion that the coming Antichrist must be a Jewish male. The Jewish community was understandably horrified, but it was made far worse by the steadily lessening trust of the Jewish community in the direction of right-wing Christian America.[38] Now here is a case where there are several old Christian traditions about who the Antichrist is, and one of those traditions is that it is a Jew, but Falwell, for whatever purpose, chooses to pick that one tradition about this dark, evil figure. Thus, this hermeneutic is combined with a cultural/psychological war that Falwell and others are engaged in to make the United States into a Christian nation, with, of course, the expected reassurances of fair treatment to minorities. It is very clear that liberal Jews, both secular and religious, stand in the way of that aim, since they are among the staunchest guardians of church/state separation.

This is more dangerous a trend than most Americans realize. The Jewish community, which has a very long memory for past eras of Christian revivalism, is worried. The alliance of conservative Christianity with a strong pro-Israel, anti-Palestinian stand, which makes conservative Christians helpful partners to certain political parties in Israel, is no real comfort to most American Jews. This trend will worsen unless there is a serious effort to intervene in this relationship.

I am particularly concerned by the tendency in conservative circles to demonize two groups in America, lawyers and anyone associated with Hollywood, two areas where Jews have been prominent. There is no doubt that there is much to criticize in American legal practice and in the media. But there is also no doubt that these professions are mere reflections of deep cultural trends in the United States. Whatever is right or wrong on television is right or wrong with the culture of America, which makes those ratings go up and down. And lawyers do what clients want them to do. There are deeper reasons why America is a legalistic culture, having far more to do with the fact that this is a young, highly multicultural society, which from its inception was bound together, not by etiquette or social custom, but by the Constitution and the rule of law.

But it is in the nature of certain expressions of religious psychology, out of bewilderment at the admittedly terrible problems of American popular culture, to search for a simple cognitive construct of reality that concocts a grand conspiracy that can be laid at one entity's doorstep, thus exonerating the rest of us. This is a compelling myth for many people, who no doubt struggle with and experience guilt over changing roles and the problems of their own families. It would be tragic if the trend, already in place, to look at Disney and Hollywood as the source of all evil—and the greatest competition for the attention of conservative Christian children, not coincidentally—moves hermeneutically into a demonization of Jewish media figures. If politics became more extreme, due to various social or ecological disasters, how difficult would it be for some on the fringe to see someone like Steven Spielberg as the Antichrist? It sounds absurd but has not Falwell opened the door to this? Spielberg would be a specifically tempting choice precisely because so many of his films have a redemptive message, which enrages those who have become obsessed with "taking America back for Christianity."[39] Of course, this is all rather distant from the American mainstream, but conflict analysis must keep a close eye on the fringes of religious society, for that is where violence often springs up, given the right circumstances.

Conflict Analysis and Situational Religious Ethics

I have offered a brief sampling of values derived from classical sources that might be considered as creative conflict resolution techniques in religious settings, a deductive method that will then allow us to move on to concrete situations. This has value as preparation for dealing with religious conflict, but, in the real situation of conflict, priority must be given to an inductive approach, which involves an empirical investigation of a conflict scenario: listening to the needs being expressed in the conflict and then exploring a series of religious ideas, values, and institutions that may be appropriate for that conflict setting.

My own work in Arab/Jewish relations and intra-Jewish conflict has led me to the conclusion that each new encounter between enemies can elicit the use of religious values and corresponding strategies of behavior that may work *only* in that setting. This is why replication and professionalization of these efforts by third-party actors must be accompanied by both a broad-based knowledge of the traditions in question, which can be drawn upon in a wide variety of circumstances, and a level of elasticity and humility on the part of interveners, which allows each new situation to dictate its own unique constellation of responses, both in terms of conflict analysis and in terms of religious texts and ideas.[40]

When I met a group of Jordanian students in a retreat center in 1991, the clear danger was that the relationship would be reduced to a series of angry exchanges about Israel. Dialogue and conflict resolution work regarding Israel was clearly the goal in this setting, but how to get to that goal was unclear. The unique circumstances of this meeting—the retreat center, the pluralistic religious context, and the personalities involved—led me to interpersonal strategies of conflict resolution that were derived from my knowledge of rabbinic Judaism. These strategies were only occasionally made explicit to the other parties. Mostly, this was an internal process: I struggled with conflict resolution techniques, my conscience, and traditional ethics. But the techniques that emanated out of that internal process, including an intensive commitment to honor adversaries, a commitment to external and internal humility, empathy, listening, and the wisdom of silence, all worked quite well in breaking barriers and creating relationships. It was a powerful motivator to me, as a party to the conflict as well as a conflict resolver, to be able to draw upon deeply held sacred traditions while engaged in the difficult and emotionally draining process of conflict resolution.

Religious Jurisprudence as a Peacemaking Tool: Prospects and Problems

There is an entirely different set of religious literature that, I would argue, could be used in fruitful conjunction with the more traditional subjects of peace studies. I refer to the use of international law in situations of conflict, arguments for international commitments to human rights, and new paradigms of global relations and mutual security based on the rule of law.[41] Another way, therefore, in which religious literature can play a role in conflict resolution is in the examination of practical values and laws as they might relate to international concerns, such as human rights. There are two possible areas of investigation here: an analysis of the correlation of religious laws and values with the basic institutions of civil society, such as human rights,[42] and an analysis of religious traditions as they pertain to conflict management and the peaceful resolution of legal disputes. Religions with strong legal traditions, such as Islam and Judaism, should be investigated regarding the management of such conflicts and studied as paradigms of intra-communal relations that could be applied to broader inter-communal dialogues.[43] The problem is that communitarian commitments are limited to the faithful. The difficulty of widening the scope of religious ethics to include outsiders or nonbelievers remains a serious challenge, especially in fundamentalist circles. This is a cognitive and emotional leap that would have to be nurtured carefully by third parties.

Extending Religious Ethical Categories beyond the Faithful: The Problem of Scope

There are two questions to be asked about nonbelievers. First, which values affirm coexistence with those outside the world of the believer, and which do not? Second, can the values that affirm coexistence be strengthened by leaders and activists in such a way that they dramatically remove the animosity toward nonbelievers?

There is an unprecedented level of interaction among people of many faiths around the globe due to patterns of rapid mobility, mass communication, and the spread of capitalism. This is deeply threatening to many religious leaders, especially fundamentalist ones. These leaders are reacting to the chaotic reality of a pluralistic society by emphasizing the aspects of their respective religions that are the most rejecting of the legitimacy and even humanity of nonbelievers.[44] On the other hand, more adherents are coming into contact with others who are not of their belief system than ever before. Clearly, religious hermeneutics that creatively engage tolerant texts of the past are necessary in order for the respective religions to flourish without building their base of support through intolerance.

It is necessary in a conflict situation, therefore, to develop a methodology of positively interacting with religious leaders and thinkers, even fundamentalists. The conflict resolution expert must elicit from this interaction the possibility of developing religious traditions that are accepting of the Other.[45] Rarely do diplomats or conflict resolution experts currently engage religious groups on their own terms and dynamically interact with their categories of thinking in order to produce a greater commitment to coexistence and peacemaking. But the effort may produce important benefits that have eluded international diplomacy until now.

These efforts will undoubtedly be complicated by the fact that religious leaders and practitioners are also influenced by the emotional and socioeconomic factors mentioned above. The complexity of mixed motivations does not negate, however, the usefulness of interacting hermeneutically with a religious tradition. It simply means that the interaction must be engaged on many levels. The religious human being in conflict must be approached on a number of planes, just like his secular counterpart. Some people think of peace and conflict rationally, in terms of the calculation of interests; others think in terms of ideological principles that necessitate conflict; and still others think in deep emotional terms. Most people tend to experience these questions in some combination of several cognitive and emotive constructs. It is exactly the same in religious life. Some people are moved to conflict or hatred by deep emotional scars, and they express this in religious terms; they clearly need to be moved from that stance by deep emotive methods of conflict resolution that emerge out of the moral guides of their traditions. Others, especially those in leadership positions, tend to think more in terms of the cognitive categories of faith, dogma, law, and institutional interests. They clearly need to come to believe that coexistence and peace are defensible legal and metaphysical possibilities within their system of belief, *and* that they are of practical benefit to their institutions as well. The successful conflict resolution expert will learn to creatively interact with all of these strains of religious life.

Leaders and practitioners must be given the chance to creatively engage their traditions, especially the ways in which difficult dilemmas were negotiated in the past. Allow me to demonstrate this by way of an example from Judaism. There are clear rules in ancient Judaism against idolatry and, in many instances, against idolaters, which would produce terrible violence if they were ever put fully into practice again.[46] But another fundamental metaphysical assumption of Judaism, based on Genesis 1:26, is that every human being is created in the image of God. That metaphysical assumption leads to a series of ancient rabbinic rules that reinforce the idea that every single human life is precious, as precious as the world itself.[47] Hillel, an older contemporary of Jesus and the most important founder of rabbinic Judaism, was motivated by this belief to call for the love of every human being as the highest calling of Judaism. Rabbi Yohanan ben Zakai, the central hero of post-Temple rabbinic Judaism in the first century, taught his disciples to greet every human being, Jew or idolater, with kindness and peace.[48] Thus, a dynamic process was set in motion that led one metaphysical assumption to overwhelm and effectively cancel the practical implications of another, and the result was a more peaceful society. This was a choice made inside the minds of religious leaders, which provides a precedent from classical sources for later generations to follow.

This ethical posture makes a place in the rabbinic universe for someone utterly Other, who will never be Jewish or even monotheistic. Furthermore, the position is not based on a hidden agenda or the motivation of a hoped-for conversion.[49] The latter, while better than violence, would call into question the ultimate acceptance of the Other who will remain different and distinct. Rather, the motivation for coexistence is the fundamental belief that God has commanded them to value all human beings.

It is apparent that much work has yet to be done in many religious traditions on constructing a theological and metaphysical approach to the Other, or "outgroups," while, at the same time, maintaining a meaningful and authentic system of belief and practice.

There is a good deal of bad precedent in the treatment of traditional Others, especially in the history of the monotheisms. Examples include the treatment of heretics, apostates, and slaves, as well as attitudes toward women. A feminist critique of religious systems would therefore be quite important in this regard and should be undertaken in order to see both the dangers of each system as well as its dynamic possibilities. Much can be learned about the possibilities within traditions by examining the steadily improved status of some of these Others over the centuries. I do not deny that the status of some groups has often risen and fallen over time, without progress. What is crucial for purposes of conflict analysis and resolution is the *dynamic* of the internal process of change, when and how a group's status has improved, and how it has been justified.

A few cautionary notes are in order before I conclude. There are two dangers to highlighting the importance of religion in conflict resolution: (1) that analysts and activists, in their enthusiasm about religion's positive contribution to conflict resolution, might overlook its violent potential,[50] and (2) that analysts will overemphasize religion's role and not see it as part of a complex array of factors that generate violence and peacemaking. It would be a profound error, for example, to attribute a conflict exclusively to religion—and, therefore, its resolution to religion—if, in fact, the society in question is plagued by problems that have been appropriately called "structural violence."[51] If a society is afflicted by gross economic inequities or tyrannized by a brutal regime, it would be seriously misguided to think that religion is all that is necessary to resolve the conflict. Worse, it could make the society more violent by masking the underlying problems and thereby, unwittingly or wittingly, taking sides in the conflict. That does not mean that religious intervention cannot be an important element in the conflict resolution process. It just means that it should not distort that process with a narrow agenda.

This brings me to my next point. Let us assume that there is a broad range of values in most of the world's religions that express a commitment to peace and elimination of violence.[52] That happy circumstance does not begin to address the problem of countervailing religious values that will, at times, override the call for peace. This struggle of conflicting values or, in some traditions, conflicting laws, is often manipulated by powerful interests that do not want peace. That does not mean, however, that the conflict of values is not a formidable reality for the average believer or cleric who struggles with his conscience. Acknowledging and dealing with those struggles is crucial for conflict resolution in a religious context.

As an example, let us take the U.S. response to Bosnian genocide. There were numerous voices in the Muslim and Jewish communities calling not only for an end to the violence on the part of the Serbians, which was certainly also vociferously being called for by the Christian community, but also calling for a commitment to arm the Bosnians to defend themselves and even to strike Serbia militarily. There are various cultural factors that could be pointed to in order to explain this rather unusual alignment of Jew and Muslim versus Christian pacifists. But it must be noted that, in Judaism, according to most readers of the traditional texts, the principle of using violence to save innocent lives in violent situations, where there is no alternative, overrides the commitment to peace.[53] In Islam, unjust injury is certainly grounds to defend oneself.[54]

These conflicting values will have to be acknowledged in conflict resolution settings and the cultural and religious differences fully confronted. There will be some interesting combinations of values that may seem unusual in the predominantly Christian West. In Christian conversations about war and peace, there is a great deal of struggle with pacifism, partly because it has such strong roots in the pre-Constantine church and partly because of a laudable degree of soul searching concerning the disastrous medieval religious wars and crusades.[55] There are some voices, both classical and modern, in Judaism and Islam, that are also pacifist.[56] But they are a much smaller voice. However, Islam, Judaism, and non-pacifist versions of Christianity all have a reservoir of sources that would commit them to aggressive efforts to limit war, pursue peace, or resolve conflicts *even if they are not pacifist*. In other words, there may be plenty of agreement on conflict resolution strategies even if not on pacifism. Conflict resolution may be a much more useful bridge between religious cultures, offering a language of discourse that may provide many more points of entry for a wide variety of religious cultures than either just war theory or pacifism. The pragmatic emphasis of conflict resolution theory and the goal-oriented nature of its methodologies allow people of many cultures to support the same processes of engagement. This has been my experience among leading conflict resolution practitioners and theoreticians, only some of whom are absolute pacifists but who, nevertheless, share a rich array of methods for aggressive conflict prevention and peacemaking. Furthermore, making conflict resolution respectful and inclusive of a broad representation of religious values, not just pacifism, can further strengthen the bond between conflict resolution practice and the behavior of religious parties to the conflict.

The Dangers of Religious Expansionism

My final cautionary note involves what appears to be one of the central tenets of several world religions, namely, evangelism, or the notion that there is either an obligation unfulfilled or a spiritual reality unfulfilled as long as the whole world does not profess the tenets of a particular religion. A corollary is the drive to convert as many people as possible to one's faith. While this spiritual disposition does not by itself require violence, it certainly has included extreme violence in the past on the part of some, both in principle and in practice, and the very drive, nonviolent though it may be, will cause more and more of the pretexts for violence in the crowded world of today. In particular, the corporate institutions of religion, for which power is dependent upon the number of adherents, tend to vie with each other in increasingly hostile ways when this issue is not confronted.

The question is: Can there be complete religious fulfillment for adherents in a world of unbelievers? What needs to be explored is what the options are in each religious tradition on these matters. The typical modern assumption is that radical change is the only possibility. However, it may be the case that shifts in emphasis will suffice or a return to other, nonevangelical classical sources or experiences or a redefinition of concepts like "mission." Each religious system must work on this in its own way. There must be, for example, great respect accorded to those who have dedicated their lives to a religious principle, such as mission, and an empathetic understanding of their inner spiritual lives. But the issue of how to negotiate the enactment of this value in the future while committed to authentic peace with others must be confronted as part of a long-term conflict resolution strategy for the world's religions.

Religious Pluralism and Conflict Resolution

More thought needs to be given to why some people find deep religious fulfillment through their particular tradition while side by side, in their minds or hearts, exists an abiding respect for other religious traditions,[57] while other people have such an intense level of identification with their own group that any affront to their group is a deep affront to their sense of personal survival, and any compromise of their group's domination is an attack on their personal legitimacy.[58]

This overidentification with one's ethnic group is also typical of patterns of over-identification with one's religious group.

I would tentatively suggest that those, like Gandhi and many others, who find it quite natural to honor and encourage other religious traditions have a sense of self that is inclusive of but not exhausted by their own religious affiliation. Their religious worldview does not confine them to one identity. They see and define themselves as religious adherents of one faith and practice but also as human beings standing in communal relation with other valued human beings. They share faith with their own group but humanity with all other humans and life with all living creatures and organisms. And their spiritual psyche values all these relations and consequent identities. It is the multiplicity of healthy identities that prevents a level of overidentification with one group, be it an ethnic group or a religious community.

Conclusion

In summary, we have analyzed a variety of issues relating to world religions that demonstrates the need to engage in a positive interaction between the study of religious texts, traditions, and practitioners, on the one hand, and, on the other, conflict resolution research. This is necessary in order to elicit from that inter-action a series of strategies for engaging in conflict resolution where some or all of the parties to a conflict hold strong religious beliefs.

Until now we have engaged in a general map of the issues surrounding world religions and their potential for violence and peacemaking. We have also indicated that a substantive interaction between religious traditions and the social science of conflict resolution would be most desirable as a way of hermeneutically en-gaging religious traditions as vehicles of peacemaking. However, this marriage of religion and peacemaking or conflict resolution has been thwarted until now by the limitations of thinking in two distinct areas of scholarship, the analysis of religious traditions on war and peace and the social science of conflict resolution. There are a variety of complex reasons for these limitations that touch upon the basic rift between liberal, secular modernity and the world of religious belief and practice. We will explore this in the next chapter.

A Critique of Current Secular and Religious Approaches to Conflict and Peace

THREE

Why Modern Culture Fails to Understand Religiously Motivated Violence

The complex nature of the interactions among world religions, peacemaking, and conflict generation in recent decades, in addition to the role of religion throughout history, warrants a special area of investigation. The need for this is urgent. As religion becomes more important in the lives of hundreds of millions of people, the political power generated by this commitment will either lead to a more peaceful world or to a more violent world, depending on how that power is utilized. Only through understanding the nature of this growing enthusiasm for religion can we hope to steer the religious world in the direction of peacemaking and coexistence. Furthermore, only if peace is, and is perceived to be, a part of a principled and meaningful fulfillment of religious experience, rather than a shady compromise with an unredeemed world, will this commitment take hold in the broadest spectrum of those who are now zealously religious. Methods of peacemaking that continue to focus only on political and intellectual elites or that fail to address the broadest possible range of religious believers are leading to systematic and potentially catastrophic diplomatic failures in key areas of the world, such as the Middle East.

There are several areas of inquiry regarding peace and war, all of which, for independent reasons, have failed to account for this complex issue. Much of the thinking about peace and conflict in terms of religion has been divided into questions about the legitimacy of war or its conduct. The contours of this long history have come to be dominated by Christian discussions of "just war" theory or, alternatively, pacifism. There have also been corresponding bodies of literature, going back thousands of years, in other religions on the legitimacy of war and its conduct.[1]

Most of this discussion has a tendency to limit the full range of possible approaches to human problems, religious or otherwise. The discussion, for example, about just war in Christianity, especially in Catholicism, is important and old. There has, however, been a far broader Christian discussion over the centuries about interpersonal ethics, human psychology, and the things inside human beings that lead alternatively to love or hate, compassion or rage, peace or conflict.

35

The same is true in numerous other traditions. There is a curious split between, on the one side, discussions of war or peace and, on the other, discussions of ethics and psychology, which are critical to the capacity, or lack thereof, to create peace. This selective approach to religious literature and experience is the first problem with just war literature.[2]

The second problem is that just war literature always focuses on a single, rather limited choice: war or not war. But this is hardly the range of choices that are available to human beings in conflict situations. One can believe that war is sometimes necessary but also believe that the choice for war, even if it rests on sound moral principles, effectively expresses a complete failure of all the other ethical or spiritual directives that are ideally supposed to guide one's actions. It is their absence that leads to conflict, and war may now be the only moral course of action possible, assuming one is not a pacifist. One such spiritual directive is a prohibition in both Buddhism and Judaism against selling destructive weapons.[3] The failure to follow this precept leads to violence and is therefore a critical component in analyzing its genesis according to these spiritual systems of belief and practice. Nevertheless, a resulting war may be necessary due to the obligation of self-defense, at least in Judaism. For example, a complete theological analysis of the Gulf War against Iraq would include a severe condemnation of the Western countries for having armed Saddam Hussein in the first place.

Another spiritual principle is the directive of boundless love in Christianity, or *metta* in Buddhism. Were it followed on a day-to-day basis with adversaries, this principle might prevent minor disagreements from turning into violent warfare. In other words, there is a range of ethical practices, spiritual experiences, laws, and codes, which are inherent in religious life, that are virtually left out of just war discussions.[4]

The broader ethical literature is the key, I will argue, to serious and constructive approaches to conflict prevention, resolution, and reconciliation in religious societies. It will also provide, if investigated well, several instructive paradigms for general conflict resolution theory and practice.

The third problem with just war literature is the lack of consciousness of the varieties of cultural contexts that form the basis of how people think about conflict, war, and peacemaking. There is a tendency to define war and peace in terms of specific religious criteria in only some faith traditions and almost exclusively in terms of biblically based religions. But many people the world over are not thinking in terms of biblically based religions. Even most of those who are rooted in biblical religion do not in practice make decisions about conflict based on just war criteria. Few of them know these criteria at all. Therefore, the entire discussion smacks of elitism and theological speculation—often after the fact—that has little to do with how, when, and why violence is generated by religious people, or why and how peace is sought and cultivated.

This has important ramifications in terms of global relations, as well as domestic relations between disparate cultural groups. Just war discussions have been valuable in the attempt to search for global standards of behavior regarding the conduct of war, harking back to their original function in the Middle Ages. Just war has also been a helpful banner around which to frame opposition to an ugly war. I do not deny the importance of evoking standards, either secular or religious, for shared behavior and values on a universal scale. Conflict prevention will require this ultimately, and certainly the building of civil societies in religious, nonreligious, and multireligious contexts requires this.

The real problem is that we cannot, while pursuing just war standards, bury cultural specificity or the unique character of all religious expressions when it comes to peace and conflict without subverting our original intention. These unique qualities must become key to the discussion if we are not simply to repeat the same mistakes of miscommunication across civilizations or to impose standards coercively on others in the name of peace. In particular, it is the broad range of spiritual beliefs and practices that could be useful in creating constructive approaches to preventing conflicts or managing constructive conflicts nonviolently.[5] From the perspective of conflict resolution practice, if we consult religious traditions only when war is imminent or on the horizon, then we ask their advice only when the real damage has already been done. By the time the sabers are rattling—or the nerve gas is cooking—the great potential of religious interpersonal values to prevent violence has already been emasculated by the dangerous and terrifying circumstances.

The field of conflict resolution theory and practice has also failed to respond to the critical role of religion in both peacemaking and conflict generation. This lacuna occurs despite the fact that an astonishing amount of the violence around the world is being justified by appeals to religious traditions. For example, millions of dollars and decades of effort have been expended by numerous governments and heads of state on the Middle East peace process. Religiously motivated violence, however, and the pressure from fundamentalist and religious nationalist wings of government have been the single greatest deterrent to this process proceeding in recent years. From Islamic radical groups to religious Jewish settlers, from suicide bombers dying for Allah's great name to a Yeshivah-trained assassin killing a head of state, all of the energy behind the destruction of the peace process comes from religion. Yet almost none of the analysis, conflict resolution strategies, and foundation grants have gone toward addressing this issue. The phenomenon of religious consciousness and commitment necessitates a reexamination of conflict analysis theory and strategies for conflict resolution.

The gap between the reality of religion and conflict and the lack of response to it by the peacemakers, both governmental and nongovernmental, both theoreticians and practitioners, suggests a deep fear of and aversion to this entire phenomenon on the part of government bureaucrats, journalists, and secular intellectuals and activists. They seem to unconsciously wish that it would go away so that everyone could continue unperturbed in simplistic diplomatic or conflict resolution paradigms. This suggests a regressive fear of a large sociological phenomenon that is terrifying to liberal religious or secular individuals. This fear has led to a strategic paralysis on the part of the very actors placed in charge of peacemaking by modern culture.

Here is the depth of the problem that we seek to address in this book. It involves two separate communities of actors, both of whom are intimidated by the resurgence of religious affiliation and its accompanying power: first, the diplomatic community and the elites of both government and the media, whose power depends on the continuing geographic and political integrity of the secular nation-state, and second, the liberal intelligentsia of the academy, who theorize about human and international relations and whose intellectual paradigm depends upon a humanist, agnostic set of assumptions. Both groups will tend to focus on those segments of society (different ones, to be sure, for each group), domestic and foreign, that reinforce that group's hold on the future.

University-based conflict resolution would rather support those cultural trends, domestic and international, that tend to strengthen the role of and legitimate space for rational, free, highly individualized inquiry. Furthermore, they will naturally seek partners in the field much like themselves. Governments, by contrast, will tend to engage in peacemaking efforts that reinforce their values and their priorities, supporting people internationally that buttress their group, namely the business and government elites. It is only natural, from a human point of view, for us to congregate tribally in our thinking and our interpersonal engagements. Too much of this very human characteristic has been projected pejoratively outward onto actual tribes or ethnic groups, without recognition that we all slip into this way of thinking and acting. It is only by constant self-examination that professionals, researchers, and peacemakers can learn to separate out the benign aspects of this human tendency from its more counterproductive elements.

Sometimes, these two groups will coalesce in supporting a cause, such as international human rights, whose agenda fits well with Western governmental efforts to open up closed societies—and their closed economic markets—and that also fits the liberal, intellectual agenda of the freedom of the individual.

There are value choices and value assumptions that lie beneath the approaches of this political and intellectual elite. These include the idea that the freedom of the individual is the highest priority, that rationality is the key to a better society, that Western and capitalist interests of opening up markets, as well as maintaining the nation-state boundaries, are the most important priorities, and many more. I sympathize with at least some of these assumptions, and as long as they are honestly confronted, there can be merit to these approaches. Many violent conflicts have been prevented or brought to a peaceful end, at least in the near term, by governmental power groups operating with the most crass level of self-interest. Furthermore, numerous dialogue workshops operating at a rather elite level of society, with rational discussion at the heart of their method, have proved absolutely critical to long-term peacebuilding efforts from South Africa to the Middle East.

I come to this work with a value bias; I assume that any effort that saves lives in the short term or the long term is inherently worthy from a moral point of view. Many successful efforts at peacemaking in the past have, in fact, been pacification. They have masked deep causes of conflict, ignored social justice issues, and ultimately failed to generate profound peacemaking. Furthermore, many efforts address the values and assumptions of just a small, elite segment of society, who, for example, may share the belief—naive, in my opinion—that rationality is the key to social change. These efforts often only have a marginal impact. But sometimes, it must be admitted, they have a major impact, such as the series of dialogue workshops and back channel conversations that eventually led to the secret Oslo meetings at the early stages of Israeli/Palestinian peacemaking.

I value any effort that saves lives in the short or long term, no matter what its cultural assumptions may be. On the other hand, its motives and its limitations must be honestly confronted if we are to maximize the amount of peace and justice achieved by the efforts of interveners and the parties to human conflicts. Thus, for example, if the diplomatic community had both embraced the Oslo peace process and also vociferously pointed out what was missing, such as its expansion to 90 percent of the population on both sides of the conflict, then we could have built on its limited success and immediately moved to a more profound process. In fact, the elites on both sides were motivated *not* to expand the process because of a mixture of fear of and disdain for the majority of the population on both sides. To be charitable, the secrecy was motivated by a fear of the violent fringe on both sides, but it still remains confusing to me. If the principal motivation for the secrecy and the elite process was fear, not disdain and distrust, why did they not want to solicit and persuade the nonviolent majority—through meetings, programs, and cross-cultural popular processes of peacemaking—in order to undermine the violent fringe? But this did not happen, and it suggests the deeper disdain for the masses that has consistently undermined Middle East peacemaking as a whole. The disdain for the populace has its roots in old authoritarian structures of governance on all sides, and the latter is one of the most important generators of intractable conflict the world over.

It should be pointed out that there is an important distinction here between governmental mixed motives and biases in peacemaking and the mixed motives and biases of conflict resolution professionals. Government intervention in peacemaking must be acknowledged to be a process in which national self-interest is built into the expenditure of public funds on international peacemaking, and the bureaucracy must demand that self-interest be high on the diplomatic agenda. This is ineluctable and needs to be confronted honestly and constructively.

The problem with the profession of conflict resolution is more subtle, not really an intentional act at all, I would like to believe. But it is necessary to begin to confront the fears and concerns of liberal peace activists as they face a large and growing, often illiberal, segment of human culture: religious militants. The militants' participation in peacemaking is vital if real progress is to be made on the basic issues of civil society and coexistence. Their absence from peace processes in the Middle East, for example, is indicative of both diplomatic neglect and the neglect of the propeace community, which seems actually threatened, at least in Israel, by a religious commitment to peacemaking, as if this upsets the peacemakers' categorization of all groups; more on this later. The fact that one subset of the religious community is decidedly against the construction of a free, civil society is exactly what needs to be addressed, and any peacemaking strategy would have to concern itself in part with precisely that subset of the community.

Returning to the problem of conflict resolution theory as it currently stands, there are several important issues.

Dialogue, Rationality, and the Dialogue Workshop

The dialogue workshop is one of the centerpieces of most conflict resolution practice. Its principal components are the direct confrontation, through verbal communication, of conflicting groups together with planning, coordination, and on-site facilitation, most often by a third party that is considered to be neutral or as close to this as possible.

There are several problems with applying this to conflicts among or involving religious people. Some of these problems will be similar to applying this method cross-culturally, especially to village-based life that is closer to premodern culture; other problems are unique to the question of religion. To begin with, hierarchy and religious authority is a major issue. The dialogue method assumes that the parties feel free to engage in open and honest communication and assumes some ability to change attitudes, opinions, and behaviors. But many, if not most, systems of traditional religious hierarchy preclude this possibility.[6] Only someone in a position of authority might be able to make new or novel overtures to an enemy. Dialogue with lesser authorities may be useful, but there would have to be an entirely different structure that allowed for a systematic process of private consultations with authorities. Or there may need to be a parallel system of dialogue in which enemies at corresponding levels of religious hierarchies could meet, then report to their superiors. This way there could be a parallel process of dialogue all the way from lay leaders to clergy, to superiors.[7]

The problem with this is that few actors at higher levels of authority encourage or even permit lower members to engage in such work, lest they subvert the hierarchy. This has been a perpetual problem in Bosnia and the Philippines, to mention just two places. The lower-level participants do come to the dialogues, but they often feel that they cannot speak. A possible solution is for the hierarchy to permit a broad range of possible topics for discussion that would not impinge on more sensitive subjects of negotiation. This could still allow for a substantive set of exchanges on personal histories, grievances, analyses of communications problems, and shared visions, to name a few.

Another problem is that hierarchies are almost never perfectly parallel between enemy groups. One group may have a clear hierarchy whose members expect to meet with those on their level. Even laypeople can often become insulted and feel they've lost face if they know that their leader is meeting with a representative of the other side who is not of the same stature. This touches on the critical issue of face saving and the honor of the group. The same attention that one gives in diplomacy to this issue must be addressed in the religious subcultures that are in conflict.

Sometimes it is not the hierarchy but rather a collective commitment to a single religious idea that is the main impediment to the dialogue model, such as the idea that a certain person or group is and must be an enemy or is an incarnation of evil. I once saw a sixteen-year-old girl on an American television talk show who was part of an extremely small Christian cult, and she was convinced that Jews were the incarnation of evil, agents of Lucifer, and responsible for all human problems. The venom that poured forth from this beautiful, redheaded girl almost overwhelmed her emotionally, even on television. I was overwhelmed, too, not by fear but by profound sadness that a beautiful young woman could be so passionately motivated by such a destructive vision. Of course, her venom was also a reaction to the atmosphere of the talk show, which was designed—as many are today—to provoke as much conflict and rage as possible from both the audience and the guests, a latter-day version of the voyeuristic and vicarious forms of ancient gladiator violence. The girl was being attacked and embarrassed by the audience. But still one could tell that the rage and the religious vision were authentic and deep.

I have wondered to this day what it would take to convince that poor young woman to feel differently about her life and her "enemy" and what it would take to teach her to deal differently with the sources of her rage. And I wonder constantly what is the usefulness of peacemaking if it cannot really speak to a girl like this, because it is this type of person who comes to the fore and takes power when society is deeply stressed by war or economic collapse. Her rhetoric and style of delivery was little different than Hitler's and what was obnoxious to this American audience at this point in time was quite appealing in 1930—and not just in Germany. If all we can do is speak to civil people in a dialogue, then what are we doing as conflict resolvers? Conflict resolution theorists must have the courage to confront this. That young girl may be a rarity right now in the West, but she is representative of tens of thousands who marched across Europe during the Crusades and of many who took control of Europe in the 1930s and 1940s. What would we have said to them back then if we had managed to get them into a workshop? More important, would a workshop have made any sense, or was something else necessary?

I leave this question open for debate, but it is not merely hypothetical or heuristic, and it is certainly not meant as a joke. We often make light of the religious fringe, because it relieves our tension about what they betray about the human and the religious human condition, and we also, in the process, enrage such people even more by not taking them seriously.

In one form or another, we often come across in conflict resolution a worldview that permanently and authoritatively affixes a label of enemy on some group. These labels are not subject to negotiation. Now, it is true that in general conflict resolution theory we are already familiar with the challenge of dialogue participants who are subject to a higher authority, such as a government, and are therefore hardened into certain positions. But some religious contexts involve a fixed view of the world that is deeply threatened by a change in assumption about the identity of the enemy. To change this would, at the very least, require authoritative permission to see the enemy in a new way so as not to threaten the entire structure of the ideological system.[8] Alternatively, some consensus-driven process of the faith group would have to come to a new perception of the enemy before the individual felt permitted to do so.

I have been working with many people, mostly Christian peace activists, in conflict resolution training that is specifically geared to religious problems. In my most recent training, I was struck by the forthcoming and bold nature of my Catholic students' presentations. They were unusually honest about the past crimes of the church against many groups and about how those crimes may have been rooted in old church doctrines. They were also the most creative group in envisioning and practically constructing a different future. Here I was, a Jewish rabbi, and my fellow trainer was a Mennonite, both of us from groups that had suffered persecution from the church, and we were witnessing an extraordinary level of serious transformation. Absolutely critical to the Catholic groups' presentations were extensive quotations from Vatican II documents, the statements of recent popes and bishops, and the changes in catechisms, among other things. I am also convinced that the public acts of contrition of various Catholic hierarchies in the 1990s concerning the Holocaust had a hand in making this the boldest presentation by Catholic students in the last three years of my training sessions. Thus, although the Catholics in my class were highly independent, critical thinkers, it was vital to their sense of who they are that the changes in their image of the enemy were following the path of their church, not destroying the basis of their religious identity. Other students, who were equally committed to peacemaking as a vocation but who came from religious subgroups that had not in the recent past openly talked about their past mistakes, had a much harder time confronting and specifying the problems in their own community. The exercise of collective self-examination often causes a minor crisis in many of my students, but it is not as traumatic for those who come from groups where the leaders themselves have boldly admitted the mistakes of the group.

Now, I am overemphasizing hierarchy to a degree. Clearly, many religious people today, in almost all the religious traditions that I have studied, including the Catholics, think and behave far more independently than their clergy would like. It is perfectly possible, and it happens quite frequently in my trainings, that people show great courage in confronting the problems of their community, with or without permission to discuss them in public. On the other hand, hierarchy and religious precedent are always in the background and often set the tone in terms of the permission that individuals feel to enter into such a painful dialogue process, whatever their private feelings may be. Add to that the already difficult psychological threshold of participation in open communication, and we have a formidable challenge to the dialogue model when applied to religious people.

This has implications as to how to structure or retool dialogue workshops that include religious groups. The religious person is carrying an immense burden of fealty to his group, which also provides him with his entire value system and worldview. To have those challenged in a dialogue with enemies is possible, and many courageous people do it. But it would be easier for the vast majority to engage in this process if the workshops were embedded in a much larger negotiation among religious groups that made this kind of process legitimate, an acceptable—even good—deed for religious people to be engaged in. It may need to take place after or in conjunction with highly public displays by religious leadership or perhaps after members of each group prepare each other and receive permission from the group to engage in such a dangerous exercise.

There may have to be deliberations over the spiritual legitimacy of such conversations. Often what needs to be talked about borders on blasphemy or sin, according to the most fundamentalist interpreters of a tradition. It may be prohibited to say anything bad about one's own community. It may be a sin to say that a pope is mistaken, according to some Catholics. It may be a desecration of the divine name that is placed on Israel to admit in public something about Jewish crimes that is not generally known, according to some interpreters. It is a violation, according to others, to speak of something bad about the land of Israel.[9] According to some, admitting that a rule in the Qur'an might be intolerant is blasphemy.

These are not simple matters to negotiate but, as I said earlier, there are many generations of hermeneutics at work here. If we give these communities a chance to engage in this process on their own terms, it is quite possible that creative ways can be found to engage in these discussions without the discussion being rejected as blasphemy or a betrayal of basic principles.

Fortunately, there are many members of these communities who are already willing, on their own and without hierarchical permission, to engage in cross-religious dialogue and conflict resolution, when or if the diplomatic community and the conflict resolution community start to include them. But we must also conceive of ways that even the most fundamentalist members of a community might be included, for it is they who often form the political bloc in contemporary conflicts that is in danger of being in violent conflict with the larger, secular cultural and political constructs.

A more fundamental question of religion, conflict resolution, and the dialogue workshop involves the issue of how people change. The culture surrounding the efficacy of the dialogue workshop assumes that direct verbal dialogue is a path to deep change within people. There are many roots to this assumption, including a culture that values rhetoric and debate as a means of governance and social legislation, with precedents going back to Greece, Rome, and rabbinic Judaism. There is also, in my opinion, some deeply Christian and particularly Protestant assumptions about the spirit of God residing among those who engage in conversation. The Protestant belief, stemming no doubt from the importance of the word and dialogue in Jesus' interactions, also has roots in ancient Jewish assumptions about the spirit of God residing among those who share the words of Torah.[10] This represents an important trend of human culture that no doubt resonates in many parts of the globe, such as in Buddhism.[11] But, in whatever culture this occurs, it does favor those with good verbal skills and those who express themselves spiritually through the use of conversation, which eliminates many of the styles of religious behavior and practice with which I am familiar. It also favors people with higher education, and they are a tiny percentage of the human community.

Alongside the highly verbal and conversational character of much spiritual or religious change, there exists a wide variety of other avenues to change a person or the character of a human relationship. In parallel with other cultural critiques of the dialogue workshop, many religious processes of conflict prevention and conflict resolution are indirect, through third parties, or they are accomplished through deep symbolism that resonates with the age-old memories of individuals and spiritual communities.

Let us take an example. Maha Gosananda, the supreme patriarch of Cambodian Buddhism, has spent a great deal of his time and the efforts of his students and fellow travelers literally walking across all of Cambodia as a way of peace-making and reconciliation.[12] We know the power of walking and marching in human history. Armies march not only to gain ground but as a profoundly symbolic act of conquest. Marchers continue in Ireland to this day in order to proclaim conquest. But people also march to affirm their identity. It is a profound statement far beyond the power of words. The most creative social change activists of this century, Gandhi and Martin Luther King, Jr., used marching in ways that literally changed history.

Maha Gosananda, however, is using marching, or walking, to be more precise, as a form of meditation that leads to reconciliation. It is a walking meditation with the purpose of transforming those who engage in it, as well as those who witness it. Why? What is this rather silent, mostly wordless method of conflict resolution, and why does it make sense in Asian or Buddhist culture? Why is it so significant to the people that the monks dip flowers in buckets of water and sprinkle the water on the shops and homes as they walk? Why has it resonated so deeply with the Cambodian people, even with many members of the Khmer Rouge? How did Maha bring himself to meet and even include in the peace marches Ieng Sary, who took part in the Khmer Rouge war in which so many innocents were brutally tortured and murdered? Why, when he writes down a saying of the Buddha suggesting the futility of violence and gives it to a soldier, does it have such a deep impact? Is it because the soldiers know that the Khmer Rouge murdered Maha's whole family, and here he is calling for an end to violence, and it thus shocks them into reconciliation or even some limited rapprochement? Are they frightened for their future, knowing what they have done, and feel safer to return to civil society in the presence of Maha? Does his example of nonviolence, despite his losses, overwhelm them emotionally, because they too have lost so much but have not found a nonviolent way until now to express that loss? Or is there some ancient cultural power in Cambodia in the act of receiving the word of the Buddha on paper from a venerated monk? There are many unanswered questions here, details that remain to be investigated, ethnographic studies of religious transformation in the context of extreme violence to be researched, and last but not least, theories and practices that need to be built upon these studies.

Maha began his walks as early as 1992, as far as I can tell. Originally, it was called the Walk for Peace and Reconciliation, the *dhammayietra* (pilgrimage of truth). In 1994, for example, the march coincided with the Khmer New Year, and it ended a month later, on a Buddhist holy day. Maha passed through regions riddled with land mines and utterly deforested.[13] He said to the people, as they passed through these places:

> We must remove the land mines in our hearts which prevent us from making peace—greed, hatred, and delusions. We can overcome greed with weapons of generosity, we can overcome hatred with the weapon of loving kindness, we can overcome delusion with the weapon of wisdom. Peace starts with us.[14]

He uses important Buddhist cultural referents in these statements and, at the same time, draws upon the brutal reality around him. But he transforms and overwhelms the violent symbols and metaphors by turning them into metaphors of transformation, healing, and peace. He uses the terminology of land mines and weapons but turns them toward inner reality, the inner life, where Buddhist tradition holds the greatest sway over the human being in this culture and where it has the greatest potential to make a Buddhist into a nonviolent sentient being.

Maha gave out books on wisdom, according to pictures that I saw, right in front of a huge portrait of a legendary figure called Finger-garland. Finger-garland was a warrior who terrorized many villages. His bloodthirsty nature was so severe that he walked around wearing necklaces of fingers, taken from the villagers that he had killed. He was transformed by the Buddha's wisdom, however, and he then was told by the Buddha to go back and face the villagers, who kicked him and taunted him. But the Buddha told him that the price was well worth it, because otherwise he would be paying with a thousand more deaths after this world for the crimes that he had committed.

Maha Gosananda knows exactly what he is doing. He knows that there is no way for Cambodia to recover without the dismantling of the Khmer Rouge. He found his own way to offer the Cambodian people a path back out of the hell of their own creation. The soldiers, who committed unspeakable atrocities for many years, truly are today's Finger-garlands, and Maha, today's Cambodian Buddha, is helping them come back to wisdom from the delusions of Pol Pot's mad vision. He invites them, under the portrait of Finger-garland, to change now, to endure the humiliation of return to the people they have damaged in order to avoid a thousand lives spent in repayment for the suffering that they have wreaked. The repetition of mythic history lived and felt by the Cambodians in this context, in the presence of this extraordinary monk, must be positively awe-inspiring, emotionally devastating but hopeful at the same time. It offers criminals the rhythm and ritual of violence, remorse, return, and punishment in order to transcend the suffering of a thousand lifetimes.

It is interesting that Maha does symbolic acts. He also speaks. He also gives out books on wisdom to be internalized by those who read them. But he does not conduct dialogue workshops. It seems that in Asia, in general, suffused by ancient wisdom traditions, the idea of giving out a book or holding a book in one's hand is widespread as a path to enlightenment. Recall the famous photos of tens of thousands of Mao's followers in China holding high his red book. Maha Gosananda now uses this cultural tool to return Cambodians to a path of sanity for their country or, as he would say, a path of generosity, loving kindness, and wisdom. He does not do this by engaging in verbal debates but by accessing deep symbolic places in the culture, by using his moral authority to get people to read, on their own, the wisdom of their own tradition. He thus empowers the individual, deepens the inner life, and moves his people to a new inner reality, which then generates a new outer reality. This is Buddhist conflict resolution at its finest. Of course, it cannot replace the need for a democratic political structure that will hold everyone to a standard of civil liberties. But he is playing a vital role in giving his people a deep way to move out of the hell in which they find themselves. Few have even approached his methods in terms of the depth of its cultural persuasiveness.

Some might scoff at Maha Gosananda's effort, assuming that there is no way to truly measure what effect he really has, how many Khmer Rouge he has really transformed. But evaluation is the great burden of all conflict resolution practice. There have been countless efforts at first- and second-track diplomacy and many workshops on Cambodia, which failed miserably for years while more people died. Do we assume that all these secular efforts are part of a slow and steady success story, despite the initial failures, because slowly Cambodia is achieving some normalcy, while the Buddhist priestly peace marches are not? The peace marches are a deeply Cambodian and particularly Buddhist way of social change, profoundly symbolic and completely serious in their intent to accomplish every bit as much as a dialogue workshop, in terms of personal and intergroup transformation.

The policy implications, which we will discuss in detail at the end of this book, seem clear. We must actively pursue a number of avenues of intervention in conflict. But, in particular, the most creative intervention strategies may require funding dialogue in one place and a march in another, or funding one kind of activity for university-based citizens and an entirely different kind of activity for villagers. It may mean a completely different approach to project conceptualization, choosing often to fund a human being with extraordinary leadership qualities in a given culture rather than a gathering, a conference, or a workshop. It may mean funding symbols rather than verbal exchanges. Of course, any authentic funding strategy must emerge from a deep familiarity with what has worked and what could work in a particular cultural milieu. But we will leave a full discussion of this for chapter 9.

Nothing we have said suggests that the dialogue workshop cannot work together with these cultural methods or even that they cannot be incorporated into the structure in some way. But this has to be thought through carefully. I participated in a Richmond, Virginia, event that has now become the national Hope in the Cities Project. It was a gathering on racial conflict. Moral Re-Armament was the chief initiator of the event. There were some workshops, more in the form of mini-classes or discussion groups to express one's feelings. In classic MRA fashion, there was a plenum that was not like the typical dialogue workshops of conflict resolution. The plenum was more in the form of public confession and included moments of contrition about past wrongs. But it was the classic model of using words and verbal exchanges to transform people. More to the point, however, is that as a predominantly Christian, (Protestant) group with old evangelical roots, the attendees were "inspired" to make a pilgrimage, which they called a walk through history. We walked as a very large group, black and white, the path of the slaves from Richmond's past. The participants became like the slaves for a time by engaging in this journey. Finally, we did a symbolic act of empathy or identification or, perhaps, burial. The group's emissaries threw thousands of flowers into the water where the slaves first came off the boats. We watched from high above as the flowers floated away.

This concept of the walk through history, or what I would call the walk through the pain of the Other, is something that various peace activists will be experimenting with in many other places. It was profoundly moving for those who participated, as powerful—or perhaps more powerful—than what could have been achieved through dialogue.[15] It seemed transformative, in distinct ways, for both the blacks and the whites in the group. Furthermore, for this Christian group, it resonated deeply with their mythic ritual attachment to Jesus' path of suffering and redemption, which is a foundation of the Christian yearly calendar. The notion of pilgrimage also has deep biblical roots beginning with Jewish cyclical pilgrimages to Jerusalem, and the mythic roots of the Jewish odyssey in search of the Promised Land while guided by God's presence through uncertain and hostile desert terrain. Therefore, this symbolic practice would resonate deeply in many religious cultures.

Another problem with conflict resolution based on dialogue involves the internal life. The way to change violent interpersonal behavior, according to the ethical treatises of many religions, is inseparable from the question of how to change the internal workings of the human being.[16] In fact, most religious traditions and cultures approach the question of conflict in terms of the personal morality of the individual and the dynamics of her internal life. The question of *how* a person trains herself to act in a peaceful way, however, is answered in divergent ways, even within the same religious traditions, let alone between them. But the work of the internal life is vital. Whether it be meditation in Eastern traditions or prayer and self-evaluation, confession and repentance in the Western traditions, religious peacemakers cannot think about dialogue as the only path to eliminating violence or conflict. They cannot separate violent behavior from the inner experiences of jealousy, anger, and rage that generate violent reactions to the world. Thus, a dialogue workshop that does not take this into account would systematically disenfranchise those religious people or spiritual leaders who discover change by other means, such as internal work on one's anger or jealousy.[17]

Timing is another crucial factor in regard to religious conflict, as it is in all conflict resolution theory.[18] Workshops are often appropriate at one stage and not at another in the dynamic of a religious community's development. Other measures may often be necessary before individuals and leaders feel comfortable accepting the dialogue process. For many in religious societies, dialogue itself is already a major concession, a recognition of the Other as a legitimate, moral counterpart that may in fact be the essential challenge of conflict resolution, the end, that is, of the process, not its beginning. This then requires a special analysis of the timing and sequencing of relationship building and dialogue. It may be, that there are earlier, more subtle stages and gestures of prosocial religious morality that might be enacted vis-à-vis the enemy Other before the bold breakthrough of dialogue is achieved. I can think of any number of prosocial gestures that I could convince even the most isolationist and the most wounded of my coreligionists to engage in, justified hermeneutically in any number of ways, before I could ever convince them to sit down for a formal dialogue with an adversary, be that adversary a Catholic priest, a Buddhist, a Reform rabbi, or a Palestinian. Authentic dialogue is one of the most challenging activities that we humans ever attempt. But there is much that can be done in religious morality short of dialogue to engage in conflict resolution.

For some societies, the dialogue workshop itself violates the system of authority. That authority system may be the key to authentic change and to alienate it at the outset is counterproductive. Many people change across the world because their leaders say and do symbolic things that transform their own attitudes, or at least open them to new possibilities. This is not the ideal Enlightenment model of the free, rational citizen choosing to engage in conflict resolution with his enemy. But it is foolish to make believe that everyone acts this way today. It is unclear how many people operate as free agents even in a democracy, given the demonstrable manipulative power of advertising. Leadership and authority figures, be they religious leaders, politicians, or rock stars, have an enormous impact on human consciousness, but they have even more impact in many religious societies.

This leads to a deeper issue. An important assumption of conflict resolution theory and practice—and an assumption beneath the surface of the dialogue workshop—is the centrality of "rationality," however one defines it, in conflict resolution. There is also a tendency among some theoreticians to assume that emotions are at the root of conflict and violent behavior, that emotions originate in a "lower" form of human evolution, and that only critical thinking leads to peacemaking.[19] There are some pivotal cultural assumptions here that may or may not be rooted in Western, male, and/or secular biases. But these biases do imply that the construction of a civil society that is rooted in deep emotional reactions and not based on rational constructs is inherently inferior and bound to create far more violence.

The rationality and pragmatism of Western thinking has led to the creation of a number of democracies, which have created many improvements in the quality of human life for many people while also leading to misery for the poorest members of society. But the benefits for many millions have been undeniable. Rational thinking has also led to the greatest concentration of brain power in the history of the human race, much of it focused on the most efficient way to commit mass destruction in a matter of hours. I speak, of course, of the scientific and technological resources dedicated to weapons production and particularly to nonconventional warfare. No "nonrational" human society, no religious culture, no animal species has ever managed to achieve this level of preparation for large-scale murder. Thus, rationality does not always lead to conflict prevention, as it has not in the scientifically based, mechanized mass murders of twentieth-century warfare. In fact, if rationality is defined as the search for pragmatic ways to achieve one's own interests, one has to wonder about who is really rational: the magic-infused culture of a tribe that has a high but stable infant mortality rate, a rather short lifespan, but a completely sustainable agricultural life with permanent, inexhaustible resources, or, a culture with a low infant mortality rate, long lifespans, resources that are steadily depleted, and a defense system that puts everyone at risk of germ warfare and nuclear holocaust? It is beyond any of us to pass judgment on whole civilizations, but we can safely say that rationality is not the only path historically to peacemaking or social stability. I would argue that at some juncture in adjudication and conflict resolution, in every culture that I have studied, there are what one would call rational discussions about compromise, the just division of resources, and so on. But there are many other factors that go into whether people reach this stage of conflict resolution, and most of them are not really what one would call rational.

There is much evidence that prosocial emotions are key to a stable nonviolent society.[20] It is only reasonable to assume, therefore, that conflict resolution practice should have a much more constructive approach to, and even embrace of, emotions and intuitions, spiritual or secular, as critical to peacemaking and reconciliation.[21] Even anger and rage are not necessarily dark libidinal impulses but normal responses to impossible circumstances or traumas. These violent emotions can and should be used in the process of moving people toward conflict reduction and even reconciliation.[22]

Western interest in the prosocial emotions goes back to the Scottish Enlightenment. It is a caricature of the Enlightenment, or at least one side of it, that it made a virtual religion of rationality. In fact, the Enlightenment brought with it an ever-increasing interest in the role of the emotions in human psychology.[23]

In the context of religion, it is clear that emotions, in religious communities across the world, play a central role in the processes by which people prevent conflict or resolve it. It is the inculcation of these prosocial emotions, such as love, empathy, and honor, that is the key to intracommunal harmony. Often they act as the very vehicle of conflict resolution, such as the spirit of remorse and forgiveness that leads to penitential reconciliation between adversaries. This is not to say that rational means of adjudication have no place in religious traditions; they absolutely do at the appropriate times. But it is clear that there is a critical role for emotions.

A conflict resolution culture that defines itself as exclusively rational tends to see itself as categorically opposed to religious systems of belief and practice, which are characterized, or caricatured, as rooted in the irrational. That cuts off the possibility of constructive engagement with religious societies and traditions in all of their complexity.

The Needs of the Individual

Another direction of thinking in conflict resolution that needs to be looked at is human needs theory.[24] The focus of this theory is that deprivation of the needs of the individual leads to conflict. As vital a contribution as this theory is to our understanding of conflict, there is also a reductionism about it that leaves little place for human behavior motivated by other than individualized need fulfillment. This leaves little room for the religious psyche that, at least in Judaism and Islam, sees itself as motivated much more by a free will, not by needs, and by a sense of duty to a community or an exalted being or beings, all of whom rise beyond the realm of the individual's needs. This is additionally true of many African religions.[25]

Now it may be the case that the social scientist will nevertheless assert that religious behavior is based on needs, not duties and not a free will. But this is certainly not the perception of the religious actors, and one has to question the usefulness of a social conflict theory whose essence cannot be communicated honestly, in terms that can be agreed upon or understood, to the very people it is trying to help emerge from conflict. Whereas to a person who has no spiritual interests, one can speak about exploring his needs, in the context of engaging in a conflict resolution intervention, it is hard to know exactly how the intervention would proceed with those who feel that they are not acting at all on their needs but on high ideals that defy their own personal needs.[26]

Human needs is also a theory deeply rooted in Western prioritization of the individual. Once again, numerous cultures and religious traditions globally, centralize the community, not the individual. It is fine to critique these cultures and religions from a liberal, moral point of view and, therefore, to advocate social change and even conflict resolution that guarantees the rights of the individual and the freedom of the individual. But this must be acknowledged as a moral position of the outside interveners. Otherwise, we will find ourselves in terrible trouble, for example, trying to negotiate the rights of a woman in a particular tribe versus the group's rights. In other words, preferring the needs of the individual over the group, or vice versa, is a value judgment that has a variety of nuanced answers in many civilizations. This has clear effects on conflict, its conduct, and its resolution. It would be fine to argue for the rights of a woman versus her tribe, but one should do so as an advocate for her or at least acknowledge, after self-examination, to the adversaries that you do have certain nonnegotiable values as an intervener.

The job of the intervener is, in my opinion, to be as self-aware as possible, to know one's moral predisposition, and then to act in as transparent a way as possible. Human needs theory that does not take into account the centrality of the communal in religious life will not deal effectively with the challenges faced by the parties to a conflict. Many people see their needs fulfilled by the guarantee of the safety and security of their group and the continuity of their group's traditions. Many others, despite or sometimes because of their particular view of spiritual truths, consider the individual's needs to be paramount when it comes to certain fights with religious authority. I do not have a solution to this moral conundrum, but I am certain that theoretical constructs of conflict that place sole emphasis on the religious individual and ignore the role of group identity will misunderstand some conflicts and miss opportunities for creative solutions.

This is not to deny that human needs theory has not contributed significantly to the conflict resolution discussion. Its frames of reference are useful and important in understanding the behavior of religious societies, and my analysis of conflicts often incorporates a review of the basic human needs that are unmet on all sides. But there are fundamental assumptions of the theory that need to be expanded or redesigned to understand religious society and even religious individuals. We must be able to develop a theory that will explain why so many people will go against their basic human needs, such as food, water, or social acceptance, in order to fulfill a religious precept. Certainly, the most blatant examples are religious suicide bombing or self-directed destruction, such as the self-immolating Buddhist monks or the self-immolating wives in old Hindu tradition. Certainly, one can theorize a basic need for ultimate meaning that is so fundamental to some people that all other needs collapse before it.[27] This must be studied further before the theory can be an effective aid in intervention when religion and culture are deeply rooted phenomena in the conflict.

Psychological Reductionism and the Cognitive/Social Structures of Religious Meaning

The same questions can be raised about psychoanalytic approaches to conflict resolution, namely that they tend to assume that beliefs and practices are reducible to emotional needs. Hatred of or violence toward a specific enemy is reducible to a manifestation of traumatic injury to the psyche or to projection and so on. This school of thought has contributed enormously to conflict analysis, and there is no argument here that it is irrelevant to religious life. On the contrary, it may well help to illuminate numerous aspects of religious culture. However, it is not the whole story nor can it explain the hold that sacred traditions involving enemies have on people. There are commitments here to systems of practice that go well beyond deep injury. For example, if a certain antisocial belief about a given enemy is inextricably related to a system of traditions whose structure would fall apart, from a fundamentalist perspective, if one piece was taken out, then the persistence of the antisocial belief cannot be explained simply as a reaction to trauma. It may have been at one time, but now its persistence is due also to the complexity of meaning systems and how they often resist evolution and hermeneutic development. Thus, the resistance to change may not be part of holding onto an objectified enemy but rather may be a holding onto a cognitive meaning structure that cannot survive without this piece. Equally important, the authority structure of clerics is often threatened by calling into question any piece of a meaning system whose legitimacy depends on its inerrancy or on its appearance of permanence. The cleric may not be attached to the enemy image embedded in the system as much as to his obligation, and that of his colleagues, to a meaning system under fire from secular culture. In their eyes that system would lose its legitimacy if it simply removed an ancient enemy image or an antisocial law, whose roots in hoary antiquity provide their own kind of legitimacy.

I have known many Orthodox rabbis, for example, who would be happy to ensure that a holiday such as Purim, with its obligatory reading of the Book of Esther, which culminates with the slaughter of the people—including their children—who tried to exterminate the Jewish people, would never be used to justify the killing of anyone today. They certainly are deeply ashamed by Baruch Goldstein's mass murder at the Hebron mosque, which was inspired in part by Purim. And yet, their hands are tied. They cannot simply abolish an ancient holiday nor change the reading of the text. They can and do give moralistic sermons, and they can and do interpret the story in less violent terms. But they cannot remove the ritual without calling into question their own legitimacy as guardians of the law. Are they frozen by Jewish trauma, or are they frozen by a meaning and authority system that gives them little room to maneuver? This dilemma is the foundation of liberal modern religion—in many traditions—that says effectively, "Yes, we do change things from time to time, gladly." This is the basic dilemma we have in conflict resolution, as we insert ourselves, whether we like it or not, into the thorny theological choices of modern human beings in search of meaning systems that make sense to them.

This has critical implications in terms of a strategy of intervention. It may mean that creative hermeneutics on the part of leadership or even individuals may be the key to a solution. It may also mean that solutions take a long time to take hold since the new interpretation of a religious symbol is not something that one can turn on and off like a faucet. Human beings become attached, in early youth sometimes, to a certain meaning system, and it is only their children who can accept a new interpretation that is more peaceful.

The hermeneutic give and take of Purim is but one example of the way in which a deeply embedded tradition will not disappear even when many people reject its implicit message of violence. It can be reinterpreted but not easily discarded. The same is true of many other systems of belief and practice. Is this because the trauma that gave rise to the holiday—the threat of annihilation—still resonates with recent traumas and that the wish fulfillment—the fantasy of strength over enemies—is still deeply longed for by this tiny people? Perhaps.

The irony is that now there is a great deal of strength over enemies that Jews experience. And yet that is not the self-perception of the community. In fact, the community acts often as if another Holocaust is about to happen at any moment. Would Purim recede into insignificance if the community slowly shed itself of the trauma of historical oppression? It is not likely in the current climate of religious revivalism, but it is possible that the violence of the story could be overshadowed with time by the numerous benevolent characteristics of the holiday, such as aiding the poor. This is what happened historically in the disempowered atmosphere of exile. The focus of the holiday was celebration, gifts to the poor, and gifts to neighbors. The risk is in the present, in a dangerous combination of living in the shadow of the Holocaust together with unprecedented military power, when Jewish empowerment allows for a new hermeneutic that could centralize the violence of the story.[28] If the political situation were to rapidly deteriorate, it is conceivable that Purim could become for radical Jews what Ramadan has become for radical Muslims in Algeria, a killing season.

There is no doubt about it: religious rituals are potentially dangerous. But even the rituals that flirt with violence mean much more to people than simply a rehearsal of trauma or a revenge for trauma. There is a persistence of Purim, for example, even among many who do not have a paranoid or fearful view of the Christian world. They cling to this holiday simply because wiping out an ancient holiday would undermine the entire meaning system of rabbinic Judaism. Even the most radically pacifist religious Jews that I know do not eliminate this holiday, although they do not really know what to do with sacralized violence yet and are only now evolving a spiritual and ritual reworking of traumatic and violent episodes, such as the Exodus and the drowning of Pharoah's armies, commemorated on Passover.[29]

Thus, psychological theory can help to decipher the labyrinth of religious culture, but it must respect its internal meaning systems and value systems and not reduce everything to libidinal impulses of the individual. It is much more complicated than that. Furthermore, it must help to evolve intervention strategies that respect meaning systems in addition to addressing deep injuries that might be causing the conflictual behavior.

Culture and Religion

The cultural method of conflict analysis is the most akin to research on religion and conflict resolution. Some caveats apply, however. Religious beliefs and practices often span many cultures. Therefore, religion must be considered, for investigative purposes, an additional or different principle of organization of analysis. Despite protests to the contrary from narrow interpreters of religion, there are values and assumptions that religiously oriented people hold in common in many parts of the world; these occur in a wide variety of cultural expressions. Some examples include the importance of spiritual as well as physical modes of existence, the importance of the inner life, and the importance of various moral precepts, such as honesty, justice, the protection of human life, and the veneration of elders. All of these would affect a religiously constructed conflict prevention and resolution strategy.

The main point is that religious values or metaphysical orientations regroup human beings into separate sub- or supercultures that cross other cultural lines and that, therefore, deserve independent analysis. It is possible, for example, that biblical monotheists from widely different cultures may share a great many values and even ritual patterns that would be critical for the construction of conflict resolution strategies among them. One could say that biblically based religions globally, consisting perhaps of 3 billion people, constitute a superculture that has its own problems and possibilities. On the other hand, the analysis of the interactions of the religion and the local cultures would be critical in anticipating what strategies of peacemaking that appear on the surface to be shared by many religions would be subject to debate as one tried to use the strategies cross-culturally.[30] For example, forgiveness is a basic theme in monotheistic traditions, but its character and parameters are interpreted in widely different ways across religions and across cultures as it pertains to reconciliation.[31] Its theological significance and, more important, the parameters of its use in peacemaking are completely different among, and even within, the various religious expressions of the monotheisms. To utilize this as a method of peacemaking without cross-cultural and interreligious awareness would be a mistake.

To take another example, in Bosnia there are at least five faiths involved in the conflict: Catholic, Muslim, Orthodox, Jewish, Protestant. And yet, there is a common language here. On one level, there used to be a common culture in Bosnia per se, especially in Sarajevo. And yet, it is the vastly different cultural meaning systems of Croatian, Serbian, and Bosnian consciousness that could give rise to the most horrific results of the war. On the other hand, the same religions that served to justify the war and the killing at the hands of some also have within their reservoirs the metaphors and values that could heal this society. There may be cultural assumptions about peacemaking, restitution, and tolerance that would be vital to understand in dealing with all the representatives of religious society in this region. Thus, there are times when, and ways in which, culture may be a unifying or a disunifying factor and other times when religion may be the important unifying or disunifying factor. A great deal depends on the interpretive initiative and zeal of the parties to the conflict.[32] Both religion and culture are potentially vital but complicated assets to peacemaking.

Rethinking Conflict Resolution Theory for Religious Societies and Subcultures

There are two things that need to occur in order to further analysis of religion in terms of conflict: first, conflict resolution theory must always consider how and whether its constructs of conflict analysis, conflict prevention, and resolution can be understood or framed in a way that includes religious societies, and second, world religions and their practitioners must be investigated with an eye to conflict and peacemaking.

Both the field of conflict resolution and the study of the religions need to begin to ask new questions. We cannot limit ourselves to negative or crisis-oriented questions, such as what makes conflict happen, or how to defuse a conflict, particularly when it comes to religions. We need to ask other questions, including: Why does conflict *not* happen in and between some religious societies in various historical settings? Why is there so little violence at a particular place and time? How did a particular community achieve such a high level of altruism or public service? When does a large portion of a community abhor violence? What values are cited or referred to by those who embrace nonviolence or even a prosocial, accepting response to others who are different? What prosocial behaviors, emotions, and principles lead to a nonaggressive or even loving response to outsiders? What social systems of justice and fairness, on the level of the distribution of scarce resources, as well as on the level of personal status, have led to harmonious interaction among human beings, especially human beings who are different? What kinds of mutual behavior between the genders leads to the least amount of conflict, violence, or miscommunication and the most amount of respect or love? All of these questions are directly related to what goes wrong in conflict and violence, but framed this way their answers can include a host of religious traditions that have not been utilized by conflict resolution theory nor, for that matter, by political science or sociology. These questions address the prosocial underpinnings of religious society by focusing on when and how religious people have successfully coexisted with each other and with others beyond their group.[33]

World religions have been particularly astute in offering answers to these questions, which fall loosely in the range of conflict prevention, whether or not one agrees with those answers. On the whole, most world religions have been weaker at resolving crises or conflicts with enemies and outsiders once these emerge, although this is not universally true. It seems to be the case, especially with biblically based religions and some tribal religions, that the reification of evil in the estranged Other, be it a heretic or an unbeliever or a foreign traditional enemy, is a deeply embedded phenomenon. Conflict analysis theory can help explain and expose this side of organized religion. But it does a disservice to its own constructs, as well as to the study of religions, to avoid asking why and when things go right as opposed to why and when they go wrong. We deprive ourselves of entire areas of investigation in social psychology and psychotherapy by not probing these prosocial constructs. Furthermore, by evading this inquiry, the current discussion of religion and conflict guarantees that religious systems will not be able to positively interact with or even contribute to the subject of peacemaking.

Distinguishing the Phenomenal and Epiphenomenal
Causes of Religious Violence and Peacemaking

Academic theory can be helpful in the process of distinguishing between phenomenal and epiphenomenal causes of religious conflict and peacemaking to the degree to which it can offer a *partial* account of these phenomena. For example, economics is important to understand the genesis of conflict between minorities and majorities,[34] but minorities often have that status due to cultural or religious differentiation. To the degree to which the genesis of conflict can be explained by the inequality of scarce resources among poor groups that are competing, or between poor and wealthy, this will help explain why a particular religious group may be developing an antisocial attitude and behavior. It may explain why a group may be hated by Others, even if the hate appears to based on theological necessity. It may also explain the opposite, namely, why at a particular point in time a religious tradition develops a benevolent attitude toward Others who are either not in competition economically or who are engaged in a mutually beneficial arrangement.

The same is true of psychological study. Let us say, for example, that a particular group is developing a middle class that is privileged economically. Furthermore, this class is removed by time and geography from some deep and horrific trauma in the group's history. Yet, a portion of this group is displaying more and more antisocial approaches to Others than their forebears, who were poorer and suffered more persecution; these attitudes are also expressing themselves in religious beliefs and behavioral priorities that are more violent or exclusivist. Here, economics is inadequate as an explanation, while psychology may be quite helpful in understanding the persistence and the strengthening of the effects of trauma over generations, the guilt that is felt more sometimes by generations one step removed from a traumatic event, precisely because they now have privileges while their parents or grandparents suffered horribly. There is also often a sense of anomie and rootlessness that comes with a life of economic privilege that pales in comparison, at a deep existential level, with the clear and dramatic moral and spiritual challenges of a previous generation that was poorer and more brutalized—but also more spiritually authentic. Or there may be an embittered, unconscious rebellion against economic privilege, the price of which is highly isolating suburbanized living that deprives one of the deep level of community that older generations had. Thus, despite the current privileges, there is an irrational longing for the very life that their parents sought to help their children escape. And so, the children or grandchildren begin to recreate religious belief systems that confirm their identity as poor and persecuted, thrust in the midst of a hostile world; their only escape is the deep, protected womb of communal religion, even angry communal religion.

One can make the case that this explains the odd behavior of many immigrants to the United States, whose politics are far more radicalized than those of their parents or than the people in their native country, who had or presently have much more direct experience of prejudice. We have the unique phenomena in the United States of Jews supporting the most extreme political positions in Israel with millions of dollars, Arab immigrants doing exactly the same thing by major financial support for Hamas, people of Irish extraction being the main source of money for many years of the IRA military operations, and Cuban exiles lobbying for the most militarist approaches to Cuba. The examples multiply.

Certainly, this is the result of the simple economic reality of American wealth having great power over poorly funded causes abroad. But it goes deeper and seems to reflect the way in which the guilt associated with expatriates' current privileges and their absence from a struggle in the homeland is channeled into financial aid for the most extreme causes; they prove their patriotism by "outpatriotizing," to coin a phrase, the indigenous patriots. Religious beliefs alone would be insufficient to explain this phenomenon.

This is an example of how two fields of research, socioeconomics and psychology, can explain epiphenomenally what happens to religious life over time in terms of peace and conflict. But it is not the full story. There is an internal dynamic to both individual and collective religious life, especially with the added factor of time, even generational time, that creates its own logic and pattern of development. If some catastrophe occurs to a religious community, there is not one day a trauma, and then a moment of healing, and then suddenly every belief and practice changes. There is an internal coherence and logic to religious patterns of being that form the basis of their attractiveness as persuasive systems of meaning. These develop over decades, even centuries. It is the very stability and conservative character of these meaning systems that attract people to believe and follow their strictures. Thus, change happens slowly to the group, if it is a group-oriented religious tradition.

What happens to the individual or to the community confronted by external changes is much more complicated and varies enormously with the personality characteristics and upbringing of individuals. The results are affected by the ways in which the religious beliefs, stories, and practices have been internalized and, above all, *which* of these have been internalized. A new event, such as massive loss of life, loss of a specific loved one, a natural catastrophe, or increased experience of hostility from outsiders, may cause a radical break with religion or confirm its teachings or lead to a profound and arduous search for new meaning inside the traditions. Those who choose to leave a religion, as so many have in the modern period, no longer affect the character of the community. Those who stay and reinterpret it in light of external events have the most impact.

These external events, these traumas, have enormous power over the evolving character of the community. At least in the Abrahamic faiths, one of the central challenges theologically is the reality of evil befalling the innocent. If a group suffers massive injury, this is a direct challenge to faith in a providential deity, unless the trauma is seen as part of some divine plan. The traumatic events then become the center of the spirituality. Responding to this violence becomes the crux of religious faith.

For the Jewish community, the Holocaust looms over everything as the prime example of what I have just described. But how that trauma is interpreted is the difference between those who embrace peacemaking and those who embrace a belligerent resistance to the rest of the world. Holocaust survivors find themselves on both sides of this equation. What is more surprising is the way in which second- and third-generation responses have been more and more belligerent. There are many factors involved in this development, including the uses of the Holocaust for Jewish education, often with little else to create a sense of collective self beyond persecution, and the uses of the Holocaust as part of a Zionist myth of history in which the state of Israel is history's, and God's, only acceptable reply to the Holocaust; the cry of "never again" is central to this mythology.

Another factor is the general loss of meaning systems in contemporary materialist societies. This void is increasingly being filled by people searching their ethnic origins for traumas that organize their response to the world, that give them a reason to live beyond the accumulation of wealth. There are often remembered traumas that are built into the community's history and cultural construct, such as the Civil War for southerners of the United States, or slavery for the black community of the United States. But it is often the unfulfilled deep needs of individuals in the context of contemporary materialist society that may drive one individual to highlight past traumas to the point of destructive obsession, whereas others, also keenly conscious of their history, may learn to live with their past in a much less angry fashion. The latter often learn from their group's traumas the skills of building a world that minimizes the trauma to underprivileged or suffering groups. Victor Frankl's response to the Holocaust comes to mind, as does Martin Luther King's to slavery and Nelson Mandela's response to almost three decades in prison and the enslavement of his community under apartheid.

One note of caution here is vital. The inner dynamics of communal religion and, in particular, the individual's experience, are utterly complex in the deepest sense, defying any serious generalization. This is particularly important because so many radically and violently religious groups are composed of individuals who are sometimes not guided by a religious authority at all but have come to their place of violent religious expression through an internal dynamic and hermeneutic engagement with their religious tradition often in opposition to family and community expressions of the same religion. They subsequently will gravitate to a religious authority who shares the same views, and the radical leader will feed off of these lone individuals, creating a new religious communal dynamic that is very violent. This is the prototype of the religious terrorist. The origins of this phenomenon are in the individual's own psychological odyssey, his own history of abuse, for example, by a parent. However, once all of this is set in motion, and these damaged individuals gather together, and do their damage, it can then have a dramatic impact on the entire community, especially as power shifts to those religious authorities who embrace the violent individuals who look to them for leadership.

We need a vastly improved working knowledge of religious traditions and their hermeneutic processes of change over time if we want to engage in serious conflict analysis and conflict resolution theory that is attuned to the reality of these communities. We must be able to trace the origin of violent trends in interpretation, when they wax and wane, and which subgroup of the culture is embracing these interpretations. Sometimes economics will help explain this trend. Terrorists are often part of some abused, disenfranchised group, deeply identified with the misery in their own group. Sometimes psychology is critical. Terrorists and fomenters of violence are often people who have been physically abused or, at least, emotionally abused. Religion is the vehicle through which radical political action is channeled, yet it is modified in the process and proceeds according to the complex dynamics of religious consciousness and hermeneutics.

At this point I should say a few words about religious hermeneutics. By this I mean the broadest way in which stories, institutions, rituals, texts, precepts, and values are being reinterpreted all the time, seen in a new light by virtue of the interactions between the individual or the community and the environment and life history in which they find themselves. I assume that even those who believe their religious beliefs and practices to be static or see themselves as changing only in order to revert to some idealized past structure are, in fact, engaged in subtle but very real processes of development. There is, to be sure, a great deal in religious traditions that remains the same over time. The science of hermeneutics, especially as interpreted by Hans Gadamer, merely suggests that much more is changing than is generally realized, not that there is nothing consistent in a tradition, an argument that would be demonstrably contradicted by empirical evidence.

The story of the Exodus, to take an example, is a clear part of the Hebrew Bible and therefore a component of literature sacred to Jews and Christians. How central it is, however, is always changing, depending on time and individualized interpretation. Furthermore, what it signifies—the importance of violently overthrowing unjust governments; the importance of destroying God's enemies; that only God, not man, wreaks vengeance on the wicked; that only God acts in political history; or that only through human leadership, as exemplified by Moses, is justice ever achieved—depends on one's horizon of understanding and the context of one's belief and idea structure.

Regarding the question of the relationship to violence and peacemaking, we need to know several things about hermeneutics, religion, and time. What are the precedents for change, in one direction or another, within traditions regarding attitudes toward outsiders or traditional enemies? When the traditions express a prosocial approach to Others, how does this express itself interpersonally, communally, symbolically? How does it manifest itself in the internal life in terms of prayer, study, meditation, ritual, repentance, and change? How are good relationships maintained? Most important, what are the boundaries of prosocial attitudes? Does it extend only to the faithful or to Others with certain conditions? Do these boundaries ever expand or contract over the course of history and, if so, why? What are the epiphenomenal and phenomenal motivations of that change? What resources in the tradition address the question of envisioning new or future realities? Are those realities violent in an overt or subtle fashion or are they peaceful? The key is to investigate how traditions have changed, and how they could change, based on the internal hermeneutic dynamics of the tradition.

The Elicitive and Cross-Cultural Methods of Conflict Resolution and the Diversity of Global Religious Expressions

It is manifestly clear that the infinite diversity of possible directions that religious faith and practice can and do take requires a method of conflict intervention that is at the very least deeply in tune with the particular characteristics of the groups and/or individuals in question. Furthermore, I am in agreement with the general thrust of elicitive methods of conflict resolution.[35] There is no true way to accomplish long-lasting peace, which truly addresses the needs of all parties, without an elicitive and relationship-building process built into the intervention. This is particularly true for religious societies, for several reasons. First, it is self-evident how individualized this process of hermeneutic engagement with tradition is, in addition to the unique complexity of the interface with epiphenomenal factors. This, in itself, makes the basic components of the elicitive method crucial to evolving a new hermeneutic of one's religious orientation. It is only over an extensive period of time and through hearing the stories, traditions, and internal struggles of a particular religious community that a third party could ever hope to be helpful to the peace process. He must elicit patterns of human interaction that sustain what peace there is, help to resolve conflicts, and especially find creative ways to traverse boundaries. The intervener must work on ways to reduce conflict between ingroups and outgroups whose adversarial relationship has been for generations built into the religious and cultural constructs of reality. She must enter into the patterns of meaning in a given culture when it comes to those who are Other or outside the community of faith, if they are the ones with whom there is a conflict. He must understand how the Others are viewed and then discover how they can be related to in peace.

Religious traditions have such a variety of ways to express the deepest human intuitions and patterns of growth in relationships that it is impossible to make this into a prepackaged formula; which would shut off an infinite number of possible creative expressions of religious peacemaking. These span the spectrum, from deeply internal processes, such as reflection on personal values or efforts to eliminate anger, to the most public, mass-communication methods involving symbolic gestures, such as those performed in the past by Gandhi or Maha Gosananda. One creative possibility might be directed toward the most elite forms of transformation in key religious leaders, who, in turn, affect populations quickly or over a long period of time, while another might be something simple and profound that will change every person's attitude slowly, over time, such as the Catholic church's changes in the catechism in order to eliminate anti-Semitism from its community of believers.

There is little point to narrowing the richness of an entire religious culture's possible responses to peacemaking into one dialogue workshop between privileged members of the enemy groups. Even in a single room of religious individuals, there may be one person who longs to write the definitive book on peace in his religion, another who wants to create an interfaith group of clergy, another who wants to engage in interfaith charity work as a vehicle of peacemaking, another who wants to create a public event of collective remorse and repentance to be coordinated with members of the enemy group, yet another who needs to sit with mothers from the other side and cry over the lost children, and still another who may want to find his way to making peace by playing a sports game with someone from the enemy group and having a drink afterward. Finally, not to be forgotten, there will be one in the group who wants to sit and rationally work out a plan for coexistence and the construction of a civil society. To cater to only the last person in one's intervention method, as many outside interventions do, is not only shortsighted and a waste of human resources, it borders on the cruel in the way in which it imprisons those who yearn the most to heal their culture and that of their enemy. The multiple paths that I have just described hypothetically—and many more—can be discovered in real people by drawing ideas out of them, slowly creating relationships, listening to and sharing in the pain of their loss, and then helping to tease out the contours of creative future visions and practical action plans.

I saw a variation of the elicitive method in Panchgani, India, in 1997, not directly in a conflict scenario, but at a gathering of Indians that included a fascinating mixture of prominent activists, intellectuals, people of wealth, and many simple people seeking social change. An Indian businessman named Aneel Sachdev and his partner coordinated a procedure involving about a hundred people at this gathering in such a way that *every single person* was invited to devise new methods of social change, to caucus with others in the room who might be interested, and to create concrete plans for the future. The ideas could range from new organizations to individual book projects to public acts of reconciliation. Anything was possible to put on the table, and everyone was free to vote with their feet as to which ideas appealed to them the most. The result was an astounding burst of energetic creativity from the group.

I watched in wonder as the group was released to form whatever they wanted. The loud, joyous chaos was riveting in its similarity to the character of Indian village life. There was great comfort in a thousand directions of energy, reflecting the embrace of a thousand Hindu manifestations of divinity that, in itself, mirrors the Indian self-image. This was Indian culture at its best.

At this event, however, there were Hindus, Christians, Parsis, Sikhs, and Buddhists but hardly any Muslims, and thus the event did not address deeply enough what I believe to be the central wound of Indian life, which is Hindu/Muslim conflict and violence. This has recently been confirmed by steps toward nuclear catastrophe taken by India and Pakistan, one all-Muslim and one predominantly Hindu state that emerged out of what once was all of India. Nevertheless, the conference was a fabulous exercise and a step in the right direction.

This Indian group had the time and the distance from their problems to truly engage their creativity. Conflict resolution interventions, by contrast, have a tendency to be crisis-driven and problem-focused. This limits creative potential. Also, as we said above, crises often evoke the worst patterns of behavior and attitude from organized religion. By contrast, eliciting long-term strategies of coexistence well before a crisis, in a way that draws out the religious tendency across many cultures to dream and conceive of better realities and work toward them, positively engages religious traditions when they are not driven into extreme positions by the passions of conflict and the suffering of their constituencies. In other words, patterns of intervention that emphasize creative vision may fit much better the strengths of a religious society, than a problem-or conflict-focused intervention, which evokes from many who are motivated by a religious consciousness the pattern of locating ultimate evil in some distant object, person, or group.

This is not to say that, as a peacemaker, one should submit to a common characteristic of religious gatherings, namely, the tendency to sweep problems from view or to pretend that there is no crisis. But in the course of one's intervention one may find that an emphasis on creative vision may tap into the natural instincts of a religious society, whereas an overfocus on problems may attack the very thing, religion, that many in the group are holding onto as their source of strength in a violent or conflict-ridden situation. There is a tension here between brutal honesty, which is at times necessary, and the deliberate protection of that which people hold as their central anchor of meaning and comfort. This is something that must be adjudicated differently in every intervention.

In a certain way, religion accentuates the deepest emotions and intuitions of the human being, and we have a choice as to whether to elicit the best from religious consciousness or the worst. We must be aware of how we affect religious thinking and feeling by the constructs of intervention that we present. Interventions that emphasize creative vision tap into the best resources in many religious societies, whereas the focus on problems tends to bring out the worst. The latter was suggested by some of my religious students who are peacemakers that, in pointing out the sources of violence in religion, I was destroying the one source of goodness that they held dear in the midst of conflict.

This is a difficult matter, and it often pits the natural desire of conflict resolvers and justice advocates to expose the full truth of history against the understandable need of many people in the worst conflicts to have one sure anchor of goodness. I have found no simple way to do this, but we have compromised in our trainings by emphasizing vision and the prosocial elements of a faith tradition while also delving into the violence that religion has produced, its origins and contours. Often we err on one side or the other, based on the dynamics of the group. This is almost unavoidable, but it is the combination of the elements of the training that I believe works for most broad-minded religious people. For fundamentalists, with a narrow or defensive view of their own religion, a different kind of intervention and training would be necessary, one that would minimally criticize the religion directly, unless they do themselves, which does happen surprisingly often in safe contexts.

Another issue is the unique role of religious identity in times of crisis. The likelihood of a preset, formulaic method of intervention and mediation leading nowhere or being counterproductive is quite high in the settings we have described. Especially in conflict-ridden situations, the tight relationship between identity, personal legitimacy, and the drive to create religiously unique cultural expression is high. Effectively, the worse a situation is the more that there is a tendency of some to hold fast to unique expressions of religious identity that mark an identity in opposition to an Other. This is the critical place of what I call "negative identity." Religious identity tends to focus on what makes me the most different precisely when I feel the most mortally and existentially threatened by an enemy, whether he be real or imaginary.

At the height of conflict, we find ourselves precisely at the point when formulaic interventions that are foreign and that do not appeal to our uniqueness will be the most suspect and will remind us the most of our enemy and what he wants to do to us—eliminate our unique identity and our right to live independently or at all. It is vital that the process of change and healing be indigenous at precisely this time in the crisis in order to wean people from this very understandable overattachment to what makes them religiously unique and, therefore, belligerent to outgroups. This cannot take the form of a weaning from religious identity as such, which a formulaic intervention would be perceived to be, but rather must take the form of a shift to a hermeneutically reworked sense of religious identity.[36] It is a process in which the person and group can come to feel that "a person of my religious tradition does not kill and commit acts of cruelty," for example, or that "the circumstances under which I would commit violence should be limited to situations whose time has passed now," "a person of my tradition and our community does the opposite ideally." That shift in mentality should be the end goal of the interveners. In my experience of observation, intervention, and training, it is the rare religious fundamentalist today who revels in the opportunity to shed blood, despite the notable exceptions that we all see splashed across our television screens. Most religious advocates of violence whom I have encountered do so reluctantly, feeling compelled by religious authority, by threatening circumstances, and by prevailing hermeneutic readings of their tradition. A slow and steady process of exposing them to the humanity of their enemies combined carefully with exploring alternative hermeneutic religious paths often creates a quiet revolution in religious thinking, both individually and collectively. Of course, these paradigm shifts are rarely acknowledged in fundamentalist contexts that prize the image of "no change." In fact, these changes do occur, regularly, and they go unnoticed because they are overshadowed by those news-grabbing fundamentalists who crave an opportunity for violence. This is not to say that one cannot find sanction for violence in these traditions. But the modern fundamentalist community in all parts of the world is more subtly divided on these matters than one sees from the outside. What conflict resolution needs to do, at the very least, is utilize that division to bring as wide a circle of religious enthusiasts as possible into the orbit of peacemaking.

In some other part of an intervention process, perhaps with a more moderate section of the religious community, one can raise the possibility of universal human commitments that might form the basis of a multicultural and multireligious society. But for many of the most extreme religious people committed to violence, those human commitments can only come about well after the deeply perceived threat to identity and existence has abated.

This is not to deny that with many other religious people and institutions in the same conflict one could actually begin the intervention with universal appeals and common principles. The two efforts, with both the more liberal and the more radical religious constituencies, could in principle proceed simultaneously. But I would argue that, especially during a crisis, it is vital that we elicit that which is most unique and most sacred as a source of prosocial practice and social change, if we truly want to move the *entire* religious culture to a new and lasting commitment to peacemaking. This is the only measure that will draw most people away from extreme violence. It must be felt as an authentic hermeneutic of tradition in its deepest phenomenal sense, as well as a reasonable response to the pragmatic external needs of the community. It must honor and speak to what religious people are safeguarding the most and are in the greatest fear of losing: their unique spiritual identity, for which they and their ancestors have lived and died for centuries or longer. This is the best way for them to eventually come to a place of shared humanity with estranged Others: after their unique identity and religious reality has been safeguarded and vindicated. Intervention can either help this evolution to take place or it can hinder it, depending on the quality of that intervention.

In this chapter we have examined the strengths and weaknesses of general conflict resolution theory as it may be useful in understanding conflict involving religious people or communities. In the following chapter, we move toward an internal analysis of two religious traditions. We will demonstrate how religious scholars over history have discussed the problem of war and peace, and why this discussion is inadequate, as it currently stands, to the task of generating authentic religious commitments to peacemaking and conflict resolution, particularly with nonbelievers, "heretics," and members of other faiths.

FOUR

What Is Missing from Religious Approaches to War and Peace

Judaism and Islam as Paradigms

War has been the subject of centuries-old discussions in both Judaism and Islam, and there have also been separate discussions in each tradition regarding peacemaking and the ethical relationships between human beings, both between fellow believers and between believers and Others. Rarely, however, are these discussions integrated in a way that illuminates the question of warmaking and peacemaking as a whole. It is as if war is a separate category of human experience, having nothing whatever to do with the full spectrum of ethical challenges of human intercourse, and as if these phenomena have no causal interconnections at all. Furthermore, there is a tendency to engage in these discussions in an ahistorical fashion, as if there has been no fundamental movement over time in attitudes toward these phenomena.

The modern study of hermeneutics has facilitated the investigation of the dynamic relationship of text, reader, and the historical horizon of each reader.[1] This ever-shifting horizon, depending on the reader, the time, and the place, will help explain the many paradoxical attitudes toward our subject. Furthermore, the social science of conflict analysis and conflict resolution can be a useful tool in understanding the shifting, dynamic attitude toward violence, war, and peacemaking in the Jewish and Islamic traditions. In addition, conflict resolution theory may help to extend the discussion of our subject in Jewish and Islamic ethics beyond its current state of ambiguity.[2] I will examine principally the evolving Jewish tradition, especially as it reinterprets religious traditions based on contemporary challenges, and make some comparisons to Islam.

War and Its Hermeneutic Transformation

Let us begin with the attitude toward war. There is significant importance attached to the relationship of God and war in the Hebrew Bible, illustrated by phrases such as "the wars of the Lord" (Num. 21:14; 1 Sam. 18:17) and "war for the sake of the Lord" (Exod. 17:16). Furthermore, wars commanded by God to Israel play a critical role, and the wars involving *herem* (complete destruction) are among the most famous, or infamous, of these.[3]

There has been a long and interesting debate concerning the Hebrew biblical concept of war as "holy war" since the appearance of von Rad's classic.[4] This concept has interesting implications in some surprising ways. For example, von Rad himself acknowledged that implicit in this holy war tradition is the way in which, at the hands of various biblical authors,[5] it actually suggests a passivity on the part of the human agent. God conducts the war, while the job of the human agent is to trust in him.[6] This suggests significant tension within the biblical text regarding the human role in God's wars. On the one hand, there are commandments to go to war, and yet there are also significant statements suggesting that war is truly the province of God. This sets the stage for the hermeneutic dynamics of rabbinic debates regarding war and peacemaking.

The term "holy war," however, is problematic in the analysis and comparison of Jewish and Islamic religious obligations, in that it does not do justice to the concept of war in either religion, as they have evolved. The laws regarding war are a composite of centuries of reading and rereading of biblical literature in both communities and of Qur'anic literature in Islam. At the heart of Judaism is a rabbinic interpretive reading of the Bible, often a deeply subversive reading. At the heart of Islam is the Qur'an, the *hadith*, and numerous oral stories, which see earlier sacred texts through a particular lens. The biblical concept of God fighting battles for Israel, the biblical institution of *herem*, the rabbinic *halakhic* analyses of *milhemet hova* (obligatory war), *milhemet mitsvah* (war as a fulfillment of a positive deed before God), and *milhemet reshut* (optional war), on the one hand, and, on the other, the rabbinic celebration of *shalom* (peace) and *pikuah nefesh* (the preservation of life) as ultimate values, various strands of rabbinic pacifism, rereadings of violent texts, and recreations of biblical warriors in a nonviolent light[7]—all must be considered part of the complex legacy of Judaism regarding war.

Qur'anic uses of the term *jihad* are only the first level of analysis of the Islamic approach to war. There are later distinctions between state *jihad* and religious *jihad*, as well as reflections on quietism and "waiting" that have legal ramifications, expressed by the words *fitna* or *taqiyya*. There are, in addition, the peaceful and violent versions of the Mahdi tradition, the pacifist and neopacifist traditions of Ahmadi Islam and Sufi Islam, Islamic celebration of life-preserving values,[8] and general principles of interpersonal ethics. All of these need to be examined, each on its own terms, in the varying and often contradictory contexts in which they appear and only then compared to concepts from other religious systems.[9]

In both Judaism and Islam, there have developed an extensive body of secondary literature confronting the question of war and its prevention, promotion, and/or regulation, in addition to larger issues of social justice that have a direct impact on conflict.[10] In each tradition there are, in the course of centuries of legal and religious reflection, countervailing trends that emphasize alternatives to conflict, the practice of conflict resolution, and the promotion of ethical values critically related to coexistence, peacemaking, and even pacifism.[11]

There is a clear dichotomy between these two strains of literature, one emphasizing moral values that tend to deplore conflict and violence while actively seeking to train people through moral discipline in the prevention of conflict and the other strain suggesting the legitimate means by which to engage in terrible violence and to conduct wars.

There is also yet a third trend in which clearly bellicose themes from ancient texts are hermeneutically reworked by later authorities, and these rereadings have some implications for our subject, implications that are sometimes clear and sometimes ambiguous. Let us begin our examination of Judaism by analyzing one of the most representative texts regarding God and war in the Bible, namely, the God of Israel represented as a "man of war" in the great battle against Pharaoh and his army in the Sea of Reeds. "The Lord is a man of war, the Lord is His name!" (Exod. 15:3). *Mekhilta de Rabbi Ishmael* records the following midrashic discussion, which completely reworks the implied military character of God. In fact, Rabbi Judah turns the many references to God in military terms on its head:

> "The Lord is a man of war, the Lord is His name!" Rabbi Judah says: Behold this verse is rich [in parallel verses]. In many places it is told that He revealed Himself in all manner of weapons. He revealed Himself as a hero bedecked with a sword, as it states, "Gird your sword upon your thigh, O hero"[Ps. 45:4]. He revealed Himself to them as a horseman, as it states, "And mounted a cherub and flew, gliding on the wings of the wind" [Ps. 18: 11] He revealed Himself as a bow and arrows.... He revealed Himself as a shield.... I might have thought that He requires these qualities. Therefore it states, "The Lord is a man of war, the Lord is His name." With His name does He fight, and does not fight with any of these instruments.
>
> There is the [human] hero of society for whom, once zealotry and power envelop him, even his father and even his mother and even his relative, all of them he strikes in his wrath. But the Holy One, blessed be He, is not like this. "The Lord is a man of war, the Lord is His name." "The Lord is a man of war"—that He fought the Egyptians. "The Lord is His name"— that He has compassion on his creatures [beriot], as it states, "The Lord, the Lord, God, merciful and kind" [Exod. 34: 6].... A human king goes out to war, and [meanwhile] local authorities come and ask for the things they need. They are told: He is angry, he has gone to war, when he is victorious and returns then you will come and ask for their [the people's] needs before him. But the Holy One, blessed be He, is not like this. "The Lord is a man of war"—that He fought Egypt. "The Lord is His name"— that He hears the prayers of everyone who inhabits the world [bo'e olam], as it states, "All of humankind comes to You, You who hear prayer" [Ps. 65:2].[12]

What is remarkable here is the rabbinic hermeneutic reworking of this most violent biblical description of God as a man of war. God's full name, emphasized in the second half of the verse, serves to circumscribe the violent image. God punishes violently the guilty while *simultaneously* hearing the prayers of all creatures, serving their needs and having compassion upon them. The terms *beriot* and *bo'e olam* indicate a specific rabbinic intention to emphasize that God's compassion is universal—not just for Jews—even as he punishes Egypt. Thus, the dichotomy of divine behavior that the rabbis wish to emphasize is not between Jew and gentile in this case but between the righteous and the wicked. Furthermore, in a most startling reversal, Rabbi Judah claims that the very multiplicity of descriptions of the divine use of military weapons indicates that God has no need of them, only needing his name, which simultaneously functions in all of the aforementioned nonviolent contexts.

This passage does not eliminate the concept of God as a man of war nor does it categorically reject it. It cannot if it is to remain committed to the sacredness of the biblical text. And that is the essential challenge that all historical religions have in needing to embrace the sacred character of earlier texts. A traditional Jew could not reject the term "man of war" as referring to God; neither could a Muslim reject Mohammed's violent program of conquest; nor could a Christian reject the wholesale reference to Jews and Pharisees as *the* main challengers of their Savior, despite all the tragedy that this led to in European history. But all three groups can and periodically have completely reworked the violence in their tradition by hermeneutic means, which maintain the religious commitment but see the sacred as operating at a deeper level than the overt violence or hatred that may appear on the surface of a particular text.

This is also a critical device in the process of trying to make some sense out of inherently contradictory systems of thousands of verses that preach love, justice, and compassion but then also imply or command rejection, hatred, or violence. Thus it is inherent in the monotheistic religious consciousness to engage in this creative, hermeneutic activity. It has been at the heart of the monotheistic program since the first centuries before the Common Era when the earliest expressions of or precursors to rabbinic Judaism began. The above text is a typical example of a later effort to ameliorate or mitigate the violence of a particular theological construct.

Legal Religious War in the Contemporary Context

These depictions of God and war exist alongside another body of rabbinic literature governing legal and nonlegal attitudes toward human warmaking. The legal attitude toward warmaking is subject to extensive debate in the earliest sources. What emerges from that debate is a conception of three types of war: *milhemet hova*, *milhemet mitsvah*, and *milhemet reshut*. The first two, for all practical purposes, appear to be the same (at least the way that they have been received in traditional Judaism), namely, a war that is obligatory or considered a *mitsvah*.

These wars include the war against the ancient Amalekite nation and the war against the Canaanites and other tribes occupying the land that became Israel. Only these latter wars involve the killing of every man, woman, and child. Virtually all talmudic authorities conclude that the war against the Canaanites is finished because they no longer exist. The Amalekite case is different. Some authorities compare them to the Canaanites in the sense that they no longer exist. Others delay the battle with Amalek to the premessianic era.[13]

The latter poses a problem in the sense that, at least according to some authorities, what is pervasive in the popular religious Jewish consciousness is the belief that implacable enemies of the Jewish people truly are, in some sense, the Amalekites. The fact that once a year it is obligatory in Orthodox Judaism to recite, hear, or read the biblical verses declaring eternal war on Amalek has strengthened a continuing sense among some Jews that there will always be people who, when they demonstrate an implacable need to kill Jews, can be considered like Amalek. Furthermore, part of the struggle in Israel today over its future relationship to Arabs, Palestinians, and the territories involves a minority of religious Jews, who actually do consider this period of history to be the premessianic period of struggle, which means that war against Amalekites could be operative potentially. Furthermore, every time there is a bombing in which the purpose of the bomb is to kill as many Jews as possible, with no other objective, it confirms in many religious minds that, on a theological plane, Amalekites exist, and they are the Palestinians, just as they used to be the Nazis. Nevertheless, it is important to point out that the vast majority of *halakhic* authorities do not consider this kind of war to be operational. The final kind of obligatory war is the war of self-defense. If it is clear that an enemy has attacked a Jewish self-governing entity, then it is obliged to defend itself. The texts seem to indicate that this obligation is limited to defense in response to attack and does not include preemptive strikes.[14] Preemptive strikes are a major issue today in the missile age, in the sense that waiting to be attacked could mean waiting to suffer massive losses and even defeat. Thus, there has been considerable discussion in the literature on preemptive strikes, particularly in light of Israel's decisions in 1967 and the questions surrounding the Lebanon war of 1982.[15] The fact is that it remains extremely difficult to justify preemptive strikes as obligatory according to Jewish law, despite the existence of some authorities, such as R. Menachem ha-Meiri (d. 1315) who did, because of several important authorities who specifically defined obligatory war as a response to attack.

This then leaves the category of *milhemet reshut*, discretionary war. Here we have an interesting set of disagreements. Jacob David Bleich summarizes the traditional attitude toward discretionary war by stating quite clearly that it is precluded in modern times and in fact has been precluded since at least the end of the second Jewish commonwealth (70 C.E.), if not earlier. Discretionary war requires a Jewish king, presumably of Davidic descent, a Sanhedrin (ancient Jewish high court), and the *urim ve-tumim* (a breastplate worn by the high priest, consulted to give its miraculous indication of whether or not to wage war). All three of these institutions have been assumed to be impossible to recreate before the coming of the Messiah, according to traditional Judaism. This point of view is typical of ultra-Orthodox Judaism in modern times, which has been quite reluctant to follow the lead of religious Zionism in terms of reconstituting Jewish institutions of power before the Messiah arrives. This represents a subtle but deep fissure regarding Jewish use of state force.

Reuven Kimelman has done extensive work on the parameters of Jewish warfare. He cites the idea, based on precedents in Maimonides, among others, that the Sanhedrin requirement is meant to act as an expression of the needs of the people and to be a counterbalance to the needs of the sovereign. Furthermore, the Sanhedrin would be in a position to evaluate the rights and wrongs of going to war and conducting it in an *halakhic* fashion. He also points out, following Chief Rabbi Goren, that the key element of the Sanhedrin is its representative authority.[16] Furthermore, the *urim ve-tumim* is no longer necessary for consultation now that it is defunct, according to some authorities.[17]

The Sanhedrin would provide a counterbalance to the ruler(s) in making the decision to go to war, thus balancing the state's interest and the people's interests (though not those of the adversaries) in deciding to go to war.[18] In the immediate background of this formulation, especially regarding Kimelman's citation of Chief Rabbi Goren, seems to be a suggested justification of warmaking in contemporary Israel when the elected government and recognized *halakhic* leaders agree on going to war, though I am uncertain of this. There appears, however, to be some confidence that the agreement of the state and the representative *halakhic* body would be enough to ensure that the war is conducted for "moral" reasons.

It must be noted, however, that Kimelman, like many previous scholars, weds this argument to an extensive effort to circumscribe both the legitimization of war and the conduct of war by a broad series of ethical/*halakhic* guidelines. This includes not engaging in wars that will involve more than one-sixth of one's forces as casualties, allowing escape routes for retreating forces, and conducting negotiations before besieging a city, "calling out to it in peace first." Destruction that is unnecessary for the achievement of military aims is disallowed. Destruction of the surrounding environment is not allowed. The killing of noncombatants is not allowed.[19]

This raises an issue, not really addressed by Kimelman, which is the problematic nature of targeting anything near civilian populations with explosive weapons. In general, I would argue that explosive weapons, from rocket-launched grenades to F-16s and certainly including weapons of mass destruction, make it extremely difficult to comply, in any contemporary warfare, with the *halakhic* rule that requires giving even combatants, let alone unarmed civilians, a way out of conflict, a path of retreat.

It would seem that Kimelman hopes to limit war due to the nature of the *halakhic* institutions that would need to support a war and that in some fashion represent the interests of the people. In principle, I would agree that getting the consent to go to war from those who represent the average person's interests is no longer easy in an age where the brutality of war is available in the living room of every parent who would send a child to the battlefield. But a present-day *halakhic* body would not necessarily be the equivalent of a democratic or even representative institution by any means, especially in a largely nonreligious and at times antireligious society in Israel. On the other hand, the Knesset, which *is* a representative elected body, hardly operates in terms of *halakhic* guidelines on issues of national security and morality surrounding the taking of life, nor can its members in any way be seen as having *halakhic* authority. Thus, we are still left without a clear way to conduct a modern Jewish war or even a mechanism to determine which wars are justified.

David Novak, reflecting on Jewish attitudes toward wars conducted by gentiles, which Jews must decide whether to support (in this case, the Vietnam War), employs the now-infamous *rodef* law, made famous by the assassin of the late prime minister, Yitzhak Rabin. The *rodef* law requires person A to intervene and stop B from killing C. But A may not use any means whatever, unless it is clear that killing B is the only way to stop him. And, in fact, A can be guilty of murder if he does not need to use deadly force. This law is used rabbinically to justify abortion when the fetus is threatening the life of the mother. Rabin's assassin and his rabbis[20] extended this law to politics and made the case that, in their minds, Rabin was a direct and immediate threat to Jewish life, a position that the vast majority of rabbinic authorities have repudiated.

Novak extends this law to justify exactly the opposite of killing in the case of Vietnam. If persons B and C, argues Novak, are not clearly defined, and we do not know who exactly is trying to kill whom, then the law of *rodef* does not apply, and another *halakhic* principle, namely, not destroying one life for another or not considering one life more valuable than another becomes morally paramount. Who was really the pursuer in the Vietnam War is dubious from an ethical point of view, argues Novak. Whether it was a war of aggression by the North, a civil war, the Cold War fought by proxy, or all three is unclear. Furthermore, the United States was hardly in a position to make a moral judgment on this, considering the fact that its strategic interests were paramount, and its decisions about the war were certainly not based on the Jewish law of *rodef*.[21] Thus, it would be complicated to justify the war as a religious Jew, argues Novak.

I would point out the rather circumscribed nature of the *rodef* law in that it only justifies use of force in the limited circumstances of "hot pursuit," as far as I have been able to tell.[22] The danger of the political extension of this law to war and wholesale killing or the use of this law to justify premeditated killing when there is no hot pursuit seems clear. While Novak's use of the *rodef* law to limit the justification of war is understandable, I think that its extension at all by theorists to situations beyond hot pursuit of one person by another that you see before you is ill advised.[23] It confuses political calculus and the *halakhic* challenges of individual decisionmaking in very particular situations.

There seems to be very little to justify Jewish war today, except when being attacked, and even then a set of circumscribing *jus in bello* laws apply. It is also not clear to me whether even this category is legitimate, because the state of Israel is not a *halakhically* constituted state, but neither were the many Jewish communities in the premodern era. The very category of *halakhic* war is only discussed by the mishnaic and talmudic rabbis in the context of a highly theoretical construct of the *halakhic* state. Many rabbinic discussions in general—most of the discussions in certain areas of law, in fact—are completely theoretical in nature because the current circumstances make the law's applicability impossible. I am not satisfied that it has been proven that these talmudic war discussions apply to any circumstances beyond the Second Temple period, or could in principle. Furthermore, it is questionable whether the rabbis, even in the period of the second Temple, ever had a sovereign construct in which their guidelines for war were operationalized.

This leaves us with two curiously overlooked Jewish principles. One is that saving of life, *pikuah nefesh*,[24] justifies the abrogation of most other laws, and the other is the principle that if someone comes to kill you, you are obligated to kill him first in self-defense.[25] As far as the former, one is permitted to do almost anything to save one's life and the lives of others, with the exception of incest, idolatry, and premeditated murder. However, I cannot kill someone else, who is not attacking me. Thus, even if person A, ordering me to kill person B, will kill me instead if I do not comply, I cannot follow the order. Now it is clear that war is a very different situation from this, where an attacking army is directly threatening one's life and the lives of many others. The people that I kill are the people who are attacking. Once again, however, it would be problematic to kill civilians or those not directly threatening one's life, based on this law, with, for example, indiscriminate bombardment of enemy cities. The same would apply to the second rule. These two principles seem to me to justify the use of violence in very limited circumstances of attack and to make organized war in an environment of many civilians problematic.

Individual Religious Ethics versus Religious Warfare

This limited notion of self-defense in specific circumstances highlights the way in which Jewish law and religion is supremely wedded to individual circumstance, which has several ramifications. One of the fundamental challenges to the moral evaluation of war in general, not just Jewish war, is the way in which the word "war" includes such a vast array of unpredictable circumstances, especially modern war. How is the individual who is committed to a personal code of morality expected to suspend all of those values in the context of war? When is the personal code, or the *halakhic* code in the Jewish situation, to be suspended and when is it not to be suspended? When does the obligation to kill, steal, or destroy things as a part of warfare override all of the everyday laws that absolutely prohibit these activities? When exactly is there a suspension of the numerous *halakhic* moral safeguards governing one's internal life and external behavior, which often prohibit even the hint of violence, such as tale bearing or losing one's temper?

Michael Walzer attempts to get at some of these issues by looking at the details of war situations, but it is a difficult enterprise.[26] The same is true of the dichotomy between the extremely high standards of conduct demanded by *halakha* and Jewish pietistic literature as applied to individuals versus the behavior that is apparently acceptable and expected in war. We see from Kimelman's sources that indeed the rabbis expected some complex interaction between these two spheres. But the interaction remains extremely nebulous, as far as I can tell, as if there is a vacuum of experience in this regard. Indeed, there is little experience that rabbinic Judaism has of organized warfare in the last two thousand years in which Jews are the combatants, not the victims. The vast chasm between the life of warfare and the talmudic and medieval pietistic insistence on an utterly sanctified day-to-day, even moment-to-moment, interpersonal lifestyle seems to be insufficiently confronted.[27]

Let us take an example. Person A is part of a group that has expressed hostility to *some* Jews at some point in time, such as Christians in medieval Europe or Arabs today, but has not attacked a Jew himself. Does one treat person A as an enemy, as if war has been declared, or does one owe him all of the moral obligations of the Jewish tradition: honoring him as a creature of God or as an elder (if he is older), greeting him with peace, honoring his property, even loving him as a creature of God, as Hillel did to all gentiles,[28] and so on? Is this stranger perhaps in an in-between state? How can one immediately classify all Christians, Arabs, or Muslims in one category, simply because some of them at some point in time have engaged in hostilities? How does one determine the contours of enemy, friend, righteous gentile, and, most important from a realistic as well as psychological point of view, those who are in-between, neither friend nor foe? These questions are particularly relevant today to Jewish/Arab relations, for example, but have never really been analyzed in Jewish legal tradition due to reasons that wait to be uncovered.

A far deeper problem with the secondary literature on war in Judaism is that it suffers from a compartmentalized and fragmented approach to life. It is only one part of a religious system of belief and practice that actually governs all human interactions. But the literature reads as if the question of war and violence can be discussed and then acted upon utterly divorced from the rest of Jewish morality. In this way, it models itself on discussions of *jus ad bellum* and *jus in bello* in Christian tradition, which have a long history. The latter, however, may be accused of the same thing. Both discussions divorce the subject of war from the rest of the range of religious values applied to the individual, as if these other religious values, such as humility, compassion, and justice, which are incumbent on the individual, were abolished during war or are irrelevant to the decision of whether to participate in a war; the discussions ignore the question of whether there are other avenues of dealing with adversaries short of war and proceed as if the moral imperative somehow disappears on the battlefield. Most important for our subject, regarding the transition from war to peace or peace to war, it is as if the decision to engage in war with an enemy is somehow divorced from the entire set of human interactions that brings groups of people to the brink of conflict, violence, and bloodshed.

Here is the most important point. War, according to all schools of conflict analysis, does not happen in a vacuum without any causal chain leading to it. Furthermore, war is not neatly separated from other human interactions. War is first a distant possibility, then it becomes reality, and then it disappears again. Or it grows, is waged, but suddenly stops due to any number of complex socioeconomic, psychodynamic, and political factors. In other words, whether war happens, how it proceeds, and how and why it ends is a sufficiently complex human phenomenon that it cannot be separated from the range of human choices and behaviors that lead up to it or that interact with it in complex ways. There are innumerable contributing factors that bring people to a state of war, and these factors themselves, be they political, economic, psychological, or ethical, can be further broken down to many individual choices that helped create the atmosphere of war. These innumerable individual choices are precisely the kind of choices that most interest rabbinic *halakhic* Judaism, especially the sources that ask continually, "What brings people to bloodshed?" But this aspect of *halakhic* thinking does not become part of the *halakhic* analysis of war in the scholarly literature.

It is also clear from conflict analysis that war often exists along a continuum from deeply embedded friendship to miscommunication to peaceful but cool coexistence to serious disagreement, and then on to small-scale isolated conflict, large-scale isolated conflict turning into chronic conflict, isolated bloodshed, organized massive bloodshed, and sometimes genocide. This continuum is in itself complex, and it does not always follow a predictable order. But this more nuanced understanding of warmaking as well as peacemaking means that many of the circumstances leading up to war are, in fact, governed morally by other parts of Jewish moral and *halakhic* tradition which apply directly to the individual and to the spiritual community (the *kehillah* in the medieval and modern period), not just to a sovereign or a Sanhedrin. The latter emerge as more important when being attacked. But even afterward they do not supplant the individual's moral decisionmaking in key choices that he makes on the battlefield, as we have seen.

Far too little attention is given, by contrast, to all of the circumstances leading up to attacking or being attacked, how to avoid a conflict that turns into war, which religious values prevent conflict and bloodshed, or what to do when the war or acts of violence are over in terms of mourning, recovery, and reconciliation and the moral laws and values that come into play for this crucial stage of human relations. Rabbinic sources are filled with advice on these matters, but their interpretations are somehow cut off in the secondary literature from the war discussion. This is a distortion—though probably not conscious—of the complex panorama of rabbinic Judaism.

Unprecedented Contemporary Circumstances, Hermeneutics, and Antimodern Backlash

The contemporary period has given rise to circumstances that have never been encountered before in rabbinic Judaism, namely, the juxtaposition of the most detailed codes of personal moral piety, developed over millennia, with a level of Jewish military ability to kill in war that is far greater than anything that ever occurred before in rabbinic history; this is especially true due to the massive and unprecedented killing power of modern weaponry. This juxtaposition is a critical example of what I would call a time of hermeneutic intensity, namely, a period when the personal horizon of those who read and internalize sacred texts and traditions has been virtually assaulted by the broadest set of unprecedented circumstances of history.[29] Thus, reading, rereading, and reading in the context of lived experience become paramount. Furthermore, one of the most important religious, and certainly rabbinic impulses, as demonstrated by the Tosafists and classical compilers of *halakhic* compendiums in earlier centuries, is the drive to integrate sacred literature, that is, to make it internally coherent. This, as an end in and of itself, forces the hermeneutic enterprise to unprecedented readings. When this is wedded to unprecedented shifts in one's hermeneutic horizon, this leads to or can lead to especially unprecedented readings.

At the same time, however, there has been a global backlash of fundamentalist traditions against precisely this process of reading and rereading, at least as a conscious process. There is plenty of rewriting of history and claims to authenticity in fundamentalist circles, but the rage against the liberal state, the antireligious thrust of some expressions of the Enlightenment and socialism, and the barrenness of the materialist global civilization, which some blame specifically on modern thinking, have driven many to a conscious unwillingness to see innovation and rereading as anything but destructive to their only line of defense against a world bereft of truth and certainty. On the other side, many of those Jews who have broken with *halakhic* Judaism as an authoritative guide to life see no need to address with a new hermeneutic the violent sources of Judaism or those dealing with war. They simply reject them.

Little of this rereading of text and tradition has been done, therefore, by the majority of conservatives and liberals, other than in a few exceptional circles. Furthermore, there are separate provinces for war literature, peace literature, and personal ethics literature, with little integration. Those who have embraced the political value of Jewish warfare, for various contemporary reasons, have tended to focus exclusively on *milhama* and its limits. Those who are particularly horrified at the prospect of modern warfare seize on the *shalom* texts, pacifist-oriented, personal, pietistic virtues that appear throughout rabbinic literature, while those who recoil utterly from the use of Jewish power in the modern world continue to study, teach, and write about the ethical piety literature, as if Jewish military power did not exist.

There is yet another contemporary alternative with some deep implications for the future of Judaism, the Jewish people, and the Jewish state. There are those who divorce entirely the ethics of personal and communal piety from Jewish issues of the use of power when that power is used against or in contention with gentiles. In other words, the ethical piety literature becomes a racial category, exclusively for Jews, while the war (*milhama*) literature is for gentile relations. This has an eerie relationship with the medieval Islamic categories of values that govern *dar al-harb* versus those that govern *dar al-islam*, though the latter was not a racial division, and both categories could apply to born Muslims, depending on their status in the faith.[30] But it suggests a dangerous direction of Jewish ethics to reserve all the subtlety and beauty of prosocial piety for one group, namely fellow Jews—and sometimes only fellow religious Jews of one group—while focusing the war literature on gentiles.

This must be seen in the larger context of the human tendency to bifurcate one's universe into a sphere of ultimate violence against some constructed Other and the focus of prosocial life on some limited group. In extreme circumstances of clan warfare this reduces down to prosocial ethics extending only to members of one's own family.[31] There is, in fact, an insidious, cannibalistic tendency of these bifurcations that, over time, reduce further and further the amount of people who reside inside one's moral universe. One could see this in the progressively more ubiquitous violence of European fascisms, national socialism, and Leninism/ Stalinism, which all started out with some chosen group for special care, such as a racial or ethnic group or a group of workers or farmers. But everyone is eventually terrorized, except for "party" members, and they are eventually terrorized as well. Hitler eventually relished burning his own cities and killing Aryan children who did not join his dying army.

This bifurcation is not necessary to human ethics or religious ethics. It *is* a human tendency but one that can be modulated, as we clearly see in the hermeneutic history of religious ethical traditions, which at times excels regarding the Other and at times fails miserably. Improving the general state of ethics does not require that everyone be treated absolutely equally, in the extreme form resulting in not caring for your own child or parent more than others. But it does require a self-conscious effort to work with difficult life circumstances, especially life-threatening conflicts, in order to find a way to extend prosocial ethics wherever and whenever possible, while also protecting one's own life and the lives of loved ones and even one's ethnic or religious group. It requires a self-conscious process of avoiding the worst pitfalls of bifurcating one's moral universe.

Conflict Analysis and Resolution Theory in Relation to Religious Ethics

The key reason that a new hermeneutics is essential for the future of Jewish thinking on the subject is the new analysis that is emerging in the contemporary world about the nature of conflict, its prevention, and its resolution, particularly as these insights are applied to ethnic groups and their unique cultural expressions.[32] Jews and Judaism will become a critical topic of this literature, particularly because Jews and Judaism have, as minorities and a minority religion, respectively, been particularly subject to conflict, often deadly conflict.[33] An integrative conception of Jewish attitudes toward peacemaking, conflict, and warmaking will have to include not only an internal or phenomenal analysis of Judaism and its hermeneutics but also an epiphenomenal analysis of the place in the world in which Jews have found themselves situated; the latter, however, is beyond the confines of the present study.

Conflict resolution theory has been critiqued for its tendency to be culturally rooted in a secular but neo-Protestant Western context that tends to make universal assumptions about what works and what does not work in conflict resolution, peacemaking, and the reconciliation of parties. As the literature cited above indicates, what is conflict-resolving activity in each culture often involves unique ritual expressions, a unique constellation of values that work together to reduce tension, facilitate communication, and ultimately reconcile parties. In some traditions this is a highly developed art, whereas in others it is either undeveloped or deeply embedded and unarticulated at the present time.

The fact is that all three monotheistic traditions have extensive systems of interpersonal ethics, much of which directly addresses the challenges of human relationships and directly confronts the human tendencies that can lead away from or toward conflict, violence, and war. The sources in Judaism, for example, that address the question of war, discussed above, actually only occupy a handful of pages of the Mishnah, Talmud, and later *halakhic* collections. On the other hand, there are thousands of rabbinic sources on a broad range of ethical values, which are specifically designed to prevent economic disagreement, misunderstanding, disrespect, callousness, conflict, hatred, revenge, violence, and bloodshed. Effectively, a large portion of Jewish ethics governs behaviors that, each in their own way, constitute broad and complex areas of human intercourse that lead toward or away from conflict.

More specifically, *shalom* is mentioned more than twenty-five hundred times in classical Jewish sources. There has also been a respectable contemporary literature that builds on the classical sources that extol the ideal of peace in Judaism.[34] More important for our purposes than peace as a metaphysical value are at least thirty eight references to the *mitsvah* of peacemaking (*redifat shalom*) as a practice, which have pragmatic strategies for preventing or resolving conflict. For example, *perek ha-shalom*, the Chapter on Peace of the Babylonian Talmud, has a variety of ethical insights that include conflict resolution techniques, such as shuttle diplomacy, empathy, and unilateral gestures to evoke a response in the other party to a conflict.[35] The literature on repentance involves a range of activities designed to make peace between people, including confession of wrongdoing, commitment to a change of behavior in the future, asking of forgiveness, and offering of forgiveness.[36] There are many other traditions, including the Hebrew biblical commitment to aiding an enemy and its expansion by rabbinic texts to suggest that the law in Exodus 23:5 is designed as a conflict resolution device: "When you see the ass of your enemy lying under its burden, and would refrain from raising it, you must nevertheless raise it with him." Helping the enemy with a burden would change his opinion of you.[37] It is a classic example of a strategy involving unilateral gestures, which cause cognitive dissonance in the enemy, which, in turn, is specifically designed to cause a rethinking of the cognitive structure of self and enemy.

This is directly relevant to one of the key themes of conflict analysis theory. Human beings are content with and even enjoy moderate levels of cognitive dissonance. It stimulates intellectual and emotional growth and is actually enjoyable for the curious mind. But, at a certain juncture, especially in the midst of conflict, the world begins to overwhelm the senses and the emotions. This is when members of combating communities need to simplify the universe. The conflict must become a cosmic battle of good and evil, and it is vital, for the sake of emotional consistency, that there is nothing redeeming in one's enemy.

Biblical Judaism, buttressed by rabbinic amplification, made the case that a way to jolt the combatants out of what Mack calls "the enemy system"[38] is by mandating that there must be gestures of aid and sharing even with the enemy. Proverbs 25:21–22 cryptically suggests, and the rabbis amplify, the psychological strategy of breaking the enemy system of cognition, thus allowing for the possibility of negotiation and even reconciliation to take place. The Bible in other places may recommend calling out to a city in peace first—which is reminiscent of initial negotiation efforts in conflict resolution practice—but the text above suggests that this negotiation can only take place successfully when the psychological impasse has been overcome.

Toward a Jewish Ethic of Conflict Prevention and Resolution

We will amplify this theme in a later chapter, but let us briefly make some suggestions now. A Jewish conflict resolution theory, applied to individuals as well as to large groups, would have to include strategies of this psychological sort—authentic gestures of aid to an enemy or an enemy group—in order to fulfill the letter and spirit of this Exodus law. For large groups in conflict, this would have to entail extensive gestures by many individuals to members of the enemy group.[39] Furthermore, they could not be perfunctory gestures, if they are to fulfill the rabbinic amplification of this biblical law. They have to be sufficiently authentic and clever that they truly cause the enemy to experience real cognitive dissonance, a real questioning of previously held assumptions. This, by all accounts of conflict resolution theory, takes a great deal of work. Thus, the *mitsvah*, the divinely taught good deed, of *redifat shalom* would entail an extensive understanding of the attitudes and feelings of the enemy, in addition to a good working knowledge of psychology and conflict resolution practice. Just as some medieval Jewish philosophers argued that fulfilling the *mitsvah* of knowledge of

God required years of training intellectually, and most *halakhic* authorities would argue today that the *mitsvah* of saving a life requires a doctor to have years of arduous training, I would argue that the *mitsvah* of Exodus 23:5, the *mitsvah* of conflict resolution, if it were to be taken seriously in the discourse of Jewish ethics, would have to entail years of training and a good working knowledge of general conflict resolution theory and practice.

Exodus 23:5 is also an expression of a unique conflict resolution strategy of shared activity, which humanizes the enemy, removing his status as an objectified embodiment of evil.[40] You work with the enemy on some shared project, in this case helping a distressed animal, which, in their times, meant also helping the enemy with the transportation system for his livelihood. This method of building human relationships has deep resonance in Jewish culture, with the latter's emphasis much more on behavior and less on dialogue as a solution to human problems. The rabbinic relationship-building process is far more attuned to doing things and sharing things, both as moral acts in and of themselves and as symbolic acts that convey to the enemy a conciliatory intention that is not merely words but something that has been concretized as deed.[41]

This speaks to another critical conflict resolution tool: trust building. It may very well be that deep in Jewish traditional and cultural responses to the world is the perception or intuition that actions are the only things to be trusted and, therefore, are the only real tools of peacemaking. This has enormous ramifications in terms of the development of Jewish thinking, culture, and even the *halakha* itself, as the subject of conflict resolution is hermeneutically engaged in the years to come. It also has important ramifications for those who would attempt to engage in peacemaking with significant portions of the Jewish community.

Islamic Possibilities and Contemporary Impasses

The methodology of investigation of peace and conflict that we are proposing here can also be a bridge to Islamic and Arabic cultures, which also highly value symbolic ethical gestures from one person or group to another, especially involving gestures of honor and magnanimity and the moral values that these gestures embody.[42] It may be that both traditions have been unsuited to attempts thus far to engage them in terms of Western styles of dialogic peacemaking. While it may be the case that Western efforts and interventions in the Middle East have resonated with those in the local cultures who are Western educated and sympathetic to Western thinking, these same efforts may not have resonated with those who consider themselves to be more closely connected to or actual guardians of their indigenous cultures. Of course, this failure at cross-cultural communication is not the sole problem with Western involvement in Middle Eastern conflict, but neither should it be ignored as an important underlying factor.

Conflict resolution through dialogue has special resonance in the West, particularly in Protestant cultures where the spirit of God is discovered through the communion of the faithful by way of harmonious conversation.[43] Western styles of conflict resolution certainly have more than this one source, including the legal tradition of disputation and negotiation, which also has early European roots. The case has been made, however, that there are numerous styles of conflict resolution around the world and that we have only begun to uncover these indigenous sources.[44] The Exodus source cited above, in addition to rabbinic sources that have Aaron, the high priest, engaging in particular methods of peacemaking that do not involve face-to-face negotiations, suggest that rabbinic Judaism has its own indigenous methods of conflict resolution that would be vital to uncover in order to develop a full picture of rabbinic attitudes toward warmaking and peacemaking. This also suggests that there are methods of peacemaking in Judaism and Islam that may yet affect the continually evolving hermeneutic constructs of the respective religious communities.[45]

The Problem of the Scope of Monotheistic Ethical Concern in Relation to War and Peace

A key challenge to peacemaking in all of the monotheistic traditions is their tendency to limit prosocial ethical values to members of the religion, or ingroup, as mentioned above. This is certainly true but only up to a point and certainly not universally. More investigation needs to be done on exactly how outsiders are viewed theologically and how they are treated in various historical circumstances over large spans of time, both in principal and in practice. Which religious subgroups of the respective religions have limited the scope or expanded the scope of their ethical universe? The scope of religious ethics, that is, who it includes, is a critical determinant and prognosticator of the system of ethics' contribution to violence or conflict resolution.

I do not mean to imply that only those religions, or interpretations of religion, that unconditionally treat everyone equally will contribute less to war. It may be impossible to create religious institutions without special systems of care for adherents nor is it necessarily desirable to do so. Many would question the moral wisdom of an ethical system without any distinctions or preferential treatment for loved ones. Furthermore, universalist religious traditions that claim to care for all have done at least as much damage historically as those religions that have preferential treatment for fellow believers. There has been a fine line, often crossed in the history of European culture, between universalist concern, on the one side, and, on the other, majority oppression, when it comes to issues of religion and culture. The two unconsciously fused in the minds of the most liberal thinkers of the Enlightenment and, therefore, caused great damage in the long run.

The real issue is the *degree* to which distinctions are made between believers and nonbelievers by a religious tradition and the nature of the treatment of the nonbelievers. This is the key question in terms of future attitudes toward war and peace. Contrary to standard modern assumptions that the only good society is a universal society where there are no distinctions, I would argue that boundaries between religious—and other—groupings are a fundamental feature of human life. They seem to play a crucial role in terms of the human need to belong to groups that give them unique identities. The real question is how does one's group negotiate the boundaries between self and Other. Do those boundaries require dehumanization of the Other or not, do they require war, or do they require compassion, justice, or even love toward those who are beyond the boundary of the group? This is what has been subject to great hermeneutic diversity over the centuries and especially in the modern era.

There is a tendency on the part of many traditional Jewish commentators emerging out of premodern Europe to see most prosocial ethics of religious Jews to be focused on fellow religious Jews. There are, to be sure, extensively developed laws regarding treatment of the gentile and the obeying of secular law that essentially make the Jew, according to *halakha*, a law-abiding citizen in a predominantly non-Jewish society. There are prohibitions against murder and theft from non-Jews, among other things. But what about the deeper interpersonal laws of which I spoke above? Here we see that often traditions stemming from interpretations of the Talmud will limit those laws to fellow law-abiding Jews. A good example is Leviticus 19:18, "And you shall love your neighbor as yourself." This is limited to fellow religious Jews by most premodern authorities. Thus we have the coexistence of several laws designed for law-abiding coexistence with non-Jews but few of the prosocial laws applied universally.

The problem is that the prosocial laws, I would argue, are especially relevant for the questions of war and peace, for how to prevent and resolve conflicts, for how to reconcile with enemies that have really hurt you or that you have hurt. The modern period, *before the Holocaust*, however, elicits some changes in this regard from some key authorities and commentators. Ernst Simon records the fact that Rabbis Mecklenberg and Hoffman directly suggest that this verse is to be applied universally.[46] Simon has trouble with this development, assuming that it is merely apologetics, a lame effort to show that Jewish law is not backward in the liberal nineteenth-century context. He claims that we should see this as a clandestine effort on the part of these men to suggest that there is something higher than the law in Judaism, whether it be ethics or conscience.

We cannot here delve into the complex theoretical problem of the interrelationship of law and ethics in general or, in particular, regarding this matter in Judaism. But I would argue that Simon has imposed his own definition of Jewish law on the traditional sources and then argues for the rejection of that structure of law as immoral. In other words, he takes honest attempts, in classic Gadamerian fashion, to develop the law hermeneutically within its own bounds, declares this process to be mere apologetics, and then argues for the rejection of those laws. What is "apologetics" to Simon, however, may be to another person or religious authority the dynamic and vibrant process of hermeneutic interactions among a highly valued religious traditional body of law, the changing facts of the world, and the conscience of the responsible lawmaker. Those *halakhic* decision makers, such as Me'iri, who saw their relationship with gentiles as profoundly different, in fact much better, than that of their predecessors, had to come to the conclusion that many prosocial laws that previously had excluded gentiles must now apply to gentiles in the current circumstances. Why? Because the world had changed, and a good legal system responds dynamically to new situations. Personal interviews that I have had with Rabbi Dr. Joseph Soloveitchik, the leading twentieth-century Orthodox interpreter of talmudic law, yielded the same results, namely, that many antisocial laws of the medieval law codes were meant to be used in circumstances of absolute or potential violence between Jews and gentiles, when it was a threat to Jewish life to trust gentiles or when it would make Jews mortally vulnerable to engage gentiles socially. This is a common assumption among many modern Orthodox thinkers in the last couple of hundred years.

Similarly, Samuel David Luzzatto (d. 1865) was for forty years the central figure at an Orthodox Jewish rabbinical seminary in Padua in the early nineteenth century. A moral sense theorist, deeply influenced by David Hume and Jean Jacques Rousseau, but also a leading figure of and defender of Italian Orthodox Judaism, he developed a Jewish *halakhic* ethics founded upon prosocial emotions, as we will see in later chapters. He stated, "Compassion in Judaism is required toward all. It extends, like [the compassion] of God, to all of His creatures. No one is excluded from the Law [Torah], because all human beings, according to Jewish teachings, are brothers, are children of the same father and are created in the image of God."[47] Now, is Luzzatto, one of the greatest authorities of his century on Jewish texts, after forty years of teaching Orthodox Judaism, knowing full well all the premodern sources, simply engaged in facile uninformed apologetics, or is he hermeneutically engaged with a conservative yet dynamic, changing legal tradition? Religious law, even conservative religious law, changes with the circumstances of human relationships. Even the more jarring elements of worldwide religious conservatism today have depended on change, though it is completely denied.

This reality of choosing, subtle though it may appear on the outside, has a direct bearing on decisions made about the negotiation of conflict, and, therefore, the conclusions that individuals and communities make about war. There are dynamic choices made concerning war and peace and, especially, regarding the extension of the moral boundaries of religious community, that is, who is considered included or excluded by the highest expressions of a tradition's moral universe. This is by far the most important ingredient in the discovery of prosocial traditions that directly affect issues of peace and war.

Islamic Parallels

Nineteenth-century Indian Muslim reflection on *jihad* and its relationship to the state is another example of our thesis. Despite a long tradition of dividing the world between *dar al-harb* and *dar al-islam* and, according to Khadduri, an extensive tradition of *jihad* fought in a variety of circumstances, *ulama* (religious leaders) emerge in India to proclaim that anywhere that Muslims enjoy religious freedom there is no justification of *jihad* against a state.[48] Now, who agrees with this in what time periods and who disagrees under what circumstances is what is most interesting in terms of the dynamic of warmaking and peacemaking in religious traditions.

Even this, however, does not do justice to the full complexity of Islamic tradition. The Islamic view of *jihad* is no more complete a picture of the variety of Islamic attitudes toward the tragedy of conflict, violence, and war or to the phenomenon of interpersonal ethics than is the limitation of either tradition to a discussion of biblical holy war.

Medieval Islamic ethical theories entailed highly developed systems of moral interpersonal behavior. Much of the earliest expression of these ethics is directly rooted in what Fakhry referred to as scriptural morality, morality directly derived from a close reading of sacred scriptures, namely, the Qur'an.[49] Key components here are the concepts of goodness (*khayr*) and righteousness (*birr*). Related to these, and deeply important to Islamic tradition are the values of *al-iqsat* (equity), *al-'adl* (justice), and *al-haqq* (truth and right). These concepts naturally have their counterparts in other religious traditions, though each tradition has its unique hermeneutic and ethical applications of these values. For example, Luzzatto makes Genesis 18:19, regarding justice and righteousness, the quintessential mandate of Judaism.[50] These values provide an interesting bridge of interpersonal ethics between Islam and Judaism, even assuming different histories of interpretation. Yet, if the analysis of Islam is limited to texts on war, we never see the full range of traditional approaches to problems of human interaction.

Yahya ibn 'Adi (d. 974) developed a set of cultural values, emanating out of his tradition, that included dignity, forgiveness, friendliness, compassion, loyalty, confidence keeping, humility, purity of intention, generosity, and magnanimity. Vices included greed, cruelty, and treachery.[51] In the long history in which Islam was the dominant religion in particular regions, where there were many non-Muslims, such as Jews, living with them, we must assume that, in addition to philosophical and political deliberations over *jihad* and other rules of a dominant political order, there were also countless interreligious relationships in which the values we are discussing here played key roles. There is no way, that Jewish/Muslim relationships could have flourished at certain points in Spain and North Africa without extensive positive interpersonal values being practiced daily by thousands of people of both faiths and with those values applied to members of another faith. And yet, if we limit the discussion in Islam regarding conflict to justifications of *jihad*, we never understand the subtle complexity of its moral tradition, and we never see the prosocial elements of a large, long-standing religious society. When it came to the wars of the caliphs and wars of expansion, there is an extensive body of law justifying—as well as limiting—the conduct of war, as can be seen in Khadduri's writing.[52] War, despite being constrained in theory by certain moral laws, clearly involves the suspension of the prosocial values discussed here. Nevertheless, we cannot have a full conception of the attitudes toward conflict, conflict prevention, and even prevention of full violent hostilities if we do not include an analysis of the range of interpersonal values embraced by a religious tradition, which have clearly been operative in the lives of millions of its adherents throughout history.

Conclusions: Hermeneutics, Religious Ethics, and the Negotiation of Conflict and Peacemaking in Traditional Societies

We have the opportunity as conflict theorists, if we seize upon it, to use the knowledge of what interpersonal values are prominent in a particular religious tradition and culture to understand better the genesis of a conflict or even a war. If dignity, nobility of character, and confidence keeping are essential characteristics in a certain culture, as they are in several Islamic traditions, we might expect that the violation of these values by members of the faith—but especially by outsiders—will likely generate conflict, possibly leading to violence and even to war. In other words, as important in understanding war as concepts such as *jihad* and *milhemet mitsvah* may in fact be, the real challenge may be to discover the interpersonal values most highly prized by a culture and how an enemy at some early stage of the relationship violated those values, thus intentionally or unintentionally striking at the heart of the relationship. This is one of my most important points. These moral failures, conflict resolution theory should argue, are early but crucial indicators of how wars get started and how they are eventually justified. The rhetoric of war, even in deeply religious societies, almost never simply states a legal or moral obligation to kill on a massive scale. Generally, the enemy needs to be portrayed as utterly corrupt, an infidel, or not human altogether. This is not just a result of the cynical manipulation of interhuman imagery by a leadership bent on war. People often gladly embrace this process of dehumanization, which suggests that there is often a dismantling of human moral relationships that occurs much earlier than actual war. This, in turn, suggests that there is much in the prosocial interpersonal values of a religious tradition that exists to prevent conflict and to build human relationships. Without understanding their presence in a tradition, we do not understand how their absence is a key progenitor of war. And without understanding their absence as a progenitor of war, we will not understand how the introduction of prosocial religious values, or their reintroduction, across enemy lines becomes a key method of indigenous and culturally profound conflict resolution.

I would suggest that in order to truly understand war and peace in these religious traditions and, most important, to understand this murky space in between war and peace where people and civilizations really make the fateful decision to humanize or dehumanize the Other, it is vital to learn the broad range of interpersonal and communal ethical ideals that have served as the cohesive force of sustainable communities since their beginnings. Often these ethical ideals have been applied to members of other faiths, paradoxically coexisting with laws and values designed to undo that very relationship or even to justify war against people of those other faiths. It seems that the hermeneutic of applying values and laws to ever-changing human societies and social constructs has always been a dynamic, paradoxical process. Therefore, it behooves us when speaking of war in religious traditions to speak not only of the justifications for war or the limitations of its conduct but also of the primordial prosocial moral/spiritual values that so often undermined the genesis of internecine and interreligious warfare, preventing war from ever breaking out.

We have a tendency, perhaps due to an understandable fear of war, to highlight its prominence in history, including religious history. But we distort that history if we do not ask why that state of war did not exist or does not presently continue *all the time*, since there are laws that justify it and even require it, such as some of the laws that we have discussed. What prevented a permanent state of war, a perpetual struggle against infidels, apostates, idolaters, or enemies of the people? What were the interpersonal values that constituted the framework of the years of coexistence? And how did that state of peace break down at some point and then yield to a new religious hermeneutic of war? Those are the theological, sociohistorical, and anthropological questions that will truly complete our understanding of war in religious traditions. Clearly, there have been in most religions mandates for coexistence with Others that occasionally reign supreme. They may not be a perfect equivalent of the more unconditional guarantees of civil equality that we seek today, but they could form the basis for a healthy coalescence of goals with even the most fundamentalist representatives of a religion.

There are some things about the past and its context that remain elusive, however. It is true that we can never know completely, for example, the context of the biblical *herem* laws. Were they ever carried out? Was this a myth to frighten syncretistic Israelites into monotheism, or was it a real genocidal plan of action? We simply do not know enough about the *sitz-im-leben* (the text's cultural and social context). But we do know enough to say that in the developing hermeneutic of Judaism, the *herem* law about conquest was discontinued by the rabbis at a certain juncture, not to be applied again to the indigenous inhabitants of Israel. On the other hand, as part of a sacred tradition, the text never disappears, and the possibility of a new hermeneutic exists as well. Part of the conservative character of Judaism and Islam is that all the texts that are believed to be divinely revealed, those that extol war as well as those that model peacemaking, will always remain sacred, though which texts within that body are favored and highlighted will always be changing. Despite the best efforts of religious authorities to control the direction of the hermeneutics, the texts will always be there to be reinterpreted. Essentially, war is a permanent part of the texts of both Islam and Judaism. In the other great monotheism, Christianity, the sacred story will always have to contain a space for some group that rejects Jesus, someone who betrays him, and someone who kills him. But equally embedded in these traditions are the profound prosocial values and the resulting conflict prevention and resolution strategies that lie embedded in the respective histories of these ethical systems. Which texts, stories, or laws gain the upper hand depends on the hermeneutics of the generation, which, in turn, depends upon the subtleties and intricacies of the human relationships of that generation.

War never occurs full-blown in religious history out of thin air. It takes a great many human relationships to fail and a great many interpersonal values of a religious system to be violated in order to bring war here and now to full religious consciousness and acceptance. Thus, if we are to fully understand war in these monotheistic traditions, we must understand the full range of religious values that break down in human relationships, which, in turn, makes war into an attractive religious alternative to religious peacemaking. Furthermore, peacemaking, with all of the requisite moral values that it entails, remains a continual hermeneutic possibility within each tradition, awaiting a reader or readers to rework the sacred traditions, symbols, and values in terms of relationship building both before and after conflict.

Finally, the scope of ethical concern is always being renegotiated by the readers of the texts, whether those readers be authority figures or anyone with access to the text and a creative, daring approach to his religion. Thus, the scope of ethical concern may be restricted to only members of my subgroup of my religion, who are the truly observant, faithful, or saved. But it may also be extended by me to include every human being, every animal, and even the earth itself. These traditions really contain both possibilities at the same time, and it is the reader or readers and the generation, influenced by all the complex economic and social psychological phenomena that evoke peace or violence from human beings, that determines which readings will become paramount.

In this chapter we have examined the limits of the religious just war discussion in addressing the deep causes of conflict and responding to them. In the next chapter, we will examine the problem of creating theological constructs of religion in the modern period that favor peace and tolerance. Liberal forms of the world's religions have flourished in all parts of the globe in the last hundred years, and they tend to favor constructs of civil society that make peacemaking and conflict resolution into religious experiences. On the other hand, the more conservative expressions of these same religions have tended to house militant approaches to Others that is conflict generating in a variety of ways, some directly through violence, others through intolerance, prejudice, or aggressive forms of proselytism.

Any strategy of conflict resolution in religious societies would have to be able to address the section of the society that is the most conservative, because it is from there that the violence usually comes. It will be instructive, therefore, to examine in the next chapter the construction of two modern, conservative approaches to tradition, which combine conservatism with a benevolent approach to the rest of the world. It is in the analysis of such constructs that one finds clues as to how conservative religious culture is capable of change and capable of generating those skills and qualities that we normally associate with conflict resolution and the construction of a civil society. It is also instructive to explore what the limitations are of these constructs in addressing the practical questions of conflict resolution, coexistence, and the construction of a contemporary civil society that has a large, dominant secular structure.

FIVE

Modern Jewish Orthodox Theologies of Interreligious Coexistence

Strengths and Weaknesses

The level of contact between people of many faiths in the last hundred years has led to some unprecedented developments in religious belief and practice. It is true that an approach to faith and practice that acknowledges the existence of other religions has been a staple of human religious experience since the dawn of civilization. But after many centuries of extremely intolerant monotheistic religious warfare, there is a decidedly important group of monotheists who have embraced multifaith contacts and exchanges. This, in turn, has led to some interesting shifts in religious consciousness. From the Parliament of World Religions in the late nineteenth century right up to our own time there is more and more conversation both on what makes us all different in the scores of world religions and on what binds us together. It is the latter that has led to a distinctive form of religious humanitarianism that suggests an important hermeneutic evolution of religion, at least for those who have come to subscribe to this kind of humanitarianism.

Let me be more specific. If one looks at a sampling of multifaith documents of recent decades, one discovers a remarkable level of commonality of both goals and values expressed by leaders of many world religions.[1] There is clearly a trend among some, especially those whose education runs wide and deep, to engage in a selective hermeneutic of their traditions that emphasizes what they share in common with the liberal humanitarianism of the Enlightenment.

This has also led, however, by way of reaction probably, to those who hermeneutically engage in the opposite, namely, the interpretive selection of that which makes their tradition distinctive, superior, and particularly opposed to the Enlightenment, or opposed to the kind of liberal humanitarian values expressed in the Universal Declaration of Human Rights.

What is most crucial for conflict analysis and resolution, when it comes to religion, is a focus on those hermeneutic trends that are felt to be authentic by a large portion of believers. Conflict resolution theory and practice must be interested in those trends that embrace values that could be commensurate with peacemaking and coexistence both inside the religious groups as well as between them and Others. Despite the fact that there are liberal elites in each religion who embrace tolerance and coexistence, if this is not embedded in the experience of the majority, then we must understand this and work with it, rather than pretend, as many liberal institutions do, that it is not there. Pretensions of dominant groups always leave us poorly prepared for the conflict and violence that lurks beneath the surface of a given culture.

Let us take an example. It is quite wonderful if the majority of liberal Protestants in universities embrace nonracialist thinking in South Africa. But more to the point in terms of conflict resolution is whether the rank-and-file members of, say, the Dutch Reformed church, as well as the church hierarchy, truly embrace nonracialist thinking and behavior. It is the masses of people in a country that determine its ultimate character. How do these rank-and-file people change? It happens by a decidedly new hermeneutic of Afrikaner Christianity that may perhaps now evolve. It happens when active members of the church engage in a serious hermeneutic of their own tradition and then teach that to the lay community. Most crucial of all, people change when a new hermeneutic is inserted into the symbolic and ritual life of the religious community. This is the most effective way to change the broadest spectrum of citizens in a society. This is a method of transforming opinions, giving people the cognitive and behavioral capacity to engage in peacemaking and tolerance, while at the same time maintaining the authenticity of a tradition with those members who guard that authenticity zealously. Guarding the authenticity of tradition is a deep human need in many people; it is a defense of the existential identity of a group and its members. The most effective way to enlist the guards in the cause of peacemaking is not to destroy what they need to protect but to hermeneutically engage their traditions in a way that *enhances* their sense of pride in what they guard so carefully. It is fine to work with those whose religious hermeneutics lead them to a wide and pluralistic embrace of wisdom from many sources, including documents such as the Universal Declaration. But these are not the people, by definition, who resort to violence in the name of religion. Peacemaking strategies must speak deeply to those who are the most at risk to create destructive conflict in the name of their religion.

As we move to the Jewish community, it is important to understand that the attitude of Jews and Judaism toward the rest of the world is a key litmus test of their embrace or nonembrace of a range of values related to conflict resolution. After at least a millennium of persecution, or certainly memory of persecution, in Christian lands, in addition to some internal hermeneutic developments within Judaism that are intolerant, the pressure on normative Judaism to be something less than peaceful in reaction to non-Jews is high today, especially now that Jews are a majority somewhere in the world, specifically in Israel.

Nineteenth-century Western European Orthodoxy is particularly interesting because it was one of the few Orthodoxies[2] to have flourished in a somewhat more hopeful and less anti-Semitic environment, unlike its Eastern European counterparts and unlike the Orthodoxies of today, whose theologians and rabbinic guardians are reeling from the trauma of the Holocaust. I am particularly interested in this subgroup precisely because the question of whether there can be a peacemaking, tolerant Orthodoxy is one of the central issues today facing the Jewish people and, indeed, the Middle East. This is the case because of the meteoric rise in prominence and power of Orthodoxy in contemporary Jewish culture and political life. In many ways, today's Orthodoxies are still in crisis mode, engaged in emergency measures to rebuild everything that was lost in Europe. But let us turn to the nineteenth century for the moment and then return later to contemporary analysis.

Ever since the beginning of the Enlightenment, there has been a markedly tolerant shift in the philosophical and ethical stance of Jews and Judaism toward non-Jews and their religions. This is certainly true in the social sphere, in political conceptualization of the liberal society, and in the extension of ethical commitments to non-Jews.[3] But this has generally been considered typical mostly of liberal Jewish thought and in opposition to Orthodox philosophical and *halakhic* constructs. But a closer look at the details of the philosophical and ethical positions in this matter yield some surprising results.

While in the practical realm there was a considerable degree of acceptance of gentiles among liberal Jewish philosophers of the Enlightenment and the nineteenth century, there was also a significant effort to articulate, especially in Germany, the supremacy of Judaism over all other faiths. Among some philosophers there was even a perpetuation, at least on a philosophical level, of the need to destroy false religions.[4] For example, Hermann Cohen, the great exponent of ethical monotheism and the ethical treatment of the stranger, stated:

> The worship of the unique God unavoidably exacts the destruction of false worship. In this respect there can be no pity and no regard for men. . . . Therefore the worship of false gods must be annihilated from the earth.[5]

On the other hand, some modern Orthodox formulations of Judaism are astonishingly accepting in principle of gentile religions. This is particularly true in Italy.

Samuel David Luzzatto's philosophy was a careful construction of a moral sense theory out of the sources of the Bible and rabbinic literature. It demonstrates a profound relationship to the Scottish Enlightenment school of moral sense theory and to figures such as Rousseau, Hume, and Shaftesbury.[6] Luzzatto's benevolent attitude toward gentiles stemmed from his early childhood as amply demonstrated in his *Autobiografia*.[7] But the moral commitment to gentiles was not just a personal or sentimental one. It is at the heart of Luzzatto's construction of Jewish philosophy and the ethics of *halakha*. The most important moral sense in his construct is the Italian moral sense of *compassione* or the Jewish moral sense of *hemlah*. By definition, this sentiment extends universally, even to nonhuman creatures. *Halakhah*'s object is to strengthen this sentiment and formalize it in terms of virtually all human relations.

Further acceptance of gentiles is found in some rather astonishing biblical hermeneutics regarding monotheism and idolatry. Luzzatto argued that biblical Judaism's main problem with idolatry is immorality and, particularly, brutality *not* its metaphysical errors. This sets him apart from most Jewish philosophers, even among modern liberal theologians.

Elijah Benamozegh (1823–1900), the Orthodox rabbi of Livorno (Leghorn) for more than a half century and a Kabbalist philosopher, demonstrated in his post-humous work, *Israel et Humanité*, and several other rare commentaries a bold interest in and embrace of Christian and pagan religious symbols and ideas.[8] In his philosophy, all of the most significant theosophical concepts in the major religions stem in one way or another from the eternal truths of Kabbalah. Even the Trinity, a concept generally considered anathema in Orthodox circles, is considered derivative of the lower portion of the *sefirotic* structure and merely "mistaken" in its translation into physical incarnation.[9] Benamozegh further strengthens his commitment to the gentile world through his non-Jewish student, Aimé Pallière, who he converts to "Noachism," not Judaism.[10]

These models demonstrate the need to reanalyze the nature of modern Orthodoxy, the hermeneutic dynamics of modern traditional thought, the ever-present question of Jewish particular and universal moral commitments, and the question of Jewish universal versus particularist self-perceptions and self-definitions.

Luzzatto, or Shadal (the acronym of his full name), was one of the most pragmatically oriented thinkers in the history of Jewish thought. His assumption was that the entire structure of Torah beliefs and practices is geared toward the creation of the good person, particularly the compassionate person. As such, even the central axis of monotheism, the rejection of a plurality of deities, was subject to his pragmatic/ethical cross-examination. Luzzatto asked an astounding question regarding the second commandment of the Torah: Why does God care whether people believe in his unity, or whether they worship gods other than him? "For does the worship of idols harm human society?"[11] The answer for Luzzatto was that, indeed, idolatry is socially harmful. The belief in many gods allows for the possibility of worshiping evil as a separate sacred entity or god, and therefore it encourages people to become evil.[12] This is an astounding position. Luzzatto actually can ask of this tradition what is wrong with idolatry! One would think that idolatry is the quintessential denial of the essence of monotheism and Judaism, as in the Maimonidean position. But for Luzzatto the highest good in the world is the inculcation of goodness in humanity, not the inculcation of religious dogma. God wants to foster, by his teachings, the good person, not the good theologian. This is God's highest aim, and monotheism is simply the best instrument to accomplish this. That is why Luzzatto's question is even possible.

This position has serious moral implications in terms of the treatment of non-Jews, especially idolaters, and may explain why Luzzatto has such a qualitatively different attitude toward them than philosophers with other theological orientations. It makes the boundary between the Jewish self and the gentile Other far more negotiable, based on common commitments to goodness, and far less dependent on theological or dogmatic constructs.

To return to Luzzatto's theology, evil, as he defined it, is only real in the world in atomistic form. When seen as a totality, the world is wholly good. Therefore, the amorality of belief in pagan gods, especially the Greek gods, is due to their expression of partial reality. Each god embodies characteristics, such as jealousy or war and, therefore, conditions believers to embrace evil by way of the model of the deity's behavior.

Second, the idea of one God is crucial to the idea of one human family, and the latter is a core justification of the Torah's ethics. Like other moral sense theorists, Luzzatto focused on the way that human beings extend their loving sentiments universally when allowed to do so naturally, such as upon seeing a mishap on the street and expressing a natural compassion for the car accident victim. However, these same sentiments are blocked by various prejudices and injuries, sometimes brought about by other angry sentiments. Thus, the same person, upon seeing that the victim is a member of a certain race, may lose his compassion. The Torah is designed to train one to extend the loving sentiments to all situations and to not allow them to be buried by other emotional reactions or cognitive prejudices. It is also designed, avers Luzzatto, to generate a love of the entire human family. But each tribe and nation worshiping its own deity leads to human alienation and to dehumanization of the Other, who is not a member of one's tribe or protected by one's tribal god. Thus, monotheism is an essentially moral teaching whose utility to human life is in generating a common love of humanity:

> The compassion that Judaism commends is universal. It is extended, like God's, to all of His creatures. No race is excluded from the Law, because all human beings, according to Judaism's teaching, are brothers, are children of the same Father, and are created in the image of God.[13]

It is an extraordinary testimony to the cultural shifts within Orthodoxy of the post-Holocaust period that we find a deliberate mistranslation of this paragraph by Luzzatto in his collected writings, which were translated into Hebrew in Israel in recent decades. The paragraph now reads in Hebrew, "No race is excluded from the Law, because *all Jews* [my emphasis], according to Judaism's teaching, are brothers, they are children of one Father, and are created in the image of God."[14] Apparently, it was too much to bear for a translator or an editor that an Orthodox theologian and Torah scholar could actually say that all human beings are brothers or, more specifically, that Jews are brothers with all of humanity.

This astonishing willingness to mistranslate and misrepresent a famous Jewish theologian is a testimony to the fluidity of Orthodox hermeneutics, which appear unchanging from the outside but which are, in fact, subject to the deep influences of time, place, and circumstance, on basic theological/moral constructions of the

social universe. In this case, the interpretation and translation from one generation to another reaches the logical extreme limit of hermeneutics, namely, the
deliberate subversion of the author and the destruction of the integrity of the text
by putting in a word that the author never wrote, replacing "human beings" with
"Jews" and thus undermining the author's entire premise.

The context of this rewriting of Jewish theology is entirely understandable.
Contemporary Orthodox Jewry has come to be dominated by descendants of
Eastern Europeans. As a group, their ancestors suffered the most at non-Jewish
hands since around the 1880s and have had the least positive interaction with
them. In addition, there is the overshadowing presence of the Holocaust, which
calls into question all Jewish/gentile relations. Furthermore, Western materialism
and wealth has had a decidedly deleterious effect on many minority groups, which
come to the West harboring deep injuries. Some in the group will often proceed
to take advantage of newfound wealth, not to heal, but to deepen the wounds of
the past as a way of strengthening ultraethnic and ultranationalist commitment.
This is not rational, but it is all too common among many deeply insecure
minorities around the globe, who find themselves in the throes of modern, materialist alienation and dislocation. It is for this reason that Luzzatto's love of
non-Jews would be considered bizarre by many ultra-Orthodox or ultranationalist
Jews today, at best, and, at worst, heretical or traitorous. That is why a mistranslation has gone unnoticed or is even an acceptable subterfuge.

Let us return, however, to nineteenth-century Italian Orthodoxy, which is no
less a manifestation of modern Orthodoxy than the models of today but which
has an extraordinary quality of universalism built into its worldview. There are
some interesting questions to raise about Luzzatto's ethical, monotheistic constructs. What would Luzzatto think of gentiles who, despite the lack of monotheism, lived peacefully and amicably among themselves and with Others? How
would he evaluate, for example, Tibetan Buddhist teachings on compassion,
which exist side by side with the worship of a pantheon of deities? His two great
moral concerns—the development of moral character and the peaceful coexistence of the human family—would be embraced by the Dalai Lama, for example,
but without belief in one God. Would this call into question the need for monotheism? Would God be satisfied with this religion, according to Luzzatto's belief
structure?

It certainly seems that Luzzatto's perception of the divine will is that the desire
is primarily for human goodness and secondarily for monotheistic worship. Conceivably, Luzzatto could respond that the behavior is good, and that this is the
most important thing, as far as God is concerned, even though the theology is
mistaken. It is hard to imagine that he would, therefore, not see any appreciable
advantage to Judaism. He clearly is committed to the monotheistic construct of
the world and is most certainly convinced that divine revelation insists on a
certain path for the Jewish people. But it is remarkable how unimportant theological constructs are to him next to the choice between compassion and brutality,
for example. Therefore, we cannot really say with any certainty that he would
reject nonmonotheistic systems as idolatrous—at least for non-Jews—if they em-

brace the single greatest divine teaching for him: compassion. We simply do not know for sure. Effectively, however, it is irrelevant for Luzzatto. He may or may not consider Tibetan Buddhism to be idolatry. But, pragmatically, the Jew is obligated to a universal level of benevolence and committed relationship building with even idolaters. Thus, the stakes are not high for Luzzatto as to whether Others are idolaters or not. This is quite distinct from other formulations of *halakha* wherein if the person is an idolater a whole series of laws applies that makes a normal or benevolent relationship impossible.

The importance of universal benevolence is further confirmed by Luzzatto's extended efforts to demonstrate not only a benevolent biblical attitude toward idolaters but the commitment of key representatives of normative biblical Judaism to enter into sacred commitments with idolaters, in the form of oaths and covenants. This is rooted in the institution of *berit*, the most sacred term for divine/human covenant in the Bible, which is then applied to interhuman covenantal relationships. Abraham prayed for Abimelekh's recovery, and he and his son Isaac both took oaths and established covenants with Abimelekh and the shepherds of Gerar, with Aner, Eshkol, and Mamre, as well as with the Amorites. Simeon and Levi, Jacob's children, are rebuked for the murder of idolaters on the eve of their entering into the community of *berit*, even when a wrong was committed against their sister, just as centuries later Ezekiel rebuked King Tsedekiah for breaking his covenant with the Babylonian king, who was clearly not a monotheist. Judah kept an agreement with Hirah the Adulamite, while Joseph demonstrated covenantal devotion to his Egyptian pagan master by resisting his wife's overtures. Joshua kept true to an oath to Rehab, as well as to the Gibeonites.[15]

Luzzatto's last example is especially striking because it involves Joshua, the man who probably killed the most idolaters of anyone in biblical literature—at God's command. Luzzatto argued, however, that the biblical condemnation of the inhabitants of Canaan is a singular event and is due exclusively to their moral degradation and pollution of the land, not their idolatry. It may be true that their idolatry was seen as a dangerous snare for the Israelites, but it was not the basis of their capital punishment. Numerous texts are quoted to demonstrate that idolatry is always condemned in the context of moral failure, such as in the ill treatment of the poor or the defenseless, especially in the prophetic critiques of the brutality of nations, such as those found in Isaiah and Amos.[16]

Even where there has been enmity or wrong done to the Jewish people by idolaters, the Torah commands a tolerant approach, such as not hating the Edomite or the Egyptian, despite the harm they did to the Jewish people. It must be emphasized that these biblical proof texts involve the treatment of idolaters, not simply non-Jews, and therefore suggest a far more sweeping construct of Jewish ethics requiring an almost complete universalization of Jewish moral laws.

We must note here, however, that Luzzatto is prepared to justify the killing of men, women, and children by Joshua and others for two reasons: there is a singular divine mandate for this event in history, and their society, according to the biblical story, is steeped in so much brutality that they have lost their right to live. Luzzatto does not enter into the moral problem of exactly how a child is condemned to death for the sins of his culture, nor why this is not counted as at least as cruel as the condemned cruelty of the culture.

Luzzatto seems not to have a choice here. He is investing the literal words of the Bible with ultimate authority. His critique of rabbinic institutions that are chauvinistic are based on a return to the Bible as he has interpreted that document. This is somewhat parallel to Protestant critiques of Catholic accretions to the New Testament, although Luzzatto is completely beholden to the rabbis on most interpretations of Jewish law, unlike the Protestant/Catholic split. What Luzzatto cannot do then, as long as he remains Orthodox, is ignore where the Bible directly mandates cruelty. What he can do is circumscribe it to the degree that it is never to be repeated, and he can explain it in terms of a higher purpose of compassion, namely, others will learn what happens to civilizations that were based on cruelty.

This is a difficult position to sustain. Luzzatto is making the case that compassion is God's supreme concern. He is also suggesting that God will decide in very rare instances to suspend compassion and to punish the guilty, such as in Sodom, where God justifies wiping out an entire city for the ultimate purpose of teaching what happens to those who live based on brutality. But the destruction of the children, together with the parents, in the biblical extermination laws is well beyond the Sodom episode. After all, in the latter Abraham does ascertain that God is *not* condemning the innocent together with the wicked. But the extermination laws do demand the murder of the innocent together with the guilty, as far as we can tell, although this seems to be directly contradicted by other biblical discussions of this subject.[17]

Here Luzzatto, and perhaps Orthodoxy itself, is backed into a corner, a corner whose parameters suggest that one cannot reject as wrong a biblical position mandated by God. Luzzatto works mightily to make that corner more "livable" by making it a singular event in history. Ironically, it is the *herem* war laws that were subsequently used as the justification for much of the religious wars of monotheistic traditions in the last two thousand years, especially against the peoples of the Third World. One can hardly avoid the irony that these wars, especially the Crusades, claimed thousands of Jews as victims through so many centuries. Essentially, as long as those biblical words were and are considered to be expressive of something that God wills, or willed at one time, it will always be more difficult theologically to categorically reject the morality of a war that systematically slaughters the innocent, if they are nonmonotheists or not of one's faith. Of course, one cannot hold Luzzatto or Orthodox *halakha* responsible for the uses of biblical scripture for murderous purposes at the hands of others, especially when rabbinic Judaism would seriously circumscribe the applicability of the *herem* laws. But the logical difficulty of Luzzatto's position seems to me to remain, and the militarist purposes to which these laws have been put in biblically based religions continues to adversely affect history.[18]

Luzzatto did not deny that there is differentiated treatment of Jews and gentiles in biblical Judaism. However, as part of the structure of his major work, *Lezioni di teologia morale israelitica*, Luzzatto focused heavily on universal moral obligations in which no distinction between Jew and gentile is made, while the particularist obligations, though documented, received much less attention.[19] Essentially, Luzzatto traced the necessary *halakhic* differentiations to five areas: interest, loan cancellation, loan guarantees, responses to the enslavement of a Jew, and revenge. Anywhere that the text distinguishes *ahikha* (your brother) and *nokhri* (foreigner), the text is acknowledging special obligations of the Jewish family to itself.[20] Luzzatto allowed for the special commitments of families and indeed structured his moral lectures around family commitments. The Jewish people are a family in his theology, but they are also committed to a family of humanity, which has equal theological cogency. There are families within families within families, each with increasing levels of commitment. However, the family of humanity carries the broadest possible level of mutual obligations, while increasingly intensive levels of commitment are reserved for the Jewish family and one's personal biological family, respectively.

The case is made further that all references to *re'a* (fellow or neighbor), [21] must be considered universal, and thus the love principle of Leviticus 19:18, the commandment to "love your neighbor as yourself," is to be universally extended. Evidence is cited from various biblical sources, including Exodus 11:2, that *re'a* refers to gentiles. This is an old problem in Jewish ethics, and there are certainly other Orthodox rabbinic figures in more recent times, such as Rabbi Mecklenburg, who claimed the love of *re'a* as a universal obligation.[22] Furthermore, Luzzatto cited several places in rabbinic literature where the ethics associated with *re'a* are extended to gentiles. Even the ethics of *ahikha* regarding interest-free loans is extended to gentiles as an act of piety by Talmud Bavli. Makkot 24a, the latter directly contradicted, incidentally, by Maimonides.[23] This has revolutionary implications because the *re'a* laws of the Bible involve the deepest kind of moral relationships, including the prohibitions of envy, oppressive behavior in both business and interpersonal interactions, encroachment on another's land, and— one of the most important laws of social engagement that goes beyond contemporary morality—a prohibition against inaction when you see a neighbor being assaulted or under mortal threat of some kind. It also involves prosocial commitments to the distribution of scarce resources equitably and a moral guide as to how the poor should take what they need from the rich, but not more than their due.[24]

Luzzatto is well aware of how much of rabbinic literature contradicts his conclusion about universalizing these values. This is why much of his writing is dedicated to carefully defining rabbinic Judaism as a divinely mandated but, nevertheless, *human* process of adjusting the divine word to *makom u' zeman* (time and place). To the degree that the rabbis are successful in accomplishing this, Luzzatto applauded them. He adhered to their words assiduously in the face of mounting modern pressure to change the laws and customs that express the particularity of the Jewish people, such as in prayer, and simultaneously attacked stylistic and ritual reforms. But where the rabbis plainly violated the most fundamental biblical commitment to universal compassion and justice, due to the circumstances of their own times, Luzzatto rejected their conclusions categorically, stating:

> Whatever proposition or story that could be found in the Talmud . . . which would be in opposition to the sentiments of universal humanity and justice—which are suggested equally by nature and by Sacred Scripture—must be regarded as neither of the dictates of Religion or of Tradition, but as regrettable insinuations of the calamitous circumstances, and of the public and private vexations and cruelties to which the Jews were subjected in the barbaric centuries.[25]

In sum, Luzzatto concluded, "The difference, in religion or opinion, of a person [and ourselves] does not allow us to hate him, or to injure him, nor to refrain in any way from exercising towards him the universal obligations of humanity and justice."[26] This is a remarkable level of commitment to detheologize the question of religious ethics. What I mean by this is that Luzzatto's ethics of sentiment are simply to be extended universally, without regard to any theological evaluation of the other human being or living creature.

This is a necessary position for Luzzatto. His understanding of nature and what appeared to him to be irrefutable on a biological level led him to conclude that only the prosocial sentiments, centering on *misericordia* (compassion), have the requisite power to motivate human ethics and thus create the good society. Thus, if God's wish is for human beings to be good, as is shown by the biblical corpus, then the Torah must, in its essence, be founded upon a pedagogy that always reinforces the natural sentiment of compassion, especially for those who suffer. That compassion can have no limits, at least in principle. Luzzatto did address the necessary suppression of compassion, such as in capital crimes. But it appears that he saw the suppression of compassion vis-à-vis gentiles and idolaters or its limitation to fellow Jews to be in direct contradiction to the natural direction of compassion and also to be a direct violation of the biblical vision of a universal human family that is meant to be the recipient of the individual's feelings of compassion, love, and justice.

As far as Luzzatto's approach to rabbinic Judaism, one should note the irony here. Rabbinic Judaism, in its essence, is a hermeneutic religion; it is such a thorough hermeneutic of biblical Judaism that it is effectively now known as Judaism, having overtaken biblical Judaism. Luzzatto is one of the few traditional thinkers in Jewish history who turns this hermeneutic enterprise on its head. He is a *parshan*, a commentator, a hermeneuticist, in the classic rabbinic fashion. Yet he creates from this enterprise a return to biblical centrality that keeps the rabbis to a standard of legitimacy: they are authoritative to the degree to which they do not violate basic biblical values and goals.

Of course, the irony is double. Luzzatto is as human as the rabbis, a hermeneuticist in his own place and time who, no matter how brilliant a Bible scholar he may have been, saw in the biblical text a particular ethic of compassion and out of that central perception built his explanations for when and how the Bible makes exceptions for that ethic. This is a perceptual and hermeneutic construct that may be quite convincing, more convincing than that of the rabbis, perhaps, when it comes to interpretations of the biblical meaning of *ger* and *re'a*. It may very well be that rabbinic circumscription of these concepts is less true to inner biblical exegesis than Luzzatto's interpretation, but his is also a hermeneutic construct of his own place and time, and we have seen this hermeneutic move in other modern Orthodox thinkers, as noted earlier. But Luzzatto is one of the only ones, in classic Italian fashion, to remain in an Orthodox construct but still treat the rabbis as deeply human interpreters, capable of basic errors. And he did join other Orthodox interpreters who, as a group, hermeneutically redesigned the basic boundaries between Jew and gentile, even between Jew and idolater, in the modern period. This suggests the surprising elasticity of moral boundaries even in the most religious constructs of a religion in response to the changed circumstances of the religious interpreter.

Turning to Benamozegh, we discover a complex attitude toward Jewish-gentile relations, opposed in some key ways to the theological and ethical framework of his older contemporary and rival, Luzzatto. Whereas Luzzatto's engagement with gentiles and idolaters was entirely on the level of ethics—true to his theological orientation—Benamozegh's relationship to other traditions was almost entirely on the plane of metaphysical and mystical speculation. Furthermore, Benamozegh's attitudes changed, it would seem, over time, based on the evidence we have.

Benamozegh's erudition in Jewish rabbinic sources, in Kabbalah in particular, in world religions, and, last but not least, in Christian sacred literature, is truly astounding. In midcareer, at the age of forty-four, he wrote a stunningly bitter polemic against Christianity entitled *Moral juive et moral chrétiènne.*[27] Its main purpose was to demonstrate that Christian pretensions to supplant Judaism were ill founded from the beginning. In rather angry language, he asserts that the best in Christianity had been plagiarized from Judaism, while the adverse effects of Christian morality are documented throughout. One is struck by how much even the discussions of Jewish ethics are couched in Christian language in order to demonstrate the plagiarism still further, while in general the Jewish ethics are not particularly well developed by the author. Benamozegh states at the beginning of his essay:

Now what has Christianity substituted for the God of the Jews, the First-and-the-Last, the Author of the beginning and end of man and of the world? It has ascribed progression to God himself . . . asserting that this last bends to circumstances, to custom, even to the weakness of man—has ascribed to him the flexibility of Paul . . . and the base concessions of the Jesuits to idolaters; it has made a god after its own image, like the gods of Homer, instead of making man after the image of God, as Moses teaches.[28]

The overall impression one gets of his early polemical writings is that what Benamozegh resented the most is religious successionism,[29] the theft from Judaism of its best values and then the pretension to supplant its usefulness to mankind. Later in his writings, he also resisted biblical scholarship that suggests an evolutionary, linear progression in human history from the most primitive to the most progressive human thinking for the same reason, namely, the implied succession of Judaism by more advanced expressions of religion, philosophy, and science. This, indeed, was a commonplace, sometimes subtle, sometimes not so subtle, message of cultural/religious supremacy, which underlay modern Western scholarship.

Even in Benamozegh's early period, however, we see some remarkable and rather atypical characteristics of his thinking. As an Orthodox rabbi, he seemed to have no trouble singing the praises of Cicero, Epictetus, and Marcus Aurelius. For example, he said:

> As to Paganism, without urging the simplicity, beauty, and elevation of Greco-Roman poetry or theology, we should have to cite only from some sacred books of the East, from Confucius or Menu [Mencius? the code of Manu?)], for instance, to show what man can extract from that rich and inexhaustible soil of Divine gift, viz., the religious sentiment.[30]

We see here the beginnings of his perception as a thinker that divine truths exhibit themselves universally in all religions, even pagan ones. In fact, he has far kinder things to say about Confucius at this point than about Christianity.

By the time we revisit Benamozegh in 1885, twenty-three years later, we discover a man deeply committed to Judaism's contribution to the future of humanity. His *Israel et Humanité* is an introduction to the long posthumous work, of the same name, which did not appear until 1914.[31] He was still engaged in a debate with Christianity, though it was far less polemical. His principal concern was to demonstrate the existence of a universal religion, deeply embedded in Judaism, which could solve the problems of mankind and which could accomplish this more effectively than Christianity, as the latter was currently formulated.

The first thing to notice about Benamozegh's formulations is that ethics is not at the center of either Judaism or its universal religion: metaphysics is, although it is a formulation of metaphysics with profound moral implications. Furthermore, science and history matter a great deal to his methodology, in addition to the sciences applied to biblical literature. He did not flinch from the biblical scholarship of his time. On the contrary, he embraced it in order to demonstrate his argument.

At the heart of Benamozegh's thesis is the belief that there is a universal religion that predates Mosaic religion, the latter being specifically designed just for the Jewish people. The former, however, is far more ancient and is Benamozegh's greatest concern in terms of the fate of humanity. Its manifestations are to be felt in veiled form in every major pagan tradition. This revelation, which Jewish tradition, according to Benamozegh's formulation, associates with Noah, is monotheistic. Its principal message is the unity of God, especially as, or when, this is manifest in the unity of mankind and the unity of the universe. However, it is obvious that mankind is not united and that belief in God is hardly a uniting force in the world. Following Vincenzo Gioberti's philosophy, with which he was quite familiar, and adding a neo-Hegelian twist, Benamozegh argued for a stage-by-stage process of human religious consciousness that begins with unity—albeit a vague conception of it—moves on to complexity and multiplicity, and then returns finally to a higher unity or synthesis. Gioberti's description of the development of consciousness, the "palingenesis," or ultimate return of the existent to being, was applied by Benamozegh to human history, especially religious history.[32] Thus, the progress of history, if and when it leads to unity of mankind, also demonstrates or makes manifest the divine unity that is latently present in all of existence.

All of the multiple manifestations of deities to be found in many religions are actually vague reminders of an original conception of unity. The universal religion embedded in Judaism, particularly as this is expressed by Kabbalah, is designed to synthesize the multiplicity and diversity of the world's pagan religious expressions. It can be the glue that synthesizes a "religion of the future," which returns the human race to a higher reality of divine unity, human unity, and cosmic unity.

This is why the Kabbalistic description of divine traits necessarily contains within itself so many contradictions. It is a synthesis of the real and the ideal, the material and the spiritual, the pantheistic and the transcendent. Every aspect of nature that has been worshiped separately in the world's religions is contained therein.

It is for this reason that Benamozegh refused to utterly condemn any pagan idea or form of worship, because it always has some roots in the *sefirotic* structure of the universe.[33] That does not mean that it is not mistaken. But it is not evil in the absolute sense; it is only incomplete. All theological sins involve, argued Benamozegh, the terms *ketsots, perud,* or *hibbur.* All involve the mistake of cutting, separating, associating—in other words, not seeing the whole. Therefore, pagan gods should never be cursed.[34] They are part of the higher unity of the world but have been mistakenly separated from the higher unity of God.

Judaism's ultimate task is to resolve the duality and multiplicity that exists in humankind and to bring it closer to the synthesis and unity to be found in the authentic doctrines of divine revelation, particularly the universal revelation given originally to mankind through Noah. In answer to the "rationalist" critics of Judaism—by which Benamozegh usually meant the Bible critics—he claimed that Moses understood this original revelation well. That is why Moses, as the author of the Torah, does draw upon pagan mysteries and rites. He took from the secrets of Egyptian religion, such as circumcision, which were rites of entry for the few, for the elite, but made the whole Jewish nation into a priesthood. This was not due to pagan and primitive roots of the Torah. Rather, this was intentionally designed to create ever-larger human communities dedicated to the higher unity of God.[35]

A crucial point is that Benamozegh believed that Moses and the Jewish people encountered, in their time, a purer form of paganism than what has been studied by scholars today as the latter analyze, from a distance, the popular manifestation of those religions. Its secrets were closer to the original unitary conception of the world in the time of Noah. That is why the patriarchs, for example, can have good relationships with figures such as Malkhitsedek and why the biblical text could see him in such positive terms, even considering him a priest (Gen. 14:18, 19).

Turning to the modern period, Emile Burnouf's science of religions is an important backdrop to Benamozegh's philosophy.[36] Burnouf claimed a basic divergence of Eastern and Western religion in which the East is characterized as pagan, emanationist, and/or pantheist, while the West is characterized as Semitic and transcendent. This was completely unsatisfactory to Benamozegh, who believed that Kabbalah, which contained within it the synthesis of all religious ideas, the higher unity of human revelation, called into question Burnouf's duality. True Semitic religion has both. It recognizes at once transcendence and immanence, unity and pantheism, "where this is reasonable." By this Benamozegh meant that the mistake of many religions, including Christianity, is when they take this too far in one direction, such as in the doctrine of the *literal* incarnation of God in Jesus.

True faith in one God can unite all peoples and all religions. It can also harmonize science and religion. Benamozegh characterized modern science as the search for causal chains and singular principles, such as Newton's laws, to explain the universe. He saw himself on the same path of discovering singular truths in the universe. But he saw the challenge of religious diversity as no less important than the challenge of a world of chaos without scientific explanation. Religious diversity indicates a multiplicity of avenues to God, which awaits a higher synthesis to resolve the conflicts of religions and, particularly, sectarianism, a key concern in his intellectual milieu.

Science is based on a search for the relationship of cause and effect. But this is also the basis of religious metaphysics. Benamozegh assumed that angelology, for example, is an analysis of the causal connection of divine attributes and their effect on the world. Similarly, pagan hierarchies try to explain the same thing. But sometimes they make a fatal error in not seeing the entire causal chain moving back or up to the highest expression of a unified deity. That is why he is particularly hopeful that many non-Western traditions have within them the bases of not only scientific conceptualization but monotheism.

Benamozegh was particularly struck by how much Christian Europe was in search of a solution to its disastrous struggle with religious sectarianism and how devastating it was to human life. He offered his form of universal religion as the religion of the future, which could solve this problem of gentile life. A united God, as a synthesis of higher unity, would solve both the religious crisis and the scientific quest for singular truth.

Revelation, through the prophets and Kabbalistic constructs, was a major source of proof texts for the radically inclusive approach to multiple expressions of religion. Pantheism is seen as in dramatic tension with, but also in coexistence with, transcendent expressions of divinity in biblical texts.

Isaiah 6:3 and Isaiah 45:5 are both seen as evidence of a pantheistic side to the higher unity of Judaism. The word describing God as *kavod* is a key here, since it is translated as "glory" but is clearly related to the Hebrew term *kaved*, thus implying a substantive heaviness, a tangible reality. Isaiah 6:3 is normally translated as "Holy, Holy, Holy, the world is filled with His Glory." Benamozegh translated this as "All that fills the world is His *kavod* (glory)."[37] Isaiah 45:5 is usually translated, "I am the Lord and there is none else," while Benamozegh stressed, "I am the Lord and nothing else exists."

There is an obvious problem for Jewish identity and spirituality in Benamozegh's construct. What is the purpose of Jewish particularity if the entire theological construct is geared toward universalism? He rejected the charge that "chosenness" is racism. Here, he clearly laid great stress on the early chapters of Genesis to demonstrate the belief in one God in those early generations. The revelation of that principle universally clearly means, argues Benamozegh, that the truths of Judaism were not exclusively given to one people. Here, Benamozegh's formulation parts company with a theological construct commonly known in traditional circles, which emphasizes one midrashic myth, namely, that the Torah was offered to all nations and only accepted by Israel. But Benamozegh stressed the biblical recounting of a long period of early history in which there were many sins but not pure idolatry or absolute rejection of monotheism. Thus, there is never an overt rejection by the entire world of monotheism, as is recounted in early biblical history.

Jewish particularity, therefore, has a restorative quality and is not an exclusivist privileging act. This he shares with Luzzatto. Jewish life is a particular means to a universalist end. The only purpose is to restore the original religion of humanity by teaching a higher synthesis, which removes the need for each religion to worship in opposition to the Other, rather than with the Other. It is inconceivable, argued the rabbi of Livorno, that Jewish monotheism is not related in some way to gentile monotheism, particularly to gentile beliefs in their original form. He saw a deep affinity, not so much with Spinozist pantheism or Christology, but with sacred texts such as the Vedas. For example, each god in the Vedas takes turns at supremacy, and this, Benamozegh argued, is halfway between polytheism and the authentic theosophy of Kabbalah. Kabbalah recognizes the different faces of God and the way in which one face or expression can have more or less power at some place and time. But he denies their independent existence.[38] Polytheism, the worship of each face of God as independent, is only a later corruption of earlier thinking, which had been unitary and monotheistic. Benamozegh concluded near the end of his magnum opus, "Thus, Israel is only a means, as grand and noble as you like, but solely a means and not an end in itself. The end resides in the union of Israel and humanity that sums up the entire providential plan."[39] The particularity of the Jewish people is limited to an unredeemed present and functions as a means of preserving the universal religion. But the messianic end is unity.

Benamozegh's vision took on political implications as well, as we see from his article "Le crime de la guerre denoncé à l'humanité" (The crime of war denounced before humanity).[40] His conception of human unity precluded a violent approach to uniting humanity. This is why he denounced Roman imperialism and Christian forms of cultural domination brought about by the Christianization of the Roman Empire, despite the fact that Christianity spread monotheism. An approach of force to establish the synthesis that he seeks is completely unacceptable. Even a culturally imperialist approach, namely, a rigid monotheism that vigilantly denounces the idolatry of the rest of the world is unacceptable. He sought a higher unity through synthesis, through recovering the pure doctrines embedded in all religions. This cannot be done through violence, physically or culturally.

This approach to the world is in keeping with that of the first Jew, Abraham. Benamozegh saw Abraham in spiritual continuity with his ancient environment, purifying it, not conquering it. Malkhitsedek's blessing of Abraham and his God, el elyon (Gen. 14:18), indicates that Salem, later Jerusalem, is a capital of pagan religion, yet not a religion that rejects Abraham's God.

The names of God are an important part of Benamozegh's theory. Here, for example, Malkhitsedek's use of el elyon (roughly, "most high God," or, more radically, "the God who is the highest of the gods") is important. It recognizes a hierarchy of divinity, which for Benamozegh is the key to the ultimate synthesis of monotheism. Other biblical texts refer to God's praises being sung throughout the world.[41] Benamozegh believed that the Psalmist, among others, believed these praises to be coming from pagans.

In order to demonstrate his positions from Kabbalah, Benamozegh referred often to sefirotic syntheses that reflect higher unities of separated phenomena of the world. The most important, in terms of Jewish/gentile relations, is the conceptualization of shekhina as the plenitude of divinity in its relation to the created. Israel worships the multi-faceted shekhina, while others worship partial aspects.[42] Christianity borrowed from Judaism the multiple relations of the Trinity but limited divine manifestations to just three.

The infinity of divine manifestations, such as is found in the Vedas, was more interesting to Benamozegh than the Trinity. It seems that multiplicity is closer to the higher unity that Benamozegh sought from gentiles than the dogmatic and exclusivist faith in the Trinity or the more secular expression in his time of Spinozist pantheism. Infinite expressions of the divine intimate, by their nature, an ultimate unity, whereas a rigidly formed Trinity ultimately creates division that cannot unite nature or the metaphysical universe, while a dogmatic and exclusivist pantheistic conception does not recognize multiplicity, or transcendence as well as immanence. The Torah itself, in referring to God as tseva'ot (hosts) and making reference to angels and b'nai elohim (sons of God) recognizes multiple forces in the world. But this is why the most important name for the sefirah of malkhut (kingship) is bet ha-kenesset (house of gathering), the gathering in of all cosmic forces, which for Benamozegh is the synthesis of all the forces worshiped as pagan deities.[43] Thus, an overfocus on just three deities, or a Trinity, and the only path to that through Jesus is too exclusivist a conception to pave the way for higher unities.

Benamozegh was aware of the fact that Judaism or, more specifically, the universal, primordial religion embedded within Judaism could be accused of syncretism. More accurately, he was aware that he could be accused of developing a highly syncretistic expression of Judaism that was inauthentic to tradition. But on a metaphysical level, Benamozegh saw himself practicing the Kabbalistic doctrine of *berur*, choosing the good from multiple sources and synthesizing a higher unity. It would only be syncretistic if it did not resolve itself in a higher unity. In other words, the Kabbalistic roots of his method gave it authenticity and internal coherence as part of the primordial religion of the world, rather than being a facile, syncretistic effort to combine the superficial elements of world religions for the purpose of creating a modern culture. As mentioned earlier, he was actively engaged in palingenesis, recovering the original roots of this primordial religion and rediscovering it, but in a higher unity now, by gathering and synthesizing the divine wisdom implicit in many traditions.

Another way that Benamozegh looked at this is by a metaphysical definition of Israel. Israel is seen as the "synthesis," the central point of faith, a priesthood, and the gentiles as "analysis," the perception of divinity in the smallest objects of the world. Atomizing the worship of God into the smallest objects is a crucial cultural and metaphysical development in the history of humankind. It is a way to deepen our understanding of the divine relationship to everyone and everything. But it also requires an eventual return to or movement toward the central point of unity, the synthesis.

This is his messianic vision. It is the way in which Judaism alerts the world, through teaching, to the theosophic essence of universal religion, which Benamozegh referred to as Noachism. It is this Noachism that he taught to Aimé Pallière, who in turn wrote about it and set the stage for the development of a small sect of gentiles now known as Noachides. Some live in the United States to this day, in Tennessee.[44] Naturally, in compliance with rabbinic Judaism, it included the Seven Laws of Noah. For Benamozegh, it clearly signified a much deeper synthesis of human religious beliefs and practices, which returns mankind to the primal unity of its earliest origins. But now this is fulfilled with a higher unity, which is more deeply redemptive of the world, uniting all of humanity politically and socially—and metaphysically uniting humanity with God.

Peace is indispensable for the process of teaching this universal religion. Therefore the role of the Jewish people is to be peacemakers among the nations, ambassadors, and intermediaries. He disagreed radically with other visions of the future that suggested what he considered either incomplete visions of humanity or barbaric means of social change. He completely rejected Marxist internationalism as materialistic and incomplete, while Ferdinand Lasalle's (d. 1864) vision was poorly conceived and too one-sided, presumably because it favored only workers, but this is unclear.[45] Benamozegh also seemed to be quite nervous about revolutionary means of change as producing too much violence, thus achieving the opposite of the hoped-for unity.

Despite his universal vision, Benamozegh was not a typical internationalist of his day. He felt that pure internationalism devalues the spiritual and the providential significance of nations. He wrote, "The nations are unified historically through Adam, psychologically in the *shekhina*, the Divine Presence in the world, which is the center of all souls. . . . Each nation represents a particular idea unto itself which is its *raison d'être*."[46] Ultimately, the nation's purpose is to evolve organizationally into a higher unity of nations but not by betraying its essential character. Each nation has a *sar*, an angelic force, and it maintains its distinction while also evolving into a higher unity, which clearly parallels a dramatic Kabbalistic process of the divine presence itself. Thus, Benamozegh's vision would embrace a method of peacemaking and conflict resolution that simultaneously affirms the independent identity of all parties, while also searching for a higher set of principles and cognitive constructs of the world that serve to unify all parties.

The true way to the future for both the body and the soul of humanity, as well as for the *shekhina*, is by harmonizing, not delegitimizing, the multiple spiritual and national expressions of humankind. The Jewish people, with their commitment to the theosophic doctrines of Kabbalah, their awareness of their own distinct particularity combined with a universal vision of the future, are perfectly equipped to teach this to humankind, precisely because Jews have lived for so long with their particularity coexisting, in dramatic tension, with their existence in larger, non-Jewish cultures. They thus have a keen understanding of how to make a higher unity out of multiple particular identities.

Benamozegh is touching here on a vital principle of conflict resolution in situations of multiple ethnic and religious identities. There is a constant struggle between the search for universal principles of coexistence and the clearly demonstrable human need for particular identity. The latter seems to be a constant in human history, and it expresses itself in abundance through numerous religious constructs and rituals throughout the world. Benamozegh was suggesting a solution to this tension of the universal and the particular and also cautioning us about the ways in which an overemphasis on universalism leads to repression, while an overfocus on particularism leads to permanent conflict.

The answer lies in an embrace of particularity with the aim of creating a higher synthesis. How exactly this approach would express itself in situations of conflict is well beyond the purview of this theologian, but his ideas deserve careful study and should be considered in the future as we experiment with the construction of a multicultural, multireligious civil society. We cannot do this without careful study and experimentation on a social scientific level. But neither can we do it without a refined understanding of the ethical and theological challenges of this process.

It is ironic that Benamozegh's vision fits into neither political trend that shattered the optimism of the Enlightenment and destroyed tens of millions of lives. The particularism of World War I nationalisms and their fatuous pride led to the senseless deaths of millions of people and destroyed a generation, which in turn set the stage for the European fascisms of World War II, which were simply a more demonic form of ultranationalism. The Cold War and its innumerable deaths in proxy wars around the world, in addition to the horrors of the gulags and purges, was, by contrast, due to a universalist vision of communism, which turned into a nightmare. Western triumphalism and occasional paranoia made a bad situation even worse, but there can be no doubt that universalist political and universalist religious visions have their dark side, as Benamozegh understood well. His subtle attempt to build a political/spiritual vision that embraces both particularity and universality presaged the spirit of multifaith conversation and cooperation that has begun to take root in recent decades, as well as our fledgling but honorable efforts to create an international political community that embraces distinct nations but also a higher political unity of moral purpose.

We clearly have a long way to go, but Benamozegh's theology demonstrates how even the most conservative religious traditions can become a part of this process. An Orthodox community rabbi for fifty years, he evolved a vision that in certain ways proved superior to many progressive political ideologies of the modern period, particularly in terms of its attention to the challenges of peacemaking.

These two Italian philosophies also raise timely theological/psychological questions that are relevant to our study. How does the religious individual define himself vis-à-vis human beings who are not of his belief or believing group? Most often, especially in monotheism, this definition involves an ontological opposition to the Other, a dualistic division between the good Self—collective or individual—and the evil Other, between the saved and the unsaved.[47] For Luzzatto and Benamozegh, there is a clear differentiation of Jew and gentile but not an oppositional duality. The Jewish role is pedagogic, teaching a compassionate ethic and simple monotheism, in Luzzatto's case, and, in Benamozegh's, teaching a synthetic unity of God and humankind that includes the best expression of all spiritual human insights. For Luzzatto, the pedagogic vision is strictly in the ethical realm—simply teach a good way to live that also happens to be monotheistic. For Benamozegh, there is a grand design to teach a universal religion to all of humanity or to enable its evolution out of the sources of the world's spiritual traditions, to transform history, and to realize the messianic age, which is the hoped-for palingenesis, the regeneration of humankind.

Benamozegh's vision has all the problems associated with any universal pretension to religious truth, namely, the potential to be a coercive force in the world despite Benamozegh's commitments to peace. Luzzatto might have rejected outright the aspirations of Benamozegh precisely because, in Luzzatto's vision, compassion is at the heart of God's aspiration for human beings, both Jewish and gentile, and universal ideological aspirations are notoriously oppressive in history. Benamozegh, however, repeatedly rejected the Roman imperial character of historical Christianity and its use of force, and he also clearly embraced an extremely tolerant program of theological inclusiveness, that is, the construction of theology in such a way as to include many pagan beliefs as a part of his overall conception of divine unity. Furthermore, he made it clear that politically he would not have any part of coercive international programs of action.

Benamozegh also, according to Pallière's reports, held out the possibility of a religion, such as Christianity, being the universal religion *if* it would rid itself of the key errors of Incarnation and Trinity and the accompanying intolerance of Others who do not accept these dogmas. One of Benamozegh's problems with the Trinity and Incarnation is its classic expression of an idolatrous principle from a Jewish point of view, a move too far in the direction of God's presence in the material world. Another key problem is its limitation to just three characteristics of God and the limitation of Jesus as the sole vehicle of salvation. In other words, it is not inclusive enough, and Christianity must go through a process of self-reform in order to be more inclusive.

Of course, Benamozegh's conditions for Christian reform would wipe out precisely what gives many Christians their sense of having a unique and special sacred story. It would be similar to asking Jews to keep their religion but just eliminate the Talmud. It would rob them of what makes them unique, and I would argue that this undermines the basic human need for particular identity that many people achieve through their embrace of religious dogma and ritual, especially those dogmas and rituals that are the most peculiar to outsiders. Thus, Benamozegh's vision of one religion in particular shedding all its particularity seems a little unrealistic. More realistic is the possibility of people of many religious faiths and practices coming to agreement on higher unifying values, while still maintaining their particular religious expressions and groupings. Indeed there are tens of thousands of peace activists and others around the world who already embrace this perspective and act on it ethically in the world.

Presumably, all religions, in Benamozegh's view, could engage in some process of self-reform, thus setting the stage for a confluence of expressions of the universal, ancient religion. Benamozegh's concept of a universal religion could not be one that buries all particularist expressions of or approaches to God. True universal religion must allow for particularist expressions of relationship to God, in order for it not to become an instrument of violence.

As far as I can tell from my experience in training and conflict resolution, it is only a small portion of religious humanity, even among those committed to peacemaking, who want to embrace a universal religion in addition to their own. It should be noted that many people in the United States, for example, actively search for this very thing and discover it in various small groups, which are referred to as New Age religions. By contrast, many traditionalists are frightened by and even enraged by this syncretism. All old religious structures and cognitive constructs are threatened by new ones. Thus, it is likely that an emphasis on a new universal religion, at least in the contemporary period, would create a negative backlash that, in pragmatic terms, would not generate more peacemaking. On the other hand, Benamozegh's more subtle vision of many particular religions experiencing some higher unity as they perceive or embrace common values— while maintaining their particularity and that of their institutions—stands a much better chance of generating peacemaking trends in religious cultures.

Both Benamozegh and Luzzatto saw a separate, pedagogic, even priestly role for the Jewish people, with the need for Jewish particularist ritual, in the form of *halakhic* Judaism, to flourish and continue as an instrument of pedagogy, not as a privileged structure, separated from an unredeemed or evil world. Furthermore, these formulations require extensive attention to Jewish/gentile engagement and relations and certainly cannot coexist with any kind of spiritual or ethical chauvinism. Thus, what these theologians wanted and needed for the Jewish people is a need that all peoples and religions feel, namely, to be important and to make a unique contribution to humanity. Any serious conflict resolution work must recognize this need.

It also should be emphasized that these Italian theologies represent an utterly distinct expression of *halakhic* Judaism; they assume a level of *halakhic* acceptance regarding gentiles and their religions, even demonstrating a commitment to repudiate rabbinic statements of intolerance. But, in classic Orthodox fashion, there is also considerable *halakhic* stringency implied by these two philosophies. The stringencies, especially for Luzzatto, are in the area of interpersonal relations. The extension of Jewish ethical interpersonal requirements globally increases dramatically the burden of *halakhic* Jewish life in a qualitatively different fashion than the Judaism that was being expressed or is presently being expressed by other formulations of Orthodoxy. Benamozegh also placed on Jews an increased burden of a global pedagogy and mission.

In addition, both men placed greater *halakhic* responsibility onto the shoulders of gentiles. For Luzzatto, what gentiles do in their day-to-day lives, their morality, is far more important than their theology. However, it should be said that the vast bulk of his *oeuvre* is dedicated to Jewish ethical and ritual behavior as a universal pedagogy. Benamozegh, however, spent the bulk of his later writings persuading the *gentile* world of what it must do for the sake of the future of humankind, while also staking out a unique Jewish destiny as peaceful teachers of universal spiritual unity. His call for the unity of God and humanity, his pedagogy of insight into the multiple and fractured expressions of divine unity in the world's religious traditions, is a wake-up call primarily to gentiles. Benamozegh believed that his and the Jewish people's destiny is to express the unified vision of universal religion embedded within Judaism and to recover the separated portions of it scattered throughout the world's national cultures and religions.

There are other questions raised by these two philosophies: What is modern Orthodox Judaism? Deeper still, what is Jewish particularism? In light of these Italian models, it seems to me that we have not begun to comprehend the varied expressions of traditional Judaism. Benamozegh's spiritual vision is so universal and Luzzatto's ethics so inclusive that they radically change the standard conceptions of Jewish Orthodox life and what is normative and what is not normative. Yet, both men prayed three times a day from the same Siddur (prayer book) as all other Orthodox Jews (except, of course, the minor differences of the Italian Siddur), kept kosher and sabbath laws strictly, and observed all of the innumerable rituals of *halakhic* Judaism. Certainly, however, the religious visions of both men make them part company with *individual halakhic* decisions regarding, and rabbinic attitudes toward, gentiles. Even here, however, their *halakhic* commitment, on the behavioral level, does not challenge the requirement to keep the religious

Jew distant from worshiping God in any way that would be considered pagan. The departure from expressions of Orthodox and non-Orthodox antigentile attitudes is at once subtle and profound. To borrow *halakhic* language for a moment, it expresses itself less in *issur* (prohibition) and more in *mitsvah* (positive deed). Both men extend the realm of Jewish obligation *and* gentile obligation in terms of what both owe to God and to each other. In particular, it calls upon both Jews and gentiles to live up to a high standard of universal morality in addition to an exalted and inclusive conception of God and the spiritual life. It does not challenge profoundly the behavioral, *halakhic* expressions of Judaism, with a few exceptions, particularly in the realm of prohibition, as much as it challenges the Jewish people to a far greater destiny in human history and, for Benamozegh, in the fate of the universe itself, perhaps even the fate of God's *shekhina*.

It is beyond the confines of this chapter to speculate too much on the relationship between these doctrines and the time and place in history in which these men found themselves. But it seems clear that expansion into humanity with one's religious particularity intact is something natural to these Orthodox men, while, in contrast, withdrawal from humanity seemed more the traditional Orthodox order of the day as the late nineteenth and twentieth centuries unfolded.

Two elements seem important in the development of this withdrawal: poor relations between Jews and gentiles, especially as they escalate into extreme violence, such as in pre–World War II Eastern Europe, the Holocaust, and contemporary Israel; and a fragmented, multicultural pattern of loose coexistence, such as in contemporary America, where there is less and less of a common culture with humanity that is rooted in something more than materialistic gain. There is, therefore, little motivation in such a culture for Orthodox Jews, deeply immersed in the cultural recovery of Eastern European Judaism, which was lost in the Holocaust, to see themselves spiritually as part of the larger whole of humanity. Both of our subjects, by contrast, found themselves in a peaceful and intellectually engaged relationship to a larger Italian gentile world that was immersed in its scientific and cultural achievements. Both of them took that world seriously, and they expected to be taken seriously by that gentile world.

The contrast between these Italian philosophies and other Orthodox philosophies in the modern era suggests once again how intimate the relationships are among ideas, texts, and contexts, and the observer is struck with a "consciousness of being affected by history (*wirkungsgeschichtliches Bewustein*)" or "a consciousness of the hermeneutic situation," to paraphrase Gadamer.[48] The Orthodox hermeneutic situation is much more deeply affected by the vast differences of cultural horizon that one sees across the Diaspora than is usually assumed. There is a dramatic process of hermeneutic interpretation and reinterpretation unfolding in the many Orthodoxies of the last two hundred years. Judaism is thoroughly text-centered, and of all Judaisms, Orthodoxy claims the most text-true (or Torah-true) status, a status that is supposed to—theologically speaking—be seen as static, relatively unchanging, true to an original form of the Torah. Furthermore, Orthodoxy, especially *haredi* Orthodoxy,[49] often assumes a cultural and global horizon that is fundamentally dualistic, qualitatively distinguishing Israel and the nations, or Jacob and Esau, often set in the stark contrasts of righteousness and unrighteousness, good and evil. And yet we see here, in these two philosophies, dramatic combinations of hermeneutics, personal and cultural horizons, and theological conceptualizations of the world, which all add up to a universe or horizon of Orthodoxy that is antiseparatist to its core, that deeply engages even all of *pagan* humanity, in addition to monotheistic humanity and fellow non-Orthodox Jews. It is an Orthodoxy that is conscious of multiple Jewish identities or a complex spiritual identity, in which the individual Jew is a part of a particular people's destiny and of humanity's destiny before God, at one and the same time.[50] It is a theological and *halakhic* construct that challenges the Jewish people to a higher level of moral and spiritual existence but that also unambiguously embraces all of humanity in a shared spiritual destiny.

There is an obvious problem with using Luzzatto and Benamozegh as models of Orthodox thinkers whose philosophies could form the basis for Jewish peace-making values and practices today. It is obvious that their philosophies are *sui generis*; they are a product of their time and place. If we were to present the philosophies of these Italian Jews to a *haredi* leader today, they may well be dismissed as both bizarre and heretical. We live in an age where the bottom has fallen out of respect, even grudging respect, for modern culture and where the injuries of the last hundred years run far too deep to accept these ideas in any serious way.[51] It must be said, on the other hand, that these two philosophies point us in the right direction. They provide an intellectual blueprint for how even the most fundamentalist beliefs and practices can be wedded to a deeply prosocial paradigm of Judaism.

The real question is what it would take, emotionally, culturally, and politically, for Orthodox and *haredi* leaders today to develop their own version of a normative Judaism that works for them and their people but that could also somehow embrace the universal values that are so critical to coexistence and conflict resolution in a civil society. In order to do this, there will have to be, as far as my experience and research indicates, a great deal of trust building and relationship building with their enemies. This includes intimate enemies, namely, fellow Jews, and also more distant but far more damaging enemies in their eyes: gentiles, especially Christians. This will obviously have to go both ways and will require considerable efforts on the part of those Christians who are committed to peacemaking.[52]

This, in turn, could lead to an Orthodox evolution of a *frum* (pious) hermeneutic of the Torah that would be legitimate in their eyes. It is also the case that this hermeneutic would address issues that our nineteenth-century Italians could not really imagine. I think, for example, that it is only now historically, after Hitler, that many Jews are convinced that annihilation of the Jewish people is a real possibility. This results in a new hermeneutic of the world, which will necessarily put this issue front and center, and it is inseparable from the commitment of many identified Jews to Zionism as the solution to the lesson that Hitler taught. This is especially true of modern Orthodox, nationalist Orthodox, and religious settler Jews, who have made physical survival into the supreme *mitsvah* of contemporary life. I do not assume, however, that their new hermeneutic is a fait accompli. Experience indicates that these hermeneutic trends are constantly evolving. If we shut the door on this hermeneutic, if we shut out those who are or were associated with Gush Emunim, for example, then we consign them to an interpretation that must be conflict generating. But that is contrary to truly transformative and elicitive conflict resolution practice, which never assumes that any group is incapable of transformation. In other words, the peacemakers must engage on their own terms those for whom physical annihilation is the central issue. One can argue that this is a kind of posttraumatic pathological development. But that does not matter, and it is not even necessarily true. Conflict resolution engages communities in conflict without conditions, without prejudgments, and with complete interest in relationship building and constructive engagement.

The same is true of the *haredi* wing of Orthodoxy. Its great obsession, and the roots of its deep separatism, is a response that is similar to other fundamentalisms, namely, the strong perception and fear of cultural annihilation. The contemporary materialist society continues its assault every day on their children and on their ethics and pits itself squarely against the separatism that the ultrareligious see as their only hope of maintaining their religious lives for as many millennia as their ancestors did. Indeed, they have an obligation to make their grandchildren so committed that the traditions will last thousands of years or as long as it takes for the messianic era to arrive. Their greatest fear is to fail their ancestors and their descendants, to be the ones who lost the continual line of devotion to the Torah. Furthermore, and in a way that the nineteenth-century Orthodox could not have anticipated, the unprecedented openness and tolerance of the post-Holocaust Western world to Jews, has led to intermarriage rates of 50 percent or higher, and the material success of today's highly assimilated Western Jews has led to negative birthrates. These two elements are guaranteeing the steady demise of the Jewish people in their eyes, and this has a reasonable basis in fact. This, combined with the loss of the one million children in the Holocaust, is what makes *haredi* leaders set up a sociological construct in which *haredi* families are having between six and twelve children, sometimes more. Many of the male children are encouraged to not work but to study Torah all the time, while their in-laws and their wives support them, all often justified as a way of making up for the loss of Torah scholars in the Holocaust. The resulting poverty has been, until recently, considered acceptable by the *haredi* leadership and their followers, because they are safeguarding the Jewish future and the future of the Torah. Furthermore, there is no doubt that, as with many other fundamentalist movements, there is a use of the family and especially women (many of whom seem quite willing) to produce large numbers of children in an effort to triumph numerically over non-Orthodox Judaism.

Any effort to help them evolve a peacemaking or coexistence ethics vis-à-vis the rest of the world will have to take this contemporary context and reality into account. It is a reality filled with buried injuries, resentments, and highly adverserial interactions with the rest of the world. We are in a very different universe than that of Luzzatto and Benamozegh.

I have deliberately painted the darkest side of the contemporary Orthodox scene. The truth is that there are many Orthodox Jews who are caught in the middle of this cultural and political warfare without a voice representing their values. Many would embrace Luzzatto as a role model if they could, and there are many who do not, in principle, dislike or distrust gentiles or hold other religions in disdain. Many wish other religions well, as long as they do not demonize Jews, as in the past. This is particularly the case because rabbinic Judaism and its most Orthodox adherents do not suffer from a proselytizing drive to convert everyone to Judaism, although Judaism does have standards of intolerance of certain polytheistic practices that would place it in conflict with some religions of the world. But, as I have said, these standards of intolerance tend to relax or become more strict depending on the level of trust between Jews and Others, which brings us back to the ethics of conflict prevention and resolution.

The task of truly building a peacemaking strategy with religious Jews and eliciting a peacemaking ethic is what still remains to be done. This has been made exceedingly difficult, however, by the ongoing Arab/Israeli conflict, the almost impossible contradiction between the religious need for a reestablishment of Jewish sovereignty in the ancient lands versus the rights of Palestinians, and the siege mentality that has therefore developed among many religious Jews vis-à-vis everyone else, especially in response to the fears evoked by Arab terrorism. The latter makes them justify many terrible things and refuse to acknowledge their own part in this conflict. We will address this in some of the later chapters.

The other major challenge in this regard is that religious paradigms of peacemaking and coexistence, even the best of them, tend to assume a world in which everyone believes in God or at least conforms to some basic standards of behavior that everyone agrees on as moral. The latter assumption is something that can be adjusted to the contemporary situation to a degree. There is a widespread effort among people of many religions and the secular community to establish norms that can be shared. They have been framed until now in the secular constructs of human rights, despite the fact that most religions that I have studied tend to frame these ethical values in terms of obligations, not rights. Nevertheless, there is ample room for shared work here between the secular and religious communities. But most religious systems of the past, even the most liberal, have assumed that everyone must believe in something, and this is severely challenged today by the numbers of people who are atheist, agnostic, or believers in a particular faith who will not be subject to religious authorities on how they should interpret their religion or its precepts. This large amount of people, and their rights, are a central concern of the entire human rights agenda of modern civilization.

Can we truly say that the constructs of civil society that Benamozegh and Luzzatto, for example, would come up with could address this central concern? Another way of framing this is that we have an unprecedented theological challenge for traditional religions, which is how to construct an ethical universe in which nonbelievers can coexist equally in a given society. I believe that Luzzatto and Benamozegh would fair pretty well in this regard and that Luzzatto's supreme concern for compassion, in addition to his judgment of others' legitimacy by what they do rather than by their dogmas, would put him in good standing in a contemporary context. Nevertheless, the human rights agenda has been specifically constructed so that no human being can or should pass judgment on another's legitimacy. The human rights of an individual can only be curtailed to the degree to which an individual violates the rights of others by committing crimes.

This discussion is critical for the next chapter because we move into the complex problem of contemporary Judaism, Orthodoxy, and the modern Israeli state. It is here that many factors, only one of which is religion, have come together to create a serious challenge to religion as a peaceful element of social construction. Furthermore, the injuries of the past that both secular Jews and religious Jews feel, both from each other and from non-Jews, has conspired to create a serious religious/secular conflict that threatens the future of the state and severely complicates the prospects for a peaceful and just settlement with the Palestinians. From an analytic point of view, however, this affords us the opportunity to move our study away from theology and into the complexity of contemporary culture. It is in the midst of this complexity of today's civil society that religious human beings and secular human beings must find the resources to be peacemakers and conflict resolvers.

Paradigms of Religious Peacemaking in a Multicultural and Secular Context

Healing Religious/Secular Conflict

The Case of Contemporary Israel

Confronting the Current Conflict

We turn now to a contemporary civilization in which organized religion has been a major factor in conflict and violence. There is a great deal to be worried about in terms of Israel's future, particularly in terms of the unraveling of its domestic relations. One major reason that Israel is polarizing and is in some danger of disintegrating is the war over its identity, especially as that identity has been deeply called into question by the "terrifying" prospect of peace. Some careful analysis is required to understand the reason why this identity war between religious and secular, between liberal and nationalist, along with the slow convergence of these polar sets, is so decisive—and destructive—and why something as normally hopeful as a peace process has become the major trigger. It is true that the Hamas bombs prior to Benjamin Netanyahu's electoral victory in May of 1996 did the most to disintegrate a broad consensus for peacemaking. The threat of bombs continues to frighten Israelis in ways that one can see clearly in everyday activity but that are not readily admitted. Recently, the Palestinian Authority public television aired a program that featured Palestinian children making speeches in which they aspired to be suicide bombers, with their teacher looking on and applauding.[1] This strikes Jewish psychocultural vulnerability at its weakest point, the fear of violent loss of life at the hands of gentiles.[2]

Israeli society has faced much greater violence before, in the form of warfare. Why is the culture reaching such a difficult juncture now? This is a complex question. Sometimes it is precisely on the verge of peace that populations develop a hypersensitivity to the threat of violence, as if they are only now waking up to the enormity of what they have been through: decades of buried traumas stemming from places of origin, four wars, losses of loved ones, and older terror campaigns, among other problems.

I would argue that this phenomenon is also deeply related to an entirely different dynamic. It is the fact that peace is so threatening to those whom I have interviewed on the right wing that has intrigued me the most. A lack of a substantive Israeli and Jewish identity *for peacetime* that is widely shared is one of the principal culprits of the current crisis of Israeli culture. This is due to some of the profound conflicts that Jews have been having for centuries, and it is also due to the way in which wars and anti-Semitism have masked basic questions of identity and values until now. It is a time of reckoning and painful discovery. For anyone interested in a peaceful, stable Israel and an Israel that can discover its collective ability to meet the Palestinians in a true spirit of coexistence, this is the time for deep analysis of the conflict that is devastating its identity.

There is a long history of antagonism between secular and religious Jews, as well as among Jews of different religious orientations. At the same time, this is particularly traumatic to Jews because it calls into question some vital myths that have been the key to survival in a hostile world. The myths of Jewish brotherhood and the care for fellow Jews at all costs have been central beliefs that buttressed the struggle for survival in defiance of the wishes of religious enemies for two thousand years. Furthermore, the myth of Jewish unity has always been tied to the existence of an overarching, evil enemy.[3] But this myth has masked serious divisions within the Jewish people, which have always existed and have always been avoided, at least officially. Conflict avoidance is one of the most popular methods of peacemaking—and one of the most dangerous in the long term. The Jewish people have been particularly prone, especially in the last couple of hundred years of traumatic change, to internal strife, hidden as far as possible from public view but deeply bitter. This internal strife, *mahloket*, in the language of the Talmud, strikes deeply into the heart of the basic interpersonal and social styles of interaction.[4] It goes beyond any one conflict, such as the religious/secular conflict, and goes to the core of internal Israeli interactions.

In the contemporary situation, the tendency to be conflictual may be expressing an internalized anger and self-hatred originating possibly, at least for Ashkenazi Jews, in the brutal conditions of minority life in Europe, anti-Semitism, and the Holocaust, which would be more than enough to create internalized abuse. This alone, aside from the religious conflict, has seriously undermined the search for a truly civil society in Israel and the spirit of cooperation in numerous Jewish contexts, such as synagogues in the Diaspora. Of course, this is not true of everyone, or even most perhaps, but it is true in enough contexts as to make it a serious cultural problem for numerous Jewish organizations, synagogues, and, of course, the state of Israel.

The Arab/Israeli conflicts have, in particular, masked the problem of internal Jewish conflict for most of this century. The Arab/Israeli conflicts and the accompanying terrorism are far less frightening a prospect to many Jews than facing the fact that Israel perhaps may end up in civil war, as so many young countries do, with Jews killing Jews en masse in a way that has not been seen in two thousand years. It is far less frightening for modern Jews to expect and acclimate to what they are familiar with—an assault by gentiles—than to watch their traditional base of security, fellow Jews, fall apart at the seams. External conflict confirms the myths by which Jews have lived and died, whereas internal conflict shatters them. And nothing in life is more frightening than a world of shattered myths, even if those myths are dark or fatalistic in nature. We will return to this theme later.

Beyond the general roots of conflictual styles in Diaspora Jewish life, however, there needs to be an exploration into and exposure of that which causes the secular/religious divide in Israel at a deep level, especially the level of mutual injury that has been perpetrated for a long time, going back to Europe for the Ashkenazi community and to the first Sephardi/Ashkenazi encounters in the Yishuv (the early Zionist settlements in Palestine). These remembered injuries may sound petty next to the Holocaust. But curiously, many *haredi* Jews to whom I have talked have far more venom for what Reform Jews, Bundists, or Zionists did to their community in Eastern Europe or during World War II than they express for anti-Semites.[5] It is almost as if the pain that many *haredim* feel about the loss of virtually all their cultural centers in the Holocaust and all their families in the *shtetl* is beyond words; it is literally unspeakable. It is much less daunting to deal on a conscious level with fellow Jews who are adversaries. It also may be the case that they *expected* gentiles to behave barbarously but were deeply wounded by what they perceive as betrayals by fellow Jews since the Emancipation but especially since the beginning of the terrible European persecution and poverty from 1880 onward, culminating in the Holocaust. Much is still unknown about these attitudes.[6]

We have not even begun to understand the pain that is hidden in this reclusive community regarding the Holocaust and the European past.[7] They have been deprived of what is essential to healing and to developing a renewed trust of the world: the chance to openly face one's injuries, what one has lost, and have this acknowledged by the world, especially by that part of the world that was partly or completely to blame for that loss or perceived to be so by the victims. Their theologians may have responded at one point to the Holocaust but never has there been a truly open encounter between *haredi* Jews and non-*haredi* Jews, especially Zionists, about the loss of the Holocaust. One almost never sees *haredi* Jews at Holocaust museums. The reasons are complicated and partly attributable to Jewish legal sensibilities.[8] But it is these Jewish legal differences over the presentation of the material that embody the pain of the community. Jewish law and legal conflict often embody Jewish emotions, pain, and unresolved rage. Furthermore, there was such a legacy of shame over the Holocaust in Israel that many people, not just *haredim*, felt prohibited for years from speaking of these things.[9]

This encounter between religious and secular about the pain and anger of the past—and the healing that could come about from such an encounter—remains a distant possibility as long as conflict resolution in Israel remains at the level of select representatives of progressive elites talking to each other. It must reach the masses for it is their unresolved anger that drives the polarization of the politics and, therefore, the impasses on coexistence. Furthermore, the Knesset, with its vested interest in power informing most members' behavior—be it secular or religious political behavior—is not an ideal place either, although select members of that body may have the courage soon to show the way.

One must deal with whatever injuries come to the fore initially in these encounters, even if one suspects that something much darker, such as the Holocaust, lurks beneath the surface. It is difficult to disentangle these matters in dialogue, but it is vital to not predetermine where dialogue processes go. If I am correct about a deeper injury lurking beneath the surface, then it will emerge as relationships proceed. It is in the nature of these difficult encounters that someone breaks the silence about a deeper stratum of trauma, which others may be avoiding.[10]

There is a great deal that is hidden in Israel, so much family history, so many injuries from the results of anti-Semitism all the way to brutality imposed by fellow Jews, such as what was done to Yemenite families by some Zionist institutions. There appears to be a strong need among some Jews to project injury that was done by gentiles onto fellow Jews; this, in my opinion, is especially true among anti-Zionist *haredim*. It appears that for some people the "injuring Others," in this case European Christians, are so fearsome that to directly attack them is somehow too overwhelming or disempowering. One feels safer with family, and thus the family becomes the locus of all the anger that one feels at these larger, more fearsome sources of anger, such as anti-Semites. Anti-Semites have been so mystified in traditional Judaism (even elevated to supernatural levels) that to directly attack them is unthinkable; they are a mysterious but permanent fixture of God's universe. But one *can* attack those who one knows, or even oneself, for not living up to God's laws. This happens often to close-knit groups in crisis situations, and it magnifies the tragedy of victimhood to even greater levels. Thus, the secular Jews, Reform Jews, early Zionists, or even one's own sins become responsible for everything evil that befalls oneself or one's people.

The opposite coping mechanism is taken by other Jews, especially nationalist Jews, who project all family-related anger and injury onto an externalized Other, a demonized Other who must be evil by definition. The prospect of facing something repulsive that is rooted in an internal, family problem would destroy an already fragile family identity. This is especially rooted in the fact that the more exclusively religious is one's orientation to Jewishness and Judaism, the more one may lay blame for events with Others, even Jews, who are sinful, since God is the only one who is and must be sinless in these tragedies. The more that one's faith is focused on Jewishness itself, on the Jewish people, then the more one may be prone to lay all blame for evil on some outside group. This leads some Jews, in the contemporary period, to a desperate search for anti-Semitism. There is a need for anti-Semitism to be the locus of all evil in order to not face the fragility of one's family identity or identity as a people. This does not mean that anti-Semitism does not exist, but the search for it becomes pathological when it is a replacement for any positive Jewish identity. One finds this especially among Jews who support Jewish defense organizations in the Diaspora, but it is also found among those in Israel who have elevated the Jewish people and their holy land to a mystical level of worship. The worshiped object must be beyond reproach. One senses that it originates in a rather impoverished sense of substantive identity, what I have referred to often as "negative identity," but this is not always the case. For either response, the damage is profound and needs to be exposed and confronted.

On a deeper level, it occurs to me that some non-Zionist *haredim*, who today place all of their absolute faith in a good God, must see the evil of the world located in human beings who failed to live up to God's law, even if those human beings are fellow Jews who also died in the camps or Israeli soldiers who died in battle. This would explain the widespread practice of *haredim* repudiating the yearly Israeli ritual of standing for a moment of silence in honor of the fallen dead of Israel's wars, a practice that is deeply injurious to secular and Zionist Israelis.

For *haredim*, the critical thing to avoid psychologically is blame of God, who must continue to be their one anchor of unqualified goodness in a harsh world. For many other Jews, however, a good, perfect God is almost impossible to believe in after the Holocaust. Whether they admit it or not, for many Jews today, including many of the modern Orthodox, who are the most fiercely loyal to the Jewish state and its military, their deepest faith is in the absolute goodness and righteousness of the Jewish people and its one state. Thus, their need for projection of evil needs to go to any object other than fellow Jews or a Jewish state. If not, their one source of faith in the post-Holocaust world falls apart. It is especially the Holocaust, the overarching guilt that every Jew feels at surviving, that poisons the atmosphere so deeply. On the one hand, the *haredim* feel that the Zionists abandoned them in Europe by taking all the youth to Palestine, leaving them defenseless against the Nazis and generally impoverishing the community physically and spiritually. On a theological level, at least some of their theologians and leaders taught them that those Jews who repudiated Judaism, who became nationalists and idolaters of the state, like the gentiles, incurred the divine wrath of the Holocaust, a collective punishment against the people that took away the innocent together with the guilty.

God was involved at every stage of the Holocaust from the *haredi* perspective. The deaths were a sanctification of God's name, which brought people closer to God, and the survival of the individuals, especially the beloved *rebbes*, was seen often as a miraculous sign of God's continuing relationship with the people.

There was an angry side to many *haredi* responses to the Holocaust during those terrible years. Elhanan Wasserman, for example, saw the events as a consequence of anti-Torah activities. The behavior of some Jews, who were separated from *halakha*, brought the seed of Amalek (the ultimate symbol of gentile evil) into the Jewish people. The Jews who were responsible included communists, secular humanists, and Zionists, including religious Zionists who sinfully adopted the practices of the gentile world. In fact, the Zionists, unless they did *teshuva* (repentance), now belonged to the *sitra ahra* (other side), the evil side of the world, from a mystical point of view. They were no longer part of *klal yisroel*, the inclusive community of Israel, to use Greenberg's phrase, the members of which are committed to love and care for each other.[11]

The suffering of the Holocaust was seen by some as a means of purification, and for many thinkers, the suffering was supposed to spur the people into repentance. Hasidic thinkers of the Lubavitch sect in particular, felt the urgency, with each passing year of the war, that the Messiah could come at any time *if only* everyone repented.

From an outsider's point of view and from a psychological perspective, the *haredi* leaders lived in a universe of meaning in which the Jewish people were still profoundly empowered to control this brutal world. It was not the Nazis, with their unprecedented level of physical power, weaponry, and cruelty, who were in control but the Jewish people. The Jews who were faithless brought this plague, and, with a strong sense of urgency, many rabbis hoped during the war that if there were profound repentance, a return to Torah, or, for some, a discovery by all Jews of the deep revelations embedded in Kabbalah then the plague would end, and the great redemption would come. How bitter they must have felt when only a few listened to their method of winning the war against the Nazis.

What neither they nor the Zionists, who were equally embittered by the loss of their families, were ever able to face—something that all victims have a hard time facing without help—is that victims of overwhelming force usually have absolutely no power. That is part of the horror of victimhood. It is true that one can tinker at the edges of the Holocaust and learn how to prevent future genocides. It is true that there may have been things that should have been done differently. I have no doubt that many *haredim* were bitter at fellow Jews in America, for example, who seemed too afraid to speak out more forcefully in Washington. I have no doubt that there is great bitterness at what resources were or were not used by fellow Jews. But the important thing is that most victims would have died in the "final solution" anyway. The only response to this is shared mourning, the telling of the stories of the families, of the losses, of the bad fortune, of being saved, of fighting the Nazis, and even of the Jews saved by gentiles, who risked their lives. But this is not something that *haredi* and non-*haredi* Jews have ever really done together, not in a way that would bring healing and a greater openness again to the world, that would bring a greater trust of life and humanity.

These two communities live in different universes of meaning, and therefore, their tales of both the tragic and the heroic are profoundly different. For one, heroism may entail the creation of seventy grandchildren, fifty years after Hitler, all named for murdered family and all committed to a religion that Hitler wanted to make into a relic; this is a victory that goes to the heart of Hitler's design. For others, it may be the creation of seventy acres of Jewish-owned tilled land that used to be desert and now provides for a more permanent place of Jewish security than life among the gentiles could ever provide. For one, noble heroism at the hour of death could have involved the defiance of a Yom Kippur service, saying Kaddish (the comforting prayer after the death of loved ones) for themselves, hours before being led to the death pits outside of town. But for another, a noble death may have involved dying with a stolen gun in one hand and a dead fascist at her feet.

For a *haredi* Jew, the causal connectedness of the world involves an intimate system of action and counteraction by God and human being. At a profound level, what we do morally matters much more to our survival than our petty attempts to control destiny by military or even financial means. That does not mean that the *haredim* are impractical, not at all. But when it comes to the overarching questions of survival, this is where the two groups split so bitterly in the Diaspora and in Israel. For the *haredi* and many other religious Jews, the key to the promise of the eternity of the Jewish people is Jewish commitment in each generation to the covenant of Torah observance. This can conquer even Hitler, as long as some survive. But the abandonment of the Torah is truly the annihilation of a four-thousand-year-old identity before God. For Zionists and other modern Jews, this kind of imprisonment in the old ways of coping with cultural survival is intolerable. Furthermore, it was completely ineffective in combating European anti-Semitism. But the *haredim* respond that it is the Reform or secular Jews who, when they tried to be like the gentiles, brought on a genocide from the Germans that was far worse than anything in Jewish history, while the Zionists, by insisting on a Jewish secular state, have incurred the wrath and hatred of hundreds of millions of Muslims around the world. This argument has never been taken seriously, or at least understood empathetically, by non-*haredi* Jews.

The Zionists, living with a completely different construct of how the world works and how people live, die, or are killed, are outraged that the fundamentalist rabbis, for reasons of piety and fear of assimilation, prevented so many Jews from leaving Europe in the first place, thus massively increasing the death toll. But I would suggest that what everyone shares are feelings of profound guilt, in ways that they can hardly articulate, for being utterly powerless to help their families survive the Holocaust and for surviving themselves, without their families, in whatever ways that they did. We must keep in mind, in terms of Israeli society, that all Ashkenazi Jews, both religious and secular Jews, had family in Europe. Ninety percent of European Jews were murdered, and many of the few survivors did not recover their sanity. The hidden toll on Israeli Jews is astonishing.

Coming back to the present day, for some Jews, displacing all their anger onto fellow Jews is an escape from more fearsome enemies, real or imaginary, past or present. For others, they do not want to face the internal Jewish conflicts because that threatens one of the basic myths that sustains them in an uncertain world, namely, the myth of Jewish solidarity or, in religious terms, the "love of Israel," *ahavat yisroel.*

Until now, one of the powerful ways in which there have been temporary truces in Jewish conflict in Israel is by way of Arab bombs. Then one sees some truly admirable forms of Jewish reconciliation. But this is also where the true nature of the injuries is exposed. For example, there are intimate and respectful relations between Jerusalem police and the ultra-Orthodox group Hesed shel

Emet, whose adherents pick up every piece of Jewish flesh after Arab bombs have exploded; they work hand in glove with the police and have developed mutual admiration.[12] Yet some of the *same* group of Orthodox men have then gone to Saturday demonstrations against the police, where epithets like "Nazis" are hurled at literally the same policemen, although not by the same people. Still, this is a bizarre social interaction, and it suggests something deeply wrong with Jewish Israeli interaction. Also, the freedom with which the "Nazi" curse is used indicates how much the Nazi is still in everyone's mind, both secular and *haredi*, like a ghost that cannot be exorcised.[13]

One can hear this epithet frequently regarding the perennial *haredi* protests against various construction and archaeological digs, all involving outrage at the alleged desecration of Jewish graves. It is extraordinary how much attention is given by some *haredim* to graves that are thousands of years old, just fifty years after the biggest failure to bury Jews in all of the people's history: 6 to 7 million people not buried according to Jewish rites, their bodies violated, abused, and cremated, in complete violation of one of the most sacred obligations that Jewish families have regarding their loved ones. I cannot prove the correlation, but the fact that epithets of "Nazi" are often used in this context cannot escape notice.

The *haredim* who protest the digs are dismissed by almost all Israelis, including fellow religious Jews, as crazy extremists. I do not dismiss any behavior as "crazy," which is our word for what we cannot comprehend. To me such behavior presents a golden opportunity to see an injury; a minority may be acting upon that injury externally in strange ways, but a much larger amount of people may be feeling it.

I am going to suggest something harsh about the strange level of cooperation and affectionate care among Jews of all kinds during bombing crises, and I could be wrong. I suggest that there is a need—completely unconscious to be sure— that is being expressed here *for* the bombs, as a way of discovering the loved and hated Jewish Other. There also seems to be a need to continue to be deeply conflictual when there is no external attack. It is as if the psychocultural injury is so deep and vast that it needs an outlet in conflict that either has to be with an external Other, in which case one finds solace in the company of the reconciled Jewish Other, or the conflict has to be internal to the Jewish people, in which case one directs the anger *at* the Jewish Other. In any case, there must be conflict.

The need for bombs to bring out the best in Israelis can also be seen in how they care for non-Jews. The American embassy bombing in Kenya and Tanzania prompted an immediate engagement of numerous Israeli experts in recovering trapped victims, pulling out survivors who had been given up for dead. In Israel, this rescue operation was covered by the generally cynical media as one of the great proud moments of the Israel Defense Forces, a "flash of its old brilliance and style that had won Israeli soldiers international admiration."[14] This was viewed with extreme gratitude by the Kenyans.

It is the language of the reporting on this tragedy that is utterly inexplicable unless my thesis about the need for bombs is correct:

The carnage in Nairobi has provided a *welcome* [my emphasis] . . . respite
for the pressures the State of Israel as a whole . . . have [*sic*] felt regarding
the long-stalled peace process . . . Suddenly . . . Israelis this week were reliv-
ing the country's *good times* [my emphasis], periods when the Jewish state
basked in the warm glow of international admiration.[15]

This is an astonishing embrace of bombs and carnage as related to the "good
times" of a culture. Taken by itself, this appears quite barbaric and callous concerning the Kenyans, except when one remembers that most of the bombs that
have brought Israelis to a higher sense of who they are and their values have been
directed against *them*. *They* are the ones who have suffered the most from these
bombs. Furthermore, their very purpose in taking over the chaotic situation on
the ground in Kenya and bringing in such sophisticated equipment was to save
a few precious African lives buried in the rubble. Ironically, this effort is in the
highest tradition of rabbinic values, which places saving a human life at the
highest level of ethical/religious achievement.[16] Thus, this journalist recounts a
tragedy, which involved so much death and suffering, yet welcomes it precisely
because it is an opportunity to be "good" in a deeply Jewish way, by saving lives.
This is a tragic psychological paradox, which takes a profoundly prosocial spiritual
value of Judaism and Jewish culture and inserts it into a pathological need for
tragedy.

I see this phenomenon as an expression of an indirect longing that Jewish
Israelis have for community, to love and be loved by each other, even to be loved
by the world. There is a need to achieve a state of communal relationship, which
has always been a part of the Zionist dream, often epitomized and symbolized
by the idea if not the reality of the kibbutz. But right now they only seem able
to do this in the midst of enormous suffering that is externally generated. I have
seen this to be true among both religious and secular Jews, though expressed in
different ways.

Here is the most important point. This strange phenomenon, taken as a whole,
is an uncanny recreation of centuries of Jewish love, which was at its most intense
in the midst of pogroms. Put simply, this is an extremely bad habit of the heart,
born of tragic circumstances. It is a compulsion by some to repeat the tragedies
of the past, with all their pain and all their evocation of the nobility of the Jewish
character. But it can also be characterized as a cry for help that requires a creative
and healing response, something beyond simple, rational diplomacy. Israelis know
very well that this is not the kind of normalization of Jewish response to the
world that the Zionist founders had hoped for as they escaped the ghetto and
tried to create a new kind of Jewish life.

Of course, there are real, vital issues that divide secular and religious citizens
in the Middle East as a whole[17], real concerns on the side of the secular community for its safety, its cultural future, and its independence from religious
coercion. Those issues should be the subject of good, rational negotiation processes. The challenge to rational problem solving, however, is how to distinguish
those legitimate concerns and needs from deep psychological patterns, which are

understandable but highly destructive. This is a process that requires enormous patience, listening skills, problem-solving skills, empathy, *and* the cultural knowledge base to devise, together with the adversaries, the kind of solutions that speak to both the minds and hearts of people on all sides of these conflicts.

Solutions

The primary formulation of a new path can only really come from Israelis themselves, but I have several recommendations, which draw freely from different schools of conflict resolution theory.[18] I want to divide this into two sections: deep cultural changes, which both sides need to undergo, and practical steps for the present that will lead to the necessary cultural changes.

It is vital for all sides to acknowledge the connections among the suffering endured by Jews in the past, the effect of wars in the recent past, and their direct impact on both the tendency in Jewish life to be combative and enraged and the intolerant positions taken by the adversaries in this conflict. Both sides have strong needs that are based on old fears from Jewish history. The secular fear of coercion and their commitment to combat the influence of religion is in part a response to the past. It is their solution to past suffering. The liberal Jewish impulse in general is a direct response to the Crusades and almost sixteen hundred years of insecurity and/or persecution in unfree societies that, in particular, expressed their brutality against Jews *for religious reasons.* This is why Jews figure so prominently in the battle for church/state separation in the United States. For its strong advocates the issue goes far beyond rational self-interest. It has become a moral mission, almost a religion.

Secular Jewish identity, as it is expressed in Israel, is beginning to become aware of the limits of this social construct. They understand the problematic nature of secular modernity, the materialism, the ethical relativism, and the loss of intensive community; the latter seems to speak to a basic human need that modern secular society, at least in its large, bureaucratic manifestation, never really anticipated. But secularists—and many modern religious Jews, by the way—are willing to pay this price because the alternative is too horrible to contemplate, namely, a return to a disastrous past of persecution founded upon religiously rooted political entities.

The anger and outrage over infringements of Israeli secular society are too strong to be merely about the memory of *shtetl* rabbis and their coercive behaviors. Their outrage goes to the heart of the tragedy of Diaspora history and is an attempt by secular Jews and Israelis to heal its worst aspects.

It is also the case that Israeli culture has followed the path of contemporary European culture in terms of agnosticism and, at the very least, a rather low tolerance for organized religion. At the same time, Israelis are coerced in critical areas of life, namely, marriage, divorce, and burial, to submit to rabbinic authority. Other European societies that have a mixed model of church/state relations do not have this burden for their secular constituency. Thus, the non-

Orthodox outrage is understandable. The religious community has traditionally seen the issues of marriage and divorce as critical to Jewish survival for a variety of reasons. Thus we again come to basic existential fears.

In the religious realm, there is also a quiet, private recognition of the problems of their own subculture. They know that there is far too much fighting and distrust in the religious world. They know that there is damaging behavior in which each religious group disapproves of the group to its left and lives intimidated by the group to its right. But they believe that the price is worth it, because their children will be protected from a world that will otherwise drive them away from their identity and, at worst, put them in gas chambers. I put this in extreme terms, but it fits the emotions that religious Jews feel in their moments of anxiety. This is especially true of parents when they are making critical decisions about their children's friends and their education.

Both groups, secular and religious, have a need to perpetuate an identity, even a Jewish identity. But one does it by recreating the lost past, while the other does it by creating an utterly new future, completely divorced from the past. Both try to have victory over the horror of the recent past. The mortal threats imposed by the Arab/Israeli conflict and the deep confusion and threat to identity that the Palestinian/Israeli conflict causes make this a real, day-to-day emotional and cognitive concern. Thus the struggle over how to be victorious over the past is an immediate struggle for life and identity. The past haunts the present. There is no present and future, when it comes to identity, without the past. And yet the past often tyrannizes in a way that strangulates positive identity for the future.

There needs, therefore, to be a much greater embrace of a conversation about the future. There needs to be a way to hear what each group is really saying and feeling about the past and the future, once one gets past all the defensive rhetoric of the politicized face of this conflict. When Israelis have enough time to be honest about the past and the future, they will discover a greater consensus than they realize on the future, not full agreement, but consensus on enough to build a new civil society.

Secular Israeli culture and Jewish religious culture need to both evolve to a new place but not only a place of acceptance. That is not enough. They need to discover over time a coalescence in some overall moral and ideological framework that does not erase the boundary between secular and religious, but that allows more open borders and a higher consensus on the foundations of civil culture, culled from the best values that both communities have to offer. This can and should be done on a popular level, through meetings and conversations, and it must be done by at least one generation of courageous and visionary writers. It means giving birth to a new Israeli identity that is constructed in the context of political peace and not dependent on war or persecution. It means giving birth to a state that is secular but that deeply values and honors its religious citizens, protecting their needs and including them in the culture.

Some will argue that this internal Jewish process that I am suggesting will make Israel unwelcoming to non-Jewish citizens. This is an important critique. But I argue that it all depends on the Jewish values that are embraced and the way in which they are interpreted. I am banking on the fact that religious and secular Jews, in order to coexist, will have to discover those Jewish values from the past that would welcome the Other, embrace the stranger, and care for human beings per se, no matter what their ethnic or religious affiliation. This would allow for a legislative process that would guarantee the rights of all citizens to full civil equality and cultural self-expression. The resources for these conclusions are to be found in Judaism, even Orthodox Judaism, as we will see in the next chapter, *if* the right atmosphere is created for their exploration.

It is vital to understand that the interpreters of culture, either secular or religious, in their ongoing hermeneutic enterprise are deeply affected by their antagonists. The horizon of one's influences as one looks again and again at the texts and symbols of one's culture is deeply affected by a hostile engagement with enemies. The stronger the encounter of enemies is that entangles these people, the more likely that they will choose an adversarial hermeneutic that is directed against the attackers. Thus both sides of a secular/religious conflict have a deep effect on the spiritual direction of a particular religion. Ironically, many secular people have great power over the direction of the world's religions by being active opponents of the same. The character of secular opposition and the content of the opposition have direct impacts on the character and content of the responses to their challenge. This is true of Judaism to some degree in the Diaspora but especially in Israel. It is a natural corollary of the action/reaction dynamic of all conflicts.[19]

Whether religions advocate peace or conflict, love or hate, involves both the process of hermeneutic interpretation and the dynamic interaction of the hermeneutic process with the cultural horizon of the interpreter, the power interests at work, and the psychological state of both sides of the conflict. If both sides engage in a hermeneutic debate that is constructive, even cooperative, then the chances are strong that a religious hermeneutic enterprise will elicit the kind of values that could be useful in the formation of a civil democratic society. This is true in Israel, and I believe it is potentially applicable to other divided societies as well. But I must emphasize that the nature of Israeli relationships and the style of interaction will have a deep effect on the course of this hermeneutics.

There is no doubt that there are a variety of religious institutions that, if taken literally and applied strictly, would be conflict generating in a secular society. But the subtle reality of religious life indicates how much is left up to the interpreters in each generation. The political constraints of those interpreters in their current cultural milieu are often far more important than the actual texts of the tradition. This is rarely apparent to outside observers, and therefore the true cause of the intolerant behavior escapes notice. Potential solutions escape notice as well.[20]

The purpose of a joint exploration of these issues between religious and secular is not, however, full agreement on every issue. The purpose of effective peacemaking is not to stop conflict but to focus on ideas, interests, and needs—and not on people as dehumanized incarnations of everything that is evil and dangerous. It is the latter that creates destructive conflict.

Cultures and religions in general need to evolve prosocial models of constructive conflict, so that the cultures or religions in question do not simply revert to utopian calls for peace every time there are difficult issues; the latter effectively make the values of the culture useless in dealing with the real complexity of society. Cultures and the societies they sustain need mechanisms of constructive conflict.

The ideal kind of Jewish conflict, according to the oldest Jewish sources, is that kind of conflict, *mahloket,* that honors both sides, as the house of Hillel did at the beginning of the Common Era, and that allows for civil society or in religious language, *hibbah* (love) and *re'ut* (friendship), to survive the conflict.[21] It is also the kind of conflict that opposes, as the talmudic-era woman Beruriah did, what one thinks is wrong without inveighing curses against those people who adhere to what one thinks is wrong. On the contrary, the latter model espouses praying for, or hoping for, the other to change.[22]

In other words, a crucial form of indigenous Jewish conflict resolution is not the elimination of conflict but the reformulation of its character. This is what could create a better civil society in Israel today, across all shades of Jewish commitment. Needless to say, such a prosocial way of conducting conflict could only help stimulate new ways of relating to Palestinians as well, treating them with the honor and respect that they justifiably expect.

The other unavoidable reality, in response to the question about non-Jewish citizens, is that rabbinic Jewish values, having never previously confronted the task of coping with a multicultural society that is predominantly Jewish, will now have to find the humility to share space with other cultures, to fully embrace their expression, and even to insist on it as a peacemaking gesture between Jews and non-Jews. This too can be found in rabbinic Judaism—for those who are willing to look for it and to develop it hermeneutically for the current circumstances.[23] Conveying these ideas to *haredi* society, however, will require delicate processes of relationship building, trust building, and negotiation.

I want to emphasize at this point that none of the recommendations that I am making will directly solve the ongoing struggle between secular and religious *political* parties nor will they solve the current legislative wars over who is a Jew— or who is a rabbi. These legal battles will go on, but they are unlikely to solve the deep social crisis described here. That is not to say that they should not be pursued by those who seek a just Israeli society. But in the end they become a war by nonviolent means rather than the creation of a future based on a reasonably agreed-upon social vision, which is the only thing that will create a truly stable, vibrant society.

If there is greater effort in this direction and the social vision agreed upon is inclusive of religious and secular sensibilities, I predict that religious people will begin to vote along a much greater range of the political spectrum. This would help significantly to prevent the polarization of the country along lines that combine religious and political allegiance, a dangerous combination for any democracy. In other words, if the social and cultural processes that I am recommending are followed, it is highly likely that the religious political parties will remain but will not continue to be the exclusive representatives of religious people, which is already partially the case. This will decouple religion and political affiliation, which is vital for the stability of a democracy, because religious identity can at times become so strong that, if it is affiliated exclusively with one party, it can turn the normal give and take of party-based democracy into a life-and-death struggle for ultimate identity.

There is one legislative issue that does seem a must for the future of Israel and that is the guarantee of civil liberties, which Israel does not presently have in constitutional form. Without those at some basic level, there is danger ahead. Unfortunately, a consensus on a constitution will only occur if there is a profoundly new process of trust building between the secular and religious Jewish communities, in addition to the essential inclusion of Israeli non-Jews in the effort to create a constitution.

Practical Steps

First, there needs to be a bilateral process of discovery of the respective communities. This takes on three aspects: What motivates the heart of each community, what are its highest ideals and values? What are its deepest pains and past injuries that might be shared in common with the other community? What are at least some elements of its vision for the future.

The means of this discovery is most important. Certainly, dialogue in small and large groups needs to be extensively pursued. These dialogues should be guided by intelligent and sensitive principles of mediation, which are geared toward accommodating the cultural needs and psychological peculiarities of each group.

But dialogue is insufficient by itself. The reason why an exclusive reliance on dialogue groups is insufficient is that Western styles of conflict resolution and social transformation have been too intellectual thus far. They are too focused on spoken communication, at which only a limited amount of citizens are generally capable. Dialogue involves verbal skills and, more important, the ability to articulate extremely difficult, emotionally wrenching issues. This favors certain people and eliminates others. Often it is the least articulate people, whether they are educated or not, who have difficulty verbalizing their emotions, who become prone to violent solutions to difficult dilemmas. Thus, it is essential to creatively devise alternatives that will widen the circle of prosocial engagement.

These methods can be universal in nature, devices that could work in all cultures. But the most effective will speak deeply to the specific cultures in question. I can think of several untapped alternatives related to the unique cultural constructs of the Jewish community.

We have failed to understand the peculiarly Jewish drive for activism, for social justice, which is still strong in Israel despite the damaging effects on human relations of the wars, the occupation, and Palestinian/Israeli relations. What I mean by this is the drive to aid those who are suffering, at least when the sufferer is not from an enemy group.

There is also still in Israel a strong drive to build society, to create something out of nothing in new circumstances, as members of the Yishuv did and Jewish immigrants have done for thousands of years. These two drives, building and social justice, run deep in Jewish religion and culture. They are also survival mechanisms of two thousand years of exile. In the Diaspora, they express themselves through a powerful Jewish presence in causes of social justice, particularly defending the underdog. Often Jews were the underdog, and therefore there is a finely honed sense of injustice when society is treating groups differently. Of course, I am speaking of the best impulses of the community, not its worst, because a community's best self-image is what one must build upon in conceptualizing with them a conflict resolution strategy.

Cooperation among the conflicting groups on these two Jewish impulses, building and social justice, could be a vital form of peacebuilding and transformation of relationships among enemy groups. This might cross the lines of affiliation between secular and religious. In fact, it did for many years when the Jewish community in Israel felt a strong external threat. We know that the more complex we make the affiliations and connections among enemy groups on matters that make them interdependent the less prone they are to violence.[24]

How exactly would the opposing groups manage to cooperate on these shared tasks? Translation of values between radically different subcultures into practical projects or civil activities, especially when they are rooted in values that are deeply honored and prized, is a difficult affair, easily devolving into injury to the Other, where one meant no harm. But patient allowance for experimentation and error over time can eliminate this problem.

A related method is the process of honoring the highest ideals of each community, finding the ones that can be honored. The free gift of honor is an ancient method of discovery of the Other in Jewish life, and it has dramatic effects on conflict and interpersonal injury.[25] It is simple intellectually but exceedingly difficult emotionally for people of all educational backgrounds and will require nonverbal gestures and symbols, visual evidence, and ceremonies. The smaller these bilateral engagements are, in terms of participants, the more authentic and effective they are likely to be. The more national and political, the more endangered they are in terms of the perception of politicization and hypocrisy. On the other hand, true societal change requires a large-scale effort. Thus, a broad-based national effort that has many local outlets would be best.

Another key method of relationship building is sharing in the suffering of each community in a way that is felt to be authentic by all parties. This is also most effectively done through symbol and ceremony. All of these gestures must be created indigenously by a wide range of Israelis, especially young, creative Israelis from both camps.[26]

The next major step in conflict resolution in this case is the bilateral discovery of injuries that each group has perpetrated on the other in the last couple of hundred years. What is especially important in this regard is the use of narrative, the stories of both the different subgroups and individuals, because people believe personal narratives in a way that they believe nothing else from an adversary. There are various ways for this to happen, and all of them will have to be mediated with great skill, allowing for much pain to be unleashed in this process. But this is the kind of pain that is constructive. The most obvious means is open popular meetings. However, ongoing closed meetings among leaderships and various cultural elites, as well as living room meetings among many average citizens would be vital as well, especially in cooperatively devising future steps for the society as a whole.

The bilateral nonverbal gestures that I mentioned above would be especially relevant in confronting the injuries in each community, especially if we are interested in a truly broad-based process of social transformation.[27] This may include public symbols of deep respect or apology or simple care. It may involve intentional interpersonal gestures of aid, like visiting the sick or helping struggling children from all groups, which take on deep significance when intended as conflict resolution gestures.

Additional methods involve educational curriculums, perhaps the most important long-term step for social transformation. Various programs involving education for democracy already exist in Israel, funded by Israelis and progressive American Jews. I must emphasize, however, that at present some of this education is not deepening a consensus in Israel but further polarizing the community. The values of only one segment of Israel, the secular liberal community, are being propagated. They do not represent a consensus, and they are perceived, at present at least, as alien and extreme by the *haredi* community. That is not to say that these values are wrong, but that the teachers of these values need to acquire a method of extending their efforts into all segments of the society.

Through the trust-building methods that I am outlining here, there is at least a possibility that education for democracy, for example, could be a broad-based, deeply cultural process of Israeli social transformation. Otherwise, the educational system becomes yet another battleground, not a place that teaches universally accepted civic virtues. Many will respond that this is not possible because the religious community is not committed to democratic values. But we cannot know this until there is a profound effort to build trusting relationships, and then we can see whether some middle ground can be found on the tough issues that divide. As of this writing, this is beginning to happen. The Adam Institute, for example, is sponsoring more and more religious/secular study and dialogue on democracy.

An important catalyst to these methods is the commitment of the cultural leadership of the respective communities to these processes. It has been amply demonstrated how vital leadership is to the formation of human values, secular or religious, whether or not this offends our championing of human independence and individual conscience.[28] This is the psychological reality. It is not the case, however, that the top leadership is indispensable, and it is often the leadership that is *not* at the pinnacle that is the most useful for making change, especially if the individuals are not currently in political office. Far too much energy is expended on speculations about or influence on a prime minister or a major rabbi and not enough on their immediate surroundings; it is the actors inhabiting the latter that most often determine whether leaders have room to move politically or not.

It is also the case that many of the new directions of society begin on its fringes, for better or worse. In this regard, it would be useful to discover and actively support those individuals who are at the margins of each group, the *haredi* thinker, for example, whose tolerant attitudes have been neither accepted in his own community nor appreciated in the secular community. This aid to those at the margins could be crucial in building a new common consensus. The aid could be overt or confidential, depending on what is useful, and the venue could be financial or in terms of recognition or honoring, for example. I have met such figures, and they need and deserve major support as at current, they are virtually unknown. Such support could revolutionize their impact on their culture.

A key method of addressing the present situation is the training in peace-making and conflict resolution of as many members of each community as possible, especially the leadership. These skills have universal validity and have been useful around the world, even in nonsecular contexts, *if and only if* they are aligned with the cultures in question. They must speak to the highest Jewish values that are relevant to human interpersonal and communal behavior. There should be mutually agreed-upon parallel processes of training, one secular, the other religious. The religious process could be under the rubric of typical religious ethical educations but it would have a much more activist, engaged training process that weds conflict resolution research and methods with religious values. This should emerge from creative religious people. For example, training for religious people may involve experiments with public *middot* (morals) education or campaigns in *derekh eretz* (civility).

I must caution that this training will lead to *greater* division unless there is serious effort to coordinate culturally the two communities' efforts and to acknowledge the differences in methods, and even some goals, and learn to deal with those differences. Let us take a counterexample to demonstrate what needs to be avoided. The mistakes are subtle. In a lecture I heard recently on a certain project of peacemaking in Israel, the highly talented secular researcher evaluated the results by how much the two groups, especially their teenagers, were more prone to integrate and interact. The secular ideal here is a complete mixing of groups as vital to conflict resolution. Intermarriage is perfect in a certain sense. But this is a nightmare for religious people, who really do see a constant threat to the continuation of their culture all around them. Their one hope for perpetuation is the commitment of their children to the group. This fear and concern is as true of the Israeli religious community as it is of any indigenous, minority cultural group around the world whose existence is threatened, especially when the dominant group is pressuring them to integrate and thus lose their identity. How can we deal with this?

In secular forms of conflict resolution currently in vogue, it would be scandalous to engage in peace efforts with teenagers separated by sex. But this would be a necessary condition for *haredi* groups. Would it be seen by the Left in Israel as giving into sexism? Some will see it this way, but others may see that it is only sexist if the efforts of the boys' and girls' groups are valued differently. Some may discover that we can honor the differences of these communities and find ways to share overarching goals.

It must be emphasized in this regard that one basic error of universal or social scientific methods of peacemaking is the lack of recognition by progressive, secular peacemakers that they are propagating a certain underlying moral and social vision. Their goal often, especially in Israel, is to make a society of people who have secular, liberal values: tolerance, human rights, integration of all peoples, and the slow disappearance of religious, cultural, and ethnic divisions. Unlike their adversaries, however, they have no interest in promoting some moral code between the sexes. In fact, they would be horrified at this invasion into personal morality. But their own methods and programs clearly do express many moral values, just not the traditional ones associated with religious communities. In other words, both groups champion a set of moral values that underlie their styles of interaction and even styles of peacemaking.

The problem is that making peace only from the cultural position of the Left will mean in practice that conflict resolvers could only make peace among themselves or with those who hold their values. We must constantly be alert to how to engage in peacemaking with people who do not share all the same values. In the case of the religious/secular conflict, it may be that sexual mixing or, at the least, mixing of religious and nonreligious teenagers is a concern for many modern Orthodox people, but it is a central concern for the *haredi* community. Does it mean that there is no possibility of conflict resolution or peacemaking in its widest sense, or are we limited only by our imaginations? This remains to be discovered and will depend on the ingenuity and courage of the respective communities.

I do not believe it is impossible in principle. What we are speaking of here are the boundaries and borders of sectarian groups, which often define those borders by values that they hold dear. Is the only solution integration and the dissolution of boundaries? I have spoken and written elsewhere on religious sectarianism, and I have argued that it is never boundaries that create conflict but the *interpretation* of those boundaries, how they are negotiated, and in what ways they may be temporarily crossed. Furthermore, much conflict arises globally because of the *lack* of clear boundaries, which give one a clear and confident sense of identity.[29]

The most important goal of conflict resolution and peacemaking should be the humanization of the Other (or in Jewish religious terms, the perception of God's image in every Other), the treatment of the Other with absolute dignity, even love. It should not be the complete immersion of all parties into one, a position into which liberal visions, as well as fundamentalist visions, sometimes unconsciously slip. This merging has often been accomplished by extreme tyranny in history and does not have a good track record in the human community. It always has been and remains the dark side of universal love or global aspirations generally.

Sectarianism and separation breed all the problems that bring us to the subject of violent conflict. But it is in the negotiation of this inescapable human dilemma of integration, interaction, and boundaries that answers are to be found, not in the suppression of the problem by the merging of groups by force, by manipulation, or by cultural domination, Left or Right, religious or secular.

Another source of religious/secular conflict in Israel is the attitude toward the concept and practice of pluralism. In general, there always has been criticism of the concept of pluralism, in the sense that what it really means is ethical relativism and that, basically, "anything is permissible as long as you do not hurt the next guy." This is the caricature of the concept in many religious circles. In fact, I am told that it has become a kind of dirty word in the American Orthodox world, associated with heretics.

I do not want to go into a linguistic and philosophical analysis of pluralism now. But suffice it to say that the entire question is grossly oversimplified. Those who claim to be pluralists in Israel have more rigid values than they realize, and those who claim not to be are more pluralistic in their orientation than they admit.

Leaving this discussion aside, there is a legitimate critique underway today that says, essentially, that we cannot survive as a culture on such a thin layer of agreement as the value of pluralism. Much of what we assumed about our modern patterns of democratic coexistence has been dependent upon age-old moral values that were not clearly articulated. But now this consensus of civil values, such as honesty and fairness, is breaking down. So the argument goes.

These are difficult matters. I simply raise them because I want to suggest that, as far as I have seen in my experience of conflict resolution training, there really is a substratum of values, beyond pluralism, that seems to be indispensable in order to create a peaceful society. No matter how much understanding two groups have of each other, no matter how much they have humanized the Other and avoided demonization, there must be overarching values that bind them together, and they must actively inculcate these values and reinforce them on a regular basis. I have never engaged in a training in which the group, no matter how diverse and divided, did not consciously or unconsciously come to assume a set of values that were critical to their compromises and their conflict resolution practices. This means that, in the secular/religious divide in Israel, there is going to have to be a search for at least some common values and an attempt to mediate or articulate them in such a way that they are not only acceptable to all communities but embraced by them enthusiastically. This entails the study of each others' values and then the search for overarching consensus. The operative question must always be: What can we agree upon beyond the clear and unmistakable distinctions? Here Israelis are going to have to stretch themselves culturally. They are going to have to put aside temporarily a typical Israeli sport, which is the enjoyment of making radical distinctions,[30] showing what is utterly contradictory between their position and someone else's, and, instead, search for a higher consensus.

As I analyze more cultural conflicts, I am starting to realize that each culture has unique challenges. In Ireland, I notice a drive to fatalism, a need to see and feel the utterly tragic, which prevents even significant peace advocates from seeing a way out of the Troubles. In Jewish society, I believe that there is exultation in the intellectual distinction of two phenomena (*hiluk*), the drive to dichotomize and therefore to fight, especially if one can express this in a way that makes oneself look intelligent and the other person or group foolish. Too many intellectual Jews are obsessed with improved intelligence, probably because it is portable and just about all the community had in the way of dignity in many places and times. Making constant distinctions also seems to be a fabulous habit of the heart that always reconfirms the biggest distinction of all, the one between the Jewish people and an intolerant dominant culture that ridiculed, threatened, and constantly prodded them to merge with the clear victors of history. This may not be dissimilar to other minorities' behaviors in the face of external pressure, and I have seen similar patterns in the styles of interaction between black and white youths in America. I have also noticed that in most places of deep conflict, intellectuals, of which there are many in Israeli society, spend a spectacular amount of time overanalyzing, because it seems to be the only thing that they see themselves empowered to do or able temperamentally to do.

This drive to demonstrate the absolute contradiction of two positions and the thirst for mental competition in the haggling over positions needs to be tempered and even overcome when it comes to communal relations in Israel today. There is much more that many citizens can do—especially the intellectual elite—than endlessly debate the "true" nature of the problem, if they have the emotional courage to rise to the occasion. Their writing skills, creativity, and ability to master complexity are critical to any practical visions of the future.

Nevertheless, Israel is a deeply Jewish society, and intellectual study can have its place in peacemaking. This has been demonstrated recently by increased Islamic/Jewish/Christian, as well as secular/religious, encounters through the medium of shared times of study. Study is a natural form of interpersonal communication in Jewish culture, with ancient roots. It is no surprise to me, for example, that the first forms of quiet but serious communication in Jerusalem between Orthodox Jews and Orthodox Muslims is not coming in the form of dialogue or interfaith prayers but in the study of sacred texts as a basis of communication and mutual respect. This activity is intellectual, but it has deep symbolic and ritual significance as well.

In light of this, I recommend an unprecedented level of cooperative, reflective study of Jewish culture—ancient, medieval, and modern; written and oral; Sephardi and Ashkenazi—with the purpose of analyzing and critiquing the foundations of ethics and civil society in Jewish tradition. This should be done separately by the secular community, by the religious communities, and by independent scholars. It can also be done together, but it would have to be done in a way that would create constructive conflict not destructive injury to the participants, such as the spectacular model being provided by the Ellul program in Jerusalem. Out of this period of study, conducted on elite as well as popular levels, there should emerge discussions on what the *minimum* set of values is that could be held in common. It is vital that this also form the basis of improved civil relations with non-Jews in Israel and with Israel's international neighbors, in order to prevent an easy projection of all problems onto a demonized Other.

This process will stir serious controversy, and accusations of heresy may fly in the religious world. But it also may create a much larger consensus for what the future of Israel could look like. The consensus that it could create may startle those on both sides, who thought that nothing could ever be agreed to, except old-fashioned political status quos and cynical religious/secular political alliances born of no real trust. This surprise, in and of itself, could generate important psychological change, which could make a united future for Israel a greater possibility and civil war less of a possibility.

The purpose of the study will be to mine the resources for civil values, values that generate the kind of human relationships that are based on respect, trust, and even care. It will also be an opportunity to discover numerous sources on peacemaking and conflict resolution in Jewish tradition, both in its narrative and its legal expressions. The challenges to coexistence and pluralism in Jewish tradition are self-evident. What is less evident are the prosocial possibilities because so few have seriously explored them hermeneutically for the unprecedented circumstances of Israeli society.

It must be kept in mind that in the history of very old religions, such as Judaism, it is interpretation, vision, and the attention of great thinkers and interpreters that have shaped the values of each generation, not rigidly defined texts. There is a great deal of room here for creative visions of even *haredi* Judaism in the future, *if* many of the processes that I have mentioned generate greater trust, respect, and forgiveness between secular and religious Jews.[31] The interpersonal and intercommunal healing that I have outlined is the essential prerequisite that could turn the more intellectual enterprise of the search for common values into a realistic undertaking, rather than an exercise in futility.

The Jewish values that I am speaking of are in some ways self-evidently parallel to secular ideals, but in other ways they will provide a unique contribution to general peacemaking and future conceptions of coexistence. For example, Western society has never understood the conflict-generating character of arrogance and the lack of humility, as is plainly evident in many of its Third World relations in the last fifty years. Humility, by contrast, is a powerful method of peacemaking in Judaism. It is a key prosocial device of Jewish ethics, which makes good human relationships possible. But it has never been analyzed in a contemporary setting as a method of peacemaking or as a factor in successful conflict resolution.[32] A Jewish approach to this work would necessarily include this moral value, among many others, in the way that enemies begin to treat each other.

Eventually, this can lead to a coalescence of shared values across many cultures in the Middle East, each of which has a contribution to make in the construction of civil societies. Honor and shame, for example, are important to Jewish religious methods of moral interaction, as I mentioned earlier, but they are also at the heart of Muslim and Arab religious and cultural priorities.[33] Thus, while to some what I am suggesting sounds too particularist or provincial, it can actually form the basis of some rather deep means of trust building across cultural divides.

A classic ancient Jewish method of peacemaking is coming to the aid of someone who is suffering, as mentioned earlier. This is a biblical-peacemaking device (Exod. 23:5), which we analyzed in chapter 4. It could provide an interesting and perhaps unique model for how to utilize the normal problems of human existence as a way to create peace.

This method of conflict resolution is deceptively simplistic. Furthermore, it is rarely if ever to be found in secular literature. The focus of secular peacemaking is mostly on dialogue, and I have detailed my reservations about this as an exclusive tool. Here we have the opportunity to explore and experiment with something that is at once simple, easy to implement, and model; that is deeply indigenous to Jewish culture; and that is also a challenging new approach to general conflict resolution, even from a secular perspective. This is exactly what those of us in conflict resolution research are hoping to discover in indigenous cultures around the world.

This method is deeply compelling on a psychological level for Jews. It explains, in a much more positive way, the strange behavior that I mentioned earlier of the Hesed shel Emet group and the police. The one thing that is missing in some Israeli reactions currently is a conscious commitment to take this deeply ingrained cultural drive to join with others in aiding victims or those who are suffering and make it into a conscious, self-aware, process of reconciliation, the beginning of new relationships involving apologies, forgiveness, and numerous other moral/ emotional commitments. These last elements of apology and forgiveness have deep roots both in psychoanalytic approaches to conflict resolution and simultaneously in two thousand years of Jewish commitment to prosocial processes of interpersonal change in behaviors and attitudes.[35]

There needs to be a conscious attempt to replicate these accidental moments of secular/religious peace and make them into a *national* effort at reconciliation. This needs to be initiated by many subgroups, such as women's groups, children's groups, and men's groups. It could unite people across religious lines to work together for those who are suffering, for the poor, the sick, the disabled, the mentally ill, the imprisoned, even endangered animals and environments (in line with the spirit of compassion for animals of the biblical law just cited, among others). The one requirement is that all these efforts be constructed and crafted in ways that are appealing to both the secular community and the religious community.

There is another method that has ancient Jewish roots and that is also underutilized by secular conflict resolution. Referred to in diplomatic circles as shuttle diplomacy, it has deep talmudic roots. Several versions of a single story are told about Aaron, the high priest, brother of Moses, in which he is described as the paradigmatic peacemaker.[36] Aaron was mourned for so long by the Jewish people in the Sinai desert because he used to make peace between everyone, even husband and wife. Thus they named all their children after him, because they never would have found or restored loving relationships that led to children without Aaron's intervention.[37]

Aaron's method in this rabbinic narrative is my greatest concern. He did not sit people around a table and conduct a dialogue or negotiation. He went to one party to a conflict, listened to all of his pain, told him soothing things, waited until the pain left his heart, and then went to the other one and did exactly the same thing with her. The elements here are: shuttling, which honors both sides by entering into their own spaces and honoring the boundaries of their world; engaged listening; emotional comfort; lengthy engagement with the parties, thus building trust over time; and prodding efforts to create a new relationship between the alienated parties. The end result of this process, according to the rabbinic narrative, is that the two people would meet and embrace each other, both concluding that they had misjudged the other.[38] The results of conflict resolution would not just be a problem solved, or a compromise found, but the kind of reconciliation that leads to physical embrace.

Now, I am not suggesting that anything in the Talmud should be acceptable automatically to all Israelis as a way of behaving. It is a far too literal reading of the Talmud, in any case, to believe that one has to do exactly what Aaron did in order to be a pursuer of peace (*rodef shalom*). But working with these traditions interpretively among a broad spectrum of Israelis would create an extraordinary bridge of great cultural depth. It could both stimulate the creation of indigenous conflict resolution methods and simultaneously offer a healing connection between Jews that until now has only been provided pathologically in the shadow of exploding bombs.

Finally, it is beyond the scope of this chapter to elaborate on how the same methods that I have outlined here of building a broad-based cultural form of reconciliation among Jews in Israel can and must be extended to building serious intercultural bridges among Jewish Israelis, Arab Israelis, and Palestinians. Suffice it to say that it is eminently doable if a sufficient number of cultural leaders on all sides become committed to this process and if the political leaderships allow it to happen.

I want to emphasize, in conclusion, that nothing that I have said precludes the possibility, as well as the absolute necessity, of tough negotiations between the religious and secular communities that must ultimately, ineluctably, be subject to rational compromise. But no rational process can proceed, not deeply, unless the human communities involved, with all of their complex history in mind, begin to develop new relationships based on true knowledge of the Other, care for the Other's pain, remorse over the past, commitment to a joint future, and the discovery of some higher values that can be held in common. If rational negotiation over power is the soil in which the plant of democratic society is rooted, then decent human relations are the water that gives life to that plant. There is no escaping it. Building a sustainable Israeli society at peace will involve slowly freeing Israel from the conflicts of the past, as well as freeing it from the pathological need to live in conflict.

Now we move on to another community, which is also small in number and very significant in influence, at least in peacemaking. The Mennonite community, like the Jewish community, has a strong memory of suffering that is part of its cultural identity. But the circumstances of history have allowed the Mennonites to negotiate that trauma in a very different way.

SEVEN

Conflict Resolution as a Religious Experience

Contemporary Mennonite Peacemaking

My experience with the Mennonite community began a number of years ago, when I participated in a conflict resolution training with John Paul Lederach at Eastern Mennonite University in Harrisonburg, Virginia. Since then I have become quite involved in this community, and I consistently teach a seminar on religion and conflict resolution at the Conflict Transformation Program of EMU. I have developed close personal friendships with Mennonite peacemakers, been privileged to engage in training a number of Mennonites in religion and conflict resolution, and I have learned much from them. I also participated in a major research project about Mennonite peacemaking; this chapter is an expansion on my research for that project.[1]

These experiences have been formative in my own analysis of religion and peacemaking, and I learned much of what I know about authentic peacemaking from my Mennonite teachers, colleagues, and students. I was challenged to learn how to translate peacemaking to and from many cultural contexts—including theirs and mine—by the vast variety of Christian cultures that I encountered among my students at EMU; there have also been other religions occasionally represented in the student body of the summer program. The Mennonite cultural context was particularly challenging—and healing—for me. In this fairly conservative Christian context, I have been challenged to confront and deal with the strange place of the Jew in Christian consciousness and culture. This is particularly complicated in this case in terms of the overidentification (caused by many Jews themselves, by the way) of the state of Israel with Jews and Judaism. This has led to admiration on the part of some conservative Christians, who tend to oppose the Arab and Muslim world, and hostility on the part of others, who side strongly with the Palestinians in their struggle against Israel and, therefore, suspect the role of Judaism in this struggle. This is due, in part, to the fact that many Christians that I have taught in these circles have little working knowledge of

Jewish tradition or contact with identified Jews. Furthermore, many have not fully confronted the role of the Jew in Christian mythology and its effect on their attitudes toward Israel, the Arab/Israeli conflict, and Judaism in general.

There are some rather striking characteristics of Mennonite peacemakers that clearly resonated with my own cultural background. Strong identification with past and present sufferers is a key element of religious experience and an important foundation of one's ethical posture. There is an endearing, if frustrating, separatism or isolationism, as in my Orthodox upbringing, that combines in a paradoxical way with a deep-seated commitment to human relationship as the single most redemptive characteristic of religious consciousness, as well as peacemaking. I found that we shared an approach to peacemaking that emanates from one's instinctive identification with sufferers. As contemporary fellow peacemakers, we were all aware that we had imbibed old patterns of internalization of others' suffering, despite our awareness of the maudlin and actually damaging elements of religious experience that overidentifies with suffering and turns it into group narcissism. Furthermore, Mennonites, like Jews, are a misunderstood minority who have had a tendency to internalize the disapproval and even hatred that they have received over the centuries. This has given them a problematic but—to me—deeply refreshing level of self-criticism and self-doubt that one does not often find in other expressions of Christian culture or in policymaking circles in Washington. They have also been historically a "minority in the middle,"[2] who were used by dominant groups and benefited from this but were abused for it as well. In general they were isolated from their neighbors in ways that made them suspect and that made them not understand their neighbors' needs well either.[3]

The Mennonite community had the advantage, in contrast to other abused minorities, of recovery from their deep wounds and their own experience of mass murder as they retreated into rural isolation and agricultural independence. Eventually, by virtue of their skill and steadfastness, they achieved moderate to extensive levels of wealth and security, especially as the value of good land has vastly increased in recent years. Those minorities who could not own land or did not have their agricultural skills were not so fortunate in Europe or in the United States for that matter. The Jewish community of Europe, by contrast to the Mennonites, stayed in the only place they were allowed, the marketplace, with all its uncertainty, incivility, and opportunity for great wealth—and also great hatred.

I have also learned that, beneath the genteel surface of Mennonite life and their idealized image as pacifist "lambs of God," there is a real sense of disquiet and even shame about certain Mennonite behavior patterns, which I will not discuss here. There is also a degree of ethnic chauvinism, in terms of their European roots, expressed by some. I was always impressed with the deep commitment to pacifism of my Mennonite colleagues but soon discovered that this stance does not extend for some other Mennonites to the political realm, to voting, for example, for politicians who are propeacemaking or at least less oriented to war. On the contrary, the priority is given by many to economic and other typical Christian conservative priorities. Furthermore, while the pacifism of American Mennonites is well known, there is a darker side to Mennonite history in Germany, including ethnic devotion to Germany, astonishingly even during Hitler's time. It appears that many Mennonites of German ethnic origin were pacifists during World War II in the United States, while a significant number of their Mennonite cousins in Europe fought in armies that were implicated in the worst genocides that the world had seen up until then, though there is no available analysis, as far as I know, about how those Mennonites behaved as part of the German army.

There may have been many authentic Mennonite pacifists in 1930s America, but the sad truth is that when the world was increasingly opposing the barbarism of the Nazi regime, too many in the German community of America were, at best, arguing for isolation and nonintervention and, at worst, were actively supporting the Nazi regime. It must be said also that even Mennonites, with their history of commitment to pacifism, have not escaped the taint of racism and Christian anti-Semitism among a significant number of their members, at least during those terrible years of fascism.[4]

This makes the efforts of the peacemakers among them to develop a conflict resolution method and philosophy and to extend this practice globally that much more admirable and even heroic. They provide a model for me of how an isolated, conservative religious tradition can evolve a peacemaking philosophy and practice that is not only adequate but is a powerful paradigm for the world. This requires great courage and vision and a capacity to stand up to one's own community's limitations. The Mennonites are, on the whole, rather reticent about their community's worst failings and have not gone out of their way to highlight them. On the contrary, it has taken me several years to discover these things. But this is their way. With some exceptions, they do not attack their own with an outraged sense of injustice, at least not in public. Rather they tend to provide alternative visions that make it clear what it is they stand for and what they oppose. This too was refreshing, for they avoid the opposite extreme, described in the previous chapter, of a damaged group whose members relish the opportunity to attack each other in highly injurious and destructive ways, which are conflict generating, to put it mildly.

Before beginning my examination of their peacemaking methods, I want to emphasize that I have deliberately, in the preceding paragraphs, pointed out Mennonite flaws in order to demonstrate the continuing theme of this book, namely, that all groups of all religions are capable of moving in directions of extraordinary courage in terms of peacemaking but also are capable of shocking failure. It does not seem to matter what the theological starting point of a group may be, no matter how much we may feel the evidence or our impressions compel us to place a group into a particular box. The possibilities are open, and often they exhibit themselves at the same time historically or within just a few decades. This represents the dynamic potential, for good or for ill, in all religious groups in terms of their role in human conflict and civil society.

In order to understand the religious foundations and unique character of Mennonite peacemaking, it is necessary to define some terms and then to explore briefly the origins of the community and how this affects the nature of their peace work. In the context of the peacemakers with whom I have been in relationship, the terms "conflict transformation" or "peacebuilding" are critical. These are difficult to define briefly, and in a certain way, their definition is the subject of this chapter. For purposes of this chapter, I use these terms to describe a Mennonite commitment to the creation of deep relationships over time that, with proper care, lead both oneself and those with whom one is engaged in the direction of a profound transformation of conflictual and unjust human relationships. In general, when I refer to "Mennonite peacemaking," I assume the conflict transformation model.

When I refer to "old order Mennonites," I mean, roughly, those groups that have emphasized in the modern period a continuation of the separatist tradition. By "modern Mennonites," I mean primarily those Mennonites who demonstrate strong affinity with engagement in the world, either through mission work or peace and justice work.

Separatism and the Evolution of Peacemaking

The foundations of the Anabaptist tradition, to which the Mennonite communities belong, are most clearly seen in the Schleitheim statement of Brotherly Union of 1527.[5] There are two key components of that statement that explain a great deal about the character of the Mennonite community and its peace work. Ironically, in terms of peace and conflict resolution, perhaps the most important feature of the statement is the commitment to separatism. The second characteristic is the commitment to meekness, in emulation of the lamb of God, namely, Jesus.

The separatist imperative is quite familiar to students of religion. The world, in this formulation, is divided into the realm of light and the realm of darkness, those who are outside the "perfection of Christ" and those who are part of the fellowship. Menno Simons, after whom Mennonites are named, said in one sermon that they are the "Lord's people, separated from the world, and hated unto death." There are those who are "called out of this world unto God," and they must not mix with the abominations of the world. This dualist worldview has deep roots in the origins of Christianity and rabbinic Judaism and the respective mysticisms of the two faiths.[6] It is the resonance with these old, theological roots that makes separatist religious communities so intriguing. They are also an important part of the history of European utopian communities.[7]

The embrace of one's hatred by Others as an essential part of God's plan is an intriguing—and disturbing—reaction that is typical of many ideological groups that begin by being hated by Others. As we have seen before, this is a typical pattern of establishing the boundaries of identity, which, at its root, sets the stage for conflict. In the Mennonite case, this is tempered by the pacifist tradition, to the degree to which the pacifist tradition is adhered. But this ideological position of being necessarily hated can be found in many religious contexts, such as in the old roots of Shi'a Islam and talmudic Judaism and in nonreligious constructs as well, such as communism, where the capitalist must repress and try to destroy the proletariat that dares challenge the ownership of the means of production.

Being hated normally generates deep injury and corresponding anger in most recipients in what I call a "conflict dance" of action/reaction. But for religious theology, there is a deeper issue at work and a deeper need being fulfilled by the theology. The obvious question is: If I am living by God's word, or if I am a good person, then why do people hate me? Furthermore: Why is a good God allowing this to happen? This is the basic theodicy question, a simple but devastating question that we often pose to ourselves when injured. Religious mythology and drama solve this by making it part of God's dramatic plan of redemption. This is especially true for biblical religions.

What effect does this answer have on those who believe in it? Does it make them more or less violent, more or less angry, more or less self-hating? This is an impossible question to answer uniformly but an important one to always keep in the back of one's mind as an analyst. On the one hand, it gives people some mythic way of coping with injury without having to treat enemies in a violent fashion. On the other hand, it not only does not remove the conflict with the enemy, it actually institutionalizes it. It seems to make people passive more than peaceful, at least for the time being.

Many modern Mennonites who do peace work globally, the main subject of this study, would be, as far as I have observed, rather uncomfortable with this separatist strain in its premodern sense or as it may be practiced even today by the Amish, old order Mennonites, or perhaps even conservative conference members of their church. The degree of separation from this world still appears to be a key defining difference along the broad spectrum of Mennonite communities. Furthermore, they would hardly be comfortable with a world in which they see themselves defined in some way by those who hate them. They would be uncomfortable with embracing a destiny of hatred because they are lambs of God. On the other hand, we will have occasion in the latter part of the chapter to discuss where and when Mennonite peacemakers, in overidentifying with who they consider the victims to be, may have a tendency to demonize one side, thereby cutting off the opportunity for peacemaking and even inviting abuse from the demonized Other as a fulfillment of the destiny of the lamb of God. Religious mythology is deeply compelling, potentially a great ally of peacemaking, but also dangerous sometimes in its reification of conflict into cosmic scenarios of suffering and redemption.

To return to the separatist trend in Mennonite life, we should note the interesting attitude toward missionizing. The Amish and the old order Mennonites rejected until recently active proselytizing, something central to other forms of Christianity. They will aid the poor or someone in distress, no matter who they may be, after the model of Jesus. But they have not tended to proselytize. This is in contrast with the Mennonites of this century, many of whom have been engaged in proselytizing, and this is a complicating factor in evaluating the issue of conflict prevention and conflict resolution, as we shall see later. On the other hand, these old order Mennonites see themselves as on a mission, just like other Christians (and other biblically based religions' adherents), except that they fulfill their mission by living a separated existence, bearing witness to the world in their separateness. How exactly this works out theologically is beyond this essay, but it is an important topic.

Persecution and Pacifism

I would like to argue that the old order Mennonite and Amish rejection of proselytizing is not just based on the separatist strain in Mennonite spirituality but also on a combination of the deeply rooted pacifist strain of Mennonite Christianity together with the historical Mennonite experience of persecution. One of the most central Mennonite teachings is that Jesus as a pacifist is deeply concerned to never interact with Others in an aggressive fashion, even with his enemies. This has its roots in Romans 12:14–21, "Bless them that persecute you . . . recompense no man evil for evil . . . avenge not yourselves . . . if thine enemy is hungry, feed him . . . be not overcome of evil, but overcome evil with good."[8] This is the essence of Christian pacifism, with roots going back as far as the Hebrew Bible.[9]

Proselytizing and encouraging others to convert has a checkered history in the annals of religious traditions, especially the biblical ones. Sometimes it has been benign, and at other times it has been deadly. But all efforts to convert Others involve a degree of assertiveness that has easily spilled over into aggression whenever the potential converts actually want to adhere to their own faith, which is quite often.

There is also a deep strain in the old order Mennonite religion of identification with the persecuted, the defenseless (*wehrlos*).[10] This too goes back very far into the biblical texts that Mennonites have studied so carefully over the centuries: "What occurs has happened before, and what will occur has already occurred, and God seeks those who are pursued" (Eccles. 3:15).[11]

Mennonites remember their persecution quite well, and it is here that the several aforementioned strains come together to illustrate my thesis. It must be kept in mind that the original impulse of Mennonite separatism was in the context of a hostile, even murderous *Christian* environment, which persecuted Anabaptists for their commitment to several distinctive practices, which the latter believed to be at the heart of Christianity, including adult baptism, an emphasis on direct study of the New Testament by laypeople, an unswerving commitment to the life of Jesus as a model, separation of church and government, and pacifism.

The *Martyrs Mirror*, a key text that documents the bloody torture and execution of thousands of Mennonites at the hands of fellow Christians, was one of the most important texts on the Mennonite bookshelf for centuries. Their murder was no doubt preceded by attempts by other Christians to cajole them back to the "true faith" and away from their heresy. In other words, they were missionized by fellow Christians in order to save their souls and bring them back to Christ. The result finally was massive persecution upon their refusal to come back.

This kind of persecution is, tragically, an easy leap for an evangelical belief system that combines with a dualist view of the world, seeing the world in terms of those who are in the fellowship of God and those who are not. Mennonite belief is based on this dualist view and could have turned aggressive. It is easy to go from mildly aggressive efforts to missionize those who are not part of the saved realm, to the step of demonization of the outgroup that refuses to repent or convert. The outgroup becomes the other half of the dualistic world, and its elimination becomes a necessity in order for good to triumph over evil. This is precisely why, I argue, Mennonites were determined to prevent the dualist view from devolving into an aggressive or violent posture vis-à-vis the world of unbelievers.   *against / standing against*

I would argue that the separatism of original Mennonitism, combined with the commitment to separation of church and state (which eliminates coercive power from the religious domain) and with the reluctance to proselytize by at least a significant group of Mennonites, all stem from the deep roots of their emulation of Jesus' pacifism and the painful memories of their own experience of religious violence.[12] In other words, in the wake of their own persecution, they maintained strictly the dualist worldview, the division of the people of God from the world's abominations. But they also ensured that this dualism would not, and could not, result in an aggressive posture vis-à-vis others, not even through proselytizing. They understood Christian history and understood that the idea of a separate realm of those who follow Jesus' model was vital for their faith, but they were determined to eliminate its violent potential. This they did through pacifism and their reluctance to proselytize. Old order Mennonite religion, in my opinion, seems to question whether active efforts to convert can truly coexist with pacifism in its deepest sense. To this day, it seems a commonplace assumption even among modern Mennonite peacemakers that Constantine's conversion to Christianity and the unification of the Roman Empire with Christianity was a tragedy in terms of Christianity's religious integrity, precisely because the aggressive and imperial nature of Rome infected religious institutional life.

The Modern Mennonite Dilemma and Conflict Transformation

Many Mennonite institutions in the modern period, by contrast, seem deeply committed to actively seeking converts to Christianity and the Mennonite faith. American evangelism has had a deep impact on the Mennonite community, and many Mennonite activists, especially those who work internationally, have either done missionary work themselves or are children of missionaries. However, it must be emphasized that "mission" is a difficult term to define in the Christian world, especially today, because there is such a varied interpretation of what it means. Furthermore, there are no data available on how many of the peace activists have been involved in mission work nor what kind of mission work they may have done.

In the Mennonite circles that I have studied, it appears that a number of them who engage in peace work are uncomfortable, at the very least, with the most aggressive interpretation of mission, namely, the active process of converting as many people to Mennonitism or Christianity as possible. Some are uncomfortable with proselytizing altogether, while others are committed to mission as a religious calling but are looking to define peace work as mission. This would make sense as a development of the Mennonite focus on the life of Jesus. They would see Jesus' principal endeavors as involving direct service, aid to and healing those in need, and the teaching of nonresistance,[13] not the construction of an empire of followers. The latter they might see as perhaps a byproduct of his work, not its focus. This does not mean that they would be displeased by more Christians in the world. It remains unclear, and it appears to be a sensitive issue.

"Mission" meant something quite significant to old order Mennonites. It meant standing for a certain faith and a certain way of behaving in the world, as Jesus did. It seems to me that the modern Mennonite peacemakers, while far more actively engaged in the world than old order Mennonites, seem to share with them a more nuanced understanding of mission than the way this is aggressively expressed by some.

In the course of my discussions with Mennonite peacemakers and in the course of trainings, it became clear that many Mennonites who are peace activists seem reluctant to proselytize due to the arrogance associated with that posture. I have been struck by how rarely they have advocated, expressed pride in, or pressured me in any way to see the beauty of Christianity or Mennonite belief. They rarely used words to describe what they loved about their faith, at least in public. They seemed to see the term "Christian" as referring to someone who lives like Jesus did, not someone who declares himself regularly to be a believer. Christian is a deeply moral and spiritual term, and it borders on arrogance to refer to oneself, for example, as a fully "successful" Christian, in the sense of being "born again." Rather, being called "born again" is an honor bestowed by others *if* one earns that title by the way one lives in relationship to others. They tell the story of a man who is asked by someone, "Are you born again?" to which he replies, "Here is a list of people—my wife, my banker, my grocer, all my associates. Ask them if I am born again."

Modern Mennonites who engage in peacemaking and conflict resolution and who are deeply committed to tolerance and pluralism are caught in a bind that is rarely articulated, although I would argue that it is right beneath the surface. Mission, as they understand it, has propelled them into the world again. They see conflict resolution, which by definition is a rather invasive process of entering into someone else's culture and problems, as a necessary means to follow Jesus' role model as peacemaker and as justice seeker for those who are injured. They also need to fulfill what they see as important Christian precepts or tenets of faith, namely mission and witness. For their ancestors and present-day cousins, witnessing could be seen as a religious task done by example of one's personal and communal life, not by engaging the realm of sin.[14]

Mennonite peacemakers are moving away from this separatist take on mission and witness. On the other hand, every aspect of Mennonite life and formation of character reinforces values, personality traits, and modes of engagement that express humility, a studied effort to emulate Jesus, and a level of benign engagement with Others that emphasizes listening, care, and gentle patterns of interaction. In other words, one can trace the roots of their peacemaking methods, especially the elicitive method articulated by John Paul Lederach and his colleagues, to the commitment to adhere to Mennonite values even as these peacemakers now enter, cautiously, the unredeemed world that so many of their ancestors rejected. Furthermore, Lederach's concept of conflict transformation[15] and Kraybill's focus on social justice,[16] emerge out of an attempt to address the evil of the worldly realm that Menno Simons rejected. It is a determination to bring into the harsh realities of a violent world the elements of ideal community, which for them are found in the example of Jesus, namely, a community dedicated to humility, compassion for and service to those who suffer, justice for the persecuted, and the act of standing with the defenseless (*wehrlos*).

Conflict resolution, a deeply activist and engaged method of affecting human relations, is being used by modern Mennonites but is also being transformed by them. It has transformed them into actively engaged members of the world community, but they, in turn, have transformed conflict resolution and the Christian concept of mission. The hermeneutic circle of receptivity and two-way transformation is clear here.[17] Conflict resolution as a method of engagement in the world has given Mennonite peacemakers a vehicle of both maintaining the deepest pacifist values of their community and combining it with a reworked concept of mission.

The idea of mission pushes Mennonites into the field, and so does a commitment to actively engage issues of justice and injustice in such a way that they can never again be accused of quietism and selfishness in the face of evil, as they were accused by some in World War II. On the other hand, the commitment to listening, patience, eliciting from Others their needs and strategies for change, the self-doubt and self-criticism that permeate their work, all reflect the character of deeply committed pacifists who know how dangerous it is to presume to change someone else's life, no matter how much that person is crying out for help. They seem to know intuitively, based on their religious pacifist training and culturally embedded historical memory, how slippery a slope this engagement is and how dangerous is the power that one feels in changing other lives, especially when those Others are in a vulnerable position economically and emotionally. They express the intuition that aggression of the subtlest forms is always a possibility for the social change activist who enters into wartorn, impoverished situations. Rarely have I seen such close attention and self-scrutiny among international development activists and peacemakers to the dilemma of intervention and the subtleties of aggression by interveners who may have the best of intentions.

Perhaps it is the very ambiguity of modern Mennonite entry into mission, their memory of brutalizing efforts to invade their lives by Others centuries before, and the ever-present model of old order Mennonites preserving a strict notion of noninterference in the world that gives the modern Mennonites the creative drive to forge a radically new way of engaging the troubled part of the world, the world of sin and violence, while also remaining deeply cognizant of the dangers of engagement.[18] They seek a way of intervention that is radically nonviolent. In such a world, they know that always "sin coucheth at the door,"[19] and that a group can easily become part of the very illness of violence that it seeks to heal.

There is also a subtle awareness, out of respect for their roots perhaps, that quietism has an undeserved negative reputation, that quietism, when taken to extremes, perhaps, is passivity and even selfishness or indifference to evil. But quietism *in small doses* is a key to a nonaggressive approach to the world; one can learn as much from not doing and not speaking and not invading the world as one can by intervention and failure.[20] This nonaggressive religious strain is present in many religious cultures that value not doing, or the refraining from doing in order to achieve high ethical ends, as much as or even more than positive ritual or proactive interaction with the world.[21] This presents a sharply contrasting model to Western patterns of intervention in the world's problems.

This awareness has generated a creative tension that, in turn, has created an unusual spiritual philosophy of intervention that is deliberately benign in its execution and mode of interaction with Others. It propels the adherents into conflict resolution and social transformation and then restrains them from the natural human urge—and urge of institutions, both religious and secular—to refashion the world, violently if necessary, in one's own image. This tension requires constant self-scrutiny and a spiritual community that restrains itself and its members from slipping into aggression.

The Stranger, Peacemaking, and the Existential Awareness of Otherness

The other element in this creative tension turns once again to the separatist roots of the community. A separatist community is deeply aware of the experience of Otherness and of being outsiders. The history of persecution as outsiders leads, I believe, to a deep respect for Otherness, for the stranger. This also has deep biblical roots in love of the stranger (*ger*) as one of the highest forms of love described by the Hebrew Bible,[22] and this is also one of the chief preoccupations of Jesus' life as recounted in the New Testament.

The stranger in biblical tradition is never to be oppressed, "for you know the feelings of the stranger, having been strangers in the land of Egypt" (Exod. 23:9). This awareness of Otherness is also an awareness of the multiplicity of identities around us. It is typical of conflict-generating thinking to formulate one's identity in opposition to another's identity, to form oneself as part of an ingroup versus the outgroup.[23] The natural response to this is to assume that the best form of identity is universal identity, namely, a self-conscious identification with all humankind or some consciousness that is akin to this.

The irony is that Derrida, among others, has alerted us to the fact that there is no easy escape from the process of creating identity in opposition to the Other, and what appears to be universal or inclusive of the universal is not at all and may, in fact, consciously or unconsciously, be a vehicle of oppression of the identity of the Other.[24] This is one reason why Emmanuel Levinas's ethics is predicated not on universal codes but on the phenomenology of the facial encounter between one human being and another. It is the encounter with the image of the Other, the awareness of Otherness, that generates the ethical responses of care, compassion, pity.[25]

It is deeply important in this regard that Gandhi did not argue that we are all human beings and, therefore, let us care for one another. He said in so many words, and through his embrace of religious and cultural ideas from around the world, that his identity is multiple in nature, that he is a Hindu, but also a Muslim, and also a Christian.[26] I have argued earlier that this awareness of multiple identities is a key characteristic of successful peacemakers, particularly in the sphere of interreligious conflict. It is clearly interwoven in its psychological foundation with the characteristics of compassion and humility, in that it involves not the suppression of personal identity but the enlarging of that identity in some way that one sees Others and then internalizes their reality.

It is vitally important, perhaps central, that a conflict resolver, in the largest sense as peacemaker, needs to be someone who understands Otherness in a deep, existential way. That Otherness need not be based on his ethnicity or religion, but it must be a self-conscious awareness of that which makes all human beings, beginning with oneself, Other to other beings in some way. Otherwise, it will be difficult to comprehend the alienation caused by and fear of Otherness that drives so much interhuman conflict.

Mennonite Otherness is key not only to their own contribution to peacemaking but to the field of conflict resolution as a whole, in terms of what is necessary, in the existential awareness of the third party, to understand parties to a conflict and to be a vehicle of reconciliation between them.

The text from Exodus, cited above, "for you know the feelings of the stranger, having been strangers in the land of Egypt," reads like a description of the evolution of Mennonites from a banished outgroup, like the Israelites in Egypt, to a group that works on caring for the downtrodden in distant cultures in remembrance of their old experience. This is crucial to their peacemaking method, namely, the deep and abiding respect for identity affirmation, or what I have termed Otherness, of each party to a conflict as well as a respect for their own Otherness.

The conflict resolvers among the Mennonites travel the globe in search of the defenseless, keenly aware of their own history as defenseless strangers. In a certain sense, each time they work toward securing the legitimacy of Otherness and the identity of a threatened group, they reaffirm the spiritual depth of their own experience. It involves caring for the Other, respecting his Otherness, and com-miting not to invade his culture. This is also, once again, an emulation of Jesus, in the sense that it means being in the world of another but not *of* that world.[27] Each time one enters into another culture, one enters as a healer but not as an invading army. In other words, one is in the world of their culture but self-consciously not of it. One acknowledges and respects boundaries between peoples as *a religious experience*, not as a barrier to that experience. At the same time, there is a feeling of deep identity with the suffering group.

This method of awareness of Otherness is crucial for the third party in conflict resolution and also for each of the conflicting parties, who often cannot accept the identity of Others because of their own doubts about identity. The third party often sets the tone and creates a model of intervention that either perpetuates the inability to recognize Otherness or that, alternatively, engenders it in the conflicting parties.

It must be admitted, however, that the vast majority of Mennonite global peacemaking has taken place in Christian cultures, where there are deeper bonds of religious unity that allow them to respect the Otherness of the group with which they are engaged from a cultural point of view. It is still unclear how well Mennonite peacemaking would work where the Otherness extends to the level of religious belief, especially with those who are not Christian and will never become Christian. The Mennonite peacemakers in such a context would be challenged to embrace the Otherness of this group in a deeper way, which would challenge their own spiritual lives. They may also have to risk being less understood as a group, where the entire frame of reference of walking in Jesus' path would be alien to the group that they are trying to engage in relationship. Some Mennonites have done peace work in Somalia among Muslims and in India among Hindus. The results of these engagements will need to be studied in the future.

Community and Peacemaking

How Mennonites manage to respect Otherness is intimately related to how they create and sustain their own community while engaging in peacemaking. This brings us to the topic of spiritual community. There are several ways in which the communal impulse is maintained, in altered form to be sure, across thousands of miles and many cultures. This is a vital component of who they are and also what the field of conflict resolution in general may be able to learn from them.[28] Men and women are sent in small groups and stay for extended periods of time, long enough to create real community where they go.

It is never simple to do this, especially in cultures where an ethnic group can settle in a region for a few hundred years and still be considered a newcomer. Nevertheless, Mennonite workers invest far more of their lives in these remote assignments than typical conflict resolvers. They may find it difficult to discover a spiritual community of Mennonites who share their values of service, and they may have difficulties being accepted in the local community. But these difficulties pale in comparison to the standard model of conflict intervention, which involves such a rapid interaction with people in conflict that deep relationships are almost impossible.

The peacemakers also stay in touch with other Mennonites globally. Mennonites in their place of origin pray for their welfare regularly, and there are prayer calendars through which workers are prayed for by people all over the world. This has roots in several communal missionary customs, including a communal commissioning of a person who is being sent off to her mission.

These methods, adapted from early support of international missionaries, have some crucial lessons for conflict resolution theory and practice. Peace and justice advocacy, conflict prevention, intervention, mediation, resolution, and post-trauma healing involve such profound challenges to the inner emotional life that it is no wonder that many people burn out from this work. Isolated, often attempting to cope with witnessing the worst human degradation, the intervener cannot live with this work for long.

The Mennonite creation of community gives peacemakers the tools to endure great psychological stress. Communal support allows them to engage in long-term peacemaking, which they believe in spiritually and which may also be far more effective. Since many conflicts are deeply rooted, it is considered arrogant to believe that intervention can be quick and invasive. Their belief is that only through building trust over years can true transformation take place. This long-term building of relationship also seems to be a healthier response to the pain of local people than coming in for ten days and leaving with a combination of relief and guilt. The building of relationships with non-Mennonite natives gives the Mennonites the psychological fortitude to persist in this difficult work. Furthermore, listening to and understanding the people of other cultures is central to their religious value system, and thus one's work is felt to be the fulfillment of one's highest spiritual calling.

This emerges out of their commitment to humility but has also evolved into a kind of cultural ethos, which Lederach formalizes, in my opinion, in the elicitive method. This way of interacting takes time. Time means isolation of the individual peacemaker, unless she has community. In fact, the reasons for the Western tendency to quickly intervene and then quickly leave conflict scenarios may not only be budgetary constraints on international agencies or political constraints. There may be an awareness of the problematic isolation of interveners. That is at least one reason why Mennonite international peace activists have been so intertwined with the Mennonite missions around the world. The missions provide a long-term presence, a network of relations, a foundation of trust with parties to the conflicts, and a secure home for the peacemakers.

Moral Character and Peacemaking

It cannot be emphasized how important to our subject is the imperative to be "meek and lowly of heart" in emulation of Jesus.[29] Mennonite peacemakers often see their habitual sense of inadequacy as a flaw, and in some sense they are right. Their cultural tendency to self-doubt and self-deprecation has had some destructive effects on them, and it has, in my opinion, been an important reason why Mennonite spiritual life is becoming overwhelmed by the supremely arrogant style of other Christian conservative groups, whose politics and attitudes are encroaching on, and I believe deleteriously affecting, Mennonite moral attitudes.

Mennonite self-doubt serves as a strength, however, in peacemaking. It leads to an extraordinary level of cross-cultural sensitivity and also leads to a deep commitment to listening and receptivity, which have prominent and long-standing places in Mennonite Central Committee methods of peacemaking.

The characteristics of listening, relationship building, and cross-cultural sensitivity are what have been the key missing ingredients of Western engagement in both peace and justice work and poverty relief. I had occasion to make some small contribution to disaster relief in the wake of the Rwandan genocide. Thousands of people were on the edge of starvation in the refugee camps, and I remember a colleague telling me that of all the hundreds of international agencies that descended into these refugee camps to save lives, only two agencies bothered to even ask the refugees if there were any doctors or nurses among them. All the other agencies imported their own! One would think that rationality alone would be enough to encourage agencies in emergency situations to utilize local talent and to engage whatever cultural resources could be helpful in dealing with a crisis. But self-interest may also encourage agencies to utilize their own experts, to demonstrate budget expenditures to donors, or some such other rational calculation. However, if a moral quality such as humility were to become part of the culture and modus operandi of an agency, such abuses of the dignity of aid recipients could be avoided and conflict with them minimized.[30]

I would like to give an example of the value of humility in international interventions. Liberia's five-year civil war, or what some have described as auto-genocide, was a brutal and complete destruction of society, which devolved into at least five fighting factions. The lived reality of that event is that many family members, who were children of intermarriage, killed each other out of fear, each member being goaded and threatened by his tribe to kill first or be killed. Thus, in addition to the human loss, there was a complete destruction of moral society. There were more than 160,000 killed in the war, mostly civilians who were massacred, and 200,000 displaced.[31]

The international community brought the warring parties to the conference table scores of times. In addition, many initiatives were funded by foundations and agencies, but in all of these initiatives, almost no one funded any initiatives that included indigenous traditional peacemaking methods. Never once were the tribal elders, who used to enact those peacemaking traditions, made an important part of the international peace process. Nor were women ever involved officially in intervention strategies, until the warlords themselves came one day to, a woman, and asked Ruth Perry to temporarily lead Liberia and help them to stop their endless bickering about a way to coexist.[32] Samuel Doe was a survivor of that war and is an extraordinary Christian peacemaker. He was one of my students at Eastern Mennonite University, and he is receiving training there. I have also been working with him on a project to help revive the life of his tribe, which was utterly decimated by the war. Doe has indicated to me that there is a largely undocumented role of women as ritual peacemakers in Liberian culture, and that this has never been acknowledged.[33] But the international community could never have known this because their initiatives never even attempted to resonate with the culture and conscience of the parties to the conflict. This requires a commitment to time spent with victims of war and particularly the capacity to humbly listen to and learn from another culture, a critical lesson that Mennonite peacemakers are teaching. Had this method of engagement been used in Liberia early on, it is possible that tens of thousands of lives could have been saved.

Almost half of those who hold guns in militias in Liberia are under the age of fifteen,[34] and almost all of them are orphans. Yet few thought that these desperate, damaged children might respond more to the deep need for parents and the guidance of mothers and traditional elders than they might to a piece of paper signed in Geneva. This level of brutal, if unintentional, deafness is too common in international affairs, and the Mennonite method of intervention, a way of humble listening, is not only a more moral path of intervention, it seems to be a more rational and less wasteful path than what prevails today on the international scene.

This method of engagement of radical humility is not just an ethical act or a strategy of intervention for Mennonites. It appears to be a part of their being, a cultural characteristic that is at the heart of their religious experience of divine closeness and emulation. Every feeling of pain before the suffering of Others is a living embrace of the life and person of Jesus. The community prayers, songs, and sermons often revolve around this theme.

How do you replicate such humility among other religious peacemakers if there is no high premium placed on the character of humility in other religious groups? How do you replicate it in the secular community of international agencies, where output and efficiency may be more important as standards of evaluation of workers than a particular personality characteristic? Furthermore, how do you operationalize humility when there is no deep metaphysical imperative to do so in the secular community?

I think humility can be and should be inserted into general conflict resolution training in some fashion. Furthermore, faith in God is not the only deep motivator of ethical character, and I believe that there could be ways to justify this training in a secular context. For example, human needs theory, a school of conflict resolution theory, is built upon a humanist conception of a wide variety of basic human needs that must be fulfilled in order to prevent violence. Some of those needs are "higher" needs, such as the need for freedom or meaning. There is quite a bit of disagreement, as noted in previous chapters, on what needs are universal to all people or whether it is fair to even posit universal needs, rather than operating with a basic assumption that there are needs that vary from group to group.[35]

One topic that seems to me to be neglected by this school of thought is the needs of the third party intervener. In general, there has been a tendency to assume this intervener to be a value-free figure capable of neutrality and infinite professionalism. It is an ideal construct, not a reality, because it does not acknowledge the third party or parties as real people with real needs. It seems clear to me that the conflict resolver's needs and, correspondingly, her character is crucial. The Mennonite model seems quite pertinent here.

I would suggest that a nongovernmental organization (NGO) or any agency could make characteristics, such as humility, a fulfillment of what it is to be part of a conflict-resolving community, where the sponsoring agency constituted itself or expressed itself as a community with certain key values. Thus, as the individual—religious or not—trains himself in these character traits he fulfills the need to be good at what he does, the need to be a good peacemaker, and the need to be a good member of the conflict-resolving community. The community of the NGO or other agency strengthens and encourages this self-definition.

Humility in international work could also be reinforced by an environmental ethic that calls on the human being to recognize her place within the totality of nature, just as much of Native American thinking expresses. Work that combines environmental justice and conflict resolution could express itself in this fashion.

It seems clear from peace work and development work in many parts of the world that this quality of humility is critical to serious work with poor people, people in conflict, or both. Thus, replication of this spiritual quality, even in some secular version, would have a powerful impact on large-scale efforts at conflict resolution and development for the poor.

Instrumentalism versus Mennonite Peacemaking

The inherent moral value of building relationships is another key ethical quality of Mennonite peacemaking. It is founded on what I would like to define as an antiinstrumentalist approach to human relations in the conflict scenario. Mennonite spirituality guides the peacemaker to build relationships in the conflict situation but not only as an instrument that produces an outcome. The standard emphasis of process-oriented workshops or conflict resolution activities is that a third party facilitates, mediates, and perhaps even makes initial contacts and gestures, all with the purpose of getting the parties to the table and achieving resolution of conflict. This is encapsulated in the phraseology of evaluation, such as "outcome-based" evaluation. While the idea of evaluating one's work and one's effectiveness would not be strange at all to the ears of Mennonite peacemakers (they tend to engage automatically in self-criticism), the idea of delimiting relationship building to an instrumentalist focus on outcome would sound rather strange. Evaluation is not the problem here. It is the reduction of the human moment of relation to its instrumentality that is problematic for Mennonite peacemakers and, undoubtedly, many other peacemakers.

We see here an often overlooked but very real clash of cultures. Emanating out of certain religious traditions and ethical schools of thought is a rebellion against the treatment of a human being or, in some traditions, even an animal, as an object that is instrumental in one's efforts to achieve some social, economic, or military goal. For Immanuel Kant, a person must always be considered an end in himself. Kant's principal ethical imperative, which he spent much of his life proving is "Act so as to treat man, in your own person as well as in that of anyone else, always as an end, never merely as a means."[36] The moral sense theorists also posited, not in Kant's categorical imperative fashion but in terms of a direct observation of nature, that the "beneficent" qualities of love or compassion are innate. There are moral acts that we engage in that are not motivated solely by the instrumental furthering of self-interest but by compassionate or loving human qualities.[37]

Martin Buber deepened the Kantian move and made it into an existential response to others of deep religious significance. I–It is instrumentalist, the relation of subject to object, whereas I–You is relational, the relation of subject to subject, and it expresses the greatest end of spiritual relation. "The basic word I–You can only be spoken with one's whole being. The basic word I–It can never be spoken with one's whole being. . . . Whoever says You does not have something; he has nothing. But he stands in relation."[38]

This is the essence of the human relations that Mennonite peacemaking at its best tries to foster. As opposed to Hobbes, Machiavelli, and the political realist school, it is a worldview that celebrates the opportunity to meet the Other in relation. There is a belief that this possibility in human life demonstrates, by the concrete reality of the bonds created, that war and violence are not the only options in human relationships.

The Mennonite religious response is different also from the utilitarian perspective, best represented by John Stuart Mill. The latter is so dominant in modern bureaucratic culture that the use of his perspective is practically unconscious. It entails the constant attention to outcome and the instrumentalizing of one human moment for the purposes of the next human moment, all leading to an abstract social goal, such as prosperity for the greatest number of citizens. The latter is a laudable method of governing society and appears to be especially necessary in the unprecedented human task of governing and fulfilling the basic needs of hundreds of millions of human beings who inhabit one society. Perhaps moral and political utilitarianism is an inevitable and necessary byproduct of overpopulation. But its level of abstraction and inattention to the subtleties of human relationships is notorious, and it often has a devastating impact on society, especially in situations of bitter conflict where deeper human interaction is vital to heal the hatreds and anger.

Conflict resolution methods have been dominated by instrumentalist and consequentialist methods of process and outcome evaluation. This is understandable and vital in many instances. But Mennonite intervention offers a different vision. The moment of relation becomes a moment of religious fulfillment, of *imitatio dei*, in their case, emulating Jesus. The person in relation becomes an end in herself. The cultivation of relationship between human beings and the careful attention to the style of interaction and the character that one brings to that relationship are the essential elements of their peacemaking activity, because they are the primary moments of religious experience and discovery of the Other in the world. The outcome of the relationship, they hope, is the creation of peace and the reduction of conflict. But it is not the sole focus of every activity.

People the world over crave authentic relationship in a time of violent crisis, and they often do not receive this at the hands of professional, instrumentalist intervention by outsiders. We need to study and contrast the net effects of instrumentalist approaches to the setting up of dialogue and problem-solving workshops versus the Mennonite method of entering into relationships.[39] We need to study the advantages and disadvantages of each approach and of the mixed models as well, which combine elements of both modes of intervention. This, of course, caricatures methods of conflict resolution of the instrumentalist sort, and there are many models of instrumentalist intervention that strive for deep relationship building, as do the Mennonites. Many Western conflict resolvers intervening in cultures have often entered into deep relationships with the parties to the conflict. But was it incidental or central? Most important, could they report this in their evaluations as a major success to foundations and agencies, or was it irrelevant to the project's evaluation by their sponsoring agencies? This is where the Mennonite model might have something to teach in terms of what we call success or failure in the field and what becomes the focus of our entry into situations of conflict.

The creation of human bonds across cultural lines, the opening up of relationships among groups through the agency of intermediaries, the solidarity expressed with those who suffer should be valued by agencies, whether or not a settlement of a particular conflict is achieved in the short term. These relationships should be considered a success in and of themselves by their board members. Evaluation would then involve the question of how well the group did at creating those relationships, in addition to evaluation of the conflict resolution outcome.

It must be admitted that, with either model, we have little information on what would occur if there were unlimited resources available to replicate either model across a given country and then examine the effects ten or twenty years later. Only then would we really be able to evaluate which model has worked in lived reality and why. Until we can create such grand experiments, we need to leave open the possibility of learning from models that have worked on smaller scales, and here the Mennonite model deserves serious attention.

This discussion should not imply that Mennonite peacemakers do not care about outcomes. On the contrary, their prayers, songs, and the evidence that I have seen all testify to a deep yearning to create real change in the lives of those who are affected by war and poverty. There is little evidence here of certain religious schools of thought that would minister to the poor and downtrodden without any genuine efforts to improve their lives. This is a mistake in some Christian relief work that I have not observed Mennonites making at all. Clearly they are working at conflict resolution methods that, on the contrary, go to the root of conflict, and they argue that real resolution involves social transformation.

All methods, including those of the Mennonites, have disadvantages or risks. A strictly instrumentalist, outcome-based, process-oriented approach to conflict resolution runs two risks. First, exclusively outcome-based approaches invite burn-out on the part of the third party or activist. Many conflicts are intractable, requiring years or decades of work. That is simply not a sustainable situation for an individual or even an agency that evaluates its work solely based on outcome. There must be other motivations built into the actual work itself, which makes the work self-sustaining even when the desired ends are not achieved. Most people in the field who I have met and most analysts who sustain this work over years develop this additional set of motivations. But it is rarely articulated or reinforced by one's community, which it seems to me, places an unnecessary burden on those who do this work.

Second, instrumentalist, goal-oriented approaches to conflict (or to other intractable problems globally) have such an obsession with the hoped-for achievement that all means to get to that goal can become justified, especially in the competition among multilateral and bilateral agency interventions. This includes the economic abuse that some NGOs perpetrate on their own workers in the name of sacrificing for the "cause." It also often descends into petty rivalries among organizations that cause harm on the ground. Furthermore, the pursuit of narrow bureaucratic outcomes leads often to astounding levels of duplication in the field, which only confuses many situations.

Gandhi demonstrated that there must be no difference between means and ends in the struggle for social change—and that the means really are the ends. This, it seems to me, is deeply resonant with Kant's kingdom of ends and Buber's I–You relations. It means that building human relations *among* peacemakers, inside organizations and communities of peacemakers, is an end in itself, with the conviction that it is also the best means to achieve the goal of peacemaking in its deepest sense. This creates a sustainable group of peacemakers because they are constantly reinforced by the deep awareness that everything that they are doing is inherently valuable, even if subject to periodic evaluations on how to do it better. It means that the community of peacemakers can count on the fact that the ends desired for conflicting parties are also the guiding standards of their own communities' treatment of their peacemakers. The ends of peace, justice, fairness, honesty, and compassion become the means by which the community of peacemakers functions. This creates trust, eliminates destructive feelings of hypocrisy, and creates a model for the conflicting parties who come into contact with these peacemakers.

It is certainly not the case that all Mennonite peacemakers behave in this fashion, nor am I suggesting that they are the perfect paragons for every conflict resolution practitioner. My point is structural and relational. Making the act of building human relations into an ethical or sacred task unifies, in principle at least, means and ends. This should be considered by all conflict resolution activists as a powerful model for sustainable conflict resolution work. John Burton and others have suggested that in order for conflict resolution to really work on a global scale, it is going to have to become part of the political ethos of modern civilization.[40] I would suggest that in order for it to really work on a global scale, it is going to have to become part of the *ethical* ethos of civilization, part of the means, both interpersonal and institutional, by which conflict resolution and peacemaking are pursued by individuals and institutions, not just an end.

One final note on instrumentalism. It should be noted that mission and building up the church is instrumentalism of a sort. The conversion of people to one's religion, the most aggressive form of mission, may be perceived by the faithful as a process of "spreading the good news," but it is definitely perceived by Others as the instrumental use of people to strengthen a church or religious structure. It complicates the relationship with aid recipients or parties to a conflict. Mission activity in many parts of the world today, such as where Christianity and Islam intersect, is often conflict generating. Furthermore, for some other Christians in the field, proselytizing is so central that the human being becomes completely an instrument of church building. Thus, the intersection of mission activities and peacemaking activities creates complications of motivations and perceptions. Just as an example, any religious Christian effort to do authentic conflict resolution work between Israeli Jews and Palestinians would have to overcome serious suspicion on the part of most Jews as to the motivations of the Christians. After millennia of being subject to public humiliation, coerced experiences of proselytism in the synagogues themselves, and even forced conversions, there is little trust in anyone who calls herself a Christian missionary. It seems clear that conflict resolution work that is confused with or in any relation with proselytism is seriously flawed in principle and will have problematic effects in practice.

This is clearly a basic theological issue and dilemma for modern Mennonites, as I noted earlier. But I would argue that the creative process—sometimes stated, sometimes unstated—that I observed regarding future religious definitions of "mission" in relationship to peacemaking should be accelerated. This could help to clarify for themselves and Others what mission really means to them.

Peacemaking versus Justice

A critical issue that has preoccupied Mennonite thinking on peace and pacifism has been the relationship of peace and justice. This has become an increasingly central though unresolved issue as the modern wing of Mennonitism becomes more engaged in the world. World War II and the shame suffered by many due to their pacifist position spurred a great deal of rethinking and critical evaluation of the quietist and separatist element of Mennonite pacifism. The call for a theology of involvement encouraged greater commitment to active intervention in the lives of others.[41] This also expresses itself as a challenge to "two-kingdom theology," which implied passivity before a world that was utterly separate from the Kingdom of God.

The starkest example of this shift is the development of the Christian Peacemaker Teams.[42] The religious characteristics of CPTs seem at first glance to set them in opposition to the style and character of conflict resolution, the elicitive method, and conflict transformation. First, they are decidedly partisan. The teams go where they are invited by one side to stand with them in their suffering. Mennonites have been doing this for a long time. But CPTs are far more aggressive and are visible forms of protest against injustice. Furthermore, the sometimes confrontational language used to describe the teams is uncharacteristic of Mennonite peacemaking in other situations. It seems in certain situations that this is an effort to invite trouble in order to witness or even highlight the injustice of the situation.

This is clearly a situation in which the religious value of peace is at odds with the religious value of justice. This dilemma has old roots in biblical tradition, where God is portrayed as a God of justice punishing the wicked but also as a merciful God who loves repentance and forgiveness. Furthermore, God has a set of ideal characteristics for human beings to emulate, which includes both peace and justice. "Execute the justice of truth and peace in your gates" (Zech. 8:16).[43] But this is a decidedly difficult set of characteristics for humans to combine, whereas God is set up as the ideal being who does successfully combine these traits. It seems to me that some of the Mennonite peacemakers appear to express a deliberate process of attempting, as much as humanly possible, to combine a commitment to peacemaking and social justice.

The CPT method makes the choice for justice very stark. This has an honorable history in terms of nonviolent forms of confrontation and protest, which Gandhi championed. In the Christian case, there is also a martyrlike element (and perhaps for Gandhi also, who was deeply influenced by Ruskin and Tolstoy) with some deep resonance in Mennonite history of preparing to be assaulted for the sake of those who are defenseless.

It is unclear to me whether such an aggressive partisanship in peace work is really peacemaking at all, but it is justice work. It appears to purposely generate conflict for the sake of witnessing and calling attention to injustice and for the sake of standing with the defenseless in such a way that one invites injury. The invitations to intervene come from one side of a conflict, and, therefore, the team is immediately entering as partisans. This makes perfect sense in pursuing justice but not in conflict resolution. Nevertheless, there is some effort of the CPTs, especially recently, to teach by example the principle of nonviolent resistance, and it would be valuable to see follow-up on how many of the people they have stood with have adopted those methods.

This entry of Mennonites into hot political situations is often done in a quicker way than the evolution of contacts and relationships that has been characteristic of other Mennonite activity. It also exposes some problems with the process of choosing one side for the sake of justice. Mennonites tend to side with whoever is not holding the guns and to view with suspicion those who do. There are obvious historical and theological motivations for their choice, but it is fraught with danger. In the immediate sense, whoever is not holding the guns is much more likely to be the persecuted group. But looks can be deceiving, and it is also easy to fall prey to popular and prevailing political perceptions of who the victims are.

As an example, I understand why CPTs wanted to send a team to Iraq when it was being attacked. But why not send a team to Kuwait to witness the brutality of the Iraqi forces? Could it be that they would have been welcomed by Saddam in Iraq as a public relations ploy but killed by Saddam in Kuwait? As another example, I could not sympathize more with CPTs in Hebron bearing witness to the terrible treatment of Arabs at the hands of some of the settlers. But would they don Jewish clothing and drive unarmed through West Bank towns with Israeli license plates in order to accept the violence of Hamas upon themselves and in order to bear witness to the evil of terrorism against unarmed men, women, and children? I understand that pursuing justice for many people involves deciding who has suffered the most harm and siding with them. But it seems to me that this involves one in some problematic choices from the point of view of peacemaking and of attempting to understand how justice and injustice are viewed by all sides of a conflict.

One also runs the risk of being used, when one is partisan, by people who have no commitment to peacemaking now or in the future. The effective conflict resolver, however, the one who builds relationships on both sides, is never subject to this danger. In the worst case scenario, he may be used in negotiations by people who have no interest in peace, but he has never lent his name to a partisan effort that turned out to be an adjunct to or a cover for violence. At worst, the peacemaking effort did not succeed, but the integrity of the commitment to peacemaking remains.

Another problem with this kind of intervention from the point of view of both conflict analysis and religious ethics is that today's victims are tomorrow's killers. One can side with those who do not have guns, but their relatives may be using guns against the other side even as you protect them. Or, a child that you stand with may in a year or two become a killer. This is where the methods of conflict resolution, transformation, and relationship building with all sides of a conflict protect you from manipulation or becoming embroiled in a conflict rather than becoming a part of its resolution. There is no question that combining peace with justice, as Mennonite conflict resolution expects, as well as many secular theories of conflict resolution propose,[44] will involve one in conflict-generating activity. Most conflict resolution theory expects constructive conflict as a part of achieving resolution. But this is quite different from entering from the beginning as a partisan.

Many Israelis and Jews think of classic Christian peacemakers as anti-Semitic.[45] It must be disconcerting for members of a peace church to be perceived in this way. The activity of the peace churches in Israel, with a few individual exceptions, for the past forty years, however, has been in solidarity with the suffering of

Palestinians, not in mediation efforts or relationship building on both sides nor in identification with the suffering that Israelis have endured due to the wars and due to terrorism. As Christians, it should be obvious to them how this would be perceived by the bulk of Jews, who came to Israel in the first half of the century in order to escape from pogroms and genocide in Christian lands. The entire ethos of Zionism, for better or worse, is founded upon a response to the centuries of persecution in Christian Europe, often fully supported by local priests if not by the church hierarchy. This must be confronted by Christian peacemakers.

The only sympathetic Christians that Israelis ever really see are waiting for the return of all Jews to Israel, Armageddon, the destruction of two-thirds of the Jewish people, the second coming of Christ, and the conversion of the Jewish remnant to Christianity.[46] Right-wing Israelis have welcomed the financial support of these Christians who, incidentally, believe that war with Muslims is inevitable. But peace-loving Israelis, and the half of Israel who voted for the Oslo accords, with a few exceptions feel mostly isolated from the Christian world. This is a perfect example of why partisan approaches to conflicts may satisfy the call of justice but do little for true consensus building and conflict resolution. The CPT group in Hebron, for example, may be doing valiant work in standing up to terrible injustices, but keep in mind that they have chosen as their adversaries the four hundred most extreme settlers in Israel out of a population of millions of Jews and tens of thousands of other settlers, most of whom would not treat them so cruelly. So as they report back to the Mennonite community about their terrible experiences standing with the defenseless and against the cruel oppressor, are they helping this peace church to continue its role in the world as a peace church? Is this helping the Mennonite community get the information and the tools that it needs to be effective peacemakers with millions of Israelis who are far less extreme but who need to be brought into constructive relationship with millions of Palestinians? Or are these reports simply making good Christians angry at wicked Jews who oppress the poor, like the Israelites of the Bible, who the prophets rebuked? In other words, I am concerned that serious conflict resolution work not fall prey to predictable cultural/religious categories of good versus evil, which do little to transform human relationships.

My instinct as an analyst is to side with the Mennonite conflict transformation school of thought on what is most necessary in the Middle East. That is not to say that the time may not come, in the face of gross injustice, to stand in non-violent protest, and I applaud this when it is the case. But how can a church decide to take this route when it has not tried the path of conflict transformation and relationship building on all sides, or only taken this path when it involves warring Christians on both sides?

The tragedy is that the work of the peace churches, especially the grassroots work of the Mennonites, is precisely what could have averted the setback to the peace process of the 1996 Israeli elections, a difference of just twenty thousand votes. The elite side of the Middle East peace process, namely the business partnerships and negotiations among political leaders, were and still are in motion. But the deep levels of fear and anger of the masses of people on both sides were not and are still not being addressed. These elite strategies of conflict resolution were set in motion years ago by key representatives of conflict resolution theory and practice. The challenge at the time was the intractable nature of the government-to-government conflict in the Middle East, including the leadership of the Palestine Liberation Organization (PLO). But it is rage at the popular level, especially religious rage, that has threatened the peace process to its core in the last few years. It is this level of conflict at which Mennonites have excelled elsewhere, and this is precisely where Mennonite peacemakers could have made and could still make a decided difference. It is also where training on both sides in conflict resolution could be effective, especially in Lederach's and Kraybill's methods, which emphasize, both scientifically and theologically, the suspension of judgment of others as one tries to transform a conflict into a process of reconciliation.

The Middle East also could benefit from an elicitive approach to the religious communities involved in the conflict. Eliciting conflict resolution and peacemaking methods from religious cultures will be crucial to the future of the Middle East, especially since so much of the violence and opposition to the peace process has come from religious communities, Hamas and Islamic Jihad on one side and the Israeli religious parties and the settlers on the other side. But that requires deep entry into both cultures and long-term trust building, especially because of old issues of both Jewish and Islamic distrust of Christian intentions as third parties. But it could be done over time, in my opinion. I would argue that there are some deep cultural challenges that the Mennonites face in moving their work from conflict situations in which both sides are at least nominally Christian, such as in Nicaragua, to other conflicts of different religious/cultural backgrounds. There is a natural affinity religiously on which they have relied in creating relationships with all sides of a conflict. If they want to expand their work to non-Christian frameworks, as I believe they should, then they must carefully think through how they are going to build relationships as successfully as they have done among Christians.

There is no clear answer for the religious dilemma of justice seeking versus peace seeking or the dilemma of peace seeking with all parties versus keeping oneself distant from military powers. They do seem to come into conflict often, and one has to acknowledge that within complex moral situations, choices for justice will be made by some and not others. But one should not make believe that justice seeking is always peacemaking. As a brilliant South African religious peacemaker, Khuzwayo Mbonambi, told me recently, "Justice preserves the peace, but it never makes peace. Only reconciliation and forgiveness do that."

The Transformation of the Peacemaker

Conflict transformation is not just the process of enabling transformation to take place in the conflicting parties. Many Mennonite interveners seem prepared to go through a personal spiritual transformation. There is an openness to learning and a sense of gratitude for the opportunity to do that. This creates a much more symbiotic relationship between the conflicting parties and the peacemakers. There is a sense that they share a destiny of change and growth that empowers all of them, rather than maintaining one as the recipient of the good graces of the other.

Conflict resolution as a field of inquiry needs to think more about how and whether the third party truly enables others to change, and whether that is possible without the third parties being transformed themselves. Furthermore, it seems quite clear that ethical traits, such as gratitude, an eagerness to learn from others, an openness to positive change, and generosity, are all critical to Mennonite conflict transformation. Its replication would require, in my opinion, training people in the development of ethical character. This is a radical idea for the field of conflict resolution, but it bears consideration.

Christian Foundations and Replicability

Prayer is an important element of Mennonite peacemaking. Prayer and song often frame the actual intervention between enemies, although this is certainly not required. Many effective Mennonite peacemakers operate in secular circumstances. For those who do engage in prayer as a frame for the intervention, it is a kind of sacralization of the experience. It generally evokes in many people their most noble aspirations for themselves and for Others, which provide a useful counterbalance to the primal fears and anger that otherwise naturally dominate one's consciousness in these meetings with enemies.

Biblical study is also key here, and I believe accomplishes something more. Biblical study, especially when texts are chosen with some relevant ethical content, insert into a deeply political and even military situation the fundamental questions of interpersonal ethics. Furthermore, it makes justice, peace, empathy with suffering, mourning over suffering into topics of intellectual study. Generally, in tough negotiations, intellectual inquiry or reasoned discussion are the bases of exchanges regarding ceasefires, distribution of scarce resources, reconstruction, election issues, and so on. The Bible study makes the issues of justice and peace into intellectual inquiries on a par with the other pragmatic issues. It makes values into pragmatic reality, which is a useful frame for discussions. It makes it more likely that, in the process of negotiations, the minds of the participants will associate with the questions of how to pursue justice or peace or reconciliation. The association may lead to more creative problem solving that interweaves pragmatic needs and ethical goals.

The one cautionary note is to acknowledge that the frame is highly culturally specific, in this case, to the culture of Christianity. Clearly, in any context that has more than one religion represented the ideal would be an artful combination or alternating frames that refer to the traditions of everyone involved. With indigenous peoples, I would assume that in most contexts it would be vital to include indigenous religions and tribal customs, unless the groups in question have converted to one religion, and they all strictly adhere only to their new religion. Certainly, if it is a mixed group of religious and nonreligious people, this would have to be accommodated as well. The last thing that a frame for discussions should do is encourage exclusion or ideological coercion. Then it tends to appeal to the worst instincts in the participants rather than the best ones.

One notes also a tendency to appeal in Mennonite writings to Christian themes of reconciliation and forgiveness. Forgiveness and reconciliation are particularly important in Christian tradition and will play an important role in conflict resolution for Christian contexts. But it is not a universally accepted method of peacemaking. At the very least, it is not as highly positioned theologically and should not be expected to be the *only* means to create peace between enemies, even religious enemies. I am still undecided about its universal usefulness, and I believe it requires further study.[47] In other traditions, such as Judaism and Islam, a shared commitment between enemies to justice, for example, may work better as a vehicle of peacemaking, although I have witnessed the powerful effect of unilateral apologies in Jewish/Islamic relations. But each religious community has different sets of traditions and high ideals, and it is out of those ideals that conflict resolution methods must emerge. Forgiveness is important in all these traditions, but *how* important it is, how it is done, and under what circumstances is clearly conditioned theologically and culturally.

Conclusion

In sum, Mennonite peacemaking methods are integrally related to their religious values. These, in turn, are formed by their historical experience, their close reading of biblical tradition, and their evolving spiritual response to the world around them. In many ways, their methods are unique to their religion and culture. But, as I have demonstrated, their methods pose powerful challenges to the general field of conflict resolution. Due to the immense power of the United States and Europe in the affairs of people, especially poor people, the world over, Western modes of interaction with the rest of the world are in need of perpetual self-scrutiny and creative growth. Mennonite conflict resolution and peacemaking offers a powerful model of human interaction that, if duplicated, would have to be altered to fit other worldviews and institutions. Nevertheless, the forms of peacemaking analyzed here have within them enormous transformative potential for the future interactions of the global community.

Mennonite peacemakers have demonstrated an ability to function in secular contexts and in multicultural contexts that are primarily Christian. The real complexity of most conflicts that I have witnessed is that they involve actors who are religious, people who are nonreligious, and members of numerous religious subgroups that are at odds with each other. Add to that the fact that the religious differences may be a major or minor element in the conflict. Also, religion may begin as a minor factor but become the major factor as it comes to symbolize the ethnic, tribal, or class differences among the conflicting groups.

Mennonite peacemaking in its ideal form fulfills certain basic necessities of peacemaking that emanates out of a religious position. Mennonites feel less of a need to publicly proclaim their religious commitments, and they are comfortable with a separation of their private religious lives from the public sphere. Therefore, it is easy for them to translate their religious impulses into peacemaking gestures that do not exclude in any way secular actors. This is a vital asset in effective peacemaking for complex contemporary situations. They also have the capacity to comfortably move into a Christian context of conflict and utilize their religious tradition to deepen the process of conflict resolution among the parties to the conflict. It is in the latter scenario that there has been a relatively easy relationship between the role of Mennonites as local missionaries and the role of Mennonites as peacemakers. What is harder is the mixed model of religious, secular, Christian, and non-Christian, which is typical of many conflicts. It seems to me that the next stage for Mennonite peacemaking is to develop a model of care and intervention that engages those who are not and will not be culturally or religiously Christian.

What does the Mennonite model teach us about what is necessary so that other religious traditions can be effective agents of peacemaking? A religious tradition should:

1. have a firm spiritual foundation for engaging in peacemaking with all human beings, regardless of race, religion, or culture
2. have a method of engaging in conflict resolution that does not impose its own theological assumptions on Others, or that is at least capable of being adjusted as these cultural and religious differences become apparent
3. develop an articulated set of ethical and spiritual foundations for peacemaking that (a) make the work sustainable over long periods of time and in trying circumstances and (b) instill in the peacemaker a series of values that will have her treat those in conflict as ends in themselves, as fellow human beings to be engaged in authentic relationship
4. generate a community that is capable of and prepared to support peacemakers institutionally and interpersonally
5. develop a reasonable way to deal with the inevitable and ongoing tension of peacemaking, pursuit of justice, and other competing ethical values that are critical to the construction of a civil society, such as civil rights
6. develop the ability to truly listen to another religious reality and culture, to not be threatened by it, and to discover the spiritual resources to make peace with those who are in different theological universes
7. learn how to integrate the development of a peacemaking method and philosophy with the most authentic elements of its own spiritual tradition and to combine this in a creative way with the best secular methods of understanding and dealing with human conflict

Now we will turn to a detailed examination of another religious tradition from the perspective of conflict resolution, in order to model the creation of a religious philosophy and a method of conflict resolution where there has not been one until now. This is vital for our analysis because the goal is to evoke these insights from religious cultures in the unprecedented circumstances of the contemporary era.

EIGHT

New Paradigms of Religion and Conflict Resolution

A Case Study of Judaism

The field of conflict resolution theory has emerged in recent years with a vital and timely analysis of the deep roots of persistent conflicts in addition to theoretical constructs and practical strategies for resolving conflicts. As a field, it addresses a variety of conflicts, including straightforward disputes of a limited sort as well as deep-seated violence that encompasses the fates of millions of people. It examines the roots of conflict that stem from issues of communication, psychology, power, and a variety of other human needs.[1] The field has been mostly developed in Western, industrialized, secular contexts. As such it has been harder to integrate the results with a variety of cultures and religious contexts that have their roots in premodern categories of thinking and feeling. As noted earlier, this has led to a relative impasse in dealing constructively with those global and domestic conflicts today that have some roots in issues of religious identity.

There has been another intellectual development involving the detailed analytic study of the growth of religious militancy in the twentieth century, particularly that kind of religious behavior that involves an aggressive rejection of the modern state and a willingness to try to undermine the roots of the modern state.[2] This always involves conflict and sometimes very violent conflict.

In this chapter, I will engage in an in-depth analysis of one religious tradition, but I will do this with an eye to conflict resolution theory and practice. The purpose is to evolve a model of conflict resolution that might appeal to even the most religious elements of a particular culture, even to those who have expressed great distrust of modern constructs of human relationships. This, in turn, is meant to create a possible bridge between secular and religious cultures as they both confront the difficult issues of conflict. An important backdrop of this piece is naturally the most deadly conflict that has involved Jews and the Jewish people in recent years, namely, the Arab/Israeli conflict. It also, however, is written in the context of the legacy of extreme violence at the hands of non-Jews, especially the Holocaust, which is an indelible element of many if not most Jewish identities at this particular time in history.

The Variety of Hermeneutics on War and Peace

Religions that have survived for many centuries present a unique set of challenges in terms of conflict and peacemaking. For the most part, religions survive a long time by having within the reservoir of their resources a wide variety of responses to peace and violence. The essential problem of the interaction of religion and violence is the hermeneutic variability of responses to peace, enemies, and war. This is true intragenerationally and certainly true intergenerationally. Tracking this hermeneutic evolution is a critical method of conflict analysis in religious societies and of prognostication of religious violence.

In concrete terms regarding Judaism, the central axis of the religion is rabbinic literature. In rabbinic literature, one can marvel at the differences between, say, Hillel or Rabbi Yohanan ben Zakai and their attitudes toward the Other, to gentiles, and, at the other end of the spectrum, a man like R. Shimon bar Yohai, whose disdain for the Romans was legendary.[3] There were rabbis who loved converts to Judaism, and there were rabbis who rejected them as a foreign threat.[4] Of course, the latter is complicated by our difficulty in contextualizing talmudic statements in specific places and times, such as the effect of disaffected converts turning into spies against the community at specific points in time.

Out of this soup of rabbinic literature, the religious interpreter can and really must construct specific responses to her place and time. This the rabbis of each generation have done, each with his own lens. As these responses have accumulated, they have gelled into a set of attitudes and laws regarding issues of peace, conflict, violence, enemies, etc. But I must emphasize that this gelling effect, this developing consensus on what "normative" Judaism is, has been a selective process, unfortunately affected profoundly by the often miserable state of Jewish/non-Jewish relations for many centuries, since the end of Jewish sovereignty in Palestine.

The early rabbinic literature has a mix of texts on the subject of war and peace. There is an extensive body of literature celebrating peace as a religious value, as a name of God, and as a supreme ethical principle.[5] There is some talmudic discussion of legitimate and illegitimate wars that Jewish kings may or may not wage.[6] Maimonides (1135–1204 c.e.) elaborated and codified these discussions,[7] which in turn, has given plenty of grist for the mill to Jewish theoreticians, who, in keeping with their Christian counterparts have tried to develop in recent years some cogent thoughts on just war.

Of course the Jewish community does not have the dubious benefit of hundreds of years of religious warfare from which to extrapolate moral guidelines for warfare. It was on the receiving end of many wars but almost never in charge of them in the last two thousand years. In other words, Jewish just war theory is a heavily speculative and hermeneutic affair.

Some may argue that rabbinic Judaism's discussion of just war has always been theoretical. Historically speaking, there have never been "rabbinic" kings, that is, kings who were thoroughly steeped in rabbinic Judaism, unless one accepts the traditionalist or fundamentalist position that rabbinic Judaism existed from the beginning of Jewish biblical history. Thus, the present-day discussion rests on tenuous theoretical grounds with no practical experience upon which to draw. It seems to be a rather desperate attempt to catch up with the military realities facing a secular state—Israel—run almost completely by Jews, which is, in and of itself, a historically unprecedented arrangement.

Jewish Post-Holocaust Anger and Its Hermeneutic Effects

The Jewish just war versus Jewish pacifist discussions have not addressed creatively what Judaism has said or could say about how to prevent violence, how to keep wars from happening, how to deescalate them, or how to heal people once the war has stopped. But Judaism has many things to say about peace, violence, and conflict resolution. It just has never been documented in recent times, with a few exceptions, particularly because, on the whole, the post-Holocaust scholarly Jewish community has not been much in the mood to mine the sources of Judaism for conflict resolution, especially with gentiles. Ironically, this has had a deleterious effect on the skills of the community in dealing with intra-Jewish conflict, which is reaching serious proportions, brought on in no small part by the political choices facing the government of Israel.[8]

Certainly the section of the community that would be most comfortable with delving deeply into the *halakhic* sources as a guide to life, namely, the Orthodox community, has been particularly uninterested in confronting Jewish resources on conflict resolution, despite righteous outcries against wanton hatred (*sin'at hinam*) and conflict (*mahloket*). On the contrary, the prevailing focus of attention has been increasingly on those rituals and laws of Judaism that would buttress cultural and physical survival, which would be specifically aimed, almost as weapons rather than as religious deeds, against annihilation. These are the rituals that make the Jew different, including obligations of protecting Jewish life, education on the uniqueness of Jewish life and practice, inculcating radical levels of defense of any Jew whose life is in danger, and ritual practices that are particularist by definition, such as the dietary and purity laws. Even the laws with universal application, such as the sabbath, tend to be seen or need to be seen as uniquely Jewish.

This trend especially focuses on the minutiae of practice, which make a clear boundary between who is in and who is out of the group, who can be trusted and who cannot be trusted, rituals that become, in their modern incarnation, markers of ethnic and national trust, markers of distinction, markers of insulation from a dangerous world. The more unique and peculiar those markers the better, because only those who are especially committed to the Jewish people would do such things. By contrast, the more universally moral the behavior, such as environmental protection, the more it displays similarities to outsiders, the less useful it seems to survival, the more it is suspect.[9] Now, this does not do justice to a variety of theologians and rabbis across the religious spectrum who have addressed issues of universal concern in the post-Holocaust era.[10] But this characterization does explain a certain trend of religious Jewish life that must be understood by conflict analysis theory.

I will never forget when, in 1987, I was giving a lecture on rabbinic sources on peace at one of the most prominent universities in the United States. An old Israeli Orthodox man and his wife were sitting in the front row; he was a well-known scientist. I was expounding on a particular talmudic passage, which reflected on the relationship between peace and compassion, and I heard from this educated scientist, muttered in low tones, words that I will never forget: "He sounds like a Christian." My Orthodox rabbinic credentials did not matter; my fluency with talmudic text did not matter. What mattered was that the texts were too universal and too benign in their relationship to the outside world. And I knew then, I think for the first time, that rational discussion of shared values between Jews and gentiles was a waste of time for many people, no matter how educated. Something else, something dramatically different than logic and reason, would be necessary to heal the wounds of the past. Modern anti-Semitism has led to a certain kind of Jewish wound, a rage that is often expressed in religious observance. It is to be found in ritual practices and communal precepts that express oppositional identity, often a martyrological sense of identity based on persecution.

Fundamentalist Identity Responses to Modernity and the Rejection of Universal Values

This phenomenon is not dissimilar to trends within the other monotheisms. All of them have significant subcultures today that are selectively winnowing their traditions for what makes their adherents different from Others. Often this occurs within the subgroups that have been ridiculed and despised or whose poverty and needs have been ignored by the dominant culture. And, of course, their oppositional behavior perpetuates a cycle by making them even more despised by the dominant majority cultures, which have little tolerance for difference. This, it would seem, is a restructuring of the religious ingroup in the face of the relentlessly homogenizing quality of modernity. It creates a sense of belonging that need not and sometimes cannot include ethical constructs, which would challenge an oppositional identity or complicate an identity rooted in behavior that emerges from an aggrieved position.

As stated earlier, Judaism has many things to say about peace, violence, and conflict resolution. It seems clear that, before we can even elicit a theory of conflict resolution from Judaism's prosocial ethics, sacred stories, symbols, and mythologies, conflict theory must creatively respond to the rage that many Jews feel at the world. This is especially true in light of the Holocaust and historical anti-Semitism in the Christian world. If this rage is not addressed, conflict resolution as a vocation will be dismissed by the very section of the community that needs it the most.

Mourning, Posttrauma Healing, and Deep Conflict Resolution

The first stage of a Jewish conflict resolution theory may, for some people, be mourning. This is not as unusual as it might seem when it comes to intractable conflicts involving groups that have suffered over many centuries. Conflict resolution theory and practice must develop interventions that address the full spectrum of a particular group's responses to conflict, especially the most violent sections of that group. If an abnormal level of mourning that seems to perpetuate itself over history is a key element of the conflict, an effective religious peacemaking program must directly confront this.[11]

A peacemaking mourning process must speak to the deepest identity needs of a group and also to the group's sense of threat to its future, its fear of annihilation. Often what is mourned, but mourned in ways that create violence, is a loss of the group's honor, security, or sense of confidence in its future. There is also a sense of loss of some romanticized time—real, imaginary, or a combination thereof—in which the group had a fulfilled, secure existence.

Here is the crucial point. If mourning over this loss is to be complete, the peace process itself or that part of it that deals with past wounds should take on an indigenous, religious character. If it does not, if, for example, it smacks of some dominant culture that has been implicated in persecution of the group (Western Christian culture, in the Jewish case), then the mourning process cannot really resonate deeply, at least not for the most wounded members of the group. If, on the other hand, the process has deep cultural roots, then it *affirms* their identity and does honor to them, even as it heals the wounds of the past and simultaneously builds peace.

It is the most religious segment of a community that needs the deepest level of healing, because it is this segment that so zealously and regularly internalizes the collective identity and memory of the group through ritual, prayer, symbolism, and study. Often the religion will rehearse daily, weekly, and annually all of the most painful moments of the traumas of the past, in addition to celebrating the past glories of the group. This means that religious people will have the hardest time moving to a new stage of relationship with the outside, injuring world. They will not only have to heal emotionally. They will also need the time to create a new spiritual hermeneutic, reworked legitimately through the old one, that gives them permission to move forward in new relationships to the world and its inhabitants.

What is mourning in Judaism, referred to as *aveilus,* and how can it be integrated into conflict resolution? An in-depth analysis of Jewish mourning and its relationship to peacemaking awaits a larger study. Briefly, however, *aveilus* is the ritual process of expressing the death of a loved one. That loved one is a part of oneself, one's history, one's very being. *Aveilus* practice is the most stringent regarding parents, because they represent the entire history and origin of a human being and his relationship to the eternal religious community. *Aveilus* is the ability to acknowledge loss unabashedly, to watch the lost thing[12] or person buried in the ground, especially to be able to engage in burial yourself and to feel the full horror of it. It is to immerse oneself for a long time in the life and memory of the one who is gone, up to a year for parents. Then, in response to this, the experience of *aveilus* means that one is moved by the community and one's relationship to God toward a slow and steady recovery from the loss. The recital of *kaddish* and *yizkor* is critical to this process.[13]

There is no conflict, especially deadly conflict, that does not involve loss. More important, there is no solution that does not involve loss. Win-win is an illusion in many serious conflicts.[14] The conflict has already caused loss by the time that it needs intervention or mediation, and it usually involves much more in order to arrive at peace. That is not to say that what can be gained by peacemaking is not significant, maybe even better than what was lost. But it rarely feels that way.

These losses, often unacknowledged, are the fuel of conflict. One hopes in vain that by perpetuating the conflict and winning one can somehow make up for what one has lost. But this is illusory, and the sooner that these permanent damages are acknowledged the easier it will be to focus on the concrete moves that need to be made to end the conflict, to negotiate and compromise on the concrete differences, and to begin rebuilding people's lives.

I have argued elsewhere that the Holocaust and European persecution are at the heart of the entire style of Israeli interaction. They are also, surprisingly, at the core of *intra-Jewish* religious/secular conflict in Israel, in addition to being a principal factor in the persistence of the Israeli population's mistrust and dislike of Arabs, which has now gone well beyond the understandable fear of terrorism.[15]

As another example, my family came to the United States around 1910, but there were still relatives in the "old country," in Ukraine, Latvia, and Lithuania. Of course, whoever remained was murdered in World War II, as far as we know. My family has never, ever thought of going back nor of tending to old and neglected burial sites nor of finding out what really happened in their places of origin; in fact, it has taken years for me to decipher where we came from. This suggests a rather unnatural distance from one's place of origin, but it is typical of Jews who came from places where they were persecuted. It also suggests an uncompleted process of confronting and mourning the past. There is no curiosity; instead, there is suppression of the past.

My family is also in possession of a profound level of simple Jewish faith and spiritual commitments, which defied the enormous economic and social pressures of the melting pot in Boston, forces that made the majority of their neighbors and extended relatives into assimilated Jews whose families are mostly non-Jewish now. At the same time, despite the security of holding onto this ancient piety, many members of my extended family have become obsessed with Jewish survival, with fertility, with Israeli security in particular, and a number of them have a profound distrust (hatred in a few instances) of Arabs, Germans, and other gentiles, people whom they have never met. The battles of Israel, any battle involving Israel, in fact, always becomes a battle with annihilation, at least for some of my relatives, no matter what the political or military circumstances. It seems as if the earth of Israel is compensation for every place that they and their ancestors have known and lost for centuries. Every battle that Israel fights revives old battles that were lost in humiliation, humiliating because, as defenseless civilians, they never were even equipped to fight in the old country.

Many members of my family and millions of others have never been able to or been allowed to mourn the past in a healing way, not in a way that would allow them to live again within the universe in a trusting way. They certainly have never been comforted by their former oppressors and have never engaged in any scintilla of reconciliation with Eastern European Christians. Indeed, they have never been asked or invited by anyone to do this. Eastern European Christians at present seem barely able to deal with their own wounds from the Cold War and World War II, let alone what they perpetrated against others. But everyone suffers from this lack of attention to confronting the past. Today the global Jewish community prospers financially for the most part, and Jewish rights are protected throughout most of the world, just fifty years after Jewish lives were worth absolutely nothing in Europe. But with all of the surface vitality and wealth of the Jewish community, I often feel that we are walking among the dead, haunted by loss.

As far as the Israeli/Arab conflict is concerned, there is much that *aveilus* can teach. It seems clear to me that a profound transformation of relationship would occur if Arabs and Jews, in addition to negotiating the obvious central issues of land and resource distribution, would engage in a simultaneous process of helping each group to mourn what they have lost. The losses of one hundred years, for each group, represent an important time span, which generally includes the memories that people have directly from parents and grandparents. It is these memories that must be addressed, and the process would involve focusing on all the lost children, spouses, parents, all the lost time and resources, all the lost homes, and of course all the lost land.[16]

It would be powerful indeed if groups of Arabs and Jews, perhaps aided by sympathetic Western Christians—who also have a key role in causing and healing this tragic conflict—would begin, *in detail*, to mourn what was lost.[17] They must begin to visit the dead together, to bury them together in symbolic ways, to memorialize lost lives and lost homes. They need to talk about the losses for as long as it is necessary, to thoroughly indulge the past rather than suppress it, to let go of the fear that it would disrupt rational dialogue and conversation. We must do exactly what rational peacemakers have tried to suppress, namely, we must indulge memory. But we must do it, not destructively as it is indulged in the privacy of particular groups, but as a part of peacemaking, as part of an effort to honor each group's memories at the same time that we struggle constructively over the present.

One cannot really escape the morass of deadly conflict and discover life again after death without this kind of healing of memory. Nor can conflict resolution occur without the theoreticians of conflict coming to terms with the need that most humans have to literally be with the dead or with what they have lost. We must take care of the victims of yesterday's carnage, even if they are unsympathetic now or aggressors themselves. We must crawl together with the victims back to life, out of the mass grave of the past where their imaginations hold them prisoner, and into a more rational, hopeful space of trust building and peacemaking. Presently, we simply deny this need, and therefore it haunts and destroys peace processes the world over.

Jewish Conflict Resolution Theory in a Pluralistic Context

One of the central issues that a theory of religious conflict resolution must confront today is that religion is a voluntary affair in places where there is no theocracy or police power that enforces religious rules. Many of us are happy, to say the least, that this is the case. However, this has had a revolutionary effect on religious life, effectively concentrating *inside* religious communities those individuals who hold views that are the most blatantly militant vis-à-vis the rest of the world. People who hold divergent viewpoints have the option of leaving and do so quite often. That was not possible a short time ago and is still not in many places.

Thus the dynamic process of hermeneutic engagement with a new horizon of experience, which used to force a religious community to evolve, has been extremely attenuated, at the same time, ironically, that there are more challenges on that new horizon than ever before. This has the effect of making the orthodox elements of a community more and more orthodox, while encouraging others to leave or to promote radically different versions, or attenuated versions, of the old religion. The wall between these two groups grows higher every day, and there is no longer the mediating influence of those inside orthodoxy who must remain there and who remain by fighting for their own hermeneutic evolution of the tradition. It should be emphasized, on the other hand, that there are great debates and arguments within these closed worlds, and *they* see themselves as struggling with change. But the changes are minor from an outsider's view and often do not begin to address the dangers of destructive conflict with outsiders.

The task of conflict resolution, I would argue, would be to evoke principles, values, and ways of approaching conflict that would speak to all members of a particular culture, religious or not religious, especially those who are on, or may be in danger of moving onto, a violent path. The purpose of developing such a theory of peacemaking is not necessarily to be able to convince those who are most extreme by the cleverness of one's hermeneutic interaction with religion.

Experience suggests that deep-seated conflictual styles take much more than clever sermons to undo. Rather, the purpose is to provide a hermeneutic of religious tradition that can be appealing to everyone so that, at least in principle, it binds rather than divides. The goal is to challenge and to create a positive kind of cognitive dissonance among religious people who are in conflict, rather than create a reaction of alienation, as a thoroughly secular approach often does. In this way, one strengthens those who naturally favor accommodation, while isolating the most violent elements within a fundamentalist universe. Many secular constructs of conflict resolution are designed for failure in religious contexts because, one way or another, consciously or unconsciously, they have a habit of undermining or flying in the face of religious values, spiritual priorities, and styles of interaction. This is what must change if we are to truly engage all levels of Jewish culture as it exists today.

There are several critical guidelines. One is to utilize religious constructs to heal deep injuries and to reconstitute a cultural and spiritual identity that responds to the need for uniqueness but that does not need to do this by way of hatred of the outsider. There must be an emphasis on a unique Jewish role and style of engaging this work. This responds to the fear of annihilation while channeling it into prosocial values.

Traditional liberal constructs assume that the answer to conflict is universal standards, shared values, and so forth. While I sympathize greatly with the aims of these constructs, they do emanate from a universalist position. Many people around the world—not just religious people—perceive this as secular cultural imperialism or evangelism. It can reach levels of great intolerance. The method of engaging conflict and peacemaking that could speak to fundamentalist Judaism would not be universalism but pluralism.[18] What I mean by this is that the method must first emphasize and affirm unique Jewish values and constructs, which can then be used to communicate to a plurality of other actors. An effort to speak only in universal terms, to make everyone the same, by contrast, flies in the face of numerous religious institutions whose raison d'être in the contemporary period (and perhaps always, to a certain degree) is to maintain difference.[19]

A pluralistic approach that maintains a clearly unique role for Jewish values could then lead at a second stage to tentative statements and agreements about shared values with other groups, be they non-Orthodox Jews, secular Jews, Palestinians, or Muslims. But it must begin from a premise that acknowledges and even values boundaries between cultural entities and respects those boundaries.[20]

What concerns the Orthodox Jew is cultural annihilation by assimilation; this is the great threat to the future of Judaism and always has been for this small minority. Thus, despite universalism's appealing beauty, what is seen and heard by many Jews, not just the Orthodox, is a threat to continuity. The values implicit in many of the universalist assumptions of conflict resolution practice are good and useful, but they must be mediated in a way that does not threaten Jewish culture (or any other indigenous culture, I would argue) with annihilation.[21] This is particularly true with groups that have firsthand experience of physical annihilation, as so many ancient, indigenous groups do.

We must also recognize the excessive love for and overattachment to the group that is at the root of religiously inspired conflict. Religious people tend to make extraordinary sacrifices in their lives to perpetuate Judaism and the Jewish people. Having many children, no matter how impoverishing, is just one part of that lifestyle; it is particularly true in this post-Holocaust generation. Often in conflict research there is too much emphasis on the psychopathology of group violence or the violence of the sadistic individual who acts for the group. But this ignores the full psychological reality of conflict and violence which often stems from an extraordinary love of one's own group that, in turn, spawns violence against those who are perceived to be injuring the group.

This excessive love should not be suppressed. Rather, a visionary approach to conflict resolution would acknowledge this love and give it some reasonable place within the process of building peaceful relationships within and between groups. At the present time in Israel, to give one example, those who advocate peace and who seem on the surface to be the ones "carrying the ball" for conflict resolution, often couple their peace work with a barrage of angry rhetoric against fellow Jews. The latter are labeled extremists, zealots, bigots, murderers, criminals. Of late, some who fear and loathe the power of the ultra-Orthodox community are referring to its members with words, such as "parasites" and "vermin," that are directly reminiscent of Nazi and anti-Semitic epithets. But the language expresses the same dynamic of dehumanization that the progressives struggle against when that same language is applied to Palestinians! The progressives are therefore dismissed by the right wing as self-hating Jews. Furthermore, one hears the same kind of sad distinctions from Palestinian peacemakers: "These Jews are good, and we should work with them, but those ones are criminals." Thus, we have no true peace process here at all, only some Jews who scream peace and dehumanize their fellow Jews, and some who scream security and dehumanize Palestinians. Authentic conflict resolution moves beyond this dynamic and engages each group in its own uniqueness, affirming that love of one's group is honorable and to be encouraged, except as it manifests itself in violence against Others.

Conflict Prevention as the First Stage of Conflict Resolution: Theory and Practice

Prevention is the strongest category for religious communal values in general and for Judaism in particular. There is a utopian quality to religious ethical constructs, and part of their utopianism is the quite rigorous, almost monastic, demands of piety, which, if they are followed, often lead to caring relationships of such intensity and depth that most conflicts are nipped in the bud or never even arise. The trouble is that they are rigorous and difficult to follow. That is one of the reasons that ethical observance consistently lags behind ritual observance in almost every major religion. Ritual observance is simply easier psychologically and emotionally, even if pragmatically and materially more demanding.

Prevention is the most effective tool of all in peacemaking because relationships are easier to mend at the early stages of problems. Furthermore, the religious warrants for pious behavior are strong and can, at least in principle, withstand much of the natural resistance to moral behavior that accompanies conflict situations. It is certainly true that countless religious individuals, past and present, have engaged and lived by these values in many conflictual or violent situations.

In the interests of space, I will not go into detail about these values, but they are divided into four sections: values that focus on the inner workings of one's mind and heart,[22] values that move one to the encounter with the Other; values that move one to the encounter with a foreign, estranged, or enemy Other; and, finally, values that move one to the construction of community. All four of these ethical categories are vital for conflict analysis and resolution.

Conflict Prevention Values in Judaism

Self

benevolent care of the self (*al tehi rasha bifne, ahavah kamokha, im ayn ani li*)[23]

self-scrutiny and change (*heshbon ha-nefesh, teshuva*)[24]

acquiring a good name (*shem tov*)[25]

intellectual study for the purposes of ethical practice (*lomed al menat la'asoth*)[26]

internalizing ethics rooted in wisdom (*hokhmah, middoth talmid hakham*)[27]

internalizing wisdom as a way of creating compassion and peace (*hokhmah*)[28]

calculation and prioritization of competing laws and values, constructive conflict (*talmud torah, 13 middot she'ha torah nidreshet, halakha, mahloket le-shem shamayim*)[29]

becoming like God in the acts of benevolence and peacemaking (*ve'holakhta be'derakhav, oseh shalom b'meromav*)[30]

From Self to Other

empathy with pain, including nonhuman pain (*rahamim*)[31]

personal involvement in acts of compassion as the essence of the Torah (*gemilut hasadim*)[32]

the use of the human face in interpersonal encounter to create peace (*sever panim yafot, kabbalat panim*)[33]

the infinite dignity and value of every human encountered (*tselem elohim*)[34] favorable interpersonal judgments in moments of uncertainty (*dan le-kaf zekhut*)[35]

trust (*emunah*)[36]

love expressed by complete identification with the other's needs (*ahavah kamokha*)[37]

unilateral honor as the key to relationships (*ayze'hu mekhubad, kevod haverkha*)[38]

language as a way of building human relationships (*shemirat ha-lashon*)[39]

From Self to Estranged Other

trust as a key prevention of violence (*amanah*)[40]

engagement in constructive conflict but not persisting in conflict (*mahloket le-shem shamayim, hizuk be-mahloket*)[41]

the value of constructive criticism in making peace (*tokhaha*)[42]

the importance of compromise in adjudication (*peshara*)[43]

the love of strangers and the refusal to oppress them (*ahavat gerim*)[44]

human hatred as sin and principal cause of divinely ordained punishment (*sina'at hinam*)[45]

the destructive impact of revenge in deed or in words (*nekimah, netirah*)[46]

the use of language to humiliate as sin (*ono'at devarim*)[47]

listening as the key to wisdom and human relations (*seyag le'hokhmah, shoel u'meshiv*)[48]

listening as peacemaking (*middot ahron*)[49]

humility and the temporary suppression of self (*anivut, ga'avah*)[50]

injury to the face of the other (humiliation) as murder (*halbanat panim*)[51]

truth as a foundation to society, equal to peace and justice (*emet*)[52]

peace as a name of God and the pursuit of peace as the ultimate religious task (*shalom, redifat shalom*)[53]

seeing truth in multiple and even contradictory manifestations (*shiv'im panim la'torah, elu ve'elu*)[54]

compromise as a central element in pursuing peace (*peshara*)[55]

truth as something to be found through every human encounter (*ezehu hokham ha-lomed me'kol adam*)[56]

fostering communal consciousness among enemies through shared good deeds and mutual aid (*hakem takim imo*)[57]

transparency and truth in negotiation (*emet, massah u'matan be'emunah*)[58]

patience and training in resistance to anger (*noah likh'os*)[59] patience with another's anger, especially in order to help him save face (*she'at ka'aso*)[60]

the art of reducing rage with gentleness (*ma'aneh rakh*)[61]

the overt acts of regret, confession, apology, repentance, and atonement in the context of restitution (*teshuva, haratah, vidui, selihah, mehilah, kapparah*)[62]

From Self and Other to Community

social justice and the restoration of balance in social and economic relations, especially of the economically weak and the landless poor (*tsedek, mishpat ger, ani ve'evyon*)[63]

benevolent care of the honor and security of colleagues (*kevod haverim, mamon havero*)[64]

opening the home to community (*hakhnasat orhim*)[65]

the prevention of suffering, both human and animal (*tsa'ar ba'al hayim*)[66]

developing skills of *constructive* interpersonal and social criticism that does not lead to losing face (*tohakha*)[67]

impartial courts (*mishpat*)[68]

social justice (*tsedakah*)

the limitation of material goods as a way to communal happiness (*ta'avah, ezehu ashir, marbeh nekhasim*)[69]

a proactive *mitsvah* of seeking conflicts that need resolution (*redifat shalom, bakshehu be'makom aher*)[70]

personal and collective transformation, training in the willingness to change (*darkhe teshuvah*)[71]

the construction and perpetuation of customs of civility that prevent conflict (*hilkhot derekh eretz*)[72]

the power of greeting the face of the other in the social construction of a pluralistic universe (*sever panim yafot*)[73]

Conflict Prevention and Fulfillment of the Self

I would like to highlight two of these values as particularly interesting and leave for a larger study their exhaustive analysis. The fact that one notices in religious literature, from East to West, from Buddhism to Judaism, a careful attention to nurturing the inner life and working on the moral life from an internal perspective suggests an important critique of current conflict resolution practice. Conflict resolution needs to address the most protean origins of anger, suffering, love, and benevolence and the skills of fair play and communication. Otherwise, deficiencies of character are bound to undermine the methods that are being taught.

An example of this involves the issue of self-love, a theme taken up by many moral sense theorists in the nineteenth century as a basis for a moral system.[74] In classical Judaism, the religious psyche is meant to be self-loving in order to be loving in an other-directed sense. The classical basis of this is the Golden Rule, which comes in its earliest form from the Hebrew Bible, Leviticus 19:18, "Do not take vengeance, or bear a grudge. And you must love your neighbor as yourself, I am the Eternal God." The verse is generally assumed to mean that you must love the Other as you love yourself, which cannot be done without self-love, a practice that for many people takes a lifetime to achieve. It is also one of the hardest things for members of a hated minority to truly feel.[75]

This principle, in and of itself, might form the basis of one of the most neglected areas of conflict prevention, namely, rehabilitation work with antisocial personalities, prisoners, and war criminals, whose self-loathing is plainly apparent in many cases. But we must leave this for a separate study.

Another key point in the self-oriented values is *imitatio dei*. For the religious human being, the fact that one can be like God if one is a peacemaker is a deeply empowering psychological phenomenon. It makes one's experience larger than life, a conquest of mortality, and a unification with eternity, as well as with others past and present who have walked the same path. To the degree to which this experience could be applied to the lonely life of the peacemaker who champions benevolent values, it could have a significant impact on the psychological sustainability of conflict resolution as a vocation. This is one of the most difficult problems of the field, and it is particularly true for those people who confront intractable, deadly conflicts that last for decades.

Conflict Prevention and the Interpersonal Relationship

As we move into values that govern interpersonal relationships, there are a few that are particularly noteworthy. The importance of interpersonal meeting, especially face-to-face encounter, cannot be overemphasized. The principal biblical phrase for love is *motseh hen*, to find grace in the eyes of the Other who is encountered. The talmudic rabbis mandated that one should greet everyone with a loving, or literally "beautiful," face (*sever panim yafot*). They prohibited the kind of language and actions that make the face turn white with embarrassment, making the latter into a sin akin to murder, literally the shedding of the blood of the face. Conversely, they made the honor of the Other into a supreme *mitsvah*, the opposite of humiliation of the face of the Other.[76] Honoring of the Other, in theory, can become an experience of intense religious fulfillment.

Face is a critical category in conflict analysis.[77] Saving face is a key generator of conflict in many situations, for a variety of reasons, including the inability to back down from the action/reaction spiral of aggressive behavior due to the fear of losing face. This is especially true of leaders, who fear the wrath of their own followers who might not be able to cope with the loss of face without turning on the leaders themselves. Collective humiliation is one of the main reasons for the self-perpetuating cycles of numerous international and interethnic conflicts.

Honor, as an intentional peacemaking act, is a rather underutilized strategy of conflict prevention and conflict resolution at the current time. The better diplomats understand this well, but it is rarely made into a conscious process applied generally to the interaction of large populations. Any Jewish methodology of conflict resolution would have to focus on honor and the necessary engagement with the face of the enemy, on both the elite level and on the grassroots level.

I have utilized this ethical principle myself in Jewish/Arab relationship building on many occasions, and it simultaneously fills my need for an indigenous method of engagement with the estranged Other, and it also is far more effective than dialogue in setting the stage for difficult processes of trust building and negotiation. Honor, I have experienced, is a deep surprise to the enemy Other: it puts the relationship on a new footing and makes both parties more open to a relationship in which they are deeply valued. It is no substitute for dialogue on power and resource distribution, which must inevitably come, but it does put these negotiations in a decidedly more prosocial context.

Sometimes the ethical gesture even causes a revolution in the negotiation process, uncovering the deeper reasons that the rational negotiation processes, with their seemingly obvious compromises, turn out to be so elusive. This may be why the details of negotiation appear so absurd to the outsider. Right beneath the surface of the participants' negotiating positions is deep-seated rage for various injuries, among them humiliation, and these deeper issues insert themselves as a cancer into the fine details of the negotiation. When this ethical effort is undertaken, it causes a shock and, once the shock is overcome, allows the rational processes to progress unencumbered by free-floating angers and fears, which wait to attach themselves to and disrupt this or that detail of an agreement.

I remember speaking to the PLO representative in Washington many months after Rabin's assassination and not long after the Likud party's accession to power. When he spoke of Rabin—no deep friend of the PLO, by the way—a wistful, sad look came over his face, as he peered downward into his memory. He said, simply, "They [Rabin and company] treated us with respect." To me, that was the heart of the matter. All the details of the agreements paled in comparison to this one issue. The moment of human relationship is either the glue that makes it impossible to disentangle a conflict or it is the glue that cements a common future in peace.

From Self and Other to Community

Extension of the interpersonal values to the communal and societal sphere is critical. The following communitarian rabbinic values should be highlighted: involvement in the suffering of others in the community; taking responsibility to heal that suffering; social justice, in the form of a reasonable redistribution of resources, as a religious task or *mitsvah*; constructive social criticism, which usually accompanies the implementation of social justice, perceived as a *mitsvah* as well; a strong sense of responsibility to connect the home and the public sphere by way of the openness of the home to the "street," that is, making one's home and family open to some degree as a refuge from the inevitable harshness of the public sphere; a detailed attention to customs of civility as socially constructive and as, therefore, religious duties; a commitment to voluntarily limit one's physical needs and to discourage excessive wealth in order to make a society in which everyone can live; and, finally, a *halakhic* commitment to make conflict resolution into a social *mitsvah*, a *mitsvah* of *bakesh shalom ve'radfehu*,[78] "seeking peace and pursuing it," literally a *mitsvah* to go and seek out other people's conflicts to solve. This last *mitsvah* is particularly potent as a vehicle through which to advocate conflict resolution training in even the most fundamentalist contexts.

Conflict Management, Resolution, and Reconciliation: The Ideal Jewish Peacemaker

Some of the most important constructs of conflict resolution in numerous rabbinic sources are expressed by midrashic metaphor. The rabbis make the biblical figure Aaron, the high priest and brother of Moses, into the paradigmatic peacemaker.[79] There are a variety of motivations for the rabbis to do this, some involving the inner logic of biblical hermeneutics and others involving a contemporaneous antiviolence critique of priestly Judaism embedded in the counterexample of Aaron.[80]

It is also significant that the rabbis do not speak about conflict resolution abstractly but do so by installing those values in a particular personality. This raises some important issues, for further study elsewhere, about whether the field of conflict resolution has focused too much on skills and not enough on the formation of character, namely, the ideal personality of the peacemaker. Religion focuses heavily on role modeling and on the development of moral character. More reflection is required on whether this is simply a different way to attain the same goal as conflict resolution training that focuses on objective skills, or whether there is something that these paradigms can learn from each other. Here is a classic instance of Aaron as a model of peacemaking:

> And thus when two men were in a conflict, Aaron would go and sit with one of them. He would say to him, "My son, look at your friend, [look at what he is saying], he is tearing at his heart and ripping his clothing. He says, 'Woe is me, how can I lift my eyes and see my friend. I am ashamed before him, for it is I who wronged him.'" And he [Aaron] would stay with him until he removed all of the jealous rage from his heart. And Aaron would then go to the other man, and say, "My son, look at your friend, [look at what he is saying], he is tearing at his heart and ripping his clothing. He says, 'Woe is me, how can I lift my eyes and see my friend. I am

ashamed before him, for it is I who wronged him.' " And he [Aaron] would stay with him until he removed all of the jealous rage from his heart.

And when the two would finally meet, they would hug and kiss each other.[81]

Another version has Aaron saying everything said above but with the added words to each adversary, "Now go, with your compassion, and ask forgiveness from him."[82]

Humility and Self-Abnegation as Conflict Resolution

The context of this story is a religious universe in which the high priest has the most elevated status in the community. Furthermore, his ritual purity is more important than anyone else's purity, because he regularly represents the community in the most sacrosanct realms of the Temple. For the rabbis to make this figure into a model of intervention into the crass problems of interpersonal conflict is extraordinary. Thus a key element here is the humility and even self-abnegation of the intermediary.

Humility embedded in the character of the peacemaker is seen in rabbinic thought as a major component of peacemaking:

There is no one who is more humble of spirit than the peacemaker. Think about it, how can a person pursue peace if he is not humble? How so? If a man curses him [when seeing him], he says back to him, "Hello [peace to you]." If a person fights with him, he is silent.[83] Furthermore, if two people are fighting, he swallows his own pride [depresses his spirit] and goes to appease one, and then to appease the other.[84]

Further proof of this rabbinic theme is found in an extraordinary story about Rabbi Meir (c.135–170 C.E.), one of the greatest scholars of Jewish history. He was delivering lectures, and a married woman came to hear him speak. One lecture went late, and by the time the woman got home, the candles in the house had already gone out. The husband was so incensed that he would not let her back into the house until she spit in the rabbi's face! There are many interesting issues to deconstruct in this story. There were men at the time that hated the rabbis as intellectual elitists, and in this story, this resentment was probably compounded with the classic male jealousy when women dare to know more than men do, especially when they learn from another man. Thus, there is an intellectual/popular conflict here to which the rabbi is a party in an important way. He and his class have caused some of this marital tension, though clearly the husband's reaction is seen by the rabbis to be unreasonable and sinful. Justice or righteousness appears to be on the side of the woman and the rabbi, but peace certainly is not. The great rabbi has just created a domestic war.

Rabbi Meir's response is to go to the neighborhood of the woman, who has been out of her own home for days and quite distraught. He asks her if she knows how to do incantations over an eye that is ailing. He pretends to have an eye ailment. When she cannot recall an incantation for eyes, he tells her not to worry, and, based on his authority as a rabbi, he assures her that if she just spits seven times in his eye he will be cured. And, so the story goes, this leads to reconciliation with her husband.

This is a tale, true or mythical, taken from a simple context on one level. However, as with all Jewish hermeneutic learning, it forms the basis of deeper thought about complex moral dilemmas. Rabbi Meir is a deeply involved third party, with great power due to his spiritual position, who deliberately lowers himself to make peace. This story, then, is meant to critique a certain elite, priests or rabbis, who may think that peacemaking is beneath them.

More important, the actions of the third party are a critical role model for the conflicting parties. They demonstrate that the mediator must be prepared to lose a little face in order to do something sublime, something spiritual, a *mitsvah*. In so doing, in both cases, Aaron and Rabbi Meir prepare the parties for a crucial and difficult stage of conflict resolution or, more specifically, reconciliation, which usually involves swallowing a little pride, losing a little face. It is usually impossible to arrive at a settlement and, even more deeply, to achieve some reconciliation unless there is some surrender of previously held positions. This involves a loss of pride. Furthermore, reconciliation generally involves a certain level of remorse, which again entails a psychological loss of pride or face. This, I suggest, is a crucial psychological juncture for conflict resolution that is often overlooked. We know it must happen, but we underestimate the psychological challenge to the parties. We therefore underestimate the inducements and cultural models that may be necessary in order for them to reach this stage of peacemaking. The rabbinic paradigm suggests that, in addition to making compromise and remorse into a high spiritual accomplishment, the third party may be essential in providing a model of this excruciating task. The more upright or honorable a figure the third party is in his own right, the more powerful the model will be for change in the parties. The more that this dignified individual is willing to humble himself, the more powerful the model of peacemaking. This means that the psychological strength and moral character of the peacemaker/mediator is an essential element in conflict resolution.[85]

The Rabbinic Mediator and the Contemporary Model

This is a profoundly different role than the typical Western concept of the neutral, emotionally distant mediator whose skills are central but whose character or personal values are irrelevant.[86] Rabbi Meir deeply involves himself but in complicated ways. He clearly acts on the moral belief that marriages should be saved wherever possible. He clearly sympathizes with the wife but is sufficiently respectful of the husband's domain to not challenge the latter's mean-spirited behavior. Rather, he will find a way to reconcile them in some other fashion; he will even satisfy the need of the husband for some kind of revenge against a rabbi. The latter is one of the more astonishing elements of Meir's strategy.

There is much to reflect on here and many problems with taking too literally these rabbinic methods, which after all come from a civilization of two thousand years ago. But it raises for me the question of whether our rational, or at least prosocial, methods of face-to-face engagement in dialogue, which are meant to produce a loving engagement between old enemies, really address the rage that is inside people in conflict. Perhaps by ignoring the need to satisfy this rage we are ignoring one reason why our methods fail so often. Do we need to consider methods that can help parties to a conflict release their anger more productively? Are we afraid of the process of playing at victory and revenge, which may help save some face even as parties agree to reconcile? If we reject this as barbaric, then why do we embrace the Olympics, which have always functioned in this way? I leave this as an open question for now.

We also must consider the evolving role of the mediator/peacemaker in contemporary culture. There is an ongoing debate about whether neutrality is a figment of the imagination and whether the mediator should be more or less directive as far as the values that he shares with the parties. There is also debate about whether a third party should strictly facilitate and mediate or whether he should guide the parties to a moral transformation of themselves and their relationships.[87] Clearly there are many actors today who are engaging in a variety of models of intervention in conflicts.

It seems clear from this rabbinic model that deep involvement that is somewhat directive combined with a deliberate expression of vulnerability on the part of the mediator is crucial. Although it should be noted that in the primary version of the Aaron story, Aaron never says to the parties what they should do. He listens and evokes, albeit in a rather intense fashion. In the minor version, he does direct the parties to have compassion and forgive but not coercively, and only after he has helped the adversaries through an emotional transformation that makes them ready to have compassion. Furthermore, it must be said that this is a method that is internal to a culture in which the priest or rabbi has great moral authority. Such daring behavior could backfire if this were naively applied to contemporary intercultural and international efforts, where there is no common respected authority or agreed-upon system of values and, most important of all, no substratum of cultural trust. It will take time and creativity to glean the best from this rabbinic model without blindly applying its methods to unprecedented situations.

Listening and the Suspension of Time Constraints as Conflict Resolution

Another key element in Aaron's method is empathic listening.[88] The details of the story indicate that he speaks but also that he stays with each person for an extensive period of time: "until he removed all of the jealous rage from his heart." This combination of listening, staying with someone who is enraged, and having an open-ended time frame seems to be crucial to conflict resolution in traditional cultures in general. One is struck, for example, by the difference in time that the elders in Somalia spent in retreat on resolving their country's conflicts in contrast to the official diplomatic time frames.[89] Traditional societies, in general, have a vastly different conception of time.

The ideal Jewish peacemaker's path, as seen from the Aaron and Rabbi Meir stories, involves the development of a pious or moral character worthy of respect, the conscious creation of role models of peacemaking, purposeful acts of humility that sometimes involve personal sacrifice or loss of face, active or empathic listening, a method of helping people work through destructive emotions, and, finally, the gift of abundant if not unlimited time.

Unilateral Gestures of Aid as Conflict Resolution

A critical and unique strategy of Jewish conflict resolution with biblical roots suggests an alternative approach to the typical focus on dialogue of conflict resolution theory. It does not call into question the importance of communication to conflict resolution, but it does suggest that there are forms of communication other than dialogue. The principal source for this is the biblical *mitsvah* to help your enemy when he is faltering with a burden.[90] There are a variety of rabbinic rationales for this as a conflict resolution device.[91] Essentially, it involves what I have termed "the positive uses of cognitive dissonance." The rabbis suggested that enemies have certain set understandings of each other, which play vital roles in their commitments to hate each other. Conflict resolution theory concurs with this.[92] The purpose of this mandated change in behavior is to create cognitive dissonance, to shatter the conception of the enemy. This leads, in turn, to a moral sense of regret inside the person who is the recipient of the unilateral gesture of physical aid from the enemy. He decides that he really misunderstood his enemy or that his enemy really is not an enemy: "He could not be if he did this for me." In other words, it is designed to shatter the false image of the enemy and to make more complex the real person behind the image.

It is also, I would argue, a perfect way to make justice and peace work together as a conflict resolution strategy, rather than be at odds with each other.[93] But it does require great skill and patience. A simplistic belief that such gestures would or should work after one time is foolish and will cause a backlash. Unilateral gestures of aiding those who are suffering require repeated and surprising innovations. The whole point of cognitive dissonance is that it is undoing something that is deeply entrenched and causing great anxiety, and it will only result in a new emotive homeostasis after a great deal of time and struggle.

To take an example, it would take repeated and extensive gestures of Israelis working in Arab and Palestinian villages to build good, permanent homes before it became clear that there were Israelis who understood the Palestinian demand for justice and were serious about their desire for reconciliation and coexistence. It would take repeated gestures of religious Israelis making donations to the upkeep of mosques before it would sink in that there were many religious Israelis who did not see all Muslims as enemies. It would take repeated

Palestinian offers of condolences, visits, and gestures of comfort toward Israeli victims of bombs for it to sink in that not all Arabs wanted those bombs to go off. It would take many Islamic gestures of hospitality to make religious Jews believe that they are finally welcome back to the Middle East as permanent residents. These bilateral gestures, over time, could create a far greater moderate middle than exists currently in Israel and the West Bank. This, in turn, would shift the population matrix undergirding the rejectionism of various political parties.

This method is the only real way that political or religious leaders ever make courageous gestures for peace, but they must not get too far ahead of the mood of their people if they want to stay in power or even stay alive. They need the people to change first. Peace processes that operate with the illusion that absolute power emerges from the top of society are inherently weak. The methods that I suggest here could gently move people toward the moderate middle, which would, in turn, provide the political space for leaders, religious or secular, to make the necessary compromises.

Reconciliation and Transformation:
The Processes of *Teshuva*

As we move into conflict transformation, namely, those interhuman strategies or actions that lead to a transformation of relationship from enemy to friend or from one who is hated to one who is loved, we reach a plateau that often conflict resolution never attains. As difficult as this is, and as infrequent as it may be, it is nevertheless a desirable goal with rich rewards. In certain cases, unless there is transformation rather than simple, legalistic settlements, the deep-seated problems will reassert themselves in some fashion, despite the conflict settlements. In Jewish terms, this is best expressed by the question and answer: "Who is the strongest of the warriors? . . . He who turns one who hates him into one who loves him."[94] What sort of strategies can truly make such a profound transformation of relationship?

There is a process for Jewish transformation, roughly coming under the rubric of *teshuva*, which can mean "repentance" but also means literally "returning" or "turning toward." The prophets say in the name of God at one point, "Turn toward me [*shuvu eylay*], and I will turn toward you [*ve'ashuva aleikhem*]" (Zech.1:3). There is a covenantal mutuality built into the concept of *teshuva*, and it applies to both the human/divine form of *teshuva* and to the interhuman process of *teshuva* for wrongs done and relationships broken.

There are a number of elements to the ideal form of *teshuva*. First and foremost, *teshuva* cannot replace restitution. In other words, restitution must precede or accompany the process of conflict transformation if there have been real damages that require restitution. Beyond financial or physical restitution, however, the restorative aspect of *teshuva* must take place. This is where justice and peace have to work together, or they will not work at all.

The restorative or conciliatory stage of *teshuva* ideally involves a confession of wrongdoing.[95] It is ideal if this confession, if it involves wrongs to other human beings, be done in public.[96] Joseph Karo (1488–1575) added that the public confession convinces the wronged party that the change in his adversary is authentic and thus he forgives him.[97] Other elements of the *teshuva* process involve, according to the talmudic rabbis, the giving of charity (always a standard of Jewish penance),[98] a change in one's name or identity (and, some argue, even a change in one's place), and, last but not least, crying.[99] Maimonides clarified that all of these practices and emotional states are elements of authentic change, and he even recommends that a person cognitively dissociate from his own prior self by saying, "I am another person, and I am not the person who did those things." Maimonides continues, "And he changes his deeds completely to the good and to the straight path, and he exiles himself from his current place. For exile atones for sin, because it makes him to be humble and low of spirit."[100]

Thus, there are four basic stages of *teshuva*. There is restitution. There is an expression of deep remorse (*harata*); a detailed confession, private or public, of what one has done (*vidui*); and there is finally a commitment to change in the future, to the point of even changing one's identity (*kabbalah le-haba*).

The *teshuva* model of reconciliation has some interesting implications when speculating on the application of this internal and interpersonal process to complex intergroup, interethnic, and international conflict. We must save a detailed analysis for a larger study, but a few points are in order. It is interesting to note that, almost unconsciously, collective groups, such as postwar Austrians, postwar Japanese, and Americans in response to Native American genocide or to non-American casualties of the war in Southeast Asia, when faced with great shame over actions of their group in the past, have a tendency to invent a new prosocial identity. They act as if the past did not exist, or as if the past were some strange aberration dominated by a few chosen, demonized individuals, scapegoats if you will. It is a reinvention of collective memory.[101] Social critics universally perceive this as an inauthentic cover-up, a lack of honest confrontation with the past, a hypocrisy that is bound to recreate the problem in the future.

Viewed from the perspective of the *teshuva* process just described, this is an unfair characterization. Groups tend naturally to do precisely what *teshuva* recommends for true transformation, namely, moving toward a new definition of collective self. The tendency is not wrong or hypocritical. Rather it is incomplete, which is a profoundly different sort of criticism, which leaves the door open for positive change. The full confession stage is missing, the deep remorse, and the critical apology is often missing or grossly inadequate. This is usually due to deep insecurity that the new self is really authentic and a fear that a full confrontation with the past could easily puncture the new identity.

In moving groups forward, as far as peacemaking is concerned, one should not criticize the reformulation of self-image. Rather, one should encourage the more complete process of transformation and reconciliation that the enemy party or the injured party requires. This involves remorse, confession that is full and complete, and a reinvention of identity, although the way to do this successfully requires greater study and experimentation. This same process will be essential some day as Jewish Israelis search for a new identity in the context of confrontations with the past, with 1948, and many other things. The research presented here is meant precisely to provide a framework for how to do this in a way that does not destroy a basis for an idealized collective self.

A legitimate critique of this approach might be that groups or individuals can only move forward into prosocial behavior when they take true ownership over their complete character, including the side of them that is antisocial, which some people unfortunately refer to as their "dark" side. I think that this is a subject worthy of greater study and research. My own impression from training people in conflicts from twenty countries is that a good concept of the collective self seems vital to prosocial behavior. We seem to need to feel that our group, our religious community, is inherently good, with occasional aberrations. While it is true that this kind of idealization often leads to ultranationalist or chauvinist views of the world, it is equally true that it produces extremely righteous and even heroic peacemaking behavior in many people. They see the goodness of their collective self, group, or religion as deeply embedded in the foundations of who they are and why they make peace with Others.

My own mentor, Rabbi Joseph Soloveitchik, often would make the distinction in his oral discourses between the Jewish people and the House of Israel (*knesset yisroel*). He would, rather subtly, engage his religious audiences with the latter term as the one referring to an idealized people who are in love with God and beloved by him, as a people with a great destiny who are capable of teaching God's Torah to the world by example and witness. But this was so subtle a message that I wonder how many of his listeners understood that as a teacher, philosopher, and political leader, he was quite committed to criticizing the behavior of individual Jews, even the behavior of the state of Israel, despite the risks that this entailed for him. This ability to both idealize and criticize, to love and rebuke his people, was due to his critical theological and psychological distinction of the ideal collective self and the real collective group. Many did not understand this subtle distinction, either because they chose to ignore it or because he did not say emphatically enough what he meant. In either case, despite the failings, there is an interesting model at work here for how groups can be encouraged to engage in self-criticism while still building an ideal collective self. But it should be noted that it is easy, too easy, to get a group to listen to its own idealization, while one constantly flirts with repudiation as one criticizes them. This is a delicate balancing act—love and rebuke—that is critical to building a community that is both honest about its shortcomings and peaceful.[102]

Apology and Forgiveness as a Culmination of the *Teshuva* Process

There has been much discussion about the value of forgiveness in conflict resolution. For the most part, it seems to me that this has been a heavily Christian discussion for Christian contexts, without the recognition of it as such. Forgiveness is a centerpiece of the metaphysical reality of Christianity. Why Christian culture would see forgiveness as central to conflict resolution is perfectly understandable. On the other hand, this is not a universal position even among Christian thinkers. Furthermore, the meaning and uses of forgiveness in the world's cultures are complex affairs that only occasionally resemble the Christian discussion.

From my research, it would seem that forgiveness can only play a crucial role in conflict resolution when it is made less simplistic and when it is placed in the context of individual cultures. It does occur in many cultures and can play a vital role in some circumstances. But what it means and how it is acted upon varies greatly. It also can and does interact in complicated ways with competing moral and spiritual responses, such as commitments to truth, justice, apology, repentance, and penance, among others. Clearly, it plays a role in Jewish forms of reconciliation but only when embedded in the *teshuva* process, which is either unilateral or bilateral depending on what injuries have been sustained by conflict.

As far as the application of this approach to forgiveness and apology, I wonder how powerful a *teshuva* apology process could be on a much larger scale, involving massive injury, murder, or genocide. Surely, it would be a deeper process than simple payment for losses incurred, restitution, or the indictment of selected representatives of the war criminals. The latter is all the international community has been able to orchestrate when it comes to genocide until now, and all that this really even attempts to satisfy are the demands of justice, and it usually fails at that also. Indeed it has to. Who could construct an appropriate restitution for the loss of one's family, one's world? It seems to me that victim communities, and their tormentors, need to do much more in order to transform the past and present into a redemptive future.[103]

The sites of war, mass graves, and past horrors are critical here. They are places that do not just deserve memorials. They should be places in which confessions, apologies, and restitutions are made on an ongoing basis, not in order to inject a sense of self-loathing into former aggressors. On the contrary, it is to free everyone to develop a new sense of self, to mourn the past together with the victims, regularly, in order to foster a new future. I had a hand in creating one such ceremony in Switzerland, and it was a good beginning, although only a beginning. I have also been told by various African peacemakers, among them Hugo van der Merwe and Hizkias Assefa, that such symbols and ceremonies are numerous in African reconciliation. They have yet to be cataloged and analyzed and certainly await discovery by the international community of peacemakers and diplomats. Greater attention to this may help hasten the end of numerous intractable conflicts in Africa.

Returning to the Jewish community, I was struck recently by a letter in a Jewish newspaper. The author, a religious friend of mine, had worked with one of the investigative commissions on the Swiss banks and had done a great deal of research on the Nazi gold issue. The Jewish community was particularly incensed by anyone who aided the Nazis to sell the gold that they had stolen from the victims. Pondering the issue after the conclusion of his research, my friend decided to write a letter calling on the Swiss government to take all the gold that it got from the Nazis and bury it. Yes, bury it.[104]

From a pragmatic and rational point of view, it was a rather bizarre suggestion, but it captured my imagination as a clue to hidden things. Over time, I began to make sense of it psychologically and spiritually from two vantage points. First, the obligation to personally see to the burial of loved ones is central to Jewish mourning, as it is to many indigenous peoples. Some of the gold came from the teeth of the millions of dead Jews and should have been buried as parts of them. It is that gold that, I am convinced without a doubt, weighs most heavily on the imagination and the religious conscience of survivors, even though it is kept quiet, as all dark nightmares are. Second, my friend was expressing an intuitive desire, not for the money but for penance, penance from an entire civilization, which had reduced the value of these precious men, women, and children to the gold in their mouths. What better way to do penance than to bury the very thing that was made more valuable than those human beings, who can never be replaced? What better statement that what we are engaged in is not just pragmatic, utilitarian restitution, but rather that we are engaged in an authentic process of *teshuva*? This, I believe, was his instinctive, cultural/religious motivation in making this suggestion. This is the kind of thinking and feeling that should be the basis of deeper discussions among enemy groups, particularly groups that have suffered massive injury. And it needs to take place with the involvement of as many people as possible, not just the elites, who may, for one reason or another, focus too narrowly on economic restitution, rather than on other forms of restitution and restoration. I have found in my trainings that genius in healing is often found in the variety and diversity of the people included, who are empowered to articulate their insights.

Gender Identity and Conflict Resolution

One subtle but critical feature of Jewish conflict transformation and reconciliation involves the issue of gender and conflict. It is self-evident that, in much of human civilization, men are associated with the aggressive roles of hunter/gatherer and warrior and identified with the cold calculus of war and rational advantage. Women are commonly associated with peaceful characteristics, including a constitutional abhorrence of violence, an embrace of emotional empathy, and a strong tendency to interact with others in a deeper, more intuitive fashion.

There are numerous instances in which rabbinic Judaism specifically couched Jewish maleness in allegedly female form.[105] "Who is a warrior [gibbor]? He who conquers his evil side" is one such example. Another example, and the most important for our topic, was mentioned earlier: "Who is the strongest of the warriors? . . . He who turns one who hates him into one who loves him."[106] This was a clearly subversive effort to undermine the biblical presentation of *gibbor* in terms of physical strength.[107]

I mention this here because it seems to me that there are a series of characteristics that are critical to successful conflict resolution that have been traditionally associated with the feminine in the West. These include the passive quality of listening rather than holding forth, the ability to empathize with all sides, the capacity to help people through their pain, the ability to nurture those who are sick and angry, the willingness to help people out of violence by showing them love, and many more characteristics that are typical of the truly heroic peacemakers of our century. It strikes me as dangerous if these characteristics continue to be seen as strictly female. It certainly is helpful in the evocation of these characteristics from women. But if we persist as a global culture in identifying these characteristics as exclusively female, then we certainly shall lose the majority of men as peacemakers. They are after all the principals of war and violence, and they ask themselves regularly, consciously or unconsciously, "Am I a true man? Do I have courage? Am I a heroic man in some way?" Many peacemaking men that I know, ask themselves this constantly, due to the predominant image of the male, and this often causes them to abandon their own best instincts and engage in angry, aggressive behavior. If being a peacemaker cannot be an answer to the question "Am I a heroic man?" then we lose the very people who need the identity of peacemaker to be internalized. Here I think that traditional religions have some interesting things to say, and I certainly believe that rabbinic Judaism may be teaching an important point about how we generate both men and women who see their identity fulfilled through peacemaking.

Vision, Hope, and Celebration as Conflict Resolution

One of the attractive elements in violent interpretations of religion is actually the hope generated by various myths of what the end of time will bring. Fear of and uncertainty about the future is one of the most anxiety-inducing elements of human life, especially where there is violent conflict. Often, apocalyptic views of the end of history involve one's enemies or the "enemies of God"—which often are identical—being punished. One's own group of the righteous are vindicated, saved, and experience unparalleled joy and great comfort for the arduous and tragic path that has led up to this final denouement of history.

A truly viable form of conflict resolution must address this deep human need for future vision, for a hoped-for vindication, for comfort that is provided by the future. Indeed, there must be celebration and anticipation that is a part of the life of those committed to peace. Peacemaking strategies do not necessarily have to include the idea of apocalypse in the future. But it seems clear that vision and unleashing a person or group's longing for vision is a powerful and empowering undertaking. Vision is the antidote to the obsession with the past. It cannot replace the mourning that we have described earlier, nor should it try. But it can complement it in important ways.

There has not been sufficient attention paid to the power of vision in secular peacemaking, although there are secular visions of the future that are appealing to some and appalling to others. For example, Shimon Peres's vision of a future Middle East that is economically prosperous, perfectly integrated, and democratic sounds wonderful. But many religious people in the Middle East, both Jewish and Arab, hear in his words a vision of a future that eliminates their identities, a vision of materialism where the spiritual and moral life are irrelevant. Indeed, it is on that score that Peres's vision is ridiculed the most in the Orthodox part of Israel, although the Zionist vision has always been of the Jewish people slowly shedding its religious, exilic identity and "normalizing," becoming like other nations. It is vital, then, that communities in conflict be able to envision a future in which both may live, and it is vital that they celebrate that future together.

Celebration is another basic religious impulse that has often been missing from secular constructs of peacemaking. Celebration is a critical human need, and it is therefore a basic religious category of law and ritual. This too must enter into the construction of peacemaking in order to appeal to the broadest spectrum of people.

A friend of mine, quite secular and very astute psychologically, once got lost on his way to a peace demonstration in Jerusalem. He stumbled instead into another demonstration. He was astonished by the fact that at one there was dancing, singing, and passion, while at the other, the peace demonstration, there were speeches, and only more speeches, the telltale signs of a liberal, intellectual elite cut off from the human needs of average people. The demonstration that he stumbled into was a Meir Kahane demonstration. This must change if peacemaking is to go to the heart of the average person and her needs. Religious contributions to peacemaking can readily help this, if the alliance of religious and secular peacemakers is done well.

Limitations of Religious Conflict Resolution

There is one major caveat to the construction of conflict resolution or the ethics of conflict prevention out of traditional religion. In most traditional worlds that I have studied, these conflict prevention values are to be extended to fellow believers in good standing only, or are to be extended only as a means of making people convert or change from who they are. That leaves out of one's ethical construct most of the population of the world, who do not plan on changing. I argue that this same limitation applies to the other monotheistic universalist traditions, such as Christianity and Islam. Despite the fact that many Christians, for example, quite laudably see and have seen in the past their ethical values extending to everyone, that is not how things have played out in many cases. Historically, if you were not saved through Christ, then you could easily be treated as different or inferior, in the best of circumstances, and in many tragic circumstances, dehumanized altogether.

This is the great danger that all religious traditions must face. In Judaism, there are ways in theory that this can be overcome, and in practice it is overcome in some circumstances. This is something that can be worked on *if and only if* there is greater trust that develops between secular and religious people committed to conflict resolution. Then religious adherents can develop the skills necessary to encourage this hermeneutic growth within Jewish tradition. Indeed, we have seen steady progress on this, with regard to attitudes toward gentiles and women in Judaism, *when and only when* there is a respectful but powerful interaction between secular, democratic values and a serious investigation of Jewish tradition.

This can and will lead to envisioned constructs of civil society in which cultural and religious values can play a positive role but do not in any way threaten the rights and independence of other religious groups or secular individuals and groups. This was part of the dialogue that was being engaged in 1997 between the Israeli Orthodox party Me'imad and members of the political party the Third Way, for example. Other efforts should continue and multiply but they are hampered by the deepening hatred among Orthodox, non-Orthodox, and secular Jews in Israel and a desperation in all groups to protect their interests, needs, and place in the future of the country. No one group feels secure about its future or its safety in the long run.

Essentially, after all of the internal work on a religious tradition and its possible relationship to conflict resolution is done, the most important question facing the interaction of religion and conflict resolution theory is the multicultural, multireligious, and secular nature of most contemporary social settings. Religious traditions, such as Judaism, tend to operate in their theological and moral constructs as if no other system exists. This means that, as we think about these traditions in pragmatic terms, it must be remembered that we study religious peacemaking not in order to suggest an imposition of those traditions on society. Rather, we do this in order to creatively interact with those who *are* religious, to be prepared to creatively integrate prosocial religious traditions with secular, democratic constructs or with constructs from other religions and cultures. Further, we do this in order for the secular community to have the courage and humility to learn from the religious community as well.

What I mean by learning is that the first stage of elicitive work with other communities,[108] with engaging religious people who are in conflict, is a thorough grounding in what currently exists in their worldview. Second, we should explore what could *potentially* exist in that community from a theological and moral point of view. This is a process that involves careful preparation and a strong knowledge base for the intervener. But it also entails extraordinary openness to the ways in which the communities themselves can evoke from their own traditions the skills necessary to make peace.

Any deep conflict resolution to prevent a civil war in Israel between religious and secular is going to have to involve a relationship-building process with the ultra-Orthodox, *haredi* community. This group is deeply separatist and in such a different reality than most Israelis that it will take great skill and, I believe, an elicitive method, to span the gap between them and many leading Israeli intellectuals and leaders, who are often vehemently antireligious.

An authentic conflict resolution process would begin with extensive interviews, inquiries into what the highest values are of all the communities, the deepest concerns, and the most pressing problems, the hopes and visions for the future, and the attitudes toward outsiders. When I engage *haredi* leaders, this is how I begin. I then ask them their insights as religious leaders on current events and on the future, a critical avenue into conflict resolution discussion. In the process of this kind of relationship building, based on my knowledge of their traditions, I begin to ask probing questions about their enemies, about their interpretation of the rabbinic values, stories, and laws that may be relevant to a constructive approach to their adversaries. This is an approach that emphasizes humble learning and probing, not lecturing. Nevertheless, the probing must be intelligent and informed. In Jewish religious life, trust is built on an extraordinary substratum of common knowledge and cultural reference points, which an intervener ideally should have. These reference points help the outsider enter into a private world with respect and a demonstrated commitment not to harm or injure, authentically seeking a peace that does not annihilate his interlocutors or their world. Above all, no matter how intellectual the conversation, I always probe most deeply about the injuries of the past, about the Holocaust, which looms over everything, in their family histories. Nothing intellectual is as important as this.

Consequently, the purpose of writing this chapter is not to articulate an exact blueprint of what must happen in Jewish life in terms of peacemaking. Secular and non-Orthodox people will not simply submit to a form of conflict resolution because it is rooted in Jewish law or texts. On the contrary, in a place like Israel, the secular/religious antagonism is so deep that it could produce the opposite effect. What I argue here is that digging deeply into old cultural constructs, learning them well, and then translating them into actions and peace processes that emanate from these old constructs often resonates with even the most secular Jew or Israeli. Despite themselves perhaps, they still have many Jewish cultural instincts about what is fair and unfair, what is effective and realistic, what speaks to the core of their beliefs and what does not. It is here that building a theory of peacemaking inspired by a religious tradition can have great effect, as long as it is operationalized with great subtlety and respect for all parties to the conflict.

As far as the Orthodox are concerned, it is entirely likely that many, if not most, will wince at many of the arguments made here. The purpose, then, is not to "sell" a blueprint for Jewish peacemaking. The purpose is to engage in intellectual constructs that will push the theological envelope, as it were, to suggest a model and stimulate many responses, with the full expectation that Orthodox representatives, as well as secular Israelis, will reject some of the model and rework other parts. Some will reject it altogether. And some will rise to the challenge and create their own model that really does provide for coexistence with non-Orthodox Jews, gentiles, Arabs, and Palestinians. It is the same with stimulating, by example, secular Israelis to come up with new models of coexistence with other Jews, who do not share their secularism, by presenting a paradigm of deep Jewish cultural commitments to peacemaking.

In conclusion, the development of a Jewish philosophy of conflict resolution awaits a larger study. In some ways, this will be tied to the further development of conflict resolution theory, particularly as the latter matures and becomes ready to encompass and account for the vast range of human cultural and religious experiences.

IV

Conclusion

NINE

Systematic Recommendations for Intervention in Contemporary Conflicts

The following conclusions can be drawn from our study:

1. Religion has a dual legacy in human history regarding peace and violence. Both its contribution to violence and its contribution to prosocial values and peacemaking need to be studied by scholars both inside and outside the individual faiths with an eye to sharing this information as widely as possible. This can then form the basis of theologies of peacemaking and, more pragmatically, of creative strategies of conflict prevention and conflict resolution.

2. Conflict resolution theory regarding religious actors must examine their complex ways of making decisions about conflict and peace, including the mixed motivations typical of many actors in conflict, which are further complicated by religious values and worldviews.

3. Universal commitments, such as human rights, may play a crucial role in achieving international consensus on basic civic values, even among many religious liberals around the world. But this may not be a sufficient common denominator for people who are defining their religiosity in opposition to universal, secular values. Good conflict resolution strategy requires a method of reaching out to even the most intractable and parochial religious adherents by engaging in a serious examination of their values and culture.

4. A close examination of that culture can both prognosticate religious violence and yield prosocial intracommunal values that could be vital for conflict resolution. The culture also must be studied with an eye to extending those values intercommunally or outside the faith. We must examine what the challenges are of doing this and who could authoritatively speak in favor of this process and have a broad-based appeal.

5. Leadership in the religious world is both a bane and a boon in terms of violence. This needs to be studied in conjunction with the analysis of leadership that is emerging from the field of political psychology. If leaders are particularly constrained by the extra burden of history that is embedded in and sanctified by religion, and if they are always threatened by the accusation of heresy, we must discover what can be done to allow leaders to subtly move a situation in a more

tolerant or peaceful direction. We need to examine what are the minimal steps within each religious hierarchy that can be recommended or elicited that will give permission to lower-level actors to proceed more boldly along a path of engagement with enemies. Subtle changes at the helm of a hierarchy can create powerful ripple effects at the bottom, releasing the creative energies of many courageous actors who, while committed to the organized expression of their religion, are waiting impatiently for permission to act.

6. There are numerous religious values among global religions, many yet to be analyzed, that may provide indispensable tools in religious settings to engage in conflict prevention, conflict management, compromise, negotiation, and reconciliation. They should be studied, cataloged, and made available to all actors in first-and second-track diplomacy. They will be subject to hermeneutical debate inside traditional communities, but their usefulness as an adjunct aid in crises involving religious actors seems clear. At least as important, there may be strategies of peacemaking inspired by religious ethics and ways of interaction that can be applied beyond the religious world and that will aid us in addressing a wider variety of intractable conflicts. There is currently such an expanding number of cultural and ethnic conflicts, whose characters closely resemble religious conflicts, that religious methods of peacemaking, adjusted to different cultures, may have a much broader impact if applied beyond the confines of strictly religious conflicts.

7. The history of interfaith and multifaith interactions should be studied from the perspective of conflict resolution theory. There may be successful stages of interfaith interaction that may be replicable and generalizable to a wide range of global conflicts involving religion. There may also be a long history of interfaith blunders that may be avoidable with the help of a critique from conflict resolution theory.

8. The analysis of a conflict involving religion should never impose from above a set of religious values. Solutions need to emerge from an analysis of the unique nature of every situation combined with a hermeneutical negotiation of the religious traditions affected by the conflict. This means that first-and second-track diplomats must utilize their studies of religious peacemaking not in order to impose some version of it reformulated by the interveners. Rather, the aim is to prepare oneself to seize upon places of confluence between conflict resolution and religious values and to be ready, by virtue of one's knowledge base, to collaboratively work with indigenous members of the conflicting groups. It is in this collaboration and sharing of skills and knowledge that authentic and effective methods of peacemaking could be discovered and tailored carefully to the circumstances.

9. Traditional jurisprudence in many cultures may provide ways to interpret and reinterpret traditions in order to move religious legal institutions toward civil virtues, such as human rights or democracy, as well as toward conflict resolution.

10. The problem of the scope of religious ethical concern, often limited to only the faithful who are in good standing, needs to be confronted. A full analysis of how each tradition has negotiated the reality of Others and outgroups is critical.

There is great potential to utilize ethical religious systems whose values contribute more than a mere buttress for conflict resolution practice. The latter may be able to deepen current conflict resolution practice as we currently define it by utilizing religious ethical practices, but the far greater problem is the Othering process of many religious ethical systems, which undo their good influence by eliminating from the moral agents' purview the very groups that need most to be included in the ethical system.[1]

11. There are some crucial dangers about religion in terms of conflict resolution strategy. Naiveté about religion can lead to disaster. Millions of people have suffered in history and often been killed due to someone's interpretation of religion that combined in complex ways with political and military force. Just because secular society has reached certain impasses in the negotiation of conflict does not mean that solutions to societal problems should be automatically laid at religion's doorstep. One certainly should not enter into a complex situation blindly siding with religious institutions without investigation of their work. There is no reason at this juncture of history to reinvest organized religion with the kind of power that led to so much religious warfare in the past. Rather, I suggest here an artful design of cooperation, with secular institutions and states drawing upon the best traditions of religion in the search for peace without this cooperation becoming a coercive force in the lives of citizens. The strategy is not to invest religious people with power over others but rather to make them feel more a part of a broad culture of peacemaking that respects and shares their values wherever possible. Thus they come to have a stake in peacemaking in particular and generally in the perpetuation of civil society.

Many religious ethical values both within and between cultures are bound to contradict each other, most notably the often-conflicting values of peace and justice. There are also other values, such as the appropriate use of shaming, which may be used to justify publicly protesting unjust actions, "speaking truth to power," as the Mennonites are fond of saying. The latter is a favorite method of human rights advocates, but it is to be contrasted with the value of honoring all human beings or unconditionally displaying love to all human beings, even those you have judged to be oppressors.[2] Conflict resolution strategists must be prepared for this and must design strategies accordingly. This is part of a larger problem with conflict resolution practice, which rarely acknowledges the ethical complexity of and dilemmas posed by many conflict situations. The task in religious cultures would be to openly acknowledge the countervailing values relevant to the situation and then work with the community or group toward an intervention strategy that could best accommodate the countervailing values. For example, justice may demand protest against a cruel course of action taken by some senior members of a community, whereas honor demands the display of respect for these same people. Conflict resolution practice could accommodate both by finding ways to engage in a relationship-building process that does not ignore the injustice but at least initially would avoid a public, dishonorable confrontation. This would accomplish two things: it would give the indigenous values unconditional worth, as religion does. But it would also positively affect outcome because it would avoid strategies of dishonoring, which only make the conflict more destructive. It could also help the pursuit of justice avoid becoming a "religious football," with one side considering it religiously proper and the other side calling it a heretical violation of other values. A carefully integrated conflict resolution process could proceed apace without religion being used by either side as a weapon against the other. Of course, there will always be rejectionists on both sides who do use religion as a weapon, no matter what intervention is used. However, a conflict resolution process that has incorporated religious sensibilities and negotiated with both sides is far more likely to attract a broad level of cooperation; which is critical to violence prevention or reduction and is also a key step toward a negotiated settlement.

There is great danger in the future from religious institutions that have difficulty recognizing the limits of proselytism or who have a problem theologically with Others, who will not eventually convert. The only solution to this difficulty is for each religion, especially the monotheisms, to evolve a new notion of mission, witness, and related concepts and practices.[3] This need not affect the ultimate aspirations of the religious group or its vision of some ideal future or of heaven. Including someone in one's theology of otherworldly salvation is helpful but not as essential as pragmatic rules of engagement for this world becoming sacrosanct. This does mean a major adjustment of missionizing religions' global practices in a world that is first, very crowded and, second, resentful of those who do not respect other groups' beliefs or practices. The latter, by the way, includes that large tribe of people today who feel that they have every right and responsibility as enlightened citizens to focus their belief on the human being and on science and not on a deity, namely, the secular community. Within religions, particularly Christianity, where the proselytizing drive is perhaps the strongest and most financially supported, this caveat needs to apply also to intra-Christian relations, which are already courting disaster in places like Russia. History is crucial to conflict analysis, and we must recall how many people have suffered or died in the past due to Catholic/Orthodox, Protestant/Catholic, and liberal/conservative Christian fighting. In fact, if we delve into the origins of anti-Judaism, it really began as an intracommunal fight among the first Jews exposed to Jesus. The tragic denouement of that anti-Judaism in European history is self-evident. If we dig more deeply, we find this fighting present in the history of most religions. It is critical, therefore, to evolve a theological and moral position that offers the believer an opportunity to express those religious values that are expansive or missionary, such as "bearing witness," in a way that does not put the future of the global community in peril. Respect must also be given to indigenous groups and minority religions whose members have seared into their collective memories the injury of assault on their cultural and religious integrity by missionizing over the centuries. For them to continue to experience this assault is not only cruel but also an invitation to destructive conflict.

12. The most hopeful and heroic stories of interreligious peacemaking emerge from those rare individuals who possess a combination of deeply authentic expressions of their own religiosity together with an unconditional respect for or

love of nonbelievers as fellow human beings. This is a relatively rare combination inside the religious personality, but it bears serious analysis in terms of how this psychological and ideological disposition could be fostered among religious adherents around the world. We must learn the cognitive and developmental roots of such a position and what implications this has for religious childrearing and education. The kind of moral development that leads a Gandhi to gladly respect other people's faiths is crucial to our long-term strategies of conflict prevention. As a species, we humans are learning more about development; and we now know that emotions are critical to the development of our intelligence.[4] Thus, it may very well be that the key to the future is not just theological sophistication, though that is important, but emotional training,[5] so that we feel safe enough in our own faith positions that we are not threatened by Others.[6] Furthermore, there seems to be some basic cognitive ability of special individuals to see themselves as, say, Palestinians, but also Arabs, but also Muslims, but also human beings, but also God's children, but also living creatures on a planet of billions of creatures, and so on. And this knowledge at some deep emotional level precludes them from dehumanizing anyone or devaluing any living thing. This capacity to see ourselves in multiple identities seems to require a degree of emotional strength and maturity that we must study further, for it may be the basis for the future inculcation of belief structures that do not create a world of conflict. This harks back to the theme in chapter 1: the need to integrate and merge versus the need to be unique. It seems that these individuals have developed the capacity to live comfortably within their own unique boundaries but also to reach out far beyond their own boundaries. They do not just reach to the closest position to their own but rather, solidly rooted in their own spiritual identities, they can travel anywhere with an open, benign, even loving disposition, because they know exactly where they ultimately belong. They no longer need to consume the universe in order to find the joy of religious fulfillment. Metaphorically, they have discovered, or made, their own Eden.

Recommendations

My recommendations are divided into three distinct categories: the religious world, the world of policy formation, both governmental and nongovernmental, and regional work.

The Religious World

Here I want to reiterate recommendations that I made in chapter 7 and add to them. Religious communities[7] need to:

1. have a firm spiritual foundation for engaging in peacemaking with all human beings, regardless of race, religion, or culture. The character and intensity of that engagement with peacemaking, however, can legitimately vary based on who the target of that engagement may be. In other words, the Serbian Orthodox

church may indeed educate its believers to have some special level of love and commitment to reconciliation with other members of the church without, however, this leading necessarily to conflict with outsiders. Special love and the desire of all of us to be specially treated may be, as I have stated earlier, a basic human need that we dare not deny in the name of a liberal ideal. On the other hand, what *is* essential is that the Serbian Orthodox church, for example, develop and inculcate prosocial methods of engagement with nonmembers, even with enemies, that is firmly rooted in Orthodox faith. The good treatment of the outsider need not be identical to the treatment of the insider, but it needs to have a clearly articulated spiritual foundation with accompanying skills of engagement. Thus I am suggesting, responding to Volkan, that we do need to have insiders and outsiders in our lives as human beings. We do need to distinguish who we are and who we are not, what we believe and what we reject. But the outsiders to ourselves only become internalized as enemies to be abused if we are acculturated that way. We can satisfy the need for allies and insiders without it necessarily leading to an identification of an enemy that must be abused. This requires a careful coordination of basic prosocial childrearing that is warm and affectionate[8] from both mothers and fathers,[9] combined with theological belief constructs that buttress a prosocial view of outsiders. This has been one of the central concerns of this volume, namely, the integration of values internally generated by and for the community with values directed toward outsiders. Marc Ross cataloged the attitudes of more than 186 linguistically distinct groups in the world toward violence and found that 60.9 percent valued violence against those outside their society, while *none* valued violence against members of a local community. This is remarkable and demonstrates that the central task involves some qualified extension of the concept of community, in which there are close, small communities but also larger communities, such as the human community, of which one is a part. There will always be preferential treatment for those one knows and cares for, but this need not take the form of an extreme dualism. Theology and religious practice must come to embrace a way of relating to the world that involves care for immediate religious community but does not require hatred of Others, that embraces both greater and lesser forms of community.[10]

2. have a method of engaging in conflict resolution that does not impose its own theological assumptions on Others or that is at least prepared to adjust its methods as cultural and religious differences with outsiders become apparent.

3. develop an articulated set of ethical foundations and institutional support structures for peacemaking that make the work sustainable over long periods of time and through trying circumstances and instill in the peacemaker a series of values that will have her treat those in conflict as ends in themselves, as fellow human beings to be engaged in authentic relationship, not as pawns in some institutional desire for enlargement or empowerment.

4. generate a community that is capable of and prepared to support peacemakers institutionally and interpersonally.

5. develop a reasonable way to deal with the inevitable and ongoing tension of peacemaking, pursuit of justice, and other competing ethical values that are critical to the construction of a civil society, such as civil rights.

6. develop the skills necessary to truly listen to another religious reality and culture, to not be threatened by it, and to discover the spiritual resources to make peace with those who are in a different theological universe.

7. learn how to integrate the development of a peacemaking method and philosophy with the most authentic elements of their own spiritual tradition and to combine this in a creative way with the best secular methods of understanding and dealing with human conflict. This is a critical element because it seems that much of the attractiveness of rejectionist and militarist religion is its look and feel of authenticity, its easy fulfillment of identity needs at a deep level, especially by use of the enemy Other to define one's uniqueness. One of the weaknesses of the liberal expressions of many contemporary religions, which have been tolerant, is their lack of fulfillment of these same needs. Liberal religion has tended to be a party to the global materialist trend of the homogenization of peoples and cultures. Religious militancy is a direct response to this assault on uniqueness and the meaning that groups discover in their special forms of spirituality. Thus, the discovery of a way to fulfill deep identity needs and simultaneously generate and support a peacemaking orientation are the fundamental challenges of non-militant religion.

8. develop myths and stories, or recover them from tradition, that can replace darker myths of identity that are dependent on the existence of a demonic enemy who defines the contours of the religious world and whose elimination is an ultimate goal. One can discover dark mythological constructs of the world in most religious/cultural expressions. I was struck by how central Serbian defeats in history are to Serbian Orthodox constructs of reality.[11] It reminded me of how critical to the yearly life cycle of Judaism,[12] Christianity,[13] and Islam[14] are events that are catastrophic. Of course, they are always interpreted as leading in the end to some larger redemptive goal, but the importance of remembered injury is remarkable. Working with tragic religious symbols, which are often used in violent times to hate or destroy, is a daunting task but not as difficult as it might seem to the outsider. For example, let us take the Christian focus on the devil. If the devil or Satan is an indelible part of one's mythology, it is still open to interpretation who the devil is or how he expresses himself. Gandhi once dismissively said, "The only real devils are those running around inside our heads and hearts." In one subtle move, Gandhi, along with numerous rabbis and theologians in history who have said similar things, took a hypostasized devil, which could easily be confused with real people, and made it into an internal psychological struggle. This has obvious conflict prevention benefits. As another example, I will pose a question. Is the Exodus story a prototypical story of the inevitable conflict between the "pagan" gods of Africa and the chosen people, with an unstated need to utterly destroy pagan civilization an obvious lesson? Or is it the story of how God comes to the aid of the defenseless? Is the violence perpetrated exclusively by God's hand in order to teach human beings that only God

should punish with violence, while human beings should never take it upon themselves to punish a whole civilization, no matter how corrupt, in other words, a pacifist tale par excellence? Or is it a lesson to the "saved" as to how to go about utterly destroying, psychologically and physically, God's (your) enemies? All these interpretations and many more have appeared in monotheistic literature, with diametrically opposite historical consequences in terms of the treatment of indigenous peoples by monotheists. There are numerous shades of the hermeneutic picture here, and this is only one story! Thus, there is ample opportunity for hermeneutic development of either a violent theology or a peaceful theology and ethics.

9. train clerics at all levels in the methods of mediation and conflict resolution, encouraging them to develop their own religious hermeneutical versions of these skills.

10. discover a path to deep spiritual fulfillment that is not dependent on the religious choices of other human beings. In other words, develop ways of fulfillment that do not require the coercion of all Others to accept one's religion or particular interpretations. This will require a subtle negotiation between that which one can and should fight for in the public sphere as a good religious person and that which is beyond the pale, which enters into a level of coercion and violence to Others that flies in the face of the other values and priorities of one's tradition. For example, one must expect that religious people have the right and even responsibility to express their views about what a good education is or what wars are legitimate or not or about the death penalty. These are basic issues of life that affect everyone. But one can also expect that these arguments will include a range of other religious values that govern the way in which one relates to Others who disagree, such as honor, compassion, love, and forgiveness. All of this, however, is very different from insisting that only Buddhist prayers be said in a public setting, such as, for example, in the Sri Lankan parliament; this would be an aggressive act, in this case, one that directly assaults the place of Tamils in Sri Lankan society. It is vital to instill a sense of deep satisfaction with one's inner life that is not dependent on proselytism. Of course, this last point requires that religions start to tone down their institutional aspirations for supremacy over other faiths by virtue of numerical superiority. It will require some degree of soul searching in order to distinguish between authentic religious impulses of ministry, service, teaching, and righting the wrongs of society versus the darker impulse of organized religion to dominate by winning souls. It will require some deep psychological analysis from each community, asking themselves the simple but profound question: How many members is enough in order to make us feel comfortable that our faith and beliefs have a secure place in the future of humanity? Put bluntly, I am calling for a theological end to the war for supremacy among ever-expanding religions, a war that has lasted for millennia and that still goes on, though presently nonviolently. I am calling for a new psychological foundation for institutional fulfillment of obligations and dreams, one that focuses on the internal quality of a community's life and values, not its corporate victory over others.

The Policy World

The policy world of governmental and nongovernmental agencies is complicated by competing concerns, many of which are quite laudable. I leave aside the motive of global intervention that involves national interest and will address it later. The policy world is deeply concerned with a range of vital human needs, and peace is only one of them. Furthermore, it is a rather simplistic notion of peace that does not include concern for human rights and social justice or a sustainable environment, as I have noted earlier. The subtle weaving of peace, justice, and concern for the environment, or all of sentient life, is something that can be seen in many if not most religious traditions, though differences of emphasis and priority abound.

None of the strategies listed below in any way call into question a principled commitment to generating globally a greater commitment to the basic patterns of a civil society, including basic human freedoms and rights and the acknowledgment of the worth of each human being regardless of race, class, or religion. However, in many parts of the world there is no consensus on the foundations of a civil society. Often the conflicts involve precisely the struggle over gaining basic civil liberties. Given the deep rupture in a society that this causes it is all the more urgent for policymakers to develop an integrated strategy of intervention. We must not, for example, help build a civil society only to have it destroyed by embroiling it in a war with organized religion or, alternatively, allow repressive expressions of religion to run so rampant that a civil society becomes impossible. We must generate the coexistence of religious life of all kinds *and* the growth of civil society. The details of how this integration would be implemented are the greatest challenges of all. Here are a few recommendations.

From Analysis to Policy Formation 1. Study the fears and resentments that generate religious worldviews that are opposed to contemporary constructs of a civil society and create policies that, at the least, do not exacerbate those fears.

2. Study causal chains that link religious violence to events both internal to religious traditions and external to them, such as economics or mass traumas, as a prerequisite to policy formation.

3. Be familiar with the religious traditions affected by policy or interventions, and do not delegate this exclusively to outside consultants or lower-level operatives. The generation of policy, on the one side, and, on the other, the knowledge of those affected by that policy should go on in the same mind and heart. This is far too critical an issue for there not to be an integration of analysis, policy recommendations, and feedback from the field. One of the greatest dangers is the initiation of a policy that does not anticipate its effect on religious life, on its institutions, and its power bases.

Coalescence of Policy Objectives and Prosocial Religious Values 1. Study how and when religion or religious figures have effected profound social transformation in a positive sense in that culture and then invest in people and programs that reinforce those directions.

2. Study the highest expressions of a religion or culture's ethical constructs and let them guide you to a carefully framed set of policies for intervention, or nonintervention, that coalesce with or parallel those values. This kind of coalescence should not take the crass form of directly drawing upon a tradition or quoting it in one's public policy statements or government directives. This could be seen as usurpation, and it also unnecessarily confuses the religious and public spheres, which is certainly not a goal of the method that I am suggesting here. Rather, frame policies and interventions in such a way that religious citizens and clerics immediately recognize and resonate with the goals and practices of the intervention. They may not agree with the details, but the policy will already be in their universe, in their frame of reference, and they will be able to agree or disagree with it in a healthy way, rather than resorting to a destructive form of conflict.

3. Create policies and generate programs but invest in *people* at all levels of religious society who are already engaged in a prosocial hermeneutic of their tradition, both in practice and in their teaching. The Western concept of programming and social construction is in some ways alien to most religions, which tend to rely on age-old constructs of culture and simple society, in addition to relying heavily on the authority of spiritual figures. Thus, working with individuals who have important standing in a particular community, who are visionaries but are not receiving adequate support, could be the most seamless and effective way to move a culture along toward conflict prevention or conflict resolution.

Anticipating Religious Antisocial Values   1. As policy analysts and activists, not theologians, study the darkest expression of a religion's or a culture's interpersonal behavior patterns, anticipate what could cause them, and frame intervention or nonintervention in such a way that will counteract these possibilities.

2. Study the interaction of perceived and remembered traumas, no matter how distant, and the religious interpretation of those events. Seek to create policies that will address or even lead to a healing of those traumas. Often secular or national traumas take on deep religious significance over time. It is not sufficient to deal with them on a secular level once this has happened. The religious community must be involved in some way to heal the traumas as well, to give a religious sanction to the process of moving a culture beyond fixation on the traumas, or beyond the use of those traumas to justify aggression.

Containing Religious Violence   1. Wherever possible, bring all parties, no matter how violent or separatist, into some orbit of inclusion—symbolically, interactively, publicly, or privately—on an ongoing basis. Do not make killing and self-destructive behavior the only viable "religious" alternative for a rejectionist group. Furthermore, once you have begun to include violent groups, do not allow rejectionist rage to simply transfer from the group that now cooperates to another group that "holds up the banner" of rejectionism. Rejectionism is given great religious credence when it is seen as holding up the faith. As stated, most religious mythologies are replete with those who maintain the faith when everyone else falters and who welcome persecution for their faith. When their faith has been translated into violence, this has devastating power. The answer is to keep including the rejectionists, so that their extremists cannot escape toward suicidal, almost ritualized, descents into battle with the enemy of the religion or the religious group. Reaching out to them has the effect of short-circuiting the closed and cyclical mythological universe, which includes: isolation and persecution for one's faith, lashing out in massive destructive force against an evil world, and the experience and even embrace of more persecution, as one is hunted for one's faith. Breaking this cycle is vital psychologically and brings the militant back into a human connection with his enemies. Hopefully, through this relationship-building process he is reminded of a range of other religious humanitarian values that he believes in as well. There are few religious nihilists who have no values other than killing. I know of no group that values only torture and killing. There are always, of course, individual religious sadists, as in all other groups, and the only solution for them is deep therapy behind bars. But there are almost never religious groups whose only value is sadism. Individual militants are often murderers, but that does not mean that killing and being killed is the only way that they see themselves relating *as a group* to Others. They generally have some ideal social vision, whose pursuit has led them down a barbaric path.[15] We have to work at providing them with another avenue of communication with their enemy, as well as another ritualized way of struggling for their cause. Our aim is not to convert every hardened militant, however; that is unrealistic. Our aim is to draw in as many rejectionists as possible, so that the circle of peacemaking is as wide as possible, and the circle of violent militancy becomes smaller and weaker over time.

2. Learn to isolate the truly violent factions not by confrontation, which only strengthens them, but by cooptation, embracing their deepest grievances and addressing these grievances authentically, if possible with the aid of the religions and cultures represented. Do not allow them to be the sole spokesmen for legitimate grievances against the dominant power structures. Then you give their followers no other choice.

Vision   1. Create programs and policies that, at least potentially, coalesce with the fundamental values of the traditions involved and that point to a vision of the future that can be shared by religious traditions. Encouraging all parties to engage in a vision of the future where there is no violence is one of the most powerful exercises that you can encourage. Furthermore, it dovetails nicely with the natural tendency in most religious imaginations to indulge in future visions, while prodding them to conceive primarily of nonviolent visions.

2. Always seek to combine in creative ways policies that commit to a larger, inclusive vision of humanity and its accompanying values, together with unqualified valuation of unique cultural expressions. This will attract the broadest spectrum of religious people. It is vital that this future vision has a place for the

group's particularity enduring into the distant future, for their uniqueness now and always, so that the universal values that you advocate do not imply to them or to anyone else the cultural annihilation of the particular group. This would only give credence to the militant rejectionists, and it would be an illegitimate move from the point of view of cultural conflict resolution. In effect, the best way to get most groups who assault Others because they fear their own future is to embrace their future with them, something that many cosmopolitan liberals have failed to do, as we saw in analyzing the cultural war in Israel. Ideally their enemy should be able to embrace their future also, in word, in deed, and in symbol. For example, in terms of the age-old war between Judaism and Christianity, I often ask myself: What would it take for the Jews most angry at the events of the Holocaust to trust Christians again? It would take more than apologies and much more than money for restitution. I often think it would take what may still be difficult for many conservative Christians: the embrace of the Jew not as a person, and not as a victim, but as an enduring, unique human being with an independent and legitimate religion. Repeated offers by the local inhabitants to restore Jewish synagogues in Europe, for example, where they were destroyed, or perhaps an offer to rebuild them in today's Jewish population centers would be such a gesture. The focus of the gesture would be on a synagogue or some other symbol of Jewish *religious* continuity. After all, it was the religious legitimacy of the Jew that was the basis of the persecution for most of European history; only recently did anti-Semitism turn into a plan for physical annihilation. There are many wonderful Poles who have recently been honored for restoring Polish Jewish cemeteries.[16] This is a noble gesture and an excellent method of symbolic conflict resolution. But the most skeptical and injured Jews need to see that Christians do not want to just honor Jews in their death or to apologize for pogroms and concentration camps, which no civilized human being could defend anyway, but that Christians want Jews perpetually alive and well as fellow religious human beings. This is not about what a group justly deserves—the focus of reparations negotiations—as much as it concerns elucidating what it will take to create a profound transformation of relationship and trust in the future.

Strategies of Peacemaking in Religious Contexts   1. Generate policy in conjunction with those affected by the policy. In other words, apply wherever possible the elicitive method of Lederach and other Mennonites, referred to earlier, to religious communities. If the policy and programs involved affect both religious and secular people or multiple religions arrange an elicitive process that has all these groups represented.

2. Remain committed to human rights or global goals.[17] But do have the courage to reframe human rights values and principles in deep collaboration with religious representatives and to be honestly open to the complexity of an intercultural application of these values. Be prepared to negotiate complexity and compromise, but do not accept blindly *all* cultural arguments against universal standards that may, at the hands of some, mask deep social and power inequalities in the local setting, particularly regarding women, children, and minorities.

3. If you dare to move a religious culture, or any culture for that matter, to a completely new economic or political construct, such as democracy or the free market, do not move the top without the bottom, the bottom without the top, or even just the middle, unless you are prepared to cause bloodshed. Conflict resolution policies and practices must be carried out in negotiation with all sectors of society, not just with the elites and not just with the masses. Each segment of society is capable of undoing peacemaking if its interests and needs are not included in the future of the society. Religious culture is not just run from the top down. In fact, there is remarkable power that is diffuse, which is precisely why leaders are so constrained. It will allow everyone greater elasticity in reframing their worlds, and giving up on hating their old enemies, if all levels of the culture are being addressed simultaneously.

4. Do not move one religious or ethnic group without others to a new social reality. Bilateral work is critical in every conflict but especially in religious conflicts, where each is scrutinizing the symbols and practices of the Other from a distance. If they are changing and their enemies are not, if the cultural evolution of both is not coordinated, then you will lose their trust, and they will lose face.

5. Do not assume that everyone is represented by whoever your negotiating partners are. Often religious groups that appear to have no hierarchy do have one, and those that have a hierarchy do not concentrate as much power at the top as they would like you to think. It is best with every group to institute a broad-based process, while still paying due homage to the upper echelons of the hierarchy.

6. Do not ever make a conflict worse by reinforcing one religious or cultural entity over another, especially by means of financial investment. This is the most destructive element in old colonial methods of dividing and conquering or choosing one group over another group chosen by a rival empire. Such is the sad fate of Rwanda and the entire Hutu/Tutsi relationship, as both groups were manipulated by European empires and their respective religions. This has direct relevance to the intersection of development and conflict, particularly religiously based development and poverty relief. Thus, conflict resolvers should watch carefully for this problem by examining the totality of foreign intervention in a particular place.[18] I have also noticed repeatedly and with some frustration that the predominantly Christian peacemaking organizations that I have worked with tend to be training only Christians in peacemaking, giving them skills that others do not have. For example, I have rarely met a Bosnian Muslim in conflict resolution circles, despite the fact that they are deserving of a great investment of resources, as the majority of losses and atrocities were suffered by them. But once again, Christian Europe's network of peacemakers reaches out to fellow Christians, namely, Croats and Serbs. They seem to be the ones with the network of relations that brings them into conflict resolution training circles. And it is the same in the Middle East, where Jews are almost never brought into the orbit of Christian peacemakers, with a few exceptions. If I were an average Muslim or Jew, I would be suspicious of any peacemaking or conflict resolution group that reflected this bias. Much more effort at balance must be achieved by Western, predominantly

Christian, NGOs on this matter. Part of the problem is simply the closed world of conflict resolution, which tends to rely on its network of contacts, not realizing that this makes those in their orbit rather monolithic. But part of the problem is a deep fear of the Other, even among peacemakers. We must all face this problem squarely. It is not necessarily any one person's fault, but it must be addressed soon.

7. Generate policies that reinforce small, less corruptible programs and that discourage large-scale programming, which tends to undermine the religious, cultural, and ethical fabric of a society. Religious people will tend to gravitate to programs that are less abstract and more organically integrated into their community. It resonates with the need—so strong among religious people—for interpersonal intimacy and a sense of importance in a known universe. Small programs are also easier for participants to monitor and to trust.

8. Expect there to be inevitable conflicts between religious and culturally specific paradigms, on the one side, and, on the other, Western or universal paradigms in terms of economics, politics, and ethics. Set up conflict resolution processes to deal with this.

9. Never pursue or perpetuate a project that will cause violence and social dislocation, no matter how well intended. The price is too high and the end too unpredictable. Therefore, create the institutional permission and the bureaucratic means for lower-level operatives to stop intervention when necessary, and do not penalize them for this. No intervention at all is a better option than destructive intervention, because massive violence destroys all other accomplishments.

10. Create guidelines of intervention that limit indigenous partners at the top and bottom of society to those who are willing to abide by these guidelines. Indigenous partners are not perfect by definition. On the contrary, they may be taking advantage of your intervention to assert control that they do not have or do not deserve. They need to be just as sensitive as you are to creating a peacemaking program that truly speaks to all sectors of their community.

Institutional Directives   1. Implement intellectual and social humility as an internal bureaucratic directive from top to bottom. Integrate basic values, such as humility and the ability to apologize for blunders, past mistakes, and old traumas, into the fabric of what is considered an acceptable encounter with religious subcultures.

2. Generate an internal process of debate and discussion on how precisely to remain true to or at least balance national interests, one's institutional mandates, and your personal needs as interveners, while working toward or approximating the goals and directives listed here. In other words, recognize honestly your own needs and those of your workers, share them with those you are trying to help, and then try to honestly balance all of these competing needs. For too long, aid givers and conflict resolvers have acted as if they were the only parties in the negotiation who had no needs, as if they were godlike in their capacity to analyze and offer assistance. This is nonsense. No one is without needs, and hiding them only makes matters worse. Honesty and trust are the key, as Lederach has main-

tained, not the veneer of divinelike disinterestedness.[19] This is particularly true with religious representatives, who may respect you all the more for confronting your own ethical values—and your limitations—as an intervener.

Regional Work

I cannot be exhaustive in my analysis of regional conflicts that involve religion, but a few brief recommendations are in order. The focus on a few selected conflicts in which religion has a role, positive or negative, will demonstrate how the methods suggested above have to be adjusted to the unique circumstances of each region; in no way is this meant as a substitute for a longer study.

United States Religion in the United States has had a unique effect on cultural conflict. On the one hand, the stability of civilization in the United States appears to be secure from the kind of violence that occurs in other parts of the world and, despite religious conflict and despite occasional violence in religion's name, such as the bombing of abortion clinics, religion does not appear to be a source of violent, destructive conflict. Nevertheless, there is serious nonviolent conflict in the name of religion that has had a dangerously polarizing effect on national politics and the civil relationship between the major political parties, which has been a critical factor in the continuing stability of the United States. This has been seriously eroded recently, as numerous reports from Washington and personal testimonies to me, as well as many others, confirm. A concerted effort must be made to understand the role of organized religion in exacerbating this trend and to find ways to counter it.[20]

A less recognized but far more consequential issue for the world is what U.S. citizens fund, through their religious representatives. Religious militants from around the world, including violent groups, receive vital funds from the United States. The principal source of funding for extremist groups are the three monotheisms, which means that tensions between Muslims and Christians overseas, for example, are a consequence of funding practices of groups in the United States, which live quietly side by side here, while fomenting conflict and violence elsewhere. The same is true of Jewish and Islamic groups based in Brooklyn, as another example, in terms of their effect on the Middle East. Finally, Christian missionizing, which has caused significant conflict in many parts of the world, as noted above, is mostly funded from the United States.

This is a typical trend in human history: privileged people in one part of the world express their darker fears or aspirations through conflict or violence that they support overseas. It is also a common disease of wealth. The wealth has satisfied many needs for direct sustenance but has clearly not healed the wounds that many immigrants carry to this country. Most religious U.S. citizens do not fight wars by proxy overseas, but American wealth is sufficiently great that even if a minority of religious people express themselves this way, it has a devastating impact on conflicts overseas. This is true of the Middle East, Northern Ireland, Latin America, India, and Russia, to mention a few.

A significant amount of U.S.–sponsored overseas militant activity comes from the evangelical movements, particularly based in the American South. This has important consequences. Much more can be done in the United States to lessen global religious conflict by sensitizing American populations to the consequences of their actions overseas. In addition, much more can be done to bring together conflicting parties in the United States itself. This is usually considered to be secondary to getting the principal actors together overseas. I beg to differ, not because they can solve foreign issues by proxy on U.S. soil, but rather because American citizens do so much damage in overseas conflicts that their rage must be addressed by conflict resolution methods in the United States itself.

It is clear, for example, that were it not for American financial aid for terrorist networks in the Middle East, many of the devastating bombs that destroyed Israeli lives and confidence in the peace process might have been avoided. The fateful set of bombs that whittled away at confidence in Prime Minister Peres's peace plans were the most devastating. It cost him an election that ushered into office a coalition expressly opposed to the Oslo peace process. That means that Hamas bombs had a direct destructive effect on the peace process, and whoever financially supported Hamas anywhere in the world had a hand in destroying the peace process. Hamas had a vested interest in undermining the peace process, because it would have delegitimized their entire political position.

Furthermore, had Israeli rejectionists not mustered so much financial and political support here in the United States, it is likely that the peace process would be well advanced by now. For example, thousands of American Jewish citizens of the Lubavitch sect, with dual citizenship, rushed to Israel to vote for Likud and against the peace process. This too hurt Peres badly. The 1997 letter of eighty-one senators that put pressure on the White House not to even state publicly its negotiating positions, lest it offend or embarrass Netanyahu, is evidence of the extraordinary power that the American Jewish rejectionists have had at various times in Washington. By contrast, the Israeli left of the political spectrum has never built up sufficient support in the United States or it has failed to mobilize that support. This means that what happens in the United States matters a great deal and that those institutions that are serious about international conflict resolution had better begin to take the attitudes of U.S. citizens more seriously and cultivate a strategy of conflict resolution that includes them.

As another example, Russia passed a relatively repressive religion law in 1997 that is bound to create numerous injustices. Had there been a better dialogue here in the United States among Christian groups, especially with the Orthodox, it is at least possible that evangelical practices, which led to pressure on the Russian government to clamp down on missionaries, might have been mitigated.[21] Certainly, many leaders of the Orthodox church are not happy to see so many evangelicals streaming into Russia from the outside and converting their Orthodox laypeople. But clearly this was made much worse by the infusion of vast funds and the less-than-honorable tactics to lure people away from the Orthodox church. Perhaps if this had been subject to a conflict resolution process early on, we might not have the legal results now of institutionalized antireligious prejudice.

We need much more reflection on why so many Americans are expressing themselves in this aggressive fashion, what are its roots, and how we can respond to this in a creative way. Some may argue that much of the global aspirations of southern preachers, both in terms of the vast wealth being accrued and in terms of the large number of converts, may have something to do with lingering resentments in the South. Southern Christian whites in particular may be harboring many feelings of defeat and cultural inferiority, which have not exactly been helped by decades of insulting southern stereotypes in Hollywood productions. This may, in turn, be leading to compensation in the form of accrual of power in the poorer parts of the world, a common but understudied use of imperialism. Many colonialists historically, such as Afrikaaners, were actually compensating for inferior status at home and doing unto others what was done to them.

The solutions may then involve more aggressive work on domestic healing of North-South relations more than 130 years after the Civil War.[22] Some may consider this silly in comparison to the immediacy of other violent conflicts, but the money trail is what is most compelling here. It is only elitist bias that has seen the receiving end of a money trail of conflict more condemnable than the initiating end. This is a convenient way to avoid Western or Northern contribution to conflicts that get played out violently in the Southern Hemisphere or the Third World. Those of us in the West must be constantly alert to our own natural and normal tendency to see destructive conflict—and culpability—in others while avoiding it in ourselves. Projection is the most insidious way that human beings find to avoid facing the destructive impulses of their cultures.

I would suggest a much greater investment in conflict resolution practices, of the diverse nature described above, for American religious groups that are supporting some form of religious conflict or conflict-generating behavior overseas. This could not only ease the pressure on overseas conflicts, it might also help groups here to creatively devise solutions without, of course, imposing the solutions on others.

The irony of life in the United States is that while the United States, through individual citizens, exports religious militancy, it also is a bastion of multifaith cooperation and contact unparalleled in human history. Life in a secular, free democracy provides a golden opportunity for creative multireligious and cultural conflict resolution. This is being pursued by many people of good will but should be encouraged and expanded to face the tough issues of overseas conflicts, rather than remaining a system of dialogue and good will that does not always get down to serious problem solving.

Latin America   The place of the Cold War in Latin American conflicts received such an inordinate amount of attention that a critical side effect of these conflicts went unnoticed: the intra-Christian conflict between Protestants and Catholics. The Catholic church was considered suspect in many places due to the strong activity on behalf of the poor by the lower echelons of the church and sometimes by its most elite leaders, such as Archbishop Romero. The conservative Protestant denominations, on the other hand, were welcomed by military hierarchies. The common perception was that their otherworldly message would pacify the *campesinos* more readily, and they also functioned as a fine lever against a Catholic church that needed to be constantly reminded by the dictatorships to repress its "extremists."[23]

It is also true that some in the upper echelons of the Catholic church in numerous countries of Latin America either acquiesced or were supportive of brutal regimes, including the majority of bishops in Argentina, who supported the junta's war, which included the large-scale murder of innocents. Furthermore, I have witnessed personally in Northern Ireland that there are evangelical Protestants who have come to occupy an important place in religious peacemaking, which has gone relatively unnoticed. Thus, while there were certainly elements of intra-Christian conflict that complicated the Latin American wars, it would be a serious mistake to assume that Protestants as a rule were part of the oppression or pacification of the population, while Catholics were the heroes of the poor. It is much more subtle than this, especially in Mexico, but nevertheless an overlooked element in the confrontations.

The Cold War has disappeared, but there is ample room for greater cooperation on conflict resolution, which should be coordinated between the Catholic church and the wide variety of Protestant denominations now active in Latin America.[24] There is still a great deal of suspicion and bitterness over matters of encroachment and competition, as we see elsewhere in the Christian world. Furthermore, as mentioned previously, there are unquestionably problems of differing conflict management styles, particularly between the Catholic church and Protestant evangelicals. We are so accustomed in the conflict-resolving community to Catholic and liberal Protestant styles of interaction that we simply assume that those Christians who do not have these styles of interaction are by definition more conflictual and less able to enter the orbit of peacemaking and prosocial change. While it is certainly true that some visions of Christianity are more exclusivist, intolerant, or less open to rational negotiation with nonbelievers, it is not necessarily the case that all adherents or representatives of this worldview are less tolerant. On the contrary, sometimes they have excellent abilities, as struggling minorities, to understand other views, even as allegedly liberal sections of the community, who are the majority, demonstrate remarkably poor skills. Furthermore, as we studied earlier, there may be subtle differences due to theological and cultural fine points in the ways in which Catholic and Protestant communities send their signals regarding peace, conflict, and the willingness to change a relationship for the better. Sometimes these differing signals are either unknown to the other party or may be in direct opposition. For example, the production by the Catholic church in a specific region of a peace-oriented official paper or pronouncement may be seen as revolutionary by Catholics, a broad-minded gesture of courage. But for the Protestants, it may be just paper, "merely" the pronouncement of church leadership, a leadership that their worldview was set up to reject in the first place, and not an authentic religious experiential transformation of the people. This is a built-in miscommunication among Catholic, Orthodox, and Protestant worldviews that should be kept in mind in conflict resolution in Latin America, Ireland, and Central and Eastern Europe.

Indian Subcontinent The 1999 nuclear explosions by India and Pakistan, in addition to the three wars since 1948, indicate just how deep a failure the original diplomatic and statist solution was in 1948, when India and Pakistan were separated into two nations. Fighting has increased on the border with scores dead, and now there is no mechanism in place for either side to trust the other not to release a nuclear weapon. Not only did countless people die and suffer in that original transfer, it failed to address the deep cultural injury that continues to exist between Hindus and Muslims.

Certainly, the subcontinent is also plagued by other religious difficulties, including the plight of the Sikhs, as well as lesser known conflicts, such as between the now-Christian Naga peoples and the Indian government. The most extreme Naga separatists, who have engaged in a terrorist campaign against the Indian government and also against their own people, are actually Christian militants, devotees of several American preachers, including Oral Roberts. I have made some recommendations, and others have followed through on utilizing this religious angle to communicate with these extreme groups, which actually harbor delusions of a Christian empire on the Indian subcontinent. In addition, there is increasing pressure and attacks on Christians by Hindu militants in other regions of India.

The deepest and most dangerous conflict, however, is between Hindus and Muslims. Clearly, as I have stated repeatedly, there are geopolitical, economic, and ethnic considerations at work here. But the psychodynamic elements of this conflict have been overlooked since the beginning, as obvious as they are to the sensitive observer.[25] Who could imagine that the centuries of occupation by a Muslim empire in which Muslims were a minority in numbers but a majority in power, which has now turned into a majority Hindu state of power and numbers, would not involve deep injuries on both sides collected over centuries? Who would not think that this relationship should receive the top priority in terms of regional stability? It is extraordinary how much this situation has been neglected.

Hindu tradition and Islamic tradition both play a role in reinforcing this conflict, but they also have the seeds within them for conflict resolution. There must be broad and widespread efforts to create more Hindu acknowledgment of the problem. When I went to a religious conference on the future of India, I was impressed by the level of creativity in every area *but* Hindu/Muslim relationships. There I saw simple denial, as if it were such an explosive topic, such a deep injury, that no creative conversation could occur. And this was among the progressives.

This suggests deep injuries that remain unmourned and profound fears that remain unaddressed. The extraordinary range of Hindu philosophy and practice can and does help in isolated places to create a different kind of Hindu/Muslim relationship. Certainly this was the case in Gandhi's movement years ago, which had its parallel among the Muslim Pathans led by Ghaffar Khan. The latter group was known as the Khudai Khidmatgar, and they resisted oppression on strictly nonviolent grounds.[26] We know that there are villages in which Hindus and Christians respect and even join in each others' rituals, with some indications that there are Hindus and Muslims who have a similar relationship in the villages.[27] Of course, these interfaith relationships are overshadowed by violent confrontations and the media's focus on bloodshed. But the point is that there is fertile ground for interreligious peacemaking in India, for those who are willing to discover it.

There are clearly thousands of courageous Gandhians, Hindu as well as Muslim devotees of nonviolence, active all over India; these people would welcome a more substantive dialogue and conflict resolution process. After all, nonviolence as a concept is deeply rooted in ancient Indian thought, most clearly in Jainism,[28] which has had a profound impact on many of India's citizens to this day. But in order to reduce the most serious dangers to life and limb, conflict resolution practice must reach a sufficient proportion of the population in both India and Pakistan until there is a significant shift in government leadership. This is the only way to avoid a nuclear war, which will have horrifying results, unprecedented even for the twentieth century. There must be support for a level of conflict resolution and reconciliation between the cultures that has never been tried on a grand scale since the days of Gandhi. This is what public policy analysts and activists should be investigating.

Other regional conflicts involving religion obviously must include Sri Lanka. The animus of some of the Buddhist leadership for Tamils must be analyzed and included in conflict interventions.[29] There are independent foundations to this conflict besides religion. But, once again, ignoring this vital element has exacerbated the conflict by not including religion as a critical component in the solutions.

Asia   There are a variety of Asian conflicts in which Buddhism is playing some role and could conceivably play a more prominent role. The most obvious case involves Tibet, where the systematic suppression of Buddhism by the Chinese government and the effort to delegitimize the Dalai Lama has clearly backfired on China. On the other hand, they could not have asked for a more gentle foe. If it were not for the Dalai Lama's continual efforts to keep his people's struggle nonviolent, it seems clear that matters would be much worse right now, even catastrophic. The Dalai Lama's unique approach to enemies, and how he thinks about it and teaches it theologically has been critical to this vital struggle for social justice not turning into an even greater human tragedy than it already is.

The question is: Can there be some deeper process of cultural meeting and conflict resolution that has not been tried? Clearly, since the Chinese government is in such a vastly superior position, it is difficult to persuade it to enter into more substantive processes of dialogue and cultural communication.

The Dalai Lama has made many gestures toward the Chinese, along the lines of President Clinton's efforts to engage the Chinese in an honorable form of communication, being careful not to humiliate them in public, unlike the strategies used by human rights advocates.[30] This is a controversial method of engagement, but the Dalai Lama has clearly indicated that this method is in keeping with Tibetan Buddhist religious ethics.

It should be pointed out in this regard that beneath the surface of today's official Chinese culture is an ancient Confucian culture in which honor is a critical value and shame the most devastating punishment. Thus, Clinton's method is addressing this need on the part of Confucian culture to resist humiliation. We may wince at this because we want, for reasons of justice, Chinese human rights abuses exposed and the Chinese leadership humiliated and even jailed for their crimes at Tiananmen Square on June 4, 1989, and the crimes that still take place in numerous prisons. Unfortunately, that is not how nonviolent change works, and engaging the present leaders perhaps—and I emphasize, perhaps—may lead to a more open society in the future, in which those who have been criminal in their behavior now will be exposed later. But this cannot happen without conflict resolution methods and gestures becoming a high priority of intervention.

Taoism is also an important undercurrent of Chinese culture, and it is a central assumption of the *Tao Te Ching*, the great classic of this ancient religion, that one accomplishes a great deal more with adversaries by indirect means of influence than by violent confrontation.[31] The fact that the Chinese government itself hardly acts according to the highest values of either Confucianism or Taoism is beside the point. What matters is how these leaders perceive their adversaries or how they come to trust allies. They may only come to trust outsiders when the outsiders act according to the highest ideals of Chinese culture, even if they, the Chinese leaders, are not acting this way. This is ironic but true. Human beings often give themselves the widest latitude, while demanding the most rigorous ethical/cultural standards from their adversaries. Certainly, the Chinese officials are governed by considerations of *realpolitik* as much as any government, but they also completely lack the check on governmental arrogance that a constitutional democracy might provide. That having been said, one of the best tools we have in conflict resolution is to understand the cultural sensibilities at work. The latter can at the very least prevent missteps that make matters worse and, at best, may provide an entrée into a powerful, belligerent party's mindset. From this deeper understanding may come better strategies of simultaneously pursuing justice and peace. It seems to me that the Dalai Lama is one of the finest examples in the world today of a leader using all of his religious and cultural insights to pursue justice and peace simultaneously.

And let us not forget the work of Maha Gosananda in Cambodia, referred to earlier. These Buddhist leaders and their organizations should be taken much more seriously by Western diplomacy and conflict resolution activists. They can provide a path into cultures riven by conflict in a way that few other methods of intervention can. They desperately need more financial support and more public attention. The attention given to them helps them to do more substantive work in dangerous circumstances.

Africa   Wherever possible, the old tribal religions of Africa need to be studied for their insights on how peace is maintained and how relationships are restored between enemies. There are many insights on peace combined, as they are with all religions, with violent alternatives that also emanate from these religions. There are no romantic illusions here about indigenous cultures.[32] Rather, the assumption is that peacemaking also has a deep place in African culture and society, largely hidden by those who have been made over centuries to feel shame for their culture.

I have struggled with this a great deal as I have studied with my students from Africa. Virtually every one of my students from Africa have been either Christian or Muslim. No independent voices of animist beliefs, the original beliefs of Africa, ever reach the Western, mostly Christian, frameworks of teaching and training, in which I work, and I have critiqued this already. Nevertheless, I struggle with my students, as we elicit methods of peacemaking from their midst, to deal with the fact that they can value their present monotheistic religion, Christianity or Islam, and still recover what is rightfully theirs from their past.

This is not an easy matter, and many would disagree with me for even provoking this discussion. Am I disrespecting their current religions, or am I giving them permission in a Western context to fully articulate and embrace their ancient traditions? I come to this with a belief that many peaceful people in Africa feel shame when indigenous traditions are employed in the perpetration of barbarities, such as in Liberia, mentioned earlier. They must shrink in shame as these old spiritual institutions are used by ruthless leaders, who evoke dark powers of hypostatized evil to destroy their enemies.

I would argue, however, that those in Africa who are ashamed are internalizing what the West has been saying to them for hundreds of years, namely, that there is only darkness in their old traditions (note the use of color in describing evil), as if the peacemaking rituals of tribal women in Liberia (as reported to me by Liberian students), for example, are fiction, having no basis in history. As in all human cognitive and emotive constructs of the world, there is a reservoir of antisocial *and* prosocial values and rituals in Africa waiting to be analyzed without a preconceived bias or, as Gadamer would have me say, with a consciousness of our built-in biases and horizons.

Recently I was engaged in teaching and training at Eastern Mennonite University. As usual, I had a number of African students and, as usual, I engaged in conversation with my colleagues Cynthia Sampson and Hizkias Assefa. Hizkias is based in Nairobi and is an African Christian who has done important work for years in Africa. We found ourselves in dialogue late one evening, reflecting on culture and on the Liberian tragedy. Hizkias recalled to me how he was present at one peacemaking ceremony where there was one man in the ceremony whose task it was to wear a mask of the devil. Now, both of us were already agreed on the vital importance of ritual and ceremony in transforming cultures from war to peace. But what was agonizing was including a figure on the podium who represented a force that had been so responsible for all the killing. Yet both of us felt that this was uniquely African, that in some critical way it was important for this force to be out in the open, included in peacemaking. It was far better than pretending that it did not exist, only to have it surface in some other way in society. We both sensed that there was some unique wisdom at work here that involved keeping the forces associated with evil in some circumscribed role, rather than suppressing them or denying them, as we do so often in the West.

I remind the reader that this is particularly jarring to liberal monotheists. I, in particular, have a strong disdain for and fear of devil-centered religion. The countless deaths of my people across the centuries is due in no small measure to the reification of the devil or the Antichrist inside the Jew, even in his very physiognomy.[33] No depiction of the devil in Europe, as far as I know, ever paints him as blond and blue-eyed. Often, however, he looks exactly like my revered religious teachers, like Ashkenazi Jews. This alone has made me angry at European civilization my whole life and made the Holocaust not a terribly big surprise, at least to me.

In conversations only months before with Africans, who asked me my theological opinion about the reality of evil and demons, I rejected them categorically. Thus, I surprised myself when I immediately saw the wisdom of having that man in the devil mask at the peace ceremony in Liberia. It might not make sense at all anywhere else than Africa, but it is vital to have a sense of humility about what will work in various places and to also acknowledge our own biases as we plumb the depths of human nature and violence and look at how human beings the world over recover from and become victorious over violence.

Middle East   I have already dwelt at length on the Middle East in earlier sections. But the basic lessons from the recent past indicate the necessity of a complete overhaul in the approach to violence and war in the Middle East. It is essential that the religious parties to the conflict become an integral part of any conflict resolution process. Needless to say, this needs to be worked out delicately so that their involvement does not undermine the foundations of the civil societies that already exist or that are being sought by various groups, not the least of which is the Palestinians. But this deliberate exclusion of religious parties must end if we want to undermine terrorism and the politics of religious militancy.

Judaism and Islam contain numerous values and principles, some of which they hold in common, that can form the basis of much deeper processes of conflict resolution and reconciliation between enemies. All the caveats mentioned earlier remain. There are grave dangers to civil liberties and to peace that also exist in these traditions. But many Muslims and Jews, deeply religious people, recognize this dichotomy of the prosocial and antisocial elements of their traditions. There are extraordinary struggles being waged within the precincts of these traditions over women's rights, for example, or over attitudes toward those who are not of the faith. But the antisocial positions will only harden if the belligerent halls of power politics, such as the Israeli parliament, are the only places in which secular and religious people ever engage each other. A cross-cultural process of building the future together, secular and religious, must accompany the complex political negotiations over the future of the Middle East.

Only then will we see constructive visions of the future emerging from both the religious and the secular communities.

Europe   Finally, we note the reemergence of ethnic and religious violence in Europe. Whether it be the more contained conflicts, such as between Muslims and the state in France or the cruelty displayed toward Muslim Turks in Germany or the more overt wars in which the Bosnian Muslims were brutally murdered and shamefully abandoned by Europe for too long, it is clear that Europe only suppressed its religious problems during the Cold War. Europe exported much of its religious warfare across the globe at one time, and it is clear that Europe must face the role that religion plays in its continuing problems.

The reemergence of fascist parties, especially in Russia, is a particularly worrisome development. The development of reactionary parties is always accompanied by the reemergence of old, bizarre myths, which have motivated murder in Europe for centuries. For example, the Russian Duma itself, prodded by the Orthodox church, has devoted public hearings recently to a myth that formed the basis of centuries of Russian pogroms against Jews, namely, the charge that Jews engage in ritual murder.[34] The latest accusation is that "the Jews" ritually murdered the last czar and his family. This is a society unable to cope with its past, with its pain, and with its own sins. Naturally, the Jew resurfaces once again as the perfect scapegoat. The people of Russia have never had an opportunity to heal from the horrors of the twentieth century, and the traditional conduit of healing, the church, is broadly distrusted as having played a central role in communist control of the society. What better solution than to discover once again a conspiracy in which what appears to be real is not real and what appears impossible is a reality? The traumatic truth is that the Russian people in the twentieth century engaged in a brutal campaign of terror against each other, in the form of the communist regime, which was preceded in history by the equally brutal czarist rule, which gave rise to the 1917 revolution in the first place. The acceptable myth is that it was all caused by some foreign, non-Slavic, non-Christian, demonic power: the Jew.

Confronting this barbaric side of European culture is distasteful and embarrassing for most Europeans and for Americans of European extraction. It is easier to focus on economic issues in the hopes that prosperity and materialism will make this madness just go away. As we have stated, the latter is only a partial fix; it is unquestionably critical but not sufficient to eliminate the deep roots of hatred. Nothing less than an open and honest conflict intervention process focused on the most painful issues of the past and the most problematic elements of religious expression can truly undo the damage of the past in a way that prevents it from recurring. Furthermore, a true engagement with the Christian foundations of Europe's troubles can and should be accompanied by an openminded embrace of Christian, in this case Orthodox, frameworks for renewing the culture in a way that is not paranoid or in need of scapegoats.[35] Furthermore, the creative use of symbols and rituals of reconciliation, healing, apology, and moral change will allow this process to enter into the fabric of popular European civilization. Symbol and ritual have always been used and abused by European fascists and feared by European intellectuals. But there is nothing to fear, except one's own ignorance of how to engage people at all levels of a culture and how to bring them together in a vision of a culture and a future that no longer needs chosen enemies and demonic scapegoats.

In each of these regions of the world, there is always a balance of destructiveness and creativity that is inherent in the nature of human institutions. A pragmatic approach to organized religion in these regions recognizes its potential for tipping the world toward destructiveness. But it would be foolish to ignore the resources within these religious traditions that can tip the delicate balance of human society toward creativity, toward the prosocial intuitions that all human beings have to a degree, toward a vision of the future that is not destructive but redemptive.

Final Thoughts

It seems clear from what I have studied and uncovered that there will continue to be a significant radicalization of many religions on the part of some believers for the foreseeable future. This dynamic is likely to continue as long as the range of human needs, physical and especially spiritual, continue to be unmet by the evolving global civilization, whose principal offering to human beings is the promise of a materialist civilization in which a few become wealthy, some are reasonably comfortable but very insecure, and most are poor. This materialist, exclusivist vision of the future has turned out to be attractive on one level, motivating a great deal of economic ingenuity among some in every civilization and yielding impressive material benefits. But this global civilization, as it is currently conceived, is also turning out to be repulsive to many others. I predict that it is only when this evolving global civilization develops into a serious human community with a set of high ideals that are perceived to be and actually are substantive and attractive from a spiritual and ethical point of view, that we will see militant religion begin to wane.

Religion per se, however, is here to stay, and the myth that it would leave is now simply a myth. The character of religion, how opposed or supportive it is of science, of the human mind, of human rights, of civil society, will depend completely on the hermeneutic engagement of its adherents. That, in turn, will depend on the degree to which its adherents can honestly see a creative interaction of ancient traditions and modern constructs. But both elements of the equation, ancient traditions and modern constructs of civil society and scientific investigation, will have to be respected in this artful process of weaving the future.

It is also likely that the future will bring greater and greater communication among liberal adherents of most of the world's major religions. This is a trend of more than a hundred years that is likely to continue. Their continued cooperation, their learning from each other, and their discoveries of their own uniqueness and what they share in common are critical to evolving a peaceful vision inside the world's great religions.

Those who engage in this multireligious process will be tempted, as they always have been, to retreat to safe enclaves of broad-minded people or to find refuge in secular constructs of civilization. That is quite understandable. But someone is going to have to be the bridge between the angrier expressions of each religion and the rest of the world. This is vital to the future. The longer it takes to evolve a global civilization that does not so deeply alienate religious adherents, the harder it will be to prevent religious subcultures from plunging the rest of the world into broad religious, ethnic, and national conflicts. These conflicts will resemble, or be imagined to resemble, the destructive myths of cosmic battle and apocalyptic redemption through violence.

There must appear a cadre of broad-minded religious and secular people who develop the ethics and the skills of peacemaking and conflict resolution. They must help the emerging global civilization through this difficult birth, which is threatening to kill the infant. We have the makings, in all of the U.N. declarations and documents, of an extraordinary human future—if we can cooperate in all the ways that those documents prescribe. There is no reason why organized religions cannot in principle buttress the lofty goals of this emerging global civil society and even lead the way.

But organized religion is also the repository and expression of all the deepest dissatisfactions that human beings have. If society is corrupt, then people turn to religion. If society is stifling the human need for uniqueness, then people turn to religion. If society is grossly unjust to some, then the victims turn to religion. If society reduces the human being to a materialist unit and leaves him deeply unsatisfied, then he finds ultimate refuge in religion. In short, religion is the barometer of societal dissatisfaction and can and should be seen not as an enemy of a civil society but as a diagnostician of its failings.

If this approach is used, then those of us who want a civil society to flourish will have to pay close attention to not only the kind of religion that we like and want to see but also to things said in the name of religion that we find ugly and shameful. Indeed, it is the latter that give us the most insight on what remains undone in our search for the good society. We must not, however, view violent things said or done in the name of religion as merely an obnoxious relic from the past, which we can dismiss as the gibberish of some group that we despise; this would be just engaging in more demonizing, the great enemy of peacemaking. In a very real sense, we must see these terrible things as a part of us that we cannot simply suppress. If we are a global community, then we all share in some measure the cultural legacy that drives some people to extreme violence. But we cannot construct a peaceful future without even the angriest people among us joining that effort. And we cannot invite them along on this journey to a better society without an in-depth understanding and even valuation of what they hold dear. In that development of understanding we will find the rational and nonrational ways to engage everyone in the building of a global civilization.

Beyond the actual damage that has been done in conflicts or persecutions of the past, we have also seen in our study that there is a drive, all over the world today, to recover the uniqueness of each community, each ethnic group, and each religion. There is a deep sense of loss that hundreds of millions of people feel the more that they are the same as everyone else.

Haym Soloveitchik's thesis that the loss of distinct ethnicity has led to a widespread drive to locate authenticity in text is certainly true of the Jewish community.[36] It is clearly the case that sacred texts and the legal life drawn from them are some of the most unique aspects of Jewish identity, not its art or its architecture or its food and not a particular land until recently. This is no doubt due to the exilic and homeless character of Jewish existence whose only refuge was distinctive ethnic identity, especially as it was found in traditions passed on organically from generation to generation. Now, in the free, homogenized culture of democratic modern life, this anchor has been lost, and text, especially I might add, texts that make Jews different, even superior, have an especially important grip on religious life.

This insight must be combined, as Samuel Heilman has noted in his reaction to Soloveitchik's thesis,[37] with the experience of the utter destruction of European Jewry, which has left many *haredi* Jews and others bereft of an organic, moderate tradition of piety passed down from generation to generation. This, combined with the sweeping effects of modern, material culture, has left text, legal stringencies, and rituals peculiar to Jews—and excessive chauvinism—as the only ways to reestablish and recover some sense of old Jewish life. Underlying much of this is the fear, even the terror, of assimilation doing a more thorough job of making one's great-grandchildren lose Judaism than any repressive regime in Europe ever hoped to accomplish by force.

These fears have a tendency to undermine the very values, the universal ones, also embedded in Jewish tradition and texts, that are vital to a future of coexistence with Others who are different and to the foundations of religious approaches to a civility that is held in common with Others.

This deep sense of loss of an old way of life and fear of losing even more drives the religious violence of many religious communities around the world. Those of us who would hope to create a global civil culture that does have in common basic civil and human rights and basic freedoms had better develop the skills and creativity that are needed to create a model of a future that does not annihilate the past, especially those aspects of the past that offer human beings deep patterns of meaning and unique identities. We have to help religious communities mourn the losses of the past but also help them create global institutions and directives that do not annihilate their future as distinctive religious communities. The skills, of communication, negotiation, and conflict resolution practices outlined here should go a long way toward bringing ever-greater numbers of devout human beings into some constructive paradigm of the future.

We are presently engaged in an extraordinary and exciting process of honing our skills of listening, compassion, and relationship building in order to create a civil society of the future in which everyone will be authentically welcomed and honored. Many of us are already engaged in this effort, and as the terrible visions of Armageddon, or its equivalent in non-Christian religions, become more acceptable to some religious people, many other religious people have joined in this journey of peacemaking, in this earnest engagement with the full range of human beings on the planet. I have personally witnessed the cooperation of thousands of religious people, young and old, from every major religion and country of the world, and in my few years, I have barely scratched the surface of this world of peacemakers. In the process, these people may not create an Eden on earth, but they can certainly take steps toward Eden.

It will not be an Eden in which there is magically no need for work but an Eden in which work would not need to take place in the shadow of conflict and violence. It will not be an Eden in which there are magically no scarce resources but an Eden in which scarce resources and the struggle for them need not lead to bloodshed. It will not be an Eden in which there is magically no miscommunication among the isolated consciousnesses of imperfect human beings. But it could be an Eden in which we have the wisdom, the spiritual training, and the skill to know how to turn that miscommunication or hurt into a vehicle of restored and renewed relationship.

Finally, it is important to reiterate that we have examined in this study many facets of religious violence and how violence stems from many deep wounds that individuals and groups harbor privately for decades, centuries, millennia. Many readers will examine the depths of this pain, see it reified and codified in myth, law, and ritual, and then ask themselves: How could any conflict resolution methods begin to heal these wounds that have festered for so long? It is a good question, and we will not know the answer to this question until we use all of our resources to try to heal these wounds. The human community has barely begun to invest in this enterprise, and so we still do not know what we can accomplish.

We are privileged to live in a time when we are gathering our collective wisdom from many sources and exposing the depths of human pain that lead to religiously based violence. And we have discovered that simply raising to the surface what has been hidden in the private recesses of conscience is often revolutionary enough to set human beings on a new path. This is especially the case when former enemies have the courage and vision to acknowledge the pain that is hidden inside the collective memories of their adversaries. Thus, beyond all the recommendations that I have made, which experience indicates will be effective for many people, I urge the reader to consider the powerful impact of simply helping each community to finally face its old legacies of suffering and helping each group mourn in dignity and honor, buttressed by new support from outsiders and especially former enemies.

This process—a community telling its story of pride and pain and achieving enough trust in the world to acknowledge its pain publicly—must be met by an equally powerful response from the rest of the world, especially that part of the world that is implicated or is perceived to be implicated in the damage that was done. This is the crucial dynamic of story and response that will lead eventually to the deepest healing of all and to the creation of new bonds of intercommunal trust and friendship.

Undoubtedly, this must be accompanied by negotiations over past injustices. It will entail serious compromises and acknowledgment of the inherent moral ambiguities of trying to right past wrongs. If this process of negotiations is bereft of any deeper relationship building, it will turn into a legalistic battle that satisfies no one in the end. But if it is accompanied by the kind of healing and bilateral relationship building that I have suggested here, it will likely bury more and more the specter of old wounds.

The original, mythic Eden of the Bible was supposed to be a perfect place, but it had, as our own world has, within it the seeds of misunderstanding, loss of trust, and betrayal. But we are a long way from the mythical origins of our species. Perhaps now, wiser for the wear, we know more about what to anticipate in human relationships, and we can use our skills and collective wisdom to steel the bonds of trust against all its natural foes.

We live in a world of human beings separated physically, each from the other. And we live in a world of peoples and religions separated each from the other. We always will. Every effort, both secular and religious, to forcibly homogenize all of us has ended in disaster and generations of injury. But, as an alternative to artificial unity, we can choose to find ways to build trust across boundaries where it never has existed or restore it to where it has been lost. Building trust is a moral task, an art, and perhaps even a gift. It requires painful acknowledgment of the past and broad-minded visions of the future. This would seem to be the foundation of a future Eden or as near an approximation to Eden as humanity can ever hope to reach.

Glossary

Abraham. Mythical patriarch of the Israelite people of the Bible, founder of monotheism, according to Judaism, Christianity, and Islam; father of Ishmael and, therefore, forefather of Arabian peoples, according to Islam.

Abrahamic faiths. The three monotheisms: Judaism, Christianity, and Islam.

Ahimsa. Nonviolence in several Asian religions, particularly Hinduism and Jainism.

Angelology. The elaborate system of angels and their relationship to heaven in the three monotheisms.

Ashkenazi. Jews of the Middle Ages and modern times whose ancestors migrated to European lands since the original exile from Israel in 70 C.E.

Aveilus. Mourning according to traditional Jewish laws and customs.

Bhagavad Gita. Important Hindu scripture involving the teachings of Krishna (hero of the story), set in the context of choices faced about a great battle.

Bodhissatva. A saintly figure in Mahayana Buddhism, who reaches nearly complete enlightenment and nirvana, thus ending his cycle of birth, death, and rebirth, but who chooses to remain or come back to this world, out of compassion for others and in order to help them attain enlightenment.

Brahmacharya. In Hinduism, a life of self-discipline and self-limitation, which is devoted to higher pursuits. Sometimes associated with celibacy.

Bundists. Organized Jewish workers in Europe and America devoted to a socialist vision, major competitors to Zionism and traditional religiosity for the commitment of the Jewish masses at the beginning of the twentieth century.

Canaan. Ancient name of the biblical land of Israel; also the name for one of the original "idolatrous" tribes.

Chosen people. Concept of a people with a special bond and love relationship with God. Originally rooted in the relationship of the people of Israel and its God and then used biblically to justify the expulsion of other peoples from Israel. Later absorbed into Christianity and made into a concept that has been used over the centuries, in various denominations, to contrast a chosen few who are "saved" with pagans or idolaters, who must be converted or suppressed. There have also been, through the centuries, quite benign, prosocial interpretations of chosenness and mission, a related concept.

Compesinos. Indigenous peasants of Central and South America.

Conflict transformation. Name given to a conflict resolution school, often associated with Mennonites, that emphasizes peacemaking that changes relationships and empowers all sides, especially victims, to create new relationships with adversaries based on peace and justice.

Consequentialism. Moral analysis of actions based on calculation of whether those actions lead to a greater or lesser amount of some good, such as prosperity, happiness, or the success of a social program or experiment. As opposed to an evaluation of the inherent right or wrong of an act or its inherent valuation as, for example, compassionate, just, truthful, peaceful.

Crusades. A series of Christian campaigns of conquest of the Holy Land in the late eleventh and twelfth centuries, promoted by Pope Urban II, Bernard of Clairvaux, and others, which led to atrocities and massacres of thousands of Jews and Muslims across Europe and the Middle East.

Dar al-harb. Lit. "the realm of the sword." In Islam, traditionally the realm beyond the Islamic community with which one must struggle in order to bring those people into the realm of Islam.

Dar al-islam. Lit. "the realm of Islam," where Islamic law and Islamic life is honored and is dominant.

Diaspora. People who consider themselves part of a community that is now far-flung or in exile, but that was once part of an original community in a specific place. In Judaism, the name given to the Jewish people who do not reside in Israel.

Eightfold Path. Eight parts of a path designed by the Buddha to attain Nirvana, a state of ultimate enlightenment. Includes basic ethical precepts such as right speech and right action but also training of the consciousness, such as through right understanding and right concentration.

Elicitive method. Conflict resolution method associated with conflict transformation, which emphasizes drawing out peacemaking methods, symbols, and traditions from the parties to the conflict themselves.

Emanationist. Theory of divine relationship to the world that emphasizes a flow of the divine being that connects the material world with God.

Exodus. In biblical religion, the seminal event of Israelites' national birth, as they were freed miraculously from hundreds of years of slavery by Moses and divine intervention in the natural order.

First-track and second-track diplomacy. Coined and advocated by Joseph Montville, it is a definition of effective diplomacy as consisting, or needing to consist, of more than official, government-to-government channels of communication. It includes individuals and agencies that can be effective in healing deep-rooted causes of intractable conflict.

Four Noble Truths. Most basic teachings of Buddhism, including an examination of the truths of suffering, the true cause of suffering in desire or attachment, the overcoming of suffering, and an eightfold path to follow.

Four Sublime Moods. Four cardinal virtues in Buddhism, which include compassion, joy in the joy of others, equanimity, and loving-kindness.

Ger. In the Bible, it is "the stranger" to whom a wide range of moral and emotional obligations apply. Becomes "the convert to Judaism" in later rabbinic interpretation.

Gush Emunim. Primarily followers of R. Tzvi Yehuda Kuk's philosophy, which centralizes the significance of the land of Israel in Jewish theology. They live according to a belief in the soon-to-unfold messianic era of Jewish national life and the restoration of Jewish sovereignty in the land of Israel.

Hadith. Stories about and sayings of the prophet Mohammed that are not included in the Qur'an.

Halakha (n.), halakhic (adj.). The body of Jewish traditional law that governs religious life.

Hallal. Something that is considered religiously acceptable, such as a piece of meat that has been properly prepared for eating, according to Islamic law.

Halutz. An original Zionist settler who built the agricultural base of the Yishuv.

Hamas. Islamic fundamentalist network, which supports an end to secular states in the Middle East, an end to the State of Israel, and the imposition of Islamic law. It supports various social agencies that have helped the poor, but it also has a military wing that has conducted numerous terrorist attacks on Israeli civilians.

Haredi (adj.), haredim (n.). Ultra-Orthodox Jews, including Hasidim, who today embrace as isolated a position from the non-Orthodox world as possible; the use of secular education only for the purpose of making a living, if at all; a literal belief in revelation from Sinai, and a much greater dependency on *halakhic* or spiritual leaders to determine the contours of their lives and choices. It also entails being non-Zionist or anti-Zionist (though this is changing somewhat) in the sense of not accepting a secular Jewish state. Furthermore, the male dress is distinctly dark and includes special clothing in the Hasidic case. This too varies somewhat among Hasidic groups. The lines of who is and who is not *haredi* is blurry at the edges, with people defining themselves in various ways at the borders of all Jewish affiliations.

Hasidim. Sectarians who originated in an Eastern European religious revival movement characterized by intensive prayer, song, and devotion to masters and their extraordinary powers in interceding with God.

Hasmoneans. Jewish kings in the period of the Second Temple, who managed with some success to reestablish Jewish sovereignty in the land of Israel, despite the onslaughts of various empires.

Hebrew Bible. Judaism's canonization of the books of the Bible, all in the original Hebrew, including the Five Books of Moses, historical writings, such as Samuel and Kings, the Prophets, and various books of wisdom literature, such as Proverbs and Psalms.

Herem laws. Biblical laws that mandated extermination of the population of ancient Israel who were determined to be irredeemably corrupt and idolatrous. There were also biblical *herem* laws mandating the complete extermination of a Jewish city were it to become completely idolatrous.

Hermeneutics. The science of interpretation, especially of texts, that centralizes the role of the reader and her context in the cognitive understanding of a written work.

Holocaust. The genocide of one third of the Jewish people—more than six million men, women and children—during World War II, at the hands of the Nazis and various other fascist forces in Western and Eastern Europe. 90% of European Jewry was wiped out.

Hypostasis. In theology, something that constitutes or makes concrete the essential substance of anything, including something that is divine.

Imam. A leader of ritual prayer in Islam.

Imitatio dei. The imitation of divine characteristics as a religious experience and/ or obligation.

Immanence. In theology, that aspect of God that is felt in the immediateness of human experience of the world or of time.

Jainism. Ancient religion of India, which presently has almost three million adherents; includes a basic commitment to ahimsa (nonviolence).

Jihad. A form of struggle for the causes of Islam, which can be focused on inner processes of moral transformation or outer processes of social transformation toward a just and God-fearing society; has been used extensively in the traditional literature to refer to war in defense of Islam or as a way of attacking "the enemies of Islam," however and by whomever that comes to be defined. Jihad has also been traditionally regulated by strict notions of when and where it is permissible or obligatory.

Jus ad bellum. Medieval tradition of Christian law pertaining to conditions under which war is permissible or obligatory. Now used by others in the natural law tradition in discussions of peace and war to refer to warrants for war and peace before war breaks out.

Jus in bello. Medieval tradition of Christian law pertaining to the proper conduct of and limits to war once it is undertaken. Now used by others in the natural law tradition in discussions of peace and war to refer to proper conduct of war and its limits in the context of the battlefield.

Kabbalah. Tradition of Jewish mysticism with roots in the talmudic period but not fully developed until the Middle Ages.

King David. First Israelite king in the First Temple period to establish a sizable Jewish kingdom, with Jerusalem as its capital.

Knesset. The Israeli parliament.

Kosher laws. Jewish rules governing dietary restrictions.

Likud. Political party of Israel that came to prominence under Begin, Shamir, and Netanyahu. Home to revisionist Zionists with roots in the Irgun, Lehi, and the Stern Gang, who ran various violent operations to drive out the British from Palestine and to intimidate Arabs into leaving. Old rivals of the Labor party, with distinct cultural and class distinctions beneath the surface of the rivalry.

Mahayana Buddhism. A somewhat later form of Buddhism that reigns in a number of Asian countries.

Mahdi tradition. In Shiite Islam, the belief that a future Imam will return to be the leader of the community.

Maimonidean. Characteristic of Maimonides' philosophy or legal positions.

Mekhilta. Rabbinic *halakhic* midrash that is a commentary on the book of Exodus; entails numerous *halakhic* and some non-*halakhic* discussions.

Messiah. A figure in Judaism who will transform history, bring world peace, and restore the Jewish people to their historic home in Israel. In Christianity, it refers to Jesus of Nazareth.

Messianic era. In Judaism, the time of history in which the messiah arrives.

Midrash. Rabbinic interpretation of biblical texts; one of the most central characteristics of rabbinic thinking and the place of greatest creativity and innovation.

Mishnah. One of the earliest compendiums of rabbinic law, written down in the second century but citing authorities from the first century C.E.

Mishnaic. Of or pertaining to the Mishnah or its period in rabbinic history.

Mitsvah. The central religious act of Judaism, the fulfilling of a commandment of God that appears in the Bible, and also the fulfilling of any righteous deed that is taught by rabbinic Judaism.

Modern Mennonites. Those Mennonites who maintain many traditional beliefs and practices but who dress in modern clothing and are thoroughly at home with modern technology. They engage in study of and dialogue with the larger human community and have a range of social and political beliefs and values, from very conservative to very progressive.

Modern Orthodox Judaism. A version of Orthodox Judaism that also claims a commitment to secular education and, to some degree, to creatively interact with modern thought and values.

Mohammed. Central prophet of Islam, considered by Islam to be the last and greatest prophet in the history of the three Biblically based monotheisms.

Moral sense theory. Modern school of ethics that roots good actions in prosocial sentiments, such as the drive to justice or to be compassionate or to have courage. Ethical training is thus focused on education and the habituation of the psyche to exercising prosocial sentiments.

Mosaic religion. Benamozegh's term for the religion of the Hebrew Bible or Torah and the rabbis that is specifically meant for the Jewish people, as opposed to Noachism, also embedded in the Torah, which is meant to be a universal religion for all humankind or meant as a kind of all-embracing blueprint of a universal religion, pieces of which can be found in all spiritual traditions.

NGO. Nongovernmental organization or agency, such as Oxfam, CARE, Refugees International, the Vatican, the World Conference on Religion and Peace, or the Mennonite Central Committee. Considered by many theoreticians to be crucial to conflict resolution in complex international conflicts.

Nirvana. In Buddhism, a final state of bliss attained upon enlightenment, which is a release from the cycle of birth, death, and rebirth.

Noah. Figure in the Bible who is said to have survived a global, disastrous great flood, based on God's instruction, and who proceeded to rebuild human civilization.

Old Order Mennonites. Those Mennonites who adhere to this day to strict social limitations in terms of clothing, modern technology, and exposure to secular education and information.

Orthodox Christianity. Eastern churches that broke early from Rome and formed a distinctive Christianity, they have a set of nuanced differences regarding the sacraments, a mystical emphasis on the incarnation of God, rather than a formal commitment to transubstantiation, and a different and less hierarchical structure of authority than in Catholicism, among other differences.

Orthodox Judaism. The expression of Judaism in modern times that claims to adhere most closely to traditional Judaism before the onslaught of the Enlightenment and Emancipation. Formed in opposition to Conservative and Reform Judaism.

Oslo accords. The first stages of direct PLO-Israeli negotiations, formally signed in May 1994, which have now lead to final status talks and negotiations for a permanent peace between Israel and the Palestinians.

Othering. Often used in postmodern literature, it refers to the ways in which we make ourselves distinct and alienated from Others or the ways in which we objectify Others and separate them conceptually and phenomenologically from ourselves.

Pantheist. An approach to spirituality that sees the material world as one with God.

Peacebuilding. A term typical of the conflict transformation school of thought, which emphasizes long-term relationship building with a broad spectrum of society as the key to peace, as opposed to discrete sets of negotiations and settlements, usually between elites.

Pietism. Movements of religiosity in the monotheisms that emphasize an intensive relationship to God, a focus on the personal disciplines of moral behavior, and an active engagement with the inner life of the believer.

Pogrom. Periodic massacres of Jewish men, women, and children in the villages and towns of Christian Europe; especially common on Christian holidays, such as Easter.

Prophet, The. Common term in Islam for Mohammed.

Purim. A Jewish holiday, founded exclusively by the rabbis, that commemorates a plot to destroy the Jewish people in a mythic kingdom and vengeance that is wreaked on those who engaged in the plot.

Quietism. A spiritual philosophy that emphasizes a passive approach to worldly problems, especially violence.

Qur'an. The holiest book of Islam, considered by Muslims to be the best and most direct revelation of the word of Allah (God) through the prophet Mohammed.

Rabbinic Judaism. A transformation of biblical Judaism that occured over a period of many centuries before, during, and after the beginning of the Common Era; a hermeneutic rereading of biblical religion that is so complete that it effectively became the standard Judaism until the modern day. It emphasizes the religious deed, Torah study, and a large set of ethical and ritual acts, which comprise one's spiritual relationship to God and the community.

Ramadan. Sacred month in the Islamic calendar, which involves fasting, feasting, and a greater attention to one's life and character before Allah (God).

Rebbe. Central figure of Hasidic Judaism, major righteous leader who takes care of his community and forms a special relationship to God.

Reform Judaism. A liberal version of Judaism, beginning with the modern period, that eliminates any legal requirement to observe Jewish law and emphasizes modern, ethical monotheism, the social teachings of the classical biblical prophets, and forms of worship more typical of the dominant, Western culture.

Reframing. Common phrase in conflict resolution techniques that involves helping conflicting parties to see their opposing positions in new ways, which allows for compromise, joint activity, fulfillment of everyone's needs, etc.

Sabbath laws. Extensive set of disciplines associated with traditional observance of the Jewish sabbath; they involve prayers, social meals, study, and refraining from any invasive manipulation of Earth's resources. Thus, among many other restrictions, no creation of fire, no writing, no farming, and no business is permitted for 25 hours.

Satyagraha. Lit. "holding on to truth." A method of nonviolent resistance, according to Gandhi's interpretation of Hinduism.

Second Temple Period. Time in Jewish history beginning approximately in the fifth century B.C.E. and extending to the end of the first century C.E.

Sefirot. Realms of the divine being, or extensions thereof, in Jewish mysticism that emanate toward and interact with human life on earth. The *sefirot* function in many ways, but they have an interactive quality to them that allows believers, if they train themselves in ethical and cognitive perfection, to engage in influencing cosmic, divine phenomena of the world.

Sephardi. Those members of the Jewish Diaspora who migrated to, and then originated from, the realms of Jewish life that fell under Islamic rule or influence, such as the Middle East, North Africa, and Muslim Spain.

Seven Laws of Noah. Body of rabbinic rules, including a prohibition against murder and theft, that are supposed to be universal, and obligatory for all human beings.

Shekhina. The mystical notion in Judaism of the divine presence that dwells among people, especially if they behave in ways that meet with divine approval.

Shtetl. Small hamlets and villages of Jewish life in Eastern Europe.

Sikh. A follower of Sikhism, one of the more recent religions of India. It is a monotheistic religion beginning in the sixteenth century and now numbers about eighteen million adherents worldwide.

Sitz-im-leben. The cultural and social context in which a text is written, which influences its character.

Syncretism. A strong tendency in the history of religions for a significant number of people to creatively combine elements of more than one religion to which they are exposed; often induces a reactionary response by the guardians of the respective traditions, at least in monotheism.

Talmud. The preeminent set of volumes of rabbinic Judaism, which contains the oral debates and hermeneutic interpretations of hundreds of years of rabbis.

Theosophy. A philosophic approach to a mystical understanding of the divine operation of the world and the divine nature.

Tosafists. Traditional commentators on the Talmud of the Middle Ages who were known for ingenious legal thinking and innovation.

Transcendence. That aspect of the divine that is utterly above and removed from the world, as opposed to immanence.

Ulama. The senior religious figures of a Muslim community.

Ummah. The Islamic community worldwide.

Utilitarianism. School of ethics, typified by J. S. Mill, that emphasizes the calculus of outcomes of actions as a way of deciding, in its simplest version, how to bring the greatest happiness to the greatest number of people.

Vedas. Most important scriptures of Hinduism.

Volkish. Favored term for anything characteristic of the mythic Aryan people; a key term used by Nazi propaganda.

Worldview, worldview theory. Influenced by the work of Oscar Nudler, among others, emphasizes the roots of conflict in the completely different cognitive and emotive universes of combatants; implies a different set of approaches to peacemaking.

Yad Vashem. The preeminent Israeli Holocaust museum, where most official visitors to Israel have been taken as an introduction to Israel and its foundation.

Yishuv. The original settlement of Zionists in the land of Palestine before the creation of the state of Israel.

Notes

Chapter One

1. Less well known globally, but equally revolutionary in their context, are Badshah Khan, the nonviolent Islamic leader of the Pathans, Rabbi Dr. Abraham Joshua Heschel, of U.S. civil rights era fame, Dorothy Day, and many others.

2. Rorty is correct that rigid notions of Truth, Right, Science, or God always get us in trouble when we expect them to solve our problems. He is also right to embrace a Deweyan hope for the future, which leaves the future an open possibility that is based on human thought and action, not absolute categories. But he misunderstands that, in the history of human thinking and believing, it is also the case that "absolutes," such as Truth, God, or religious myth and ritual, are made dynamic by the endless hermeneutic drive of human beings, and therein lies hope as well. Hope does not have to exist only in a humanistic embrace; it is also in the power of human beings to constantly reinterpret the absolutes that they live by. This makes many futures possible even for religious people, with all the peril and promise that accompanies the uncertainty of hermeneutic engagement with ancient values and texts. See Richard Rorty, "Method, Social Science and Social Hope," in *The Postmodern Turn*, ed. Steven Seidman (Cambridge: Cambridge University Press, 1994), 46–64.

3. Human needs theory is a school of thought that examines conflict in terms of the needs that go unsatisfied and therefore cause destructive conflict. There is great disagreement on what are human needs and which needs are the most fundamental. See John Burton, ed., *Conflict: Human Needs Theory* (New York: St. Martin's, 1990).

4. On the centrality of identity as the basis for conflict, see Jay Rothman, *Resolving Identity-Based Conflict in Nations, Organizations, and Communities* (San Francisco: Jossey-Bass, 1997).

5. There are numerous references, but see esp. Exod. 22:20, 23:9; Lev. 16:29, 17:12, 18:26; Deut. 10:19.

6. There was an obvious need to be interdisciplinary in this work, which necessarily required a degree of imprecision in each religious tradition and many generalizations that would rankle the experts. My purpose is not to be the last word on this subject but rather to stimulate further research and better recommendations, which will be finely honed to individual religious traditions. However, as we will note, all recommendations have to include methods of interreligious conflict resolution as well, methods that assume divergent traditions adhered to by different combatants. In other words, comparative work is inescapable, with all of its inaccuracies.

7. See Amos 5:20; Joel 1–3; Zeph. 1:7–2:2; Zech. 14; Mal. 3.

8. See, for example, Rev. 16:6, where the theme of blood is central. The blood of the prophets and the innocent will be paid for by rivers of the blood of the "wicked," whoever this may be. Of course, this is what is so dangerous about violent literature: Who decides in every generation who the wicked are, and are there any controls on this fantasy of bloody revenge? Rivers of blood tend to have no limit in history and always sweep up in their furious currents the innocent together with the guilty. The Crusades are perhaps the most poignant example of this in religious history, but it is only a lack of historical records that makes us overlook parallel events in other places and cultures.

Chapter Two

1. See Henry O. Thompson, *World Religions in War and Peace* (Jefferson, N.C.: McFarland, 1988); John Ferguson, *War and Peace in the World's Religions* (New York: Oxford University Press, 1978); and Homer Jack, ed., *World Religions and World Peace: The International Inter-Religious Symposium on Peace* (Boston: Beacon, 1968).

2. See Thich Nhat Hanh, *Being Peace* (Berkeley, Calif.: Parallax, 1987); Maha Gosananda, *Step by Step: Meditations on Wisdom and Compassion* (Berkeley, Calif.: Parallax, 1988); Gosananda, *A Report from the Inter-Religious Mission for Peace in Cambodia* (Providence, R.I.: Cambodian Mission for Peace, 1988); and Cynthia Sampson, "Religion and Peacebuilding," in *Peacemaking in International Conflict*, ed. I William Zartman and Lewis Rasmussen (Washington, D.C.: U.S. Institute of Peace, 1997).

3. See, for example, Clifford Geertz, *The Interpretation of Cultures* New York: Basic, 1973), pt. 3.

4. An example of the complex interplay of economics and religious extremism might be the comparative status of the Shiite community in the Middle East and the popularity of the Iranian revolution among them, or the economic scenario of Iran just prior to the revolution. Another example might involve an analysis of the economic and social status of the followers of Meir Kahane in the United States and Israel. Kahane, since the inception of his radical activity in the 1960s, was brilliant at empowering working-class Jewish youth, who were decidedly marginalized by the upper-class mobility and intellectual accomplishments of most of their ethnic contemporaries. Kahane moved them from a relatively inner-directed anger at their social position to belligerency against hoodlums attacking elderly Jews in the United States, then to opposition to the Soviets who oppressed Jews, and finally toward hatred of Arabs. For an analysis of class conflict and conflict resolution, see Richard E. Rubenstein, "The Analyzing and Resolving of Class Conflict," in *Conflict Resolution Theory and Practice*, ed. Dennis Sandole and Hugo van der Merwe (Manchester, N.Y.: Manchester University Press, 1993), 146–57. On Kahane's class consciousness, see his *Uncomfortable Questions for Comfortable Jews* (Secaucus, N.J.: L. Stuart, 1987). On Kahane's life, see Robert I. Friedman, *The False Prophet, Meir Kahane: From FBI Informant to Knesset Member* (Brooklyn, N.Y.: Lawrence Hill, 1990).

5. Mohammed Abu-Nimer, "Conflict Resolution in an Islamic Context," *Peace and Change* 21, no. 1 (Jan. 1996): 22–40, has cautioned against the unadulterated application of Western conflict resolution methods to non-Western contexts. I am suggesting some ways in which religious traditions may serve as a bridge to help conflict resolution experts adjust their methods to each cultural situation.

6. On women's roles in the Israeli/Palestinian conflict, see Simona Sharoni, *Gender and the Israeli-Palestinian Conflict: The Politics of Women's Resistance* (Syracuse, N.Y.: Syracuse University Press, 1995).

7. See Haim Cohn, *Human Rights in Jewish Law* (New York: Ktav, 1984), 27–47; Reuven Kimelman, "Non-Violence in the Talmud," *Judaism* 17 (1968): 316–34; and David S. Shapiro, "The Jewish Attitude towards Peace and War," in *Studies in Jewish Thought*, ed. David S. Shapiro (New York: Yeshiva University Press, 1975), 1:316–73.

8. See Eliezer Schweid, "Land of Israel," in *Contemporary Jewish Religious Thought*, ed. Arthur A. Cohen and Paul Mendes-Flohr (New York: Free Press, 1988), 535–42; and Martin Buber, "The Land and Its Possessors," in his *Israel and the World* (New York: Schocken, 1963), 226–33. Buber's Zionism, however, was a radical advocacy of a binational state of Jews and Arabs; see his *A Land of Two Peoples*, ed. Paul Mendes-Flohr (New York: Oxford University Press, 1983). See also Ehud Luz, "The Moral Price of Sovereignty: The Dispute about the Use of Military Power within Zionism," *Modern Judaism* 7 (Fall 1987): 51–98.

9. On Gush Emunim, see Laurence J. Silberstein, ed., *Jewish Fundamentalism in Comparative Perspective: Religion, Ideology and the Crisis of Modernity* (New York: New York University Press, 1993).

10. See Richard E. Rubenstein, *Alchemists of Revolution: Terrorism in the Modern World* (New York: Basic, 1987).

11. See Ervin Staub, *The Roots of Evil: The Origins of Evil and Other Group Violence* (Cambridge: Cambridge University Press, 1989), 72–75, 279–81, and esp. 317, n. 15; and Alice Miller, *For Your Own Good: Hidden Cruelty in Child-Rearing and the Roots of Violence* (New York: Farrar, Straus, Giroux, 1983).

12. See, for example, *Oz Ve-Shalom*, English Bulletin series, nos. 1–8 (1982–1999). Some of the bulletin titles are instructive: "One Standard of Justice," "The Cry of Religious Conscience," "Torah against Terror," "Violence and the Value of Life in Jewish Tradition."

13. See, for example, Robert Bush and Joseph Folger, *The Promise of Mediation: Responding to Conflict through Empowerment and Recognition* (San Francisco: Jossey-Bass, 1994), 27; and John Paul Lederach, *Preparing for Peace: Conflict Transformation across Cultures* (Syracuse, N.Y.: Syracuse University Press, 1995), 16–20.

14. See Joseph Montville, "The Healing Function in Political Conflict Resolution," in Sandole and van der Merwe, eds., *Conflict Resolution*, 117–24.

15. Even though the classical expression of these virtues emphasizes their unilateral character, it seems to me that in order for it to work as a conflict resolution strategy, there has to be an agreed-upon bilateral character to these interactions, even if, as they are finally made public, the interactions have the look and feel of a unilateral event. Rarely does only one side of a conflict consider themselves victims deserving of apologies. Furthermore, proper use of this method would necessarily entail judicious choices of the third-party negotiators based on an inductive analysis of the circumstances. It may be that in certain circumstances, such as postgenocide, mutual apologies would be obscene and perceived as such. It may also be that one side has more to apologize for. These considerations must enter into the give and take of the conflict resolution scenario. Also, the object of the apology must be given careful consideration. One must analyze where the gravest injuries have occurred to particular parties. For example, it seems to me that Israelis and Palestinians, unconsciously or consciously, have managed to direct their injuries of the other precisely toward the most vulnerable areas of the adversary. The Israeli policy of demolishing homes, uprooting olive trees, expelling people, or expropriating their land in retaliation for Arab violence hits the Palestinians precisely in the most painful place: the loss of sovereignty over their land. On the other hand, Palestinian support of terrorism against civilian targets over the years has hit Jews in their most vulnerable injury: the massive loss of innocent life due to genocide in the twentieth century combined with a jittery aware-

ness of being such a tiny minority in the world. This is why Israelis are obsessed by every reaction of Arabs to the murder of a Jew, while Palestinians are obsessed with every acre of land that is under dispute. The apologies and confidence-building measures need therefore to be directed toward these areas of injury.

16. See Rafael Moses, "The Leader and the Led: A Dyadic Relationship," in *The Psychodynamics of International Relationships*, ed. Vamik Volkan, Demetrios Julius, and Joseph Montville (Lexington, Mass.: Lexington Books, 1990), 1:205–17.

17. See, for example, David S. Shapiro, "The Doctrine of the Image of God and *Imitatio Dei*," in *Contemporary Jewish Ethics*, ed. Menachem Kellner (New York: Hebrew Publishing, 1978), 127–51. "The Christian is and must be by his very adoption as a son of God, in Christ, a peacemaker (Matt. 5:9). He is bound to imitate the Savior who, instead of defending Himself with twelve legions of angels allowed Himself to be nailed to the Cross and died praying for His executioners" (Thomas Merton, *The Nonviolent Alternative* [New York: Farrar, Straus, Giroux, 1980], 13).

18. Ronald Duncan, ed., *Gandhi: Selected Writings* (New York: Harper Colophon, 1971), 33–64.

19. See, for example, Thomas Merton, "The Climate of Mercy," in his *Love and Living*, ed. Naomi Stone and Patrick Hart (San Diego: Harcourt Brace Jovanovich, 1979), 203–19; Marc Gopin, "The Religious Ethics of Samuel David Luzzatto" (Ph.D. diss., Brandeis Univ., 1993), chaps. 2, 6, 7. The entire tradition of moral sense theory, especially as it was articulated by Rousseau, is rooted in the importance of empathy.

20. There exists, however, the perennial problem in a religious context of the *scope* of the spiritual commitment. In this case, for example, can the religious adherent extend empathy toward a nonbeliever? Is she even allowed to do so by standards of that tradition? This has to be examined in advance and will depend on the type of people participating, their particular hermeneutic of their tradition, and how far that hermeneutic can be stretched to include nonbelievers. We will discuss below the problem of the limited scope of religious ethical values.

21. Douglas Johnston and Cynthia Sampson, eds., *Religion: The Missing Dimension of Statecraft* (New York: Oxford University Press, 1994), ch. 6.

22. On relational empathy, see Benjamin Broome, "Managing Differences in Conflict Resolution: The Role of Relational Empathy," in Sandole and van der Merwe, eds., *Conflict Resolution*, 97–111. Of course the concept of empathy would need to be mediated by each side of the conflict, which would have to translate the concept in terms of its own religious traditions. Naturally, this might lead to differences and debate. Furthermore, the ensuing debate may reflect casuistic nuances that actually mask deeper issues. A skilled third party might want to work at bringing both sides together on the definition of terms, while simultaneously addressing what he believes to be the underlying differences of the casuistic debate. A secular observer may quickly tire of such debates over traditions; however, these kind of debates are critical to the way some religious people negotiate their needs and claims upon the world. It is also the way in which compromise is often achieved in religious contexts. Furthermore, the very indulgence in such discussions has worth in itself, namely, the valuation and honoring of religious traditions which is completely overlooked in most first-and second-track diplomacy settings. Honoring the traditions makes compromise more possible when religious combatants are involved in conflict.

23. Mohandas Gandhi, *All Men Are Brothers*, ed. Krishna Kripalani (New York: Continuum, 1980), ch. 4; and Christopher Key Chapple, *Nonviolence to Animals, Earth, and Self in Asian Traditions* (Albany: State University of New York, 1993).

24. See, for example, Roland Bainton, *Christian Attitudes toward War and Peace* (Nashville: Abingdon, 1979), chaps. 5 and 10; Peter Mayer, ed., *The Pacifist Conscience*

(New York: Holt, Rinehart and Winston, 1966), 355–410; John Yoder, *The Politics of Jesus* (Grand Rapids, Mich.: William P. Eerdmans, 1972); and Yoder, *Nevertheless: Varieties of Religious Pacifism* (Scottdale, Pa.: Herald, 1992). On the Mennonite/Anabaptist tradition, pacifism, and the central importance of Jesus as the model human being, see Paul M. Lederach, *The Third Way* (Scottdale, Pa.: Herald, 1980). Note the critical importance of emulating God, *imitatio dei*, in establishing an ideal model of peacemaking, and see my thoughts above on leadership. This concept is a critical bridge between Jewish and Christian values—and possibly Islamic as well, in terms of emulation of the Prophet.

25. On other Western religions and pacifism see below, as well as Kimelman, "Non-Violence in the Talmud."

26. "Although Islam urges its followers to fight and die in defense of their faith, it considers suicide a sin; the preservation of one's life, to many Muslims, takes priority over all other considerations, including the profession of the faith" (Khalid Kishtainy, "Violent and Nonviolent Struggle in Arab History," in *Arab Nonviolent Political Struggle in the Middle East*, ed. Ralph Crow, P. Grant, and S. Ibrahim [Boulder and London: Lynne Rienner, 1990], 11). A Jewish rabbinic text of the first century states, "Therefore was a human being created alone, in order to teach you that everyone who wipes out a single person it is as if he has wiped out an entire world, while he who saves a single person it is as if he has saved an entire world" (Mishnah Sanhedrin 4: 5).

27. Note the overwhelming importance of interior experience in the classic studies by William James, *The Varieties of Religious Experience* (New York: Modern Library, 1936), and Rudolf Otto, *The Idea of the Holy* (London: Oxford University Press, 1923).

28. For more on the special contribution of Buddhism to the inner life and peacemaking, see Kenneth Kraft, ed., *Inner Peace, World Peace: Essays on Buddhism* (Albany: State University of New York Press, 1992).

29. "You should develop unlimited thoughts of sympathy for all beings in the world above, below, and across, unmarred by hate or enmity.... this is called the holy state. When you hold on to opinions no more, when you are endowed with good conduct and true insight, when you have expelled all craving for pleasures, you will be reborn no more" (*Metta Sutta*, in *Suttanipata* [Pali Text Society Publications] 1: 8, 143–52), quoted by Luis Gomez in Kraft, ed., *Inner Peace, World Peace*, 40. Avoiding rebirth is the great goal of Buddhist spirituality. Note the relationship between no longer holding opinions, gaining true insight, and the capacity for empathy. This has interesting implications in terms of the mental states necessary for someone to see an enemy in a new light and the possible ground rules for an indigenous method of Buddhist interpersonal engagement. Note also the focus on pleasures and desire in this regard and compare it with Gandhi's experiments, below.

30. See, however, Sulak Sivaraksa's remarkable expansion of these concepts to a contemporary, proactive—and daringly progressive—interpretation of the Eightfold Path, in Kraft, ed., *Inner Peace, World Peace*, 127–37.

31. See William Theodore de Bary, ed., *Sources of Indian Tradition* (New York: Columbia University Press, 1958), 117.

32. For a Tibetan program of training in compassion, see Tsong-kha-pa (1357–1419 C.E.), *Lam rim chen mo*, in *Ethics of Tibet*, trans. Alex Wayman (Albany: State University of New York Press, 1991), 52–57.

33. See Gandhi, *All Men Are Brothers*, ch. 5.

34. See Elise Boulding, "States, Boundaries, and Environmental Security," in Sandole and van der Merwe, eds., *Conflict Resolution*, 198: "The task of innovation may not be as impossible as it seems because people and societies have always been capable of imagining the other and different. It is an interesting fact that the image of the

peaceable garden—a localist world in which people live harmoniously with each other and with their environment, with warriors laying aside weapons has persisted in every major cultural tradition."

35. For a full account, see Eugene Fisher, *Faith without Prejudice* (New York: Crossroads, 1993), ch. 7; Fisher, "Evolution of a Tradition," in *Fifteen Years of Catholic-Jewish Dialogue, 1970–1985,* ed. International Catholic-Jewish Liaison Committee (Rome: Vatican Library, 1988), ch. 10; and Eugene Fisher and Leon Klenicki, *In Our Time: The Flowering of Jewish-Catholic Dialogue* (Mahwah, N.J.: Paulist Press, 1990). For a Jewish response to the new catechism, see Rabbi Leon Klenicki, "The New Catholic Catechism and the Jews," in *Service International De Documentation Judéo-Chrétienne* 27: 2 (1994): 9–18.

36. See David Novak's careful analysis of this issue and its relation to the Jewish community, "Jews and Catholics: Beyond Apologies," *First Things* 89 (Jan. 1999): 20–25.

37. See *The Washington Post,* Mar. 28, 1995, p. A13, on the pronouncements of Metropolitan Ioann, the Russian Orthodox primate of St. Petersburg. To be fair, I attended a meeting in June 1996 at the U.S. Institute of Peace where the archpriest representing the External Department of the Russian Orthodox church recounted, in the presence of Moscow's chief rabbi, his efforts at reconciliation and pluralism in recent years. It was somewhat encouraging, though not terribly courageous regarding past wrongs.

38. "Falwell's Antichrist Remarks Anger Jews," *Boston Globe* Jan. 28, 1999, p. A7.

39. The Catholic church has an old tradition of locating all evil in the devil. This has led recently to an updating of the practice of exorcism. The devil is seen as a cosmic liar and murderer, and the presence of the devil expresses itself in modern culture in the "idolatry" of money, deceit, and sex. See "New Vatican Guidelines Revise Rite of Exorcism," *Boston Globe,* Jan. 27, 1999. The church, it seems to me, has been quite careful in recent years not to utilize this theological tradition and practice in order to demonize whole groups, unlike the sermons that one can find on the fringes of conservative Christian life. The church, in recent years, tends to locate evil in certain practices and societal trends rather than in personages. But this requires more investigation and interfaith discussion. The entire subject of certain religious tendencies to locate evil outside the human being, in some ontic entity, is of profound concern in terms of conflict analysis and requires further study. This is especially common in African religions, and I am still investigating the effects of this on conflict and war and how to respond to it from the point of view of conflict resolution practice. There are obvious dangers, but there may also be ways to engage the reification of evil in terms of conflict resolution.

40. See, for example, John Paul Lederach, "Pacifism in Contemporary Conflict: A Christian Perspective," paper commissioned by the U.S. Institute of Peace (Washington, D.C.: July 20, 1993).

41. See W. Scott Thompson et al., eds., *Approaches to Peace: An Intellectual Map* (Washington, D.C.: U.S. Institute of Peace, 1992).

42. See John Kelsay and Sumner Twiss, eds., *Religion and Human Rights* (New York: Project on Religion and Human Rights, 1994). It must be cautioned that many religious subgroupings might welcome the introduction of a human rights discussion, for example, while some may see it as an invasion of Western values or, at the very least, a system of values that they instinctively and initially consider alien to their traditions. The third-party negotiator must decide whether the benefits outweigh the cost of introducing concepts such as human rights into a discussion between warring religious groups or whether the goals of conflict resolution can be achieved in some other way.

43. The just war legal tradition in the three monotheisms, which addresses the moral problem of violence with outsiders, is not as helpful for the study of conflict resolution as one would hope. Just war theory indicates which wars are either justified, limited, circumscribed, or prohibited. See, for example, James Turner Johnson and John Kelsay, eds., *Cross, Crescent and Sword: The Justification and Limitation of War in Western and Islamic Tradition* (New York: Greenwood, 1990); David Novak, *Law and Theology in Judaism* (New York: Ktav, 1974), 125–35; and Reuven Kimelman, "War," in *Frontiers of Jewish Thought*, ed. Steven Katz (Washington, D.C.: B'nai B'rith Books, 1992), 309–32. There are important moral arguments in these traditions that would force a religious society, in principle at least, to consider all the consequences of war before engaging in it. Furthermore, there are a series of restrictions regarding the conduct of violence, which try to blunt the impact of violence on enemies. However, such legal concepts tend to emphasize warmaking strategies and not peacemaking strategies. They tend to skew the discussion toward the abstract theological choice of war or not war, without a nuanced sense of all the stages at which aggressive interpersonal and intergroup conflict resolution may address the real needs of the situation. Thus they do not really address the dynamic possibility of human relationships among adherents and outsiders or adversaries. These laws tend also to abstract the enemy, which is a major impediment, as we now know, to conflict resolution.

44. For a full exploration of fundamentalism today in its relationship to politics, see Martin Marty and F. Scott Appleby, eds., *Fundamentalisms and the State: Remaking Polities, Economies, Militance* (Chicago: University of Chicago Press, 1993).

45. I use the term Other in the sense of anyone who is outside the community of the faithful in a particular religious grouping or to refer to a group within the religious community that is considered to have a different and/or inferior status. Emmanuel Levinas's conceptualization of the Other and the topic of intersubjectivity, in general, that he and other religious philosophers, such as Martin Buber, discuss, might prove useful in provoking interreligious dialogue on the problem of the conflict between religions. Some of the debate between Levinas and Buber on the nature of the intersubjective moment, whether, for example, it is asymmetric or equal, may have important implications for designing theories of conflict resolution. See Levinas's critique of Buber's epistemology in *The Levinas Reader*, ed. Sean Hand (Cambridge, Mass.: Basil Blackwell, 1989), 59–74, and see 37–58 for an introduction to Levinas's theory of the Other. For an introduction to Buber's philosophy of the interhuman, see his *The Knowledge of Man*, ed. Maurice Friedman (New York: Harper and Row, 1965), 59–88. An interesting area of research might be to attempt to elicit from these religious epistemologies approaches to the problems of violence between self and other, as well as between nations and religious groups. On psychodynamic approaches to the relationships among self, Other, and violence, see Vamik Volkan, "An Overview of Psychological Concepts Pertinent to Interethnic and/or International Relationships," Volkan et al., eds., *Psychodynamics of International Relationships*, 1: 31–46; Rafael Moses, "Self, Self-view, and Identity," in Volkan et al., eds., *Psychodynamics of International Relationships*, 47–56; and Bryant Wedge, "Psychology of the Self in Social Conflict," in *International Conflict Resolution: Theory and Practice*, ed. Edward Azar and John Burton (Boulder, Colo.: Lynne Rienner, 1986), 56–62.

46. See Moses Maimonides, *Mishneh Torah*, Book of Knowledge, Laws of Idolatry, ch. 7; and Thompson, *World Religions in War and Peace*, 12–17. It should be said that idolaters are condemned mostly for complete moral decadence in many biblical (Amos 1–4) and rabbinic sources (Num. Rabbah 11; Midrash ha-Gadol, Noach, 11:9; Talmud Bavli Yoma 9b), which has led a number of modern Jewish religious thinkers to dismiss the harsh anti-idolatry rules in the context of the major modern religions,

all of which have strong moral codes. See Harold Kasimow and Byron Sherwin, eds., *No Religion Is an Island: Abraham Joshua Heschel and Interreligious Dialogue* (Maryknoll, N.Y.: Orbis, 1991); and David Novak, *Jewish-Christian Dialogue: A Jewish Justification* (New York: Oxford University Press, 1989).

47. See Mishnah Sanhedrin 4:5; Talmud Bavli Sanhedrin 37a.

48. See Talmud Bavli Berakhot 17a; Avot of Rabbi Nathan, version A, ch. 12. The Hebrew term *beriot* and the amplification of the idea in the text make it clear that Hillel referred to all human beings.

49. There has been a discouragement of conversion to Judaism since the beginning of rabbinic Judaism almost two thousand years ago (see, for example, Talmud Bavli Yevamot 47a). However, in the period immediately prior to the flourishing of rabbinic Judaism, Hasmonean kings did convert people en masse, sometimes by force (see Robert M. Seltzer, *Jewish People, Jewish Thought* [New York: Macmillan, 1980], 130, 182, 193). It cannot be said with absolute certainty what Rabbi Yohanan's and Hillel's respective attitudes were toward conversion, although they were pivotal figures of rabbinic Judaism. One thing is certain: the way the texts have been received and read by rabbinic Jews—the critical issue in hermeneutics—would preclude their being an encouragement to conversion. Rather, they are methods of expressing a commitment to peacemaking and to care for all of God's creation. I make no claim, furthermore, that their words are representative of all of rabbinic Judaism; there are plenty of angry statements about gentiles in rabbinic literature. My purpose is to demonstrate the dynamic possibilities of religious hermeneutics, which are inherent even in ancient texts, not to gloss over the problems associated with premodern religious literature.

50. See David Little's important work on religious intolerance and political violence, for example, *Sri Lanka: The Invention of Enmity* (Washington, D.C.: U.S. Institute of Peace, 1994); and *Ukraine: The Legacy of Intolerance* (Washington, D.C.: U.S. Institute of Peace, 1991). The genocide of Tutsi in Rwanda in 1994 was not a religious action. However, religious institutions have been implicated. See Pierre Erny, *Rwanda 1994: clés pour comprendre le calvaire d'un peuple.* (Paris: L'Harmattan, 1994); and Gerard Prunier, *Rwanda Crisis: History of a Genocide* (New York: Columbia University Press, 1995). I have received personal correspondence from a Tutsi Jesuit priest, who lost some of his family, telling me how saddened he is that the church in Rwanda is part of the process of examining the atrocities when it itself is implicated, based on what he saw. Another Tutsi survivor, who lost most of her family, told me that she was forced to learn in religious schools why Tutsi were inferior and dangerous. On the alleged participation of priests in the genocide, see "Clergy in Rwanda Is Accused of Abetting Atrocities," *New York Times*, July 7, 1995, P. A3. Thousands of Tutsi refused to go to church as a result of the crimes of the priests. See "Rwanda Struggles with a Crisis of Faith," *San Francisco Chronicle*, Jan. 2, 1995, P. A8.

51. Johan Galtung, "Peace, Violence, and Peace Research," *Journal of Peace Research* 6 (1969): 167–91.

52. See Thompson, *World Religions in War and Peace*; and Ferguson, *War and Peace*.

53. Mishnan Sanhedrin 8:7; and Ephraim Urbach, "Jewish Doctrines and Practices in Halakhic and Aggadic Literature," in *Violence and Defense in Jewish Experience*, ed. Salo Baron, George Wise, and Lenn Goodman (Philadelphia: Jewish Publication Society of America, 1977), 87–112.

54. Abdulaziz A. Sachedina, "The Development of *Jihad* in Islamic Revelation and History," in Johnson and Kelsay, eds., *Cross, Crescent and Sword*, 39.

55. See, for example, the debates over the Gulf War in David Smock, ed., *Religious Perspectives on War: Christian, Muslim, and Jewish Attitudes to Force after the Gulf War*

(Washington, D.C.: U.S. Institute of Peace, 1992); and, generally, Bainton, *Christian Attitudes*, 66–84. See also n. 24 above.

56. See, for example, Chaiwat Satha-Anand, Glenn D. Paige, and Sarah Gilliat, eds., *Islam and Nonviolence* (Honolulu, Hawaii: University of Hawaii, and Spark M. Matsunaga Institute for Peace, 1993). On a pacifist interpretation of *jihad* by the Ahmadi sect of Islam, see Yohanan Friedmann, *Prophecy Continuous: Aspects of Ahmadi Religious Thought and Its Medieval Background* (Berkeley: University of California Press, 1989), 165–80; in Judaism, see Murray Polner and Naomi Goodman, eds., *The Challenge of Shalom* (Philadelphia: New Society, 1994); and my essay in Polner and Goodman, "Is There a Jewish God of Peace?" 32–39.

57. "I believe in the fundamental truth of all great religions of the world. I believe that they are all God-given, and I believe that they were necessary for the people to whom these religions were revealed" (Gandhi, *All Men Are Brothers*, 55). See also Diana Eck, *Encountering God* (Boston: Beacon, 1993).

58. See Wedge, "Psychology of the Self in Social Conflict," 57.

Chapter Three

1. For a representative sample of essays with accompanying bibliographies, see Terry Nardin, ed., *The Ethics of War and Peace* (Princeton, N.J.: Princeton University Press, 1996).

2. The same could be said for the secular just war tradition. There is a curious tendency to bifurcate the political and theological calculus of war and divorce it from the entire range of human ethical intuitions and principles. The latter are critical in preventing wars and ending them, yet are absent from just war discussions. Furthermore, the second subject of just war theory is the proper conduct of war. Here too there is a curious way in which different rules and values apply, as if values that address stealing, dishonor, or brutality have to be seen in some new way during wartime or even be discarded during war. Clearly, advances such as the Geneva Conventions have attempted to place back into war some of the normal, universal considerations of ethics. But just war discussions have a curious way of speaking about major cataclysms in such broad terms that the fate of individual moral decisionmaking is completely obscured. This may be a bow to military hierarchy and the loss of a soldier's personal choice. But this too has been challenged by recent conventions. Essentially the just war tradition deprives us of too much of the range of moral thinking and reflection, which are essential in situations of radical moral complexity, such as a battlefield. An exception to this is Michael Walzer's attempt to investigate the complexity of military choices. See his *Just and Unjust Wars* (New York, N.Y.: Basic, 1977).

3. See Kraft, ed., *Inner Peace, World Peace*, 129. In Judaism the prohibition is on selling weapons to someone who cannot be trusted not to commit murder with those weapons and involves the obligation not to aid someone else to commit a crime (Talmud Bavli Avodah Zarah 15b; Maimonides, *Mishneh Torah*, Laws of Murder 12:12). Of course, the sad truth is that Maimonides' same Laws of Murder also make it obligatory to kill Jewish apostates and heretics if they have refused to repent, in addition to a particularly callous attitude toward the value of a polytheistic human life (*Mishneh Torah*, Laws of Murder 4:10, 11). Hence, the mixed legacy of the classical sources, although it must be said in fairness to traditional Judaism that Maimonides was particularly harsh as a social legislator on matters of dogma. See ch. 5 of this volume for at least two Orthodox authorities who were particularly opposed to Maimonides' conclusions.

4. See, for example, John Yoder's argument, in Smock, ed., *Religious Perspectives on War*, 41ff., that a key part of the ethical evaluation of the Gulf War and its conduct should be the question of how Saddam was armed in the first place.

5. When referring to constructive conflict, conflict resolution theoreticians are generally alluding to the fact that many conflicts need to occur, and they can play a constructive role in creating more just societies or more honest relationships where everyone's needs are openly confronted. Conflict management, in such circumstances, would have as its goal not the suppression of the conflict but ensuring that the conflict does not turn into a destructive (usually meaning violent) enterprise that is self-perpetuating or intractable. With some practice, observers and activists can become fairly adept at distinguishing constructive and destructive conflicts, whether they are interpersonal, familial, or societal. See Louis Kriesberg, *Constructive Conflicts* (Lanham, Md.: Rowman & Littlefield, 1998).

6. It is true that many modern liberal forms of religious experience have placed a premium on individual decisionmaking, but this is not the reality of most religious life as it is experienced globally. Some could argue that veneration of and deference to ancestors, elders, and authority figures with access to sacred revelation or wisdom is one of the most common elements in the history of human religion.

7. Naturally, religious elitist hierarchies are just as problematic to a paradigm of authentic peacemaking as diplomatic elites or professional elites. In all cases, authentic peace processes only take root deeply when people at all levels of cultures and subcultures are allowed and/or encouraged to become part of the relationship-building process. However, in order to gain entry into some religious worlds, it is necessary to get the permission of the hierarchy. Then, one can enter into deeper processes with the mass of people.

8. One can see parallel challenges in secular constructs. For example, many authoritarian regimes, such as Assad's in Syria, are predicated on an entire educational system that locates the source of all social problems *outside* the society, namely, in Israel. A shift toward peace dialogue would be deeply threatening to the cultural construct of the society. I have had at least one Syrian student, for example, who went into crisis after going to the Holocaust Museum in Washington, because the Holocaust was supposed to be a Zionist hoax, according to everything she was ever taught. Nevertheless, the pragmatic emphases of nation-state life, such as the focus on security and the material advantages of a better life without war or with more tourism, can help citizens of authoritarian states to move toward new cultural constructs despite old indoctrination. It is harder, however, with religious constructs, which are supposed to be, or felt by the believer to be, permanent fixtures of reality. The radical Christian girl referred to above cannot be "bought off" by, say, a mutually beneficial material relationship with Jews. She will have to go through some profound transformation, even a crisis, in order to change her worldview. It is possible that a carefully constructed dialogue workshop could accomplish this, but I doubt that she would ever enter voluntarily into such a cultural space. Where are our methods of conflict resolution that would help her?

9. See, for example, *Avot of Rabbi Nathan*, ch. 20.

10. See M. Avoth 3:2 on the appearance of the *shekhinah*, the divine presence, among those who exchange the words of Torah.

11. On the importance of the exchange of words in Buddhism, see William Barrett, ed., *Zen Buddhism* (Garden City, N.Y.: Doubleday, 1956), 111–56, which includes Zen instruction and the *koan* exercises. On the importance of debate in the life of Tibetan Buddhist monks, see Dalai Lama XIV, Tenzin Gyatso, *Freedom in Exile: The Autobiography of the Dalai Lama* (New York: HarperCollins, 1990), 25–26. For an eyewitness

account of the Tibetan debates in Dharamsala, the Indian center of the Dalai Lama and Tibetan Buddhism in exile, see Rodger Kamenetz, *The Jew in the Lotus* (San Francisco: HarperSanFrancisco, 1994), 113–14.

12. Robin McDowell, "Buddhist Monks March in Cambodia," *Associated Press*, Mar. 26, 1997.

13. "Ottawa Notebook," Mennonite Central Committee, Apr. 1, 1994.

14. Alan Channer, "Twilight of the Khmer Rouge," *For a Change* (June–July 1997). See also the film on Maha, directed by Channer, *The Serene Life*.

15. I have also been a participant in a number of events of the Faith and Politics Institute, an NGO in Washington, D.C., that has a focus on Congress and finds bipartisan ways to address the members' own and the country's spiritual and ethical values. The institute organized a walk that retraced Martin Luther King's marches, and there was a bipartisan team of congresspeople, led by John Lewis and Amo Houghton, who participated. Personal interviews with the participants suggest a highly unusual transformative spirit produced by the walk. My point is that here we have a sampling of highly educated, savvy politicians whose job it is every day to use words to communicate and persuade. But it was the walking along the path of history, with their bodies, that moved them, that gave them hope and a renewed sense of optimism. This is highly suggestive of what transforms people of all backgrounds. It should also be noted that another symbolic, nonverbal gesture was critical to the transformative power of that walk. A number of congressmen, among them several blacks, chose, with some mixed feelings, to shake the hand of George Wallace as part of the journey, because he has publicly repented of his old views.

16. The examples are endless. See, for example, Bachya ben Joseph ibn Paquda (c. 1080 C.E.), *Duties of the Heart*, trans. Moses Hyamson (Jerusalem and New York: Feldheim, 1970); Meister Eckhardt (d. 1328 C.E.), "About Activities of the Inner Life and Outer Life," in *Meister Eckhardt*, trans. Raymond B. Blakney (New York: Harper, 1941), 36–42; Geshe Rabten and Geshe Dhargyey, *Advice from a Spiritual Friend: Buddhist Thought Transformation*, trans. Brian Beresford (London: Wisdom, 1984), 66, 142; and Wang Yang-Ming (d. 1529 C.E.), "Inquiry on the Great Learning," in *A Source Book in Chinese Philosophy*, ed. Wing-Tsit Chan (Princeton, N.J.: Princeton University Press, 1963), 665.

17. Even from a secular analytic point of view, one can legitimately challenge current dialogue workshop methods that do not attempt to address the deeper, internal roots of rage. Religious ethical approaches to violence can and should critique behaviorist approaches to conflict resolution that do not challenge the deeper origins of human violence. This does not mean that the workshop method is flawed, but that perhaps it is incomplete.

18. See C. R. Mitchell, *The Structure of International Conflict* (New York: St. Martin's, 1981), 165ff.

19. See Dennis Sandole's summary of these views in his "Paradigms, Theories and Metaphors in Conflict and Conflict Resolution," in Sandole and van der Merwe, eds., *Conflict Resolution*, 3–24.

20. See Alfie Kohn, *The Brighter Side of Human Nature* (New York: Basic, 1990).

21. My instinct, after years of working with and teaching people, is that the expression of the full range of emotions may be central to peacemaking. The lack of attention to this or even suppression of this reality alienates many people from peace processes the world over, but this is a subject for another study.

22. This raises another important issue of cross-cultural conflict resolution. Due to the particular matrix of Christian ethics, based on *imitatio dei*, emulating Jesus in this case, there is a tendency among some in Western religious peacemaking to think

that angry religious feelings expressed are a disaster for the dialogue and reconciliation process. But this is not so in my observation of conflict resolvers emanating out of Jewish and Islamic contexts, for example. There, strong emotions, as long as they do not dominate and destroy the proceedings, seem to be a good sign that the encounter between enemies is "real." This anger means to many of us that we are getting to the root of the problem, that we have found a way to positively redirect into the dialogue process the kind of emotions that lead people otherwise to violent politics or physically violent behavior. Mohammed Abu-Nimer, an important trainer in conflict resolution in the Middle East and a professor at American University, did a week-long training with me. Our student body was primarily Christian. We kept waiting for the time when people were going to get angry, considering how painful and controversial were the issues that were being addressed, and we often were amused and baffled that people just did not want to get angry! Our cultural orientation clearly predisposes us to favor therapeutic processes that openly accept and even welcome the need to surface the angry feelings of a conflict, as long as this is not overdone or crudely manipulated by mediators, and as long as it ultimately serves a larger constructive end. By the way, I have seen anger actually evoked by interveners, who then press the group into a seesaw of anger-remorse-joy in order to manipulate it into peacemaking. This is absolutely not my intention. I reject this method as ultimately dishonest and manipulative, and I have seen it backfire badly. But I do welcome anger, when it surfaces *on its own* in some people, as an opportunity to work with a group in discovering the depth of a problem.

23. See Ernst Cassirer, *The Philosophy of the Enlightenment* (Boston: Beacon, 1951), 105ff.

24. This theory is most closely associated with John Burton and his many writings. See, for example, *Conflict: Human Needs Theory* (New York: St. Martin's, 1990).

25. "Man is regarded as intimately related to other fellow-men and beings; and the universe is conceived as a sort of organic whole composed of supra-sensible or mystical correlations and participations" (C. Nyamiti, *The Scope of African Theology* [Kampala: Gaba, 1973], 21, as quoted in Laurenti Magasa, *African Religion: The Moral Traditions of Abundant Life* [Maryknoll, N.Y.: Orbis, 1997], 52).

26. This is an obvious problem that would come up with anyone engaged in conflict for the sake of high ideals. I am sure that those who have utilized human needs theory in interventions are aware of this. But it must be stated that there is a tension here between a theory that assumes universal natural, pragmatic motivations of self-interest, on the one side, and, on the other, the self-perception of the individual or group in conflict that they are fighting for much more than the fulfillment of needs. Most groups will probably feel insulted by the reduction of their cause to needs. That does not mean that the theory is useless, but it does require flexible and creative translation into the pragmatics of intervention and relationship building between all parties.

27. This is beside the problem, known to theorists, of the enormous variety in the attachment to needs. Most people would never dream of complete sacrifice of their human needs, while others do it regularly. Furthermore, we have to account for unusual periods of time and circumstances in which thousands of people, perhaps even most, deprive themselves of life and safety for the sake of some intangible need to do one's duty in warfare, which includes soldiers giving up their comfort and even lives, parents giving up their children, and so on. This could be reduced to a basic survival need in a defensive war, but what about wars for glory? What need is being fulfilled? This is related to the religion question in the sense that it points to human motivations that clearly sacrifice many basic needs, thus calling into question a re-

ductionist account of human choices regarding conflict and violence. It is true that Burton and others have clearly recognized identity needs that include religion, and there is also ample discussion around the problem of creating a hierarchy of human needs (see Roger Coate and Jerel A. Rosati, eds., *The Power of Human Needs in World Society* [Boulder, Colo.: Lynne Rienner, 1988]. 34–56). But there is still a problem with not comprehending the unpredictable and powerful nature of religious commitment. There are religious commitments that can drive people to do things that are perfectly in line with some pragmatic human needs, such as saving a life, being prudent in one's monetary affairs, establishing community, and so on. But religious commitment can also lead to the complete sacrifice of those very needs, in certain circumstances that demand it, such as, for example, when a group is forced by some outside enemy not to observe its rituals. On the *halakhic* obligation to endure martyrdom in certain circumstances rather than violate a Jewish law, a choice forced on many Jews in history, see Maimonides, *Mishneh Torah*, Hilkhot Yesode ha-Torah 5. See also Ronald Agus, *The Binding of Isaac and Messiah: Law, Martyrdom, and Deliverance in Early Rabbinic Religiosity* (Albany: State University Press of New York, 1988). Now, human needs theory would have to question risking life and limb, including those of one's children, all for one ritual. Many religious individuals would forgo that ritual, but others would risk their health and their children's to go on observing it. This calls into question the adequacy of human needs theory as an explanation of religious life, unless all needs are subservient, for some people, to identity needs. To complicate things, in other circumstances, the same people, when not threatened in the way I just described, might in fact act based on the full range of needs described in human needs theory. Thus, I argue that the theory needs to be not discarded but made more complex and/or adjusted to each group. To illustrate with an example, my paternal grandmother devoted her entire life to the welfare of her children. As an Orthodox immigrant, however, during the Depression, she had great difficulty with employment. But the greatest difficulty she had was being fired from each of her jobs on Sundays for not coming in on Saturdays, the sabbath. This clearly put her children at some risk, in terms of her not making enough money to provide food and shelter in those terrible years. This is precisely the point at which many other immigrants, out of concern for their family's needs, gave up the most significant legal ritual of traditional Judaism: sabbath observance.

28. This, in general, is an important prognosticator of religious violence, namely, the combination of recent traumas, a history of remembered traumas that have been sacralized, together with newfound power due to shifting political and military circumstances. On the relationship of the religious myths surrounding Prince Lazar, Christoslavism, Serbian Orthodoxy, and the Bosnian genocide, see Michael Sells, *The Bridge Betrayed: Religion and Genocide in Bosnia* (Berkeley: University of California Press, 1998).

29. Numerous progressive Haggadahs (the ancient textbook for recitation on Passover) now insert a variety of new texts, including texts on reconciliation between Jew and Arab, or recount also the suffering of Palestinians, specifically aiming at ensuring that the holiday focus on redemptive, nonviolent themes and not on the harsh punishment of the Egyptians and its potential political use today. *Tikkun* magazine regularly publishes an example of this new literature every spring.

30. Most people today in complex civilizations are part of numerous subcultures and supercultures at the same time, and any analysis that reduces a person or group to one culture without constant revision and in-depth analysis will serve conflict resolution poorly. See Kevin Avruch, *Culture and Conflict Resolution* (Washington, D.C.: U.S Institute of Peace, 1998), esp. 12–21. We would be ill served for conflict

resolution purposes in not at least recognizing the potential to communicate across many cultures due to the existence of a subtle superculture, such as one devoted to biblical myths and values. But such work must recognize extraordinary differences and nuances.

31. See Marc Gopin, "Forgiveness as an Element of Conflict Resolution in Religious Cultures: Walking the Tightrope of Reconciliation and Justice." Unpublished paper, delivered Feb. 19, 1999, at American University.

32. One wonders whether the conflict could possibly have become so genocidal without the religious hermeneutic buttress that was so zealously put into place by the political leadership immediately before the war (see Sells, *Bridge Betrayed*).

33. This in no way is meant to suppress contemporary critiques of traditional religious culture and its Othering and disenfranchisement of any number of people who were different than the majority. On the contrary, I suggest an effort to face this squarely but to also discover the roots within a religious community of its own traditions of tolerance, of when it courageously protected minorities from abuse. Armed with this knowledge, it becomes easier to elicit a just conflict resolution program. Certainly, there are junctures at which certain contemporary minority groups have to take on the tradition as such, with no precedents for tolerance upon which to build. But it behooves everyone in religious conflict resolution to build from within a traditional meaning system wherever and whenever possible, because it is the latter that stands the greatest possibility of success without creating severe backlashes.

34. See Walter Zenner, *Minorities in the Middle* (Albany: State University of New York Press, 1991).

35. See Lederach, *Preparing for Peace*, 16–20.

36. This is precisely where progressive groups around the world, who are admirably dedicated to peace, human rights, and the construction of open, civil society, become a part of the "enemy system" themselves. They are perceived to be, and often are, deeply hostile toward religious constructs of reality that compete with their vision. Therefore, they lose the opportunity to be conflict resolvers in their cultures. They may be good advocates of important causes of justice, but they are hardly peacemakers. That is one of the great challenges confronting Israeli society and one of the great failures of the Israeli Left in winning more traditional Jews to their positions on peacemaking. Presently, the lines are drawn so clearly in Israeli culture and the boundaries are so high that each society, religious and secular, threatens the other mortally. This is a virtually unrecognized key to understanding the impasse in the broader process of peacemaking between Israelis and Palestinians.

Chapter Four

1. For an overview of hermeneutics, see Richard Palmer, *Hermeneutics: Interpretation Theory in Schleiermacher, Dilthey, Heidegger, and Gadamer* (Evanston, Ill.: Northwestern University Press, 1969).

2. For the literature on conflict analysis from a social scientific perspective, see Mitchell, *Structure of International Conflict*. On social scientific methods of conflict resolution, see Mitchell, *Handbook of Conflict Resolution: The Analytical Problem Solving Approach* (New York: Pinter, 1996); and John Burton, *Conflict Resolution: Its Language and Processes* (Lanham, Md.: Scarecrow, 1996).

3. The *herem* wars involved the killing of every man, woman, and child. See, for example, Deut. 3:6, 7:2, 20:17; Josh. 8:26, 10:28, 11:12; 1 Sam. 15:8.

4. Gerhard von Rad, *Holy War in Ancient Israel* (1958; rpt., Grand Rapids, Mich.: William B. Eerdmans, 1991).

5. See, for example, Isa. 30:15–16; Exod. 14:13–14; Ps. 147:10–11.

6. Von Rad, *Holy War*, 101ff., 131ff.

7. See *Midrash Kohelet Rabbah* 7:1 on a complete revisioning of King David as a scholar not as a violent warrior.

8. Chaiwat Satha-Anand, "The Nonviolent Crescent: Eight Theses on Muslim Nonviolent Action," in *Arab Nonviolent Political Struggle in the Middle East*, ed. Ralph Crow, Philip Grant, and Ibrahim E. Saad (Boulder and London: Lynne Rienner, 1990), 32–33.

9. See, in general, Thompson, *World Religions in War and Peace*.

10. To cite just a few examples, see Everett Gendler, "War and the Jewish Tradition," in *Contemporary Jewish Ethics*, ed. Menachem Kellner (New York: Hebrew Publishing, 1978), 189–210; Kimelman, "War," 309–32; and Novak, *Law and Theology in Judaism*, 125–35. On Islam, see Majid Khadduri, *War and Peace in the Law of Islam* (Baltimore: Johns Hopkins press, 1955); John Kelsay, *Islam and War* (Westminster: John Knox, 1993); and Farid Esack, *The Qu'ran, Liberation and Pluralism* (London: One World, 1996).

11. Nachum Glatzer, "The Concept of Peace in Classical Judaism," in *Der Freide: Idee un Werwirklichug* (Leschnitzer Festschrift), ed. Erich Fromm et al. (Heidelberg: L. Schneider, 1961), 27–38; Kimelman, "Non-Violence in the Talmud," 316–34; Avi Ravitsky, "Peace," in *Contemporary Jewish Religious Thought*, ed. Arthur A. Cohen and Paul Mendes-Flohr (New York: Free Press, 1988), 685–702; and Steven Schwarzschild, "Shalom," in Polner and Goodman, eds., *Challenge of Shalom*, 6–25. On Islam, see, for example, Satha-Anand et al., eds., *Islam and Nonviolence*; Friedmann, *Prophecy Continuous*; 165–80; Abdulaziz Sachedina, "Is There a Tradition of Pacifism and Nonviolence in Islam?" Paper presented at the U.S. Institute of Peace workshop on Religious Perspectives on Pacifism and Nonviolence (Washington, D.C.: July 28, 1993); and Satha-Anand, "The Nonviolent Crescent," 25–40.

12. *Mekhilta de Rabbi Ishmael*, Beshalah, Shirata 4. See also Kimelman, "Non-Violence in the Talmud," for more sources that invert violent biblical statements.

13. Kimelman, "War," 309. We have no way to know exactly what motivated each of these rabbis to curtail or eliminate altogether the legal operationalizing of these wars. We do know, however, that this hermeneutic is made in the context of pervasive criticism in Jerusalem by many Jews of both the Hasmoneans and the priestly leadership, especially regarding violence. See M. Eduyot 8:7; Ephraim Urbach, *The Sages*, trans. I. Abrahams (Cambridge, Mass.: Harvard University Press, 1987), 575–76; 661–65, 995, n. 45. But more work needs to be done on the exact connection, if any, among pietistic antiviolence statements, talmudic legal efforts to circumscribe Jewish war, and the historical context.

14. Luzzatto indicated that the biblical text generally cited to justify war can only refer to response to an attack from a group that has made it clear by that attack that they are, in fact, an enemy. See his *Ha-Mishtadel* (Vienna: I. I. Busch 1847) on Lev. 20:11, 18.

15. See J. David Bleich, "Preemptive War in Jewish Tradition," *Tradition* 21, no. 1 (Spring 1983): 3–41, and Kimelman, "War." Recent reports about Moshe Dayan's confessions that, pressured by farming interests in the north, he provoked Syria into the 1967 war in order to make a land grab on the Golan Heights, highlight the trap of theological reflection that is dependent upon limited information from governments, especially when that information is from one side of a conflict. A provocation to acquire farming land would have entirely rewritten the moral and *halakhic* debate about preemptive strikes in 1967 (see Dafna Linzer, "Israeli Hero Reveals Hebron Regrets," *Associated Press*, May 11, 1997). There will undoubtedly be debate in the

future about Dayan's motivations. Even if it turns out that his land motivations were mixed with security calculations, this would still significantly affect the moral discussion on many war-related *halakhic* issues, such as *pikuah nefesh* and the decision to risk lives for a military (or agricultural) purpose.

16. Kimelman, "War," 312.

17. Kimelman, "War," 327, n. 16.

18. Kimelman, "War," 312–13.

19. These guidelines raise several issues. First, one-sixth of one's mobilized forces in modern warfare involves a huge amount of deaths. For example, there were 8,744,000 American forces mobilized in Vietnam. One-sixth dead would have meant approximately 1.5 million American deaths, while 58,000 actual American casualties caused a significant crisis in the social history of the United States. Great Britain, in one of the most devastating social traumas in its history, lost approximately one-eighth of its armed forces: 1 million men out of 8 million mobilized in World War I (*The 1994 Information Please Almanac* [Boston and New York: Houghton Mifflin, 1994], 385, 389). Furthermore, there is no mention in the Jewish sources of a limit on enemy soldier deaths. Thus there would be no moral calculation regarding 2 million Vietnamese dead versus 58,000 Americans dead, or 180,000 Iraqi deaths due to the war and the embargo (a rough approximation that includes mostly noncombatants, who died due to the destruction of the electric infrastructure, lack of hospital supplies, etc.; these numbers are still debated) versus about 100 American deaths. However, there would be a serious *halakhic* problem with the number of those dead who were noncombatants, the massive use of napalm, an indiscriminate weapon, and the lack of escape routes from carpet-bombing campaigns.

20. Who these rabbis were or whether anyone specifically authorized Amir is a matter of debate because everyone denies ex post facto that they supported assassination, despite their rhetoric beforehand.

21. Novak, *Law and Theology in Judaism*, 130.

22. The context in the following sources seems clearly limited to "hot pursuit" circumstances: Talmud Bavli Bava Kama 117b; Talmud Bavli Sanhedrin 72b; Maimonides, *Mishneh Torah*, Hilkhot Nizke Mammon 9:6, and Hilkhot Rotseah 1:6–7.

23. The abortion analogy would still be valid based on my analysis of *rodef*. The rabbis suggest that a caretaker, seeing that the fetus before them is threatening the mother, must then see the fetus as a *rodef* and protect the mother at the expense of the fetus. This does not extend the killing justification beyond the immediate circumstances, however.

24. See, for example, *Shulhan Arukh*, Orah Hayyim 160:22, 248:41, 329:1.

25. See, for example, Talmud Bavli Berakhot 58a; Talmud Bavli Sanhedrin 72a.

26. Walzer, *Just and Unjust Wars*, esp. pts. 4 and 5.

27. The reason for the chasm and the nebulous or near-absent examination of these issues may, in fact, be that the war literature is of a highly theoretical nature, referring to circumstances that either never occurred or that occurred many centuries before, whereas the pietistic advice of rabbinic midrashic texts, as well as those of medieval compilations, is directly rooted in the day-to-day reflections and life experiences of the authors. This makes the contemporary efforts to elicit advice about violence and war from rabbinic literature a problematic enterprise when the ancient rabbis themselves were not forced to confront a deeper integration of these two fields of morality, that is, the battlefield and all that leads up to it, on the one hand, and, on the other, everyday life, which is supposed to be wedded to lofty requirements of interpersonal morality. The historical circumstances that could have led to this disjunction in the literature is a subject beyond this chapter. But this does suggest that,

whether contemporary traditional authors admit it or not, any discussion of war, peace, and related values in the contemporary context is a deeply hermeneutic process of selecting and appropriating rabbinic principles and categories.

28. See Mishnah Avot 1:12; and S. Schechter, ed., *The Fathers According to Rabbi Nathan* (Vienna: Ch. D. Lippe, 1887), ch. 12.

29. I am working here with Gadamerian categories. See Hans Gadamer, *Truth and Method*, 2d rev. ed., trans. Joel Weinsheimer and Donald G. Marshall (New York: Crossroad, 1989).

30. What these two religious traditions hold in common is some legal tendencies to divide the world between a chosen ingroup—*knesset yisroel*, in the Jewish case, and the *ummah*, in the Islamic case—and an outgroup when it comes to peace and violence, among other issues. The highlighting of this particular strand of thinking in both traditions will clearly result in a massive increase in conflict-generating and violence-generating behavior in both communities vis-à-vis each other and the entire world. If other hermeneutic strands of thinking are developed within these traditions, other outcomes will be possible. Of late, for example, there have been high-level, informal contacts among quite conservative sheikhs and rabbis in the Middle East, and the theological hermeneutic being emphasized by both sides includes the kinship of the family of Abraham, the special obligation of love and care between those who believe in one God, and the respect due to all of God's creatures. The sources for these negotiations are confidential as of this writing and part of ongoing efforts, in which I am playing a small part, to create an interreligious peace treaty in the Middle East.

31. See Vamik Volkan, *The Need to Have Enemies and Allies* (Northvale, N.J.: Jason Aronson, 1988).

32. On culture, conflict, and peacemaking, see, for example, Douglas P. Fry and Kaj Bjorkqvist, eds., *Cultural Variation in Conflict Resolution: Alternatives to Violence* (Mahwah, N.J.: Lawrence Erlbaum, 1997); Alvin W. Wolfe and Honggang Yang, eds., *Anthropological Contributions to Conflict Resolution* (Athens: University of Georgia Press, 1996); Kevin Avruch, Peter Black, and Joseph Scimecca, eds., *Conflict Resolution: Cross-Cultural Perspectives* (Westport, Conn.: Greenwood, 1991); and Rothman, *Resolving Identity-Based Conflict*. Note Rothman's indebtedness at some junctures to rabbinic values of peacemaking, such as on p. xiii. For an excellent example of a psychoanalytic analysis of religion and conflict, see Sudhir Kakar, *The Colors of Violence: Cultural Identities, Religion, and Conflict* (Chicago: University of Chicago Press, 1996), which is a case study of the Hindu/Muslim riots of 1990 in Hyderabad.

33. See Zenner, *Minorities in the Middle*, on the historical socioeconomic role of Jews, which is one paradigm for global minorities who become embroiled in conflict as a result of their unique roles in economic and cultural life. Zenner discusses how it serves the interests of higher classes, majority cultures, or occupying empires to take advantage of the conflictual position of the minority. On colonial rule and conflict generation, see David Horowitz, *Ethnic Groups in Conflict* (Berkeley and Los Angeles: University of California Press, 1985).

34. See, for example, Shapiro, "The Jewish Attitude towards Peace and War," 1: 316–73; Polner and Goodman, eds., *Challenge of Shalom*; and Ravitsky, "Peace."

35. Perek ha-Shalom, Talmud Bavli Masekhet Derekh Eretz Zuta, ch. 10.

36. Maimonides, *Mishneh Torah*. See, generally, Sefer Mada, Hilkhot Teshuvah.

37. Kimelman, "Non-Violence in the Talmud," 319ff.

38. John Mack, "The Enemy System," in Volkan et al., eds., *Psychodynamics of International Relationships*, 57–89.

39. A critical question involves addressing intercultural or interreligious conflicts in which there are no shared strategies of peacemaking. For example, this Exodus text would be a wonderful bridge between monotheistic groups in conflict, but what if there is no such shared text, or the interpretations are so different as to make the text useless? At least part of the answer lies in the fact that many traditions come to surprisingly similar peacemaking strategies and prosocial moral constructs but by different hermeneutic means and faith-based justifications. Bilateral cooperation becomes possible when all religious traditions are respected in the unique depth analysis that each makes of a problem. Then it is more possible to investigate areas of agreement and cooperation. Of course, this kind of cooperation is in direct contradiction to the many exclusive truth claims, particularly in monotheistic traditions. But here again, it seems that the interpretive process is paramount, and obsessions with exclusive truth seem to vary with circumstances of time, place, and the state of interreligious relations.

40. See Volkan, "Overview of Psychological Concepts," 1: 40.

41. This suggests a basic cross-cultural divide that always must be recognized. There are many people across the world who value words and promises over deeds (which may or may not evoke trust) versus those who trust deeds over words. I used to think that this was a basic Christian/Jewish divide, due to Paul's and other Christians' critiques of Jewish obsession with deed over word or works over faith. But I have seen in my training of students and in my analysis of several regional conflicts that this is also a common source of miscommunication between traditional Protestants and Catholics. In fact, in our extremely interactive world today, this variable valuation of deeds and words tends to be different almost from person to person. Any decent conflict resolution process, therefore, must recognize this cultural/psychological variable and seek to intentionally accommodate both modes of trust building: word and deed.

42. See, e.g., Yahya ibn 'Adi's list of ethical values, cited on p. 83.

43. See Nader, "Harmony Models and the Construction of Law," 41–60.

44. See Avruch, *Culture and Conflict Resolution*.

45. I do not mean to imply that dialogue is a waste of time as a conflict resolution measure in Jewish and Islamic cultures. That would be absurd for a variety of reasons, including the facts that there are good traditions of debate and discussion to build upon in both traditions and that all human beings in the contemporary world resonate, whether they want to or not, with certain modern cultural phenomena, such as dialogue and international negotiation, which are by now fairly universal institutions. I am suggesting, however, that as we search for reasons why some conflicts are clearly more intractable than others—a key concern of conflict analysis theory—we consider what might be the missing cultural ingredients, which could break the logjam of stubborn conflict. Intractable conflict is related in profound ways to identity-based conflict, conflict that presents—in reality or psychologically, it does not matter—a mortal threat to the identity of a group. See Rothman, *Resolving Identity-Based Conflict*. What I am suggesting is that, at critical junctures, the excruciating task of becoming ready to trust a dangerous enemy may ultimately require the utilization of familiar religious traditions and cultural patterns of acting, thus allaying deep and understandable fear of loss of identity, which goes well beyond rational considerations of security, power, and economic well-being. The foregoing argument is particularly true in religiously divided societies, such as Israel and the Arab states, where significant portions of the religious community feel alienated and threatened by secular efforts at peacemaking and the formulation of new civil constructs. The latter are perceived often as a direct threat to the future of religious life. In this context, it would be

especially relevant to analyze the impact that culturally and religiously rooted peace-making overtures would make, in contrast to classically secular strategies.

46. "Ernst Simon, The Neighbor (*re'a*) Whom We Shall Love," in *Modern Jewish Ethics*, ed. Marvin Fox (Columbus, Ohio: Ohio State University Press, 1975), 50.

47. Samuel David Luzzatto, *Il Giudaismo Illustrato* (Padua: A . Bianci, 1848), 11.

48. Friedmann, *Prophecy Continuous*, 131. On *jihad*, see Khadduri, *War and Peace*, 55–82, 141–46, 202–22, 268–96.

49. Majid Fakhry, *Ethical Theories in Islam* (Leiden and New York: E. J. Brill, 1994), pt. 1.

50. "For I [God] have come to know him [Abraham], in order that he will command his children and his household after him, so that they shall follow the path of God: to do justice and righteousness, in order for God to bring upon Abraham all that He has promised him." This verse is one of the rarer instances in biblical literature of a divine internal conversation, reflecting, in my opinion, the depth of its theological and moral significance for biblical literature. Luzzatto, one of the greatest Jewish masters of biblical literature of his century, certainly centralized this verse in his own theology because he believed that the biblical text itself highlights its centrality. Furthermore, the phrase *derekh YHVH*, "the path of God," had great significance in the development of rabbinic ethical values, and this too would move Luzzatto to centralize this text. For Luzzatto, Abraham and the Jewish people are chosen by God, not for their own sakes or because they are superior, but rather in order to fulfill these verses by their deeds in the context of and in the presence of the entire human race. Thus, when they fulfill these verses, it is a profound sanctification of the divine name that is implanted in Israel (the second half of *yisroel* is a name of God in biblical Hebrew), whereas when they do not live up to this verse, it is a profaning of the divine name. See Luzzatto, *Ha-Mishtadel*, 5. See, generally, Gopin, "Religious Ethics of Samuel David Luzzatto."

51. Fakhry, *Ethical Theories in Islam*, 100.

52. See also the important essay by Sachedina, "The Development of *Jihad* in Islamic Revelation and History," 35–50.

Chapter Five

1. See, for example, Jack, ed., *World Religions and World Peace*.

2. I use the plural because there are several things included in "Orthodoxy." There are many versions of an approach to Judaism that have a few features in common, such as commitment to revelation at Sinai and commitment in principle to observe all Jewish laws. But what these actually mean for a variety of crucial questions of ethics and politics are enormously varied.

3. See Moses Mendelssohn, *Jerusalem, or, Religious Power and Judaism*, trans. Allan Arkush (Hanover: Brandeis University Press, 1983), and, generally, Michael Meyer, *Response to Modernity* (Detroit: Wayne State University Press, 1995).

4. See Julius Guttmann, *Philosophies of Judaism* (New York: Holt, Rinehart, & Winston, 1964), 312–26.

5. Hermann Cohen, *Religion of Reason: Out of the Sources of Judaism*, trans. Simon Kaplan (New York: Frederick Ungar, 1972; Atlanta: Scholars, 1995), 52. Cohen's very purpose in creating his magnum opus, however, was to discover a truly universal set of human commitments. Thus, his commitment to the liberal program was clear, but his intolerance of idolatry was typical of the European attitudes that led, despite the "liberal" ideals, to so much oppression of indigenous peoples' traditions wherever Europeans dominated.

6. See D. Daiches Raphael, *The Moral Sense* (London: Oxford University Press, 1947); M. A. Stewart, *Studies in the Philosophy of the Scottish Enlightenment* (Oxford: Clarendon, 1990–1991); and Robert Stecker, "Moral Sense Theory" (Ph.D. diss., M.I.T., 1975).

7. Luzzatto, *Autogbiografia di S. D. Luzzatto* (Padua: Crescini, 1878), 51. See also Gopin, "Religious Ethics of Samuel David Luzzatto," 16–17.

8. The most exhaustive bibliography of Benamozegh's considerable writings is Alessandro Guetta, "Elia Benamozegh: Bibliografia," *Rassegna mensile di Israèl* 53, nos. 1–2 (1987): 67–81. An introduction to *Israel et Humanité* came out in Benamozegh's lifetime, published by himself in Livorno in 1885. The full manuscript was massive and unedited when he died. Aimé Pallière took it upon himself to edit it and publish it as *Israel et Humanité: Etude sur le problème de la religion universelle et sa solution* (Paris: Leroux, 1914). A considerably abbreviated edition emerged in French, then in Hebrew, and most recently in English, in 1961, 1967, and 1994, respectively. See *Israel and Humanity*, trans. Maxwell Luria (New York: Paulist Press, 1994). On Benamozegh's attitudes toward Christianity, there are numerous sources throughout his writings, which deserve a separate study. But see, esp., *De l'Origine des dogmes Chrétiens* (Livourne: S. Belforte 1897), and "Affinità fra la dottrina di Gesù e quella dei Farisei," *Rassegna mensile di Israèl* 16 (1951): 51–54.

9. On Benamozegh's affinity toward non-Jewish sources, such as Christianity, see Moshe Idel's preface and appendix to Benamozegh's *Israel and Humanity*, trans. Luria.

10. Aimé Pallière, *The Unknown Sanctuary: A Pilgrimage from Rome to Israel* (New York: Bloch, 1928), which is a translation of Pallière's *Le Sanctuaire inconnu; ma "conversion" au Judaisme* (Paris: Rieder, 1926).

11. Luzzatto, *Ha-Mishtadel*, 11, I. I. Busch on Exod. 20:3.

12. This is a culturally conditioned assumption of Luzzatto's that all deities, globally, are supposed to be related to by means of *imitatio dei*. This is quite a leap for many other religious systems. India would be quite a disastrous place, in terms of its social and moral order, if the followers of Vishnu or Kali did a fraction of what their gods do. On the contrary, it seems that in many theological systems the gods do precisely what humans are proscribed from doing by that very sacred system. Second, even in Judaism this type of relationship is not wholly true. It is a limited set of divine behaviors that the rabbis suggest should formulate a model for human behavior, including compassion, visiting the sick, and comforting the bereaved (see Talmud Bavli Sotah 14a). Nowhere does it state, "Just as God utterly smashed Sodom, so shall you smash wicked cities, just as God repays the wicked by punishing their children, so shall you." On the contrary, it seems that the rabbis are highly selective, in order to inculcate a specific type of religious personality.

13. "La misericordia dal Giudaismo raccomandata è universale. Si estende, come quella di Dio, a tutte le sue creature. Nessuna razza è fuori della Legge, poichè gli uomini tutti, secondo ch'il Giudaismo insegna, sono fratelli, sono figli d'uno stesso padre, e sono creati ad immagine di Dio" (Luzzatto, *Il Giudaismo Ilustrato*, 11).

14. M. E. Artom, ed., *Ketavim* (Jerusalem: Bialik Institute, 1876), 1: 55.

15. Gen. 20:17, 21:27, 26:28, 14:13, 14:22–24, 49:5–7; Ezekiel, 17; Gen. 38:1, 39; Josh. 2:17, 9:15. The point of most of Luzzatto's citations is the focus on the language of oath and covenant and their profound moral and theological significance. It proves that the prohibitions against oath taking or establishing a covenant with idolaters, which occur in other parts of the Bible and as key features of the conquest of Canaan, are based on the *moral* corruption of those peoples. Furthermore, when the Gibeonites and Rehab make an effort to establish a moral relationship through covenant, even the conquest and its command to kill are moderated.

16. See Isa. 13–19 and Amos 1–2, for example, on the way in which the condemnations focus on the brutality of the nations. Luzzatto's expertise added significant weight to his argument that the primary import of the text is a condemnation of cruelty and only secondarily of idolatry.

17. See Ezek. 18 for the boldest biblical assertion of the divine commitment to hold every human responsible, in terms of punishment or reward, for his own and no one else's actions. I have not done an exhaustive study of rabbinic reactions to the *herem* laws. It would be interesting to discover whether there is any response to the moral problems raised here.

18. Afrikaner religion, as interpreted by many in the apartheid era, comes to mind. See Johnston, "Churches and Apartheid in South Africa," 184–88.

19. Luzzatto, *Lezioni di teologia morale israelitica* (Padua: A. Bianci, 1862).

20. The *locus classicus* of this biblical distinction regarding interest laws is Deut. 23:21. The distinction is in ritual laws as well, such as Deut. 14:21. The Jewish "family" is not a biological or racial entity, strictly speaking, nor would Luzzatto want it to be seen that way, because there have been so many converts to Judaism over two thousand years, as is shown by the racial diversity of world Jewry. However, it is a religious faith group with a heavy reliance on a certain ethnic ancestry.

21. Luzzatto translated (in his *Il Pentateuco* ([Padova: Sacchetto, 1874]) *re'a* as *prossimo*. Leopold Zunz translated it as *Nächsten* (in his *Die vierundzwanzig Bücher der Heiligen Schrift* ([Basel, Germany: Goldschmidt Verlag, 1980]). The Jewish Publication Society translated it as "neighbor" in 1958 while its 1985 edition translates *re'a* as "fellow."

22. Yaacov Tzvi MecKlenburg, *Ha-Ketav v'ha-Kabbalah* (Leipzig: 1839), on Lev. 19: 18. See generally on *re'a* and Luzzatto's interpretation of it, Gopin, "Religious Ethics of Samuel David Luzzatto," 339–48; and Simon, "The Neighbor (*re'a*) Whom We Shall Love," 29–56.

23. Maimonides, *Mishneh Torah*, Hilkhot Malveh v'Loveh 5:1; see Gopin, "Religious Ethics of Samuel David Luzzatto," 299, for a full discussion of Luzzatto's polemic against Maimonides' attitude toward gentiles.

24. See Exod. 20:14; Lev. 19:13–16; Deut. 19:14, as examples.

25. Luzzatto, *Lezioni di teologia*, 33–34.

26. Luzzatto, *Lezioni di teologia*, 38.

27. (Paris: 1867).

28. Benamozegh, *Jewish and Christian Ethics: With a Criticism on Mohammedism*, trans. From the French (San Francisco: E. Blochman, 1873), 4.

29. Benamozegh touches here on one of the central problems of religious intolerance. It has a tendency to deny legitimacy to some traditions that came earlier while simultaneously incorporating the best of those earlier traditions. This is a rather benign pattern in new, minority traditions, but when they become the majority, they can prove deadly in their artful combination of successionism and intolerance. In one generation, the successionism can appear as simple cultural embrace of an earlier, indigenous tradition, but it quickly becomes a tool to "bury the opposition." This method has been used with great skill in conquering Africa in recent centuries. Of course, as we now know, ancient Israelite religion itself, as it expresses itself in at least some biblical sources, absorbed myths and stories from the local religions and then ridiculed those religions as idolatrous. I know of no major religious tradition that has not succumbed at one time or another to this antisocial pattern.

30. Benamozegh, *Jewish and Christian Ethics*, 2.

31. *Israel et Humanité* (Livorno: Elijah Benamozegh, 1885); the larger work is *Israel et Humanité*, ed. Aimé Pallière (Paris: Leroux, 1914).

32. See Vincenzo Gioberti (1801–1852), *Introduzione allo studio della filosofia* (Brussels: M. Hagel, 1840); and Gioberti, *Del primato moral e civile degli Italiani* (Brussels: Meline, Cans, 1843).

33. The totality of the *sefirot*, variously described and symbolized by Kabbalistic authors throughout many centuries, represents the internal workings and characteristics of God, except *ein sof* (lit. without end), which is that part of God that is utterly unknowable. These *sefirot* are also reflected in a mystical structure of reality that has a direct effect on the world, as humans know it, but is also affected, in turn, by the human world. If one exclusively focuses on one of the *sefirot*, then one is indeed perceiving some aspect of divine reality, but one is also cutting it off from the whole and therefore distorting its essence.

34. *Israel et Humanité* (1885), 160.

35. *Israel et Humanité* (1914), 72.

36. Emile Burnouf, *The Science of Religions* (London: 1888); Burnouf, "La Science des Religions: Part II, Les Grandes Religions et Leurs Origines," *Revue des Deux Mondes* 6 (1864): 979–1010; Burnouf, "Part III, L'Unité des Religions," *Revue des Deux Mondes* 2 (1868): 995–1017; Burnouf, "Part IV: La Diversité des Religions," *Revue des Deux Mondes* 4 (1868): 864–889.

37. *Israel et Humanité* (1914), 76.

38. *Israel et Humanité* (1914), 121.

39. *Israel et Humanité* (1914), 718.

40. (Paris: League of Peace, 1870). It is unclear whether this was ever published or whether it was published briefly and lost, but we do have an outline of its contents.

41. *Israel et Humanité* (1914), 137. Benamozegh cites Ps. 145:14, 67:4.

42. *Israel et Humanité* (1914), 251.

43. *Israel et Humanité* (1914), 165.

44. *Jerusalem Report*, Nov. 1996.

45. See *Israel et Humanité* (1914), 272.

46. *Israel et Humanité* (1914), 387, 388.

47. The case has been made that defining oneself in opposition to another is basic to human identity from its earliest development. See Vamik Volkan, "The Need to Have Enemies and Allies: A Developmental Approach," *Political Psychology* 6, no. 2 (1985): 219–47. Whether this is necessarily the case, or is just predominantly the case, in adult formation of identity is an open question. But it is clear that the more that a theological system is predicated on this kind of dualism, which reifies good and evil in groups of people, the harder it is to generate a prosocial response to the group that represents the Other identity, the identity that is opposed, by definition, to one's own. The idolater clearly plays this role in monotheism, and the destructive influence of this dualist mythology on monotheistic colonial practices in the last two thousand years is well known. The challenge for monotheistic systems is how to promote some values and practices and reject others without this turning into a dualist universe, which must demonize whole groups of people by definition.

48. Gadamer, *Truth and Method*, 301.

49. *Haredi* generally refers to those ultra-Orthodox Jews who today embrace as isolated a position from the non-Orthodox world as possible, a use of secular education only for the purposes of making a living, if at all, a literal belief in revelation from Sinai, and a great dependency on *halakhic* or spiritual leaders to determine the contours of their lives and choices.

50. On the relationship between a consciousness of multiple layers of one's spiritual identity and the ability of the religious person to coexist with others, see Marc

Gopin, "Religion, Violence and Conflict Resolution," *Peace and Change* 22, no. 1 (Jan. 1997): 1–31.

51. This, incidentally, is along a spectrum of disappointment with the society created by Enlightenment values, which one can see from left to right in secular social criticism as well. Much of postmodern thinking, for example, is a direct assault on many Enlightenment assumptions and may well have contributed to the present cultural vacuum in which we await an alternative. A conservative religious critique of modern culture, however, has what it thinks is a ready-made alternative to the dominant culture. A separate study should explore to what degree the reassertion of a confident neo-Enlightenment culture would undermine the descent of many religious cultures into violent rejections of modern life. We have no way of knowing how many young, impressionable people the world over are falling into religious militarism simply because there is little else in which to believe. Obviously, a reassertion of the Enlightenment would have to confront the failings of modern life and then move forward with a vision, but this is beyond our present study.

52. To this end, I have been engaged in repeated attempts to encourage the traditional peacemakers of the Christian world to reach out to the most religious Jews, including the *haredim*, the most separatist of them. Mostly this effort has been in vain. In the Arab/Israeli conflict, for example, the progressive peacemakers have, unlike their sophisticated mediation in Northern Ireland, Latin America, and throughout subsaharan Africa, been almost completely partisan in their approach. The exception is probably the Catholic church, which, in its sheer magnitude and global vision, continues to maintain a wide array of sophisticated contacts, even with the religious Jewish community. The others seem to lack the infrastructure, the skills, and the courage to approach the religious Israelis, who need to hear from them the most— both the *haredim* and the West Bank settlers who are religious. Some Christian peacemakers have expressed to me fear at being rebuffed, particularly because of the Holocaust. This has made their contribution almost nil in terms of the crisis on the West Bank, for example, where authentic outside mediators, who have built up some trust on both sides, are glaringly absent. There are complicated reasons for this that deserve a separate study. They include the fact that the various Christian infrastructures for conflict resolution are often tied to Christian missions, which, on the liberal end of Christendom at least, have not dared approach the Jewish community. Furthermore, their infrastructures for peacemaking have been most effective in predominantly Christian countries. There also seems to be an old deep-seated fear of approaching Muslims and Jews who are engaged in conflict; this, in turn, may have to do with the pacifist roots of many Christian peacemakers and their revulsion at violence, especially when it is expressed by people in other religions. Much more serious analysis needs to take place in the Christian community on separating the peacemaking impulse from the proselytizing impulse, both institutionally and constitutionally. This may help clarify how a good Protestant or Catholic needs to act if she wants to rebuild relationships with Others who have no intention of becoming Christian and/or who may have old rage at past encounters with Christians. As far as the Middle East is concerned, the Christian role has not been one of mediation, on the whole, but rather one of choosing sides, with liberal churches siding with and only engaging Arab Christians and Muslims, while the conservative churches embrace the Israelis. This is not conflict resolution or mediation but aid in polarization of a conflict. In fact, not only do evangelical Christians appear to be supporting Israel as a state, with investments and tourism, they are now reaching out to *haredim* as well, with some Israeli *haredi* rabbis appearing with the most extreme opponents of church/state separation in the United States (see J. J. Goldberg, "Alabama Election Has Jewish Nerves on

Edge," *Washington Jewish Week*, Aug. 13, 1998, p. 13). *Haredim* and religious Zionists on the West Bank are not hearing from the very Christians who could play a mediating role between Jews and Palestinians. The evangelical Christians, by contrast, seem increasingly to be siding with Jews and Israelis in anticipation of a coming great war with the Islamic world, in which all Jews will either be killed or converted to Christianity in the final cataclysm.

Chapter Six

1. *Jerusalem Report* 9, no. 7, Aug. 3, 1998, p. 21

2. I use Marc Ross's terminology here, which seems the most appropriate for an analysis of the psychological condition of Israeli society, with its deeply rooted Jewish cultural consciousness (see Ross, *The Culture of Conflict* [New Haven: Yale University Press, 1993]).

3. The ancient tribe of Amalek has played this symbolic role since the dawn of biblical literature (Exod. 7:8–16). Furthermore, there is an ancient Jewish saying that is used repeatedly to this day by Orthodox thinkers and leaders: "It is a [cardinal] law, Esau hates [read: persecutes] Jacob," in which "Esau" actually is a code word for Rome, then later for the Catholic church, and has come to mean, for some Jews, all gentiles (see *Sifre* Be'ha'alotekha 69). This was a common phrase when I studied in yeshivah. This persecution has been confirmed for many by the Holocaust, during which, despite the overfocus on Germans, there were an astonishing array of European fascist nationals perpetrating the murders, benefiting from them, or covering them up, and by the Arab/Israeli wars, which for many Jews, who take literally Arab propaganda about "pushing the Jews into the sea," are always a potential Holocaust. Of course, a wide assortment of nationalities were also involved in risking their lives to save Jews during the Holocaust, to which trees on the grounds around Yad Vashem attest. Furthermore, in Arab/Israeli dialogue and debate, Arab journalists and peace-makers will repeatedly downplay Arab threats of annihilation as rather pitiful rhetoric that typically functions in Arab culture as a poor substitute for military strengths. However one evaluates these phenomena, if one wants to be paranoid as a Jewish Israeli, one can find a good rationale for it.

4. Dialogue and debate are ancient elements of Jewish culture, stemming from prophetic rhetoric and the talmudic embrace of conflict as a critical way to elicit ever greater depths from the sacred texts (see David Kraemer, *The Mind of the Talmud* [New York and Oxford: Oxford University Press, 1990]). It is difficult to separate this cultural embrace of a conflictual style of interaction from an accompanying history that has been so dominated by exile and conflictual struggle with alien environments, which could have caused a conflictual style of interaction. While this has always been a part of Jewish life, the level of conflict within the community waxes and wanes, and the question is: Why is the community now experiencing such an extreme level of internal and external conflict, to the point of the first assassination of a major Jewish leader in two thousand years?

5. There is more and more being written about the *haredi* community. See Martin Marty and F. Scott Appleby, eds., *Accounting for Fundamentalisms* (Chicago: University of Chicago Press, 1994), pt. 2, esp. the essays by Samuel Heilman, Menachem Friedman, and Haym Soloveitchik. In general, all titles by these authors are important. See also Silberstein, ed., *Jewish Fundamentalism.*

6. Idith Zertal is doing extensive work on the memory of the Holocaust and the state of Israel that will be important for our continuing research. See her *From Catastrophe to Power: The Holocaust and Israel, 1944–1948* (Berkeley: University of Cali-

fornia Press, 1998). Also of great importance is Ehud Sprinzak, *Brother against Brother: Violence and Extremism in Israeli Politics from Altalena to the Rabin Assassination* (New York: Free Press, 1999). See esp. ch. 3 on *haredi* violence. In general, no violence occurring now at the hands of religious Jews was not originally pioneered by non-Orthodox Zionists, either against the Arabs, against the British, or even sometimes against other Jews. Violence, in general, seems to have a life of its own in cultures and societies, where one generation's violence always seems to play itself out as a drama in the next generation. It is as if the radicals of one generation receive a tradition and permission from the culture to engage in the same activity as before, even if the current establishment is now shocked and horrified by actions that they themselves undertook or tolerated when it was their turn to reject an intolerable situation. The relationship of violence and drama is only now emerging. Psychodrama is being used by therapists in Belfast and Africa as a way to help heal victims of violent trauma. On the relationship between conflict analysis and drama, see Marc Ross, "Psychocultural Interpretation and Dramas: Identity Dynamics and Ethnic Conflicts," unpublished paper, 1999.

7. A critical clue to this thinking is the growing body of work by Gershon Greenberg on theological responses to the Holocaust by *haredi* thinkers during and immediately after the war. Theology is an important resource for understanding how a group in terrible pain frames its universe and creates meaning in the midst of senseless destruction. It also helps to explain the dynamics of group conflict, but this I will leave to a separate study. See Greenberg, "Ontic Division and Religious Survival: Wartime Orthodoxy and the Holocaust (Hurban)," *Modern Judaism* 14, no. 1 (1994): 21–61; and Greenberg, "Consoling Truth: Eliezer Schweid's *Ben Hurban Le'Yeshua:* A Review Essay," *Modern Judaism* 17, no. 3 (1997): 297–311.

8. This includes the presentation of nude victims of the Holocaust, which, to the *haredi* community (for whom sexual modesty is a central spiritual practice) is gross humiliation of their murdered kin. To non-*haredi* Jews, graphic photographic evidence presents the true horror of the Holocaust, something they are driven to remember and to teach the world.

9. The Holocaust was an utterly shameful event for many Zionist Jews who tried to build a new, supposedly more "manly" Jew, who would never die without a fight. The image of millions deported to their deaths, many without physical resistance, was anathema to these Jews. Consequently, when the Holocaust survivors, especially the *haredim*, came to Israel in the 1940s they had no real opportunity to share their grief or their experience. One Israeli reported to me that it was commonplace at the time to refer pejoratively to these survivors as "soap," based on the stories of Nazis turning Jewish bodies into soap in the concentration camps. Many if not most *haredim* came to Israel in these circumstances and with this cruel reception; in addition, their physical image and attire symbolized everything rejected by the Zionists in the dark European past. The image of the pious European rabbi preparing a community spiritually and ritually for death in the *shtetl* as the Nazis arrived is a classic myth and countermyth of this conflict. It does not matter whether this happened or how often. It has become an image embraced by some and abhorred by others. For the *haredi* Jew this would have been a holy act, as was done during the Crusades centuries before, a way to prepare to meet God with great holiness, as the ancestors did, when the angel of death is upon you. Dying in holiness and repentance assured one a place in heaven, far away from one's tormentors, who were equally assured of a place in hell. For the Zionist, such surrender is the epitome of the failed, effeminate, rabbinic, exilic Jew who was defeated by the gentiles—as much by his own weakness as by gentile intolerance. Combine this with *haredi* sentiment that militarist and secular Jews had

at least a hand in provoking God's wrath, which caused the death of their families, and you have a prescription for several lifetimes of mutual anger. Understanding and accepting these dichotomous worldviews is the only way that *haredi* and secular Jews are going to come to understand each other and to learn to apologize or forgive.

10. On *haredim*, the Zionists, and the Holocaust, see Menachem Friedman, "The *Haredim* and the Holocaust," *Jerusalem Quarterly* 53 (1990): 87–144.

11. See Greenberg, "Consoling Truth," 299ff.

12. *Jerusalem Report* 8, no. 10, Sept. 18, 1997, p. 19.

13. Take, for example, this quote from an extremely anti-Zionist *pashkeville* (large flyer), put up in Mea Shearim, the most religious center of *haredim* in Jerusalem, describing the fight between the police and the *haredi* sabbath protesters, "Back to Nazi Germany!... Suddenly the Zionist Gestapo storm troopers arrived ... On Saturday night they launched a pogrom in Mea Shearim ... And as true followers of Hitler, may his name be cursed, they made tens of Jews stand up against a wall" (cited in Sprinzak, *Brother against* Sprinzak, *Brother*, 96). There is a bone-chilling quality to reading this announcement as a Jew, let alone what it does to the psyches of those who really believe it. Despite its extreme quality and lack of many supporters, such a letter testifies to the depths of the injury.

14. David Landau, "Rescue Operation in Kenya Gives Israel Respite from the Peace Process," *Jewish Telegraph Agency*, Aug. 10, 1998. Even the title is astonishing.

15. Landau, "Rescue Operation," p. 1.

16. Mishnah Sanhedrin 4:5.

17. Despite my own active work on Middle East peacemaking and my exploration of Jewish pathological attachment to tragedy in this chapter, it would be foolish to ignore the need on the Arab side for similar psychological investigations. The fact that the Palestinian Authority both persists in the peace process but simultaneously funds summer camps for children where the virtues of an endless war against the Zionists are inculcated is utterly baffling. There are numerous reports of those who teach the virtues of suicide bombings, the inculcation of plans to take all of Palestine by force, and brigades of children being named after all the regions inside pre–1967 Israel that will be liberated. This is despite the fact that any attempt on the part of these young Palestinians to regain the heartland of Israel someday could only lead to a war that they could not win and that perhaps would guarantee their own destruction (see the *Boston Globe*, Aug. 13, 1998, p. A19). The attachment to suicidal war in particular runs deep in certain circles of the Palestinian world and perhaps in the region in general. Maybe it stems from a legacy of centuries of imperial occupation and humiliating defeats, but suicidal behavior is destructive to any group, by definition. The psychological scars and pathologies of some in the Arab community will have to be exposed and dealt with eventually if there is to be a real peace between Israelis and Arabs. Thus, it seems that both sides of the conflict need to deal with the scars that lead their people to self-destructive mindsets and behaviors.

18. See, for example, Burton, ed., *Conflict: Human Needs Theory*; Louis Kriesberg, Terrell A. Northrop, and Stuart J. Thorson, eds., *Intractable Conflicts and Their Transformation* (Syracuse, N.Y.: Syracuse: University Press, 1989); Avruch et al., eds., *Conflict Resolution*; Lederach, *Preparing for Peace*; and Volkan et al., eds., *Psychodynamics of International Relationships*.

19. I am combining here a Gadamerian analysis of how human beings construct their cultures with the classic conflict analysis paradigm of the action/reaction spiral.

20. A deeply religious Orthodox scholar of some fame told me recently that he used all his skills to try prevent a certain conflict in Israeli society involving Jewish law. His efforts were rebuffed and suppressed repeatedly over decades by the religious

establishment. However, behind closed doors he was told by the same authorities that they agreed with him. The real constraints were actually political and included the rabbis' own fears of being branded as heretical by some among their own constituencies. In an age where there is no effective limit to religious extremism on a psychocultural level, there is nothing protecting a rabbi or other cleric from the charge of heresy, other than strict conformity to the latest religious stringencies. Thus, an additional piece of this problem is how religious leaders can follow their consciences but not sacrifice their positions of leadership. This is not dissimilar to the political leader who, in an ultranationalist atmosphere, is immediately accused of being a traitor if he moderates his position one iota.

21. See Talmud Bavli Yevamot 14; Talmud Bavli Eruvin 13b. On Hillel's relationship to peacemaking, see Nahum Glatzer, *Hillel the Elder: The Emergence of Classical Judaism* (New York: Schocken, 1970).

22. Talmud Bavli Berachot 10a.

23. See, as one small example, "We support the poor among idolaters, visit their sick, and bury their dead, for the sake of [following] the ways of peace" (Talmud Bavli Gittin 61a). The talmudic rabbis required this in the treatment not just of non-Jews but of idolatrous non-Jews, those who could not be trusted to follow even the most basic laws of morality. Their attitude toward those non-Jews who were moral would no doubt be even more generous. Observing the letter of this law today in Israel would, in and of itself, substantially reduce the tension between Jews and Arabs.

24. See Ross, *Culture of Conflict*. It should also be noted that getting into the habit of this kind of interdependency for the sake of a common goal is reinforcing the kind of cognitive and emotive disposition that could lead to Jewish/gentile or Arab/Israeli interdependence as well. Thus, contrary to common belief, creating better social skills among Jews, and therefore more unity, would make those same skills more available to do the same thing eventually with the Palestinians, assuming that they, in turn, acquire the same skills. The power imbalance between these groups is an important complicating factor, but even as that power imbalance is negotiated, the kind of skills that we speak of here are essential to making the relationship really work.

25. The resources on Jewish attitudes toward honor as a tool of social harmony are numerous but diffuse. See, in Hebrew, C. Bialik and Y. Ravnitsky, eds., *The Book of Legends* (Tel Aviv: Dvir, 1973), 502, under the heading for *kevod ha-beriot*.

26. One note is in order about these methods of discovery of the Other and coexistence. They do require a degree of faith, which intellectuals and political leaders rarely have, in the power of human wisdom, once it is unleashed. There is among educated classes, even in democracies, a basic fear of the masses and, therefore, an overreliance on law and constitutional guarantees to solve deep social problems. While I value secular democratic legal structures, they cannot ultimately transform human relationships by themselves. Nor can they really prevent tyranny from overtaking any culture, because ultimately democratic processes are not invulnerable to tyrannical social movements. Only the building of trust, relationships, and ethical commitment can really do this. This is a prejudice of my method, which I readily admit. It does not mean that legal checks and balances are not vital to democracy nor that economics do not have an impact on human civility in a critical way. But if we are looking for the glue that truly will hold together democracies in the future, it is going to be the discovery or rediscovery of common values in the context of extensive trust-building relationships. Compare Robert Bellah et al., *Habits of the Heart* (Berkeley: University of California Press, 1996); and M. Scott Peck, *The Different Drum: Community Making and Peace* (New York: Simon and Schuster, 1987).

27. Academics, who often are those who promote peacemaking in Israel, tend as a group to resist the central importance of emotion, symbol, and metaphor in human motivation and transformation. It is difficult for them to realize just how powerful simple, nonverbal gestures can be when they are done well. The power of these gestures also appears to violate the basic intellectual assumption that only rational processes change people for the better. Meanwhile, political and military leaders in the Middle East easily embrace this psychological reality and often use this power for the most destructive purposes, if it keeps them in power. Intellectually oriented activists must force themselves to utilize the full spectrum of human inner life for the purposes of peacemaking. King Hussein, for example, was one leader who understood this well and demonstrated it in his various gestures of compassion for Israelis who have suffered, including visiting bereaved families after a terror attack by a Jordanian officer and making significant, symbolic gestures of apology. These gestures could easily be seen as lowering the dignity of a king, but that is precisely what made them so powerful. The families of the bereaved children sent a representative contingent to Hussein's funeral to honor him, another important symbolic gesture. Sadat understood this as well and used it quite skillfully. He knew how much Jewish people crave recognition in the Middle East, and he gave it to them by his symbolic entry into the Knesset. And then he proceeded to say exactly what they did not want to hear about the return of all the territories. But it was heard, at least by some, precisely because of the power of his symbolic recognition. I feel, and there is no way to prove this, that we would have had the majority necessary for the political coexistence of Israel and Palestine right then if only more Arab leaders had come and done the same thing. The current chief rabbi, Bakshi Doron, also appears to be skilled in the making of gestures. He appears headed in this direction in the meetings that he has initiated with Arab and Muslim leaders. It is no surprise that he is a Sephardi, in terms of his intuitive grasp of what is necessary in the Middle East. Rabbi Menahem Frohman of Tekoa, a West Bank rabbi is spearheading this utilization of gestures and symbols.

28. See Moses, "The Leader and the Led," 1:205–17.

29. Marc Gopin, "The Heart of the Stranger and the Transformation of Sectarianism," unpublished paper delivered in Belfast, June 1997, at the Bonds and Boundaries Conference on Religious Sectarianism. Some have argued that it was the lack of clear geographic boundaries for Germany that led to its obsession with language and blood in the first half of this century, which, in turn, led to a disastrous, boundless aggression in the European context. Something similar occurs in Russian history. Nations with very clear boundaries, by contrast, such as Tibet or India, have tended to be less expansionist; at least, so the argument goes (see John Agnew, "Beyond Reason: Spatial and Temporal Sources of Ethnic Conflicts," in Kriesberg et al., eds., *Intractable Conflicts*, 41–52). America's boundless fascination with expansion may also come from habituation to an endless frontier. Of course, one can think of counterexamples. Why did England have need of an empire, since it is so contained by the sea? Or was it a natural extension of imperial habits inherited from earlier periods of tribal war in England? These are difficult matters to prove. Nevertheless, geography's effect on culture and psychology is an important element of conflict analysis for those who want to use every clue possible to understand the intractability of a given conflict.

30. The phrase "exactly the opposite," *be-diyuk ha-hefekh,* comes to mind, originating no doubt in some artful version of Yiddish culture's embrace of the same, epitomized in the phrase *poonkt farkert.* This, together with the nature of talmudic dialectics, makes for a powerful cultural mix that embraces argumentation as a form of intellectual discovery.

31. See ch. 8 for a Jewish expression of these peacemaking methods.

32. This is why I developed a course at George Mason University entitled the Moral and Philosophical Foundations of Conflict Resolution. Eventually it will lead to several investigations, including one on the relationship between moral character and conflict resolution practice.

33. See Fakhry, *Ethical Theories in Islam.*

34. See the discussion of this method in ch. 8.

35. This requires a separate study but, briefly, acts of apology and forgiveness as ways of peacemaking raise complicated issues. They have been known to work, but they are unpredictable and can often gloss over the critical balancing act of justice and peacemaking. They are also subject to significant cultural variations in terms of how and when these gestures are successfully used.

36. See Talmud Bavli Perek Ha-Shalom. The talmudic rabbis perceived that the Bible portrays Aaron as someone far more in touch with the people and far more beloved than Moses, because he expressed his love for people through making peace between them. The rabbis were also concerned in their own generation to emphasize the role of priests as peacemakers, in contrast to how some of the priests were actually behaving in their political and military alliances, especially the Hasmoneans.

37. See more in ch. 8 on this method.

38. Schechter, ed., *The Fathers According to Rabbi Nathan,* ch. 12.

Chapter Seven

1. I am indebted to the U.S. Institute of Peace for its role in funding this project.

2. See Zenner, *Minorities in the Middle,* for a full exposition on this sociological syndrome.

3. Frank Henry Epp, *Mennonite Exodus: The Rescue and Resettlement of the Russian Mennonites since the Communist Revolution* (Altona, Manitoba: D. W. Friesen and Sons, 1966); E. K. Francis, "The Russian Mennonites: From Religious to Ethnic Group," *American Journal of Sociology* 54 (Sept. 1948): 101–7; James Urry, *None but Saints: The Transformation of Mennonite Life in Russia, 1789–1889* (Winnipeg, Manitoba: Christian Press, 1978); and James Toews, *Czars, Soviets and Mennonites* (Newton, Kans.: Faith and Life Press, 1982). I want to thank my student Larissa Fast for pointing out these sources to me.

4. This information is hard to come by, since the Mennonite community has been relatively closed to outside scrutiny. I am grateful to my Mennonite students for their honest inquiry into their own community and for these sources: Kenneth Dueck and Donald Froese, "Attitudes towards Jews Encountered among Selected Segments of Mennonites in Canada," student essay (1972) available in the libraries of Canadian Mennonite Bible College and Associated Mennonite Biblical Seminary; Ken Quiring, "Anti-Semitism and North American Mennonites in the Twentieth Century," student essay (1998) available in the libraries of Canadian Mennonite Bible College and Associated Mennonite Biblical Seminary; James F. Schrag, "The Jewish 'Protocols': An Assessment of Their Origins, Content, and Influence on American Mennonites" (1971), available from AMBS library, which has a section that addresses the American Mennonite view of Germany 1933–1935; Frank Henry Epp, "Facing the World," in his *Mennonites in Canada, 1920–1940* (Toronto: Macmillan of Canada, 1974), ch. 12; James Juhnke, *A People of Two Kingdoms: The Political Acculturation of the Kansas Mennonites* (Newton, Kans. Faith and Life Press, 1975); Epp, "An Analysis of Germanism and National Socialism in the Immigrant Newspaper of a Canadian Minority Group, the Mennonites, in the 1930s" (Ph.D. diss., Univ. of Minnesota, 1965); Epp, "National Socialism among the Canadian Mennonites in the 1930s," paper for the Fifteenth

Conference on Mennonite Educational and Cultural Problems, Bluffton College, Ohio, 1965; and John Redekop, "The Roots of Nazi Support among Mennonites, 1930–1939," *Journal of Mennonite Studies* 14 (1996): 81–95. See also information on Ingrid Rimland at http://hatewatch.org/who/rimland.html and connecting links to her Holocaust denial website.

5. See Leo Driedger and Donald B. Kraybill, *Mennonite Peacemaking: From Quietism to Activism* (Scottdale, Pa.: Herald, 1993), 22, 54.

6. See Elaine Pagels, *The Gnostic Gospels* (New York: Vintage, 1981); on Judaism, see Gershom Scholem, *Major Trends in Jewish Mysticism* (New York: Schocken, 1977), 40–79.

7. Frank Manuel, *Utopian Thought in the Western World* (Oxford: Blackwell, 1979).

8. Ron Kraybill (personal correspondence, Jan. 1, 1997) rightly points out my bias toward "proof texts" in religious life. He suggests that, more deeply than text, *Nachfolge Christi*, following the way of Jesus in his dealings with enemies, was a key resource for Anabaptist justification for this behavior. I agree, though I assume the centrality of *imitatio dei* here and suggest simply that the text is the only way for believers to learn what the way of Jesus was.

9. Several Pauline texts demonstrate the hermeneutic interaction of Paul and his Jewish biblical sources: "If someone returns evil for good, evil will not depart from his house"; "If your enemy is hungry, give him bread to eat"; "Do not rejoice at the fall of your enemy"; "If you see the donkey of your enemy struggling under its burden, you shall surely lift it up with him" (Prov. 17:13, 25:21, 24:17; Exod. 23:5).

10. Driedger and Kraybill, *Mennonite Peacemaking*, 23.

11. The Hebrew term for "pursued" is *nirdaf*, and it is questionable from the context whether this is, in fact, a moral statement about God protecting the persecuted. However, early rabbinic writings from the first centuries c.e. interpret the verse as confirming that God sides with anyone being persecuted or pursued, no matter how "wicked" they may be. In other words, there is a divine preference *in all circumstances* for the persecuted (see *Leviticus Rabbah* 27:5). This interpretation of the verse is probably familiar to Mennonites, although I have not found a source for this, and it has profound implications for religious conflict resolution that, in fact, complicates the elusive search for third-party neutrality in conflict resolution practice. See below on the struggle between peace and justice and my thoughts on the Christian Peacemaker Teams.

12. It should also be noted that this combination of faith and group experience with persecution, which leads to resistance to violence, is evident among those European Christians who risked their lives to save Jews during the Holocaust. Resistance to evil and saving lives are slightly different religious and ethical activities from peacemaking among Mennonites, our subject of study. However, they share a common commitment to engage the world nonviolently, to resist violence, and they also seem to share a willingness to be different from or go against the dominant cultural trends, which are violent, and to share a high level of empathy for the persecuted. See Phillip Hallie, *Lest Innocent Blood Be Shed* (New York: Harper and Row, 1979), on the character of the residents of Le Chambon, France. Most of the research on the roots of altruism in these circumstances stresses the importance of loving family environments, education in moral values, and a general prosocial orientation, which seem to give rise to this kind of behavior. See Pearl Oliner et al., eds., *Embracing the Other: Philosophical, Psychological and Historical Perspectives on Altruism* (New York: New York University Press, 1992). But I would argue that not enough attention has been given to the awareness of being separated, different, and/or persecuted as key motivators of human empathy, which leads individuals and groups to nonviolent interaction, altru-

ism, and peacemaking. The theological worldview of these groups builds itself around the cognitive and emotional orientation that is unique to their historical experience. This is the only way that I see to explain how deeply embedded this posture is as a Christian faith for some Christian groups or families, while, at the same time, Christian faith is being used by others, in the very same period and only a few miles away, to justify theologically the most brutal racist violence of the twentieth century. See Susannah Heschel on the theological program of de-Judaizing Christianity, "Transforming Jesus from Jew to Aryan: Protestant Theologians in Nazi Germany," The Albert Bilgray Lecture presented at the University of Arizona, Apr. 1995. The Confessing church declared in May 1939, "In the realm of faith there exists the sharp opposition between the message of Jesus Christ and the Jewish religion. . . . In the realm of volkish life an earnest and responsible racial politics is required for the preservation of the purity of our people" (Heschel, "Transforming Jesus," 4). This subject deserves a separate study. Philippe Lasserre who, as a little boy in northern France, played a key role in his family's scheme to lead to safety approximately thirty Jews over a period of several years, at considerable risk to their lives, suggested to me recently that his family's experience of and awareness of being different as Protestants in France and the history associated with that in France gave them a special level of concern for the persecuted that combined seamlessly with their religious faith. His mother was involved with an organization run by Protestants for displaced persons during World War II, after the fall of France to Germany. He also describes the powerful memories that his religious community maintains of the intense persecution they suffered in the seventeenth century, when they had to hide in the mountain caves of central France, where they sang special psalms and identified with the Jews exiled to Babylon (personal correspondence, Mar. 24, 1997). On the evolution of Christian wars, persecution, and pacifism, see Bainton, *Christian Attitudes toward War and Peace.*

13. From its earliest roots, American Mennonite missionizing appears to have focused on the teaching of pacifism (see Driedger and Kraybill, *Mennonite Peacemaking,* 29).

14. There is yet another interesting parallel here to Jewish values rooted in the Hebrew biblical conception of the people as a "kingdom of priests and a holy nation" (Exod. 19:6), with "holy" interpreted in its original Hebrew meaning as "separated" or "consecrated." It suggests a special destiny in the world but a separated one. However, other sources, such as Gen. 18:19 and Isa. 42:6, convey the notion of a people with a mission, "a light unto the nations [*or la-goyim*]," teaching to the world "the path of God [*derekh YHVH*]." One mandate suggests active integration in the world, while the other implies separation. Traditional Orthodoxy of the last two thousand years tended to see the separation as key, with the mission being expressed by one's distant example as a God-fearing and moral people. Modern liberal Judaism has emphasized, instead, a mission of spreading the prophetic social justice values of Judaism while also maintaining a distinct religious identity. This is a striking hermeneutic parallel to Amish and modern Mennonite divisions on the subject.

15. Lederach, *Preparing for Peace,* 17–23.

16. See, generally, Ron Kraybill, "Peacebuilders in Zimbabwe" (Ph.D. diss., Univ. of Cape Town, 1996).

17. See Gadamer, *Truth and Method,* 265ff.

18. It also occurs to me that Mennonites have certain advantages for healing and learning from their pain that other abused groups have lacked. They have emphasized to me on several occasions that their worst suffering, on the whole occurred centuries ago, and time does heal wounded groups to a degree. Second, their separated and

rather safe rural existence has given them the nurturing space in which to heal themselves and from that safe space to reflect on the ethical and spiritual implications of their ancestors' suffering and what it implies for all human beings. This is a luxury unavailable to most minorities around the world who are in the throes of abuse presently or who only recently emerged from it and therefore have not been given the time or the space to heal. Often they find themselves in a tense, antagonistic relationship with competing groups, either in the city or in the countryside, which hardly gives them the time or the space to work through the trauma that they have suffered. Thus, sustained injury easily turns into outer-directed violence. If my hypothesis is correct, conflict resolution strategies would need to address this and creatively seek ways for the minorities who both persecute and suffer persecution— Hutus, Tutsi, Serbians, etc.—to find or be given the time and the space to heal themselves. The Mennonite experience would be impossible to recreate, but it may provide a model for approximating measures. Ury and Fisher have already expressed the legitimacy of approximating the best possibility in negotiation, BATNA (Best Alternative to a Negotiated Agreement). See Roser Fisher and William Ury, *Getting to Yes* (New York: Penguin, 1991). Perhaps we need to think in terms of the best alternative to psychological healing for groups that cannot easily extract themselves from intractable problems. We know, furthermore, that there are always—even in the most damaged groups engaging in massive violence—those individuals for whom the violence is not passed on but who experience it as clear testimony to the futility and evil of violence itself. We should be thinking of how we can creatively support this nucleus of people, who could be at the vanguard of healing their community. Some comparative studies on the relationship between a major trauma suffered by minorities at a discreet point in time, such as a genocide, and the character of their subsequent reaction to either hostile or healing circumstances would be useful.

19. Gen. 4:7 expresses this idea by describing Cain's jealousy during an episode that is the prelude to the first murder in biblical literature. Mennonite sensibility reflects this constant attention to the thin line between good and evil intervention in the world.

20. Quietism is a common facet of Christian, as well as Jewish, pietistic groups and it shares certain features with Buddhist approaches to the world as well. Religious pietism with quietistic overtones could easily be accused of passivity in the face of evil and conflict, and this may be true in many cases historically. But it also should be studied cross-culturally for what it can teach conflict resolution about what *not* to do in human relations, what to avoid in engagement with Others, what character traits lead to violence, and how the inner life leads toward or away from violence. This is the great strength of traditions that have focused on the inner life and their potential contribution to conflict prevention, in particular, but also to conflict intervention and resolution.

21. This was expressed to me many times, over a period of years, by my teacher, Rabbi Dr. Joseph Soloveitchik, who was the preeminent theologian and legal authority of modern Orthodox Judaism in the twentieth century. He always said that the deepest spiritual experience in Judaism is not the positive ritual but the negative prohibition. He embraced precisely that aspect of Judaism that was ridiculed by Others for centuries as barren legalism and saw in it the supreme fulfillment of the inner life. It is the discipline of not eating everything available to humankind, of not having an impact on the natural world in any way one day a week (on the sabbath), of not having sex at all places and all times, of not taking everything the world has to offer but leaving some for the poor or simply to replenish the earth, which are the keys to the religious life before God. Similarly, in Buddhism, the deepest fulfillment of the

Four Noble Truths is following the Eightfold Path. But that path expresses itself in largely negative terms, mostly adding up to a variety of ways in which one is instructed to do no harm to oneself or to other sentient beings. This does not mean that positive ritual plays no role in Judaism nor in numerous cultural expressions of Buddhism. But it seems to me that the greatest exponents in these traditions perceive the key spiritual challenge in the discipline of limitation and not doing—not in positive ritual. The latter, by contrast, is notorious as a vehicle in many religious histories of avoiding true spiritual and moral discipline while simultaneously showing oneself to be righteous before man and God. See Isa. 1, among many other prophetic sources, which attacks in blistering language the use of ritual to cover up the sins of greed and murder.

22. Deut. 10:19.

23. See Volkan, *The Need to Have Enemies and Allies.*

24. See the discussion in Laurence J. Silberstein, ed., *The Other in Jewish Thought and History* (New York: New York University Press, 1994), 1–34. Silberstein also confronts a related issue: "antiessentialist" definitions of cultural identity. Essentialists argue for a singular definition of a particular cultural identity, whereas antiessentialists, influenced by postmodern thinking, argue that cultural identity, while having some essential characteristics, is evolving all the time and dependent upon the interaction and mutual influencing of many identities. Regarding conflict analysis, the latter approach is often to be found among those actors who are comfortable with their identities and unafraid of the creative process of interaction with other group identities and their accompanying values. Conversely, rigidly essentialist positions are often to be found among those actors who express deep suspicion of intergroup interactions. One possible explanation of this difference is that the very artificiality of essentialist postures, e.g., "only Christians truly understand love," "only Jews are truly compassionate," "only Germans understand culture," etc., make them highly vulnerable to deniability with extensive intergroup relations, therefore threatening this thin essentialist identity and the weak psychological life that it buttresses.

25. See, for example, Emmanuel Levinas, *Time and the Other,* trans. Richard A. Cohen (Pittsburgh, Pa.: Duquesne University Press, 1987); and Levinas, *Ethics and Infinity,* trans. Richard A. Cohen (Pittsburgh, Pa.: Duquesne University Press, 1985).

26. "I believe in the fundamental truth of all great religions of the world" (Gandhi, *All Men Are Brothers,* 55, and, generally, 54–56). In the movie *Gandhi* by Sir Richard Attenborough, he has Gandhi say at one point, in exasperation at Hindu hatred of Muslims, "I am a Muslim, and a Hindu, and a Christian!" which only made his enemies hate him more. The movie is often predicated on actual statements by Gandhi, but I have not been able to find this one as yet.

27. Theologically, Jesus is seen like the angels of the Hebrew Bible, in the world but a messenger from another world, who is not quite of this world. That there is an otherworldly character to the person who works tirelessly for the good of Others is something that every religious peacemaker feels inside herself at one or another difficult juncture, especially in the wake of extraordinary personal sacrifice. It is, therefore, deeply compelling and comforting to feel at these moments that one emulates others who have done the same. In Judaism, the model for this are the "righteous," the *tsadik,* great prophets and rabbis, and even God himself. In Christianity there are also many possible role models that people look to, but Jesus himself stands out as the quintessential linkage of this worldly life and otherworldly aims and dreams. For those who believe in it, the Trinity stands out as a mystery that embodies this unification in one person of being this-worldly and otherworldly at the same time and in the same person. Emulation of the Prophet in Islam also has this compelling

quality. In Mahayana Buddhism, the figure of the Bodhissatva, who is about to ascend to nirvana but steps back in order to serve Others, also seems to fit this theme of this-worldly and otherworldly existence combined inside the person who sacrifices himself for Others.

28. See "Peacebuilders in Zimbabwe," Kraybill, ch. 7, on community.

29. Driedger and Kraybill, *Mennonite Peacemaking*, 22.

30. In fairness, it may be the case that aid agencies choose sometimes to *not* utilize local resources in order to avoid conflict. But that should not be done summarily without first humbly engaging a community that is in need. It not only is the moral thing to do, it is the only sensible way to avoid the infamous waste of aid resources. Furthermore, conflict avoidance, while necessary sometimes as a method, is a poor long-term solution to human problems.

31. *Christian Science Monitor*, Nov. 27, 1996.

32. *Washington Post*, Jan. 26, 1997, pp. A1–2.

33. Personal communication, July 10, 1996.

34. Eyewitness report by one survivor, Samuel Doe, personal communication, July 10, 1996.

35. See Burton, ed., *Conflict: Human Needs Theory*. For a critique of the theory, see Kevin Avruch and Peter Black, "A Generic Theory of Conflict Resolution: A Critique," *Negotiation Journal* 3 (1987):87–96.

36. Kant, "The Metaphysical Foundations of Morals," in *The Philosophy of Kant: Immanuel Kant's Moral and Political Writings*, ed. Carl Friedrich (New York: Modern Library, 1977), 178.

37. Francis Hutcheson (d. 1747), for example, argues that if our motives in care were purely instrumental and self-interested, we would never express any admiration for those who love or give to Others. We also would love equally the kind of people who are kind to us but cruel to Others and the kind of people who are kind to us and kind to everyone else as well. But this is plainly not the case with our feelings, says Hutcheson. We clearly admire and have a special level of love for the saintly among us, who care unselfishly for everyone. See Hutcheson, "Concerning Good and Evil," in *The Classical Moralists*, comp. Benjamin Rand (Boston: Houghton Mifflin, 1937), 404. In general, the moral sense theorists posit that basic feelings of compassion and love, which plainly are observable in nature, should form the basis of one's ethical response to the world and that education is the key to strengthening those moral senses. This was written, of course, before the Freudian critique of conscious motivations. A moral sense theory response to the important Freudian critique is vital to our purposes, but it is beyond the scope of this book.

38. Martin Buber, *I and Thou*, trans. Walter Kaufmann (New York: Charles Scribner's Sons, 1970), 54, 55.

39. Of course, I recognize the irony that my desire to study the "net effects" reflects an instrumentalist orientation.

40. Richard E. Rubenstein, "Unanticipated Conflict and the Crisis of Social Theory," in *Conflict: Readings in Management and Resolution*, ed. John Burton and Frank Dukes (New York: St. Martin's, 1990), 325.

41. Driedger and Kraybill, *Mennonite Peacemaking*, 53.

42. There is little published on CPTs other than CPT publications. See John Stoner, *Interventions of Truth: Christian Peacemaker Teams* (Chicago: Christian Peacemaker Teams, 1993); Robert Hull, *A Chronology of Christian Peacemaker Teams 1984–1992* (Newton, Kans.: CPT Steering Committee, 1991); and Cynthia Sampson and John Paul Lederach, eds., *From the Ground Up: Mennonite Contributions to International Peacebuilding* (New York: Oxford University Press, 2000).

43. See, generally, Ps. 85.

44. See Johan Galtung, *Peace by Peaceful Means: Peace and Conflict, Development and Civilization* (Oslo and London: International Peace Research Institute and Sage, 1996).

45. See Arnold Soloway and Edwin Weiss, *Truth and Peace in the Middle East: A Critical Analysis of the Quaker Report* (New York: Friendly House, 1971).

46. For the full array of evangelical preachers' statements on the Jews and their future, see http://www.fields.org/links.htm. From here one has complete access to thousands of Christian missionary organizations, dozens of which are specifically focused on the fate of the Jews.

47. This is also complicated by the fact that "forgiveness" seems to include or mean many different things in some Christian contexts, such as unilateral apology, mutual apology, unilateral or mutual verbal expressions of forgiving, gestures of friendship, repentance, expressions of love, and acceptance. See the various ways in which forgiveness has been engaged historically in Michael Henderson, *The Forgiveness Factor* (Salem, Oreg., and London: Grosvenor, 1996). Depending on what is meant, there will be more or less in common with other cultures and religions, which often have parallel moral values and/or spiritual states but which embrace them conditionally, depending on how the forgiveness gestures are carried out.

Chapter Eight

1. For an overview of the field, see J. Folger, M. Poole, and R. Stutman, eds., *Working through Conflict* (New York: Longman, 1997).

2. For an overview, see Marty and Appleby, eds., *Accounting for Fundamentalisms.* On Jewish fundamentalism, see Silberstein, ed., *Jewish Fundamentalism.*

3. On Hillel's embrace of gentiles, see Talmud Bavli Shabbat 31a; on Yohanan's greeting to gentiles, see Talmud Bavli Berakhot 17a; on R. Shimon, see Talmud Bavli Shabbat 33, 34, and Gen. Rabbah 79.

4. See Talmud Bavli Kiddushin 70b; Num. Rabbah 8; and, generally Talmud Bavli Masekhet Gerim.

5. There is a large literature on this subject. See the following for selections of rabbinic aphorisms: Avot of Rabbi Nathan 12; Talmud Bavli Perek ha-Shalom; Lev. Rabbah 9; and Num. Rabbah 11. For some contemporary discussion, see Polner and Goodman, eds., *The Challenge of Shalom,* and the essay by Gopin in the same volume, "Is There a Jewish God of Peace?"

6. On early justifications for war, see the discussion in Talmud Bavli Sotah 44b; for a contemporary overview and analysis of the rabbinic discussion, see Kimelman, "War," 309–32 (incl. bibliography).

7. Maimonides, *Mishneh Torah,* Laws of Kings 5.

8. See ch. 6.

9. I think this was brought into sharp relief for me when a wonderful *haredi* relative of mine responded with curiosity to the risks I was placing on my career by spending so much time fighting nuclear proliferation. She said, "Isn't that a *goyish* [gentile] problem?" The fact that Jewish scientists had been and continue to be actively involved in the development of nuclear weapons did not register, nor did the fact that a nuclear exchange between the United States and the Soviet Union at the time would have wiped out most of the world's Jewish people. But this is a person whose ethical behavior often exceeds my own and that of many of my colleagues in peace work. The real problem is the scope of her ethical concern in the context of a constructed identity.

10. See, for example, Menachem Kellner, ed., *Contemporary Jewish Ethics* (New York: Hebrew Publishing, 1978); Elliot Dorff and Louis Newman, eds., *Contemporary Jewish Ethics and Morality* (New York: Oxford University Press, 1995).

11. On uncompleted mourning and conflict, see Vamik Volkan, *Bloodlines: From Ethnic Pride to Ethnic Terrorism* (New York: Farrar, Straus and Giroux, 1997); and Volkan, *The Need to Have Enemies and Allies*.

12. *Avelius* also applies to events in history and objects, such as the Temple in Jerusalem, although this is negotiated in a somewhat different fashion by *halakha*. Nevertheless, its extension to realms beyond the individual/interpersonal suggests its usefulness in dealing with overarching collective experiences of the people.

13. On mourning in Judaism, see Maurice Lamm, *The Jewish Way in Death and Mourning* (New York: Jonathan David, 1969). *Kaddish* is a formal responsive prayer said by mourners a number of times in the prayer service, when there is a quorum present, in three separate services during the mourning period. It is a prayer of praise and comfort. *Kaddish*, it should be noted, is formally required every day only for a month for most relatives but is required for a year for parents and then recited annually on the day of death, the *yohrtseit*, as it is termed in the Ashkenazi/Yiddish usage. *Yizkor*, recited several times a year collectively in the synagogue, is also central. My mentor, Rabbi Joseph Soloveitchik, said *kaddish* for his wife for several years, every day, several times during each of the three daily public prayers. It is perhaps my most vivid childhood memory of him. By contrast, unfortunately, my grandmother lost her four-year-old only son in the 1930s. She cried for the next seven years, every single day, according to my mother's testimony, and was haunted by the loss for the rest of her life. She never said *kaddish* once because women were not permitted to say *kaddish*. I have no idea whether it would have helped her recover, and to think otherwise is sheer speculation. But it is clear to me that *kaddish* is a vital element of Jewish life, which deserves more study in terms of recovery from extreme injury. I also believe that it should play a more prominent role in conflict resolution between Jews and Others, if and only if it is done in a way that respects the culture. More on shared mourning below.

14. Compare Roger Fisher and Scott Brown, *Getting Together: Building Relationships as We Negotiate* (New York: Penguin, 1988). Fisher's work and the work of the Harvard Negotiation Project have honored places in the field of conflict resolution, and many conflicts have been negotiated successfully with this wise, practical advice. But win-win concepts are obscene in certain contexts, such as ethnic cleansing and genocide. Many things in violent conflict can never be recovered, as I am sure they know, and much deeper psychological work is called for. The methods I suggest here are complementary not contradictory to rational negotiation processes, which always have their place at some stage of resolution. But I argue that the work that we suggest here goes deeper and is more essential to long-lasting solutions.

15. Marc Gopin, "Confronting the Secular/Religious Conflict in Israel: Suggested Solutions," in *Religious Secular Relations in Israel: Social and Political Implications*, ed. Ephraim Ya'ar and Tamar Herman (Tel Aviv: Steinmetz Center for Peace Research, Tel Aviv University and the Konrad Adenauer Foundation, 1998), 81–94. This essay is an early version of ch. 6 of this book.

16. It is obvious why the Palestinians feel this about land, but it is also part and parcel of Jewish religious experience even today. Every day, in numerous blessings, there are fervent prayers for the restoration of lost lands, as there has been for thousands of years. There is little acknowledgment, at least ritually speaking, that the lands truly have been restored. It is not, I believe, because not enough land has been restored, but because the restoration has not been accompanied by a deep sense of

peace or the dreamed-of utopian messianic era and because old religious habits of lament die a slow, hard death. They are part of the Jewish psyche; they have formed and preserved identity for millennia and are a source of comfort, even if today such a lament appears bizarre to the outsider because the dream of acquiring the land has already been fulfilled. There are other complicated reasons, *halakhic* and political, that these laments are preserved in the prayer texts, but that requires a separate discussion.

17. Detail is the key. Detail is the heart of narrative, and narrative is the path into the individual psyche and the collective memory of human beings. Details of personal narratives also are a powerful bridge between enemies. In their uniqueness, details paradoxically become universal. That is why powerful novels and movies about individuals affect all of us far more than statistics about war.

18. I do not mean "pluralism" in the popular sense of acceptance of the legitimacy of all expressions of Jewish practice, which is generally derided in Orthodox circles.

19. My ideas here parallel and are indebted to Bill Vendley's on primary and secondary religious language. See William Vendley and David Little, "Implications for Communities: Buddhism, Islam, Hinduism, and Christianity," in *Religion: The Missing Dimension of Statecraft*, ed. Douglas Johnson and Cynthia Sampson (New York: Oxford University Press, 1994), 307; and Vendley, "Religious Differences and Shared Care: The Need for Primary and Secondary Language," *Church and Society* (Sept.–Oct. 1992): 16–29.

20. I want to emphasize that this is no way discounts the importance of moving all groups in question toward a civil society based on shared values, shared rights, and shared responsibilities. But the way to build trust in deeply conflictual, wound-infested situations is not necessarily to start out with universal constructs, which have sent many religious enthusiasts running from secular society in the first place. It is to acknowledge lost or injured identities, to acknowledge their value and importance, to honor them, and only then to move toward shared civil constructs.

21. I was struck by the positive reactions of my secular friends to a beautiful advertising campaign that the Benetton Group published in conjunction with *Newsweek* in March 1998. It was a series of photographs of Jews and Arabs together in beautiful poses of friendship. The first thing that I saw in those photographs as a devotee of peace was the beauty of the vision of the future. Most of the first photographs (not surprisingly, emerging from the advertising firms) were of extremely handsome Arab men embracing or kissing beautiful Jewish women. And with my memories very keen of my background, I also saw catastrophe. I knew that those photographs would have the opposite of the intended effect on the community that needs visions of peacemaking the most. It is the nightmare scenario in essence. It is the loss of continuity by way of intermarriage placed right into these "peace" photographs. There are other reasons, typical of the relations between dominant and repressed cultures, that it was consistently Arab men embracing Jewish women, but that is beyond our topic. Suffice it to say that the envisioned intermarriage is precisely what keeps many religious people on the right wing of the political spectrum. From the progressive perspective, this is nothing short of racism. From a religious perspective, this kind of assimilation is nothing short of a threat to survival, as it was in Europe and is in America. It guarantees the slow disappearance of Jewish culture and Jewish people. This is a common and understandable concern among indigenous and tribal groups with low birthrates. This difference between progressive and religious approaches to integration must be confronted. In other words, there must be some shared vision of the future, despite the differences, between religious and secular groups before there can be any hope of that future being peaceful. It is the same between Arabs and Jews, with a surprising amount of agreement on these issues from

religious people on both sides. There is no reason in principle that there cannot be both a religious and a secular vision of a future that involves peaceful coexistence. Almost never, however, do the progressive forces responsible for envisioning the future allow for, or encourage, this possibility, at least not as of this writing. This was the central element missing from the visions of the "new Middle East" espoused by those who engineered the Oslo accords, and it is precisely those left out of that future vision who almost destroyed the gains of Oslo.

22. I use "mind" and "heart" traditionally, that is, metaphorically, to refer to cognitive development and affective development.

23. M. Avot 2:13; Lev. 19:18; M. Avot 1:14. I have included rabbinic phrases for each value, which will require a longer study to analyze. They are not precise formulations but rather abbreviated references to the epigrams and aphorisms of rabbinic moral formulations, but they do typify the way in which these values are referred to often in the lived interactions of religious life. The latter is vital, from the point of view of anthropologically based conflict resolution. See Avruch et al., eds., *Conflict Resolution: Cross Cultural Perspectives.*

24. See Zohar Num. 178; for overviews of the extensive rabbinic literature on repentance, see *Sefer Orhot Tsaddikim* (1581; rpt., Jerusalem: Eshkol, n.d), ch. 26; and Maimonides, *Mishneh Torah,* Laws of Repentance. The citations in this and subsequent footnotes are merely selections and not an exhaustive list.

25. Eccles. 7:1; Exod. Rabbah 48. *Midrash Tanhuma* va-Yakhel states, "One finds three names that a human being is called, one that his mother and father call him, one that others call him, and one that he acquires for himself. The best of all of them is the name that he acquires for himself."

26. M. Avot 4:6.

27. M. Avot 6:6.

28. Moshe Cordovero (d. 1570), *The Palm Tree of Devorah,* trans. Moshe Miller (Spring Valley, N.Y.: Targum/Feldheim, 1993), ch. 3.

29. M. Avot 5:18, 5:20

30. Deut. 13:5; Talmud Bavli Sotah 14a; Talmud Bavli Shabbat 133b; on peace, Job 25:2; *Sifra* be-hukotai; *Sifre* Naso.

31. Talmud Bavli Shabbat 151b; Gen. Rabbah 33; on compassion as the determining characteristic as to whether a person is really a Jew, see Talmud Bavli Bezah 32b; on the pain of animals, see Talmud Bavli Shabbat 128b.

32. Talmud Bavli Sotah 14a; Eccle. Rabbah 7, statement of Rabbi Judah.

33. M. Avot 1:15; 3:16; *Talmud Yerushalmi* Eruvin 5:1.

34. Gen. Rabbah 24, statement of Ben Azai; M. Avot 4:3.

35. M. Avot 1:6.

36. Talmud Bavli Berakhot 60; Talmud Bavli Ta'anit 21.

37. Lev. 19:18; Sifra Kedoshim; Avot of Rabbi Nathan 16; on love and fulfillment of needs, see *Sefer Orhot Tsaddikim,* ch. 5, 46ff.

38. M. Avot 4: 1, 3, 2:15.

39. Lev. 19:16; Ps. 34:13; on a range of language-related values, see Yitshak Abohav, *Menorat ha-Maor,* ed. J. Horeb and M. Katznelbogen (Jerusalem: Mossad HaRav Kuk, 1961), 94–172.

40. Talmud Bavli Shabbat 119b.

41. M. Avot 5:20; see Talmud Bavli Hullin 89b, on the capacity to contain one's rage in the midst of conflict.

42. "Criticism leads to peace. . . . All peace that does not involve criticism is not peace" (Gen. Rabbah 54, in the name of Resh Lakish).

43. Talmud Bavli Sanhedrin 6b.

44. Deut. 10:19; Talmud Bavli Bava Mezia 59b. The biblical *ger* (stranger) has been interpreted to mean "convert" in rabbinic Judaism. But this is debatable because the rabbinic category of *ger toshav*, resident stranger, may refer to a much larger group of non-Jews who abide by basic moral laws. See Talmud Bavli Avodah Zarah 64b.

45. See Talmud Bavli Yoma 9b, on destruction in Jewish life coming from wanton hatred.

46. Talmud Bavli Yoma 23b.

47. Talmud Bavli Bava Metsia 58b.

48. M. Avot 1:17, 6:6.

49. Avot of Rabbi Nathan, version A, ch. 12.

50. M. Derekh Erets Zuta 5:7.

51. M. Kallah, statement of R. Nehorai; Talmud Bavli Berakhot 43b; Talmud Bavli Bava Metsia 58b.

52. M. Avot 1:18.

53. Lev. Rabbah 9; Talmud Bavli Perek ha-Shalom.

54. See Talmud Bavli Yevamot 14a, on the relationship of the house of Hillel and the house of Shamai; Num. Rabbah 13; Talmud Bavli Eruvin 13b.

55. Avot of Rabbi Nathan, version B, ch. 24.

56. M. Avot 4:1.

57. Exod. 23:5; Exod. Rabbah 30:1; see the discussion in Kimelman, "Non-violence in the Talmud," 318–19.

58. Talmud Bavli Bava Metsia 49b; Talmud Bavli Makkot 24, story on R. Safrah.

59. M. Avot 2:15.

60. M. Avot 4:23; Talmud Bavli Berakhot 7a.

61. Talmud Bavli Berakhot 17a.

62. See n. 24 above, on repentance.

63. Deut. 16:20; Zeph. 2:3; *Otsar Midrashim*, Midrash Hashkem, 183.

64. Avot of Rabbi Nathan 15:1, 17:2; Moshe Hayyim Luzzatto (1707–1746), *Sefer Mesilat Yesharim* (rpt., Jerusalem and New York: Feldheim, 1969), ch. 19.

65. *Otsar Midrashim*, Midrash Gadol a'Gedulah, 78.

66. Talmud Bavli Bava Metsia 32b; *Sefer Orhot Tsaddikim*, ch. 8; Maimonides, *Mishneh Torah*, Laws of Murder, 13:1.

67. Lev. 19:17; Talmud Bavli Arakhin 16a.

68. Deut. 16:19; M. Pe'ah 8:9.

69. M. Avot 4:1, 2:7.

70. Talmud Bavli Perek ha-Shalom.

71. M. Avot 4:1; Talmud Bavli Berakhot 17a; Maimonides, *Mishneh Torah*, Laws of Repentance.

72. M. Derekh Erets Rabbah; M. Derekh Erets Zuta; Abohav, *Menorat ha-Maor*, 699–735, on the role of civility in conflict prevention and, generally, 696–747, on "the ways of peace and love."

73. Talmud Bavli Berakhot 17a.

74. See, for example, Francis Hutcheson, *An Essay on the Nature and Conduct of the Passions and Affections with Illustrations upon the Moral Sense* (London: sold by J. Osborn & T. Longman, 1728). Other key figures included the Third Earl of Shaftesbury, David Hume, and Adam Smith.

75. It is interesting to note that R. Akiva (c. 50–135 C.E.) considered this the preeminent principle of Judaism. However, his contemporary Ben Azzai stated that the most important principle is the idea that every human being is created in the image of God and is therefore invaluable. This is superior as a principle to the love principle, lest "someone say, 'since I have been abused, let my fellow human being be abused,

since I have been cursed let my fellow human being be cursed'" (Gen. Rabbah 24). R. Tanhuma adds, in the same commentary, "If you do this [abuse others], know who you are abusing: . . . in the image of God He made him [Gen. 5:1]." We have here, in a nutshell, what might be the thought patterns of abused people the world over who, despite good consciences, feel that, from the point of view of justice, if they have been unloved and abused, that they should treat others no differently. The statement by Ben Azzai is meant to contradict that tendency of feeling within the Jewish people of his time. It means that the only way that a Jewish person could devalue another human being would be to consider him not really created in the image of God, not really human, which manifestly contradicts the sacred text.

76. See a fine example of contemporary rabbinic hermeneutics on the relationship of honor for all people as a way of protecting human life in Micha Odenheimer, "Honor or Death," *Jerusalem Report* 9, no. 22, Mar. 1, 1999, p. 25.

77. B. R. Brown, "Face-Saving and Face-Restoration in Negotiation," in *Negotiations*, ed. D. Druckman (Beverly Hills, Calif.: Sage, 1977), 275–99.

78. Ps. 34:15.

79. See Gopin, "Is There a Jewish God of Peace?" 32–39.

80. On the violence of some of the priestly families, see Talmud Bavli Pesahim 57.

81. Avot of Rabbi Nathan 12:3.

82. *Otsar Midrashim*, Midrash Gadol u'Gedulah, 78, under the word *perek*.

83. This is probably based on the rabbinic idea that, while someone is in a rage, it is best not to respond to her but to wait until the heat of anger is gone, and more conciliatory language can be used. See n. 60 on *she'at ka'aso*.

84. M. Kallah Rabbati, ch. 3. The rabbis are, like many other cultural figures around the world, extremely attuned to issues of dignity. This is hard to understand in the crass culture of industrialized society, and this misunderstanding is the frequent cause of intercultural conflict, particularly between those who dwell in large urban centers and those who live in more traditional, less populated settings. Apparently, in rabbinic culture, even the act of engaging in other people's conflicts involves some loss of dignity, perhaps because a concerned outsider is so often rebuffed or even abused by parties to a conflict.

85. I leave aside here the inappropriateness of this story as a model for any contemporary solution to a marital crisis. Any husband who throws his wife out of the house can and should be subject to prosecution if he does not come to some more equitable way to separate, if that is what they must do. I urge the reader to see the moral tale in its context, to suspend contemporary moral evaluations temporarily, in order to see the prosocial message of the story, which is intended to teach mediators how they should behave. We do not use it as a role model for a husband's behavior or as a contemporary solution to that behavior.

86. I am caricaturing to a degree the contemporary model. For example, I have studied and watched a Jewish divorce mediator whose emotional involvement during the mediation process is quite clear. He shares why this work is so important to him, and he goes out of his way to evoke emotions by mentioning and frequently talking about the children who will be affected by the settlement or lack thereof. He does this to bring the full emotional reality of the process into the mediation, rather than suppressing it.

87. Bush and Folger, *The Promise of Mediation*; compare with Bruce McKinney, "A Critical Analysis of Transformative Mediation," *Peace Research* 29, no. 1 (Feb. 1997): 41–52.

88. As a contemporary example, Leah Green, building on the work of Gene Knudsen Hoffman on compassionate listening, has initiated the Middle East Compassionate

Listening Project, based in Indianola, Washington. It has brought a variety of American Jews to the West Bank and Israel to engage in listening to the full spectrum of Israeli and Palestinian points of view, without engaging in debate but simply involved in the discipline of listening. They are one of the only groups, to my knowledge, that listens actively to settlers as well as to the more radical Muslims on the West Bank. The Fellowship of Reconciliation also has an extensive program of compassionate listening projects.

89. See John Paul Lederach, *Building Peace: Sustainable Reconciliation in Divided Societies* (Tokyo: United Nations University, 1994), 26.

90. Exod. 23:5; Deut. 22:4; see also Prov. 25:21.

91. See Kimelman, "Non-Violence in the Talmud," 318ff, for the rabbinic sources.

92. See Volkan, *The Need to Have Enemies and Allies.*

93. Enormous amounts of human and financial resources are applied globally to fighting a variety of forms of injustice involving women, children, abused classes or races of people, prisoners, laborers, and more. Much of this work is focused on the poor and the inherent injustices of social structures. This is vital work, but it sometimes induces not only constructive conflict—which is necessary—but unnecessarily adversarial and destructive forms of confrontation. The latter cause many backlashes of a violent sort, which just perpetuate the cycle of violence and injustice. The fact is that justice seeking and peace seeking are often at odds with each other, and analysts need to confront this and suggest integrated models of social change. The conflictual styles of many people in justice advocacy, at least in the United States, are quite notorious. Indeed, part of this stems from a mistaken model of social change, which requires the demonization of one group of people and the exaggerated innocence of another group. The real world has never been that simple, and, more important, such a psychological construct is guaranteed to perpetuate the very injustices and violence that one is combating. Gandhi and King understood perfectly the delicate balance of resistance to injustice and the art of peacemaking. Many of those who engage in this work, especially when made rigid by institutionalization, do not, and they need more guidance from ethicists and conflict analysts. See Marc Gopin, "Conflict Resolution and International Development: Conflict or Cooperation?" in *Conflict Resolution and Social Injustice*, ed. R. Rubenstein and F. Blechman (forthcoming).

94. Avot of Rabbi Nathan 23:1.

95. Talmud Bavli Ta'anit 67a.

96. See Talmud Bavli Yoma 86b; Maimonides, *Mishneh Torah*, Book of Knowledge, Laws of Teshuva, 2:5

97. See Kesef Mishneh on Maimonides, *Mishneh Torah*, Book of Knowledge, Laws of *Teshuva* 2:5

98. Compare with Islam, where generosity in debt disputes, which were arbitrated by Mohammed, was seen as a central way to bring about peace between enemies (*Hadith Sahih Bukhari* 3.49.868–70).

99. See Talmud Bavli Rosh ha-Shanah 16b; and Kesef Mishneh commentary to Maimonides, *Mishneh Torah*, Book of Knowledge, Laws of *Teshuva* 2:4.

100. Maimonides, *Mishneh Torah*, Book of Knowledge, Laws of *Teshuva* 2:4.

101. Several years ago I was working with American teenagers, who came to Washington to be educated about politics. I repeatedly asked these teenagers the following question: "How many people died in the Vietnam War?" I constantly got the answer: 50,000. The collective American memory to which they had been acculturated eliminated the more than 2 million Asians who were killed in the war. I said, "people," but they heard me say "Americans."

102. See n. 42 above, on the concept of *tokhaha*.

103. The effects of the Truth and Reconciliation Commissions presently emerging are complex, especially in view of the political and military circumstances that require their creation. They are, however, an important development and require a separate study.

104. Shai Franklin, "Victim's Gold Deserves Proper Burial," letter to the editor, *Washington Jewish Week*, May 29, 1997, p. 19.

105. See Daniel Boyarin, *Unheroic Conduct: The Rise of Heterosexuality and the Invention of the Jewish Man* (Berkeley: University of Berkeley Press, 1997); and Boyarin, "Homotopia: The Feminized Jewish Man and the Lives of Women in Late Antiquity," *Differences* 7 no. 2 (1995).

106. Avot of Rabbi Nathan 23:1.

107. This requires a much larger discussion of early rabbinic efforts to create or recreate the ideal Jewish man in terms of Torah study and a restrained, semi-monastic lifestyle and their undermining of the role of men as warriors, which was popular in competing sects of the Second Temple period. This does not mean that the rabbis were pacifists, although some were (see Kimelman, "Non-Violence in the Talmud"). But there was a clear shift in emphasis toward a certain kind of peace-making Jewish man. This then set the stage for the prevailing images of the Jewish man for many centuries to come, with some notable exceptions in Spain and else-where. Another major shift in Jewish male identity came with the Enlightenment, the Emancipation, Jewish entry into various militaries, and, of course, the new Jewish man, the Zionist *halutz*. All of this history will have to be confronted as Jewish cul-ture faces in the future the question of what the ideal Jewish man is. This is brought into sharp relief in contemporary Israeli culture, where one part of the culture views manhood as essentially related to universal military service while the *haredi* part views manhood in a completely different way, with each group of men deeply re-senting the other's definition of manhood. Furthermore, for entirely secular reasons, many Israeli youths are beginning to question the centrality of the army in their male identities.

108. I refer to the elicitive method of John Paul Lederach. See his *Preparing for Peace*.

Chapter Nine

1. Of course, this problem is not limited historically to religious ethics. The U.S. Constitution and Bill of Rights come to mind, with their extraordinary guarantees of liberty and justice for *all*, which happened to not include slaves before the Civil War, or the European precedents for those documents, which did not include women or the landless. Thus, in promoting human rights, for example, we should not approach religious authorities arrogantly, as if secular culture has never faced the same limita-tions in its cultural constructs.

2. See, e.g., Sachedina, "Is There a Tradition of Pacifism and Nonviolence in Is-lam?" 7–8.

3. The Jewish community has been thinking of mission in the last couple of hundred years, in the context of newly found empowerment to influence the course of the world. The Christian community has been engaged in missionizing since its inception and is now considering how to define this concept in the light of modern life and a crowded world. But mission as a problem has not been truly confronted by the monotheisms that have traditionally missionized and prosely-tized. On the Jewish community and mission, see ch. 5 of this volume, and Seltzer, *Jewish People, Jewish Thought*, 587, 596, 600, 612–13, 617–18, 688, and 698; Abraham

Isaac Kook, *Abraham Isaac Kook: The Lights of Penitence, the Moral Principles, Lights of Holiness, Essays, Letters and Poems,* comp. and trans. Ben Zion Bokser (New York: Paulist Press, 1978), 271–75, 317; and Cohen, *Religion of Reason,* 158 and passim. On Christian concern about mission, see my comments above in ch. 7, and, for a contemporary sampling of approaches to mission, see M. Thomas Thangaraj, *The Common Task: A Theology of Mission* (Nashville: Abingdon, 1998); and Carlos F. Cardoza-Orlandi, *Mission: An Essential Guide* (Nashville: Abingdon, 1998). Interpretation of mission and, in particular, the attitude toward proselytism in Christianity tends to be an excellent marker of conservative and liberal approaches to the rest of the world or more or less aggressive approaches to other faiths. Ironically, in Judaism, the marker is reversed. More intensive discussion of mission usually indicates a greater commitment to humanity in terms of a universal moral sense of that commitment, since there has been no aggressive commitment to proselytism in Jewish rabbinic history, both practically and theoretically. By contrast, less of a commitment to mission usually indicates less care for the fate of humanity.

4. Stanley Greenspan, *The Growth of the Mind and the Endangered Origins of Intelligence* (Reading, Mass.: Addison-Wesley, 1997).

5. Greenspan argues (*Growth of the Mind,* 236–39) that the key emotional skills of conflict resolution include empathy with the emotions of Others; an ability to deal with multiple feelings inside oneself, such as anger; an affection for Others; and the ability to deal with disappointment. It would be interesting to explore a Greenspanian method to engage religious communities, to build on religious values that would dovetail with the capacities that Greenspan makes essential to peacemaking.

6. I include in this those who have faith in the Enlightenment conception of the world or faith in the marketplace or faith in the scientific method and the importance of the university. They too can either lead the way in conflict prevention or be part of the problem if they are easily threatened by and therefore intolerant of other paradigms of living and believing.

7. I mean community in two senses: (1) the largest bodies, for example, of organized Christianity and within that the Vatican, the Mennonite Central Committee, or the World Council of Churches, the last being subject to negotiations among many groups, and (2) the smallest groups—churches, mosques, fellowships—as well as regional communities, such as the Catholic communities of the Philippines. Obviously there are intimate relations between both categories, but the more local category is critical because it is in the local context that the problems of conflict are most clearly felt and understood—and where indigenous solutions can occur. On the other hand, those in charge of the religious policies of broad corporate groups are important as well. Their greatest strength is twofold: they provide a place outside local conflicts that can serve in an intermediary capacity, and they can set long-term educational policies that inculcate the values and skills that are critical to conflict resolution, especially toward those outside the faith.

8. Ross, *Culture of Conflict,* 61–63, and passim.

9. Ross, *Culture of Conflict,* 63–65, and passim.

10. Ross uses Murdock and White's Standard Cross-Cultural Sample of 186 linguistically and culturally distinct groups from around the world (*Culture of Conflict,* 79–80).

11. Sells, *The Bridge Betrayed.*

12. Tisha B'Av (the ninth of the Jewish month of Av), which always occurs in the summer, commemorates the destruction of the First and Second Jewish Temples in 586 B.C.E. and 70 C.E. respectively. It also commemorates the beginning of a two-

thousand-year exile and numerous other tragedies in history, including the Crusades. These mostly occurred in the summer because that is when premodern armies generally killed the most people in the course of their exploits.

13. The Passion of Christ, for example.

14. The death of Ali, for example, in Shi'a Islam and, generally, the escape of Mohammed from persecution in Mecca, associated with the beginning of the Islamic calendar.

15. See Kakar, *Colors of Violence*, for an excellent description of professional murderers and their ritualized role in the Hindu/Muslim struggle in India.

16. See Ruth Gruber, "Israel Honors Poles for Work on Preserving Jewish Heritage," *Jewish Telegraph Agency*, July 7, 1998. Their work included restoring cemeteries and creating museums. I once met a Christian from Krakow, through my contacts with Moral Re-Armament, who spent two years in search of Poland's surviving Jewish life. When he realized that it was almost absent because millions had been murdered, he proceeded to spend much time photographing Jewish tombstones. He showed me some of his work. Clearly, for him, this was an act of penance for the past. It moved me deeply that he would dedicate his life to this, and this was one of the first instances that demonstrated to me the power of religious gestures of change and reconciliation and how they transform both those who make the gesture and those who receive it.

17. If your arguments for civil liberties are perceived to be or are a cover for your own national interests (a tactic to open up foreign markets, for example), then you have completely undermined your credibility with religious representatives. It is vital that you openly acknowledge mixed motivations that you may have. Personal motivations are not necessarily destructive, as long as they are openly acknowledged. The United States in particular is resented in many parts of the world for always framing its arguments in moralistic terms, even when it is pursuing its own national interest. Religious people are particularly sensitive to the uses or abuses of moral principles for private motivations. That is not to say that national interest is not a legitimate concern; it simply must be stated up front. Negotiators need not be perfectly disinterested in outcomes, but they do have to be honest.

18. See Gopin, "Conflict Resolution and International Development."

19. Lederach, *Preparing for Peace*.

20. I am involved, for example, in the Faith and Politics Institute, which was founded precisely to make the spiritual life and values of individual politicians in Washington into something that binds a civil society together, rather than something that divides. It is especially meant for religious politicians to have an outlet for their values, which help construct civil society not unravel its accomplishments, and that is why an important focus of its work is on racial reconciliation. More steps must be taken in this direction, but there also must be concerted efforts to reach out to the most militant religious voices, not in order to submit to their program but to lessen, through all the methods mentioned above, the destructive character of their present involvement in politics.

21. For an exhaustive study of this problem, see "Soul Wars: The Problem of Proselytism in Russia," *Emory International Law Review* 12; no. 1 (Winter 1998). The entire issue is dedicated to the subject.

22. See Joseph Montville, "Reconciliation in America," *American Civilization* (May–June 1995), 14ff. On the tendency to export American anger overseas, see Montville, "Psychology, War, and Integrity," *Psychologist/Psychoanalyst* 11 special supp. (Summer 1991): 14–17.

23. For one example of the relationship between the military leaders and Protestant evangelism and the friction with the Catholic community that resulted, see David Stoll, " 'Jesus Is Lord of Guatemala': Evangelical Reform in a Death Squad State," in Marty and Appleby, eds., *Accounting for Fundamentalisms*, 99–123.

24. A student of mine reported extensively on a conflict between a new Protestant sect and the Catholic majority in a particularly remote region. This conflict escalated into arson and expulsion. The feelings are deeply bitter. Furthermore, the sect speaks such a different religious language than the Catholic community that, over and above the bitterness of the enemies, there are serious communication problems. Both sides see the other as heretical and malevolent. This is one small example.

25. Kakar, *Colors of Violence*.

26. See *Islam and Nonviolence*, ed. Glenn Paige et al., 66–67. On Gandhi's relation to them, see Pyarelal, *A Pilgrimage of Peace: Gandhi and the Frontier, Gandhi among N.W.F. Pathans* (Ahmedabad, India: Navajivan, 1950).

27. Corinne Dempsey, "Rivalry, Reliance and Resemblance: Siblings as Metaphor for Hindu-Christian Relations in Kerala State," unpublished paper delivered at the American Academy of Religion, 1996.

28. *Ahimsa* (nonviolence) is the first of the Five Great Vows of Jain monasticism. See Thompson, *World Religions in War and Peace*, 74; and Koshelya Walli, *The Conception of Ahimsa in Indian Thought according to Sanskrit Sources* (Varanasi, India: Bharata Manisha, 1974).

29. Little, *Sri Lanka*, and Stanley Tambiah, *Buddhism Betrayed? Religion, Politics, and Violence in Sri Lanka* (Chicago: University of Chicago Press, 1992).

30. See, for example, Maura Moynihan, "Enter the Dalai Lama," *Washington Times*, Apr. 22, 1997; and Stephen Johnson, "Dalai Lama Recommends Middle Path: Leader Warns against Bad Signals to China," *Houston Chronicle*, Sept. 7, 1995.

31. See for example, Lao-tzu, *The Tao of the Tao Te Ching: A Translation and Commentary*, ed. and trans. Michael Lafargue (Albany: State University of New York Press, 1992), 125, 150.

32. As noted above, Ross found that 60.9 percent of the indigenous groups around the world that he studied valued violence against other societies, while only 6 percent disapproved (*Culture of Conflict*, 80).

33. See Joshua Trachtenberg, *The Devil and the Jews: The Medieval Conception of the Jew and Its Relation to Modern Anti-Semitism* (Philadelphia: Jewish Publication Society, 1993).

34. *Jerusalem Report* 9, no. 8, Aug. 17, 1998, p. 12.

35. I want to acknowledge here the important work of René Girard on sacred violence in understanding the importance of scapegoating in religious traditions (see Girard, *Violence and the Sacred*, trans. Patrick Gregory [Baltimore: Johns Hopkins University Press, 1979]. While I agree that the latter is an important element in religious violence, it is also an oversimplification to assume that all religious violence is based on the need to sacrifice the scapegoat. I have tried to show that there are many complicated reasons for religious violence and, therefore, a variety of measures need to be taken to counteract it. That having been said, Girard has described a deep cultural impulse that seems to me to particularly capture at least the outer characteristics of European bloodletting in the name of God; this seems especially relevant to understanding European anti-Semitism and its culmination in the Holocaust.

36. Haym Soloveitchik, "Rupture and Reconstruction: The Transformation of Contemporary Orthodoxy," *Tradition* 28, no. 4 (1994), 64–106; and Soloveitchik, "Mi-

gration, Acculturation, and the New Role of Texts in the Haredi World," in *Accounting for Fundamentalisms*, ed. Marty and Appleby, 197–235.

37. See June Glazer, "A Transformed Orthodoxy Explored at Harvard," *Yeshiva University Review* (Winter 1998), 27–28, which reports on comments by various scholars on Soloveitchik's thesis.

Bibliography

Abohav, Yitshak. *Menorat ha-Maor.* Edited by J. Horeb and M. Katznelbogen. Jerusalem: Mossad HaRav Kuk, 1961.

Abu-Nimer, Mohammed. "Conflict Resolution in an Islamic Context." *Peace and Change* 21, no. 1. (Jan. 1996): 22–40.

Agnew, John. "Beyond Reason: Spatial and Temporal Sources of Ethnic Conflicts." In *Intractable Conflicts and Their Transformation,* edited by Louis Kriesberg, Terrell A. Northrop, and Stuart J. Thorson. Syracuse, N. Y.: Syracuse University Press, 1989.

Agus, Ronald. *The Binding of Isaac and Messiah: Law, Martyrdom, and Deliverance in Early Rabbinic Religiosity.* Albany: State University Press of New York, 1988.

M. E. Artom, ed. *Ketavim.* Jerusalem: Bialik Institute, 1976.

Avruch, Kevin. *Culture and Conflict Resolution.* Washington, D.C.: U.S. Institute of Peace, 1998.

Avruch, Kevin, and Peter Black. "A Generic Theory of Conflict Resolution: A Critique." *Negotiation Journal* 3 (1987): 87–96.

Avruch, Kevin, Peter Black, and Joseph Scimecca, eds. *Conflict Resolution: Cross-Cultural Perspectives.* Westport, Conn.: Greenwood, 1991.

Bainton, Roland. *Christian Attitudes toward War and Peace.* Nashville: Abingdon, 1979.

Baron, Salo, George Wise, and Lenn Goodman, eds., *Violence and Defense in Jewish Experience* (Philadelphia: Jewish Publication Society of America, 1977).

Barrett, William, ed. *Zen Buddhism.* Garden City, N.Y.: Doubleday, 1956.

Bellah, Robert, et al. *Habits of the Heart.* 1985. Reprint. Berkeley: University of California Press, 1996.

Benamozegh, Elijah. *Moral juive et moral chrétiènne.* Paris: 1867. Reprint. 3rd ed., Neuchâtel: Edition de la Baconnière, 1946.

———. "Le crime de la guerre denoncé à l'humanité." Paris: League of Peace, 1870.

———. *Jewish and Christian Ethics: With a Criticism on Mohamedism.* Translated from French. San Francisco: E. Blochman, 1873.

———. *Israel et Humanité.* Livorno: Elijah Benamozegh, 1885.

———. *De l'Origine des dogmes Chrétiens.* Livourne: S. Belforte, 1897.

———. *Israel et Humanité: Etude sur le probléme de la religion universelle et sa solution.* Compiled and edited by Aimé Pallière. Paris: Leroux, 1914.

———. "Affinità fra la dottrina di Gesù e quella dei Farisei." *Rassegna mensile di Israèl* 16 (1951): 51–54.

———. *Israel and Humanity.* Translated by Maxwell Luria. New York: Paulist Press, 1994.

Bialik, C., and Y. Ravnitsky, eds. *The Book of Legends* (Hebrew). Tel Aviv: Dvir, 1973.

Bleich, J. David. "Preemptive War in Jewish Tradition." *Tradition* 21, no. 1 (Spring 1983): 3–41.

Boulding, Elise. "States, Boundaries, and Environmental Security." In *Conflict Resolution Theory and Practice*, edited by Dennis Sandole and Hugo van der Merwe. Manchester, N.Y.: Manchester University Press, 1993.

Boyarin, Daniel. "Homotopia: The Feminized Jewish Man and the Lives of Women in Late Antiquity." *Differences* 7, no. 2 (1995).

———. *Unheroic Conduct: The Rise of Heterosexuality and the Invention of the Jewish Man*. Berkeley: University of Berkeley Press, 1997.

Broome, Benjamin. "Managing Differences in Conflict Resolution: The Role of Relational Empathy." In *Conflict Resolution Theory and Practice*, edited by Dennis Sandole and Hugo van der Merwe. Manchester, N.Y. Manchester University Press, 1993.

Brown, B. R. "Face-Saving and Face-Restoration in Negotiation." In *Negotiations*, edited by D. Druckman. Beverly Hills, Calif.: Sage, 1977.

Buber, Martin. "The Land and Its Possessors." In *Israel and the World*, translated by Olga Marx and Greta Hort. New York: Schocken, 1963.

———. *The Knowledge of Man*. Edited by Maurice Friedman. New York: Harper and Row, 1965.

———. *I and Thou*. Translated and annotated by Walter Kaufmann. New York: Charles Scribner's Sons, 1970.

———. *A Land of Two Peoples*. Edited by Paul Mendes-Flohr. New York: Oxford University Press, 1983.

Burnouf, Emile. "La Science des Religions: Part II, Les Grandes Religions et Leurs Origines." *Revue des Deux Mondes* 6 (1864): 979–1010.

———. "Part III, L'Unité des Religions." *Revue des Deux Mondes* 2 (1868): 995–1017.

———. "Part IV: La Diversité des Religions." *Revue des Deux Mondes* 4 (1868): 864–889.

———. *The Science of Religions*. London: S. Sonnenschein, Lowry, 1888.

Burton, John, ed. *Conflict: Human Needs Theory*. New York: St. Martin's, 1990.

———. *Conflict Resolution: Its Language and Processes*. Lanham, Md.: Scarecrow, 1996.

Bush, Robert, and Joseph Folger. *The Promise of Mediation: Responding to Conflict through Empowerment and Recognition*. San Francisco: Jossey-Bass, 1994.

Cardoza-Orlandi, Carlos F. *Mission: An Essential Guide*. Nashville: Abingdon, 1998.

Cassirer, Ernst. *The Philosophy of the Enlightenment*. Boston: Beacon, 1951.

Channer, Alan. "Twilight of the Khmer Rouge." *For a Change* (June–July 1997).

Chapple, Christopher Key. *Nonviolence to Animals, Earth, and Self in Asian Traditions*. Albany: State University of New York, 1993.

Coate, Roger, and Jerel A. Rosati, eds. *The Power of Human Needs in World Society*. Boulder, Colo.: Lynne Rienner, 1988.

Cohen, Hermann. *Religion of Reason: Out of the Sources of Judaism*. Translated by Simon Kaplan. 1972. Reprint. Atlanta: Scholars, 1995.

Cohn, Haim. *Human Rights in Jewish Law*. New York: Ktav, 1984.

Cordovero, Moshe. *The Palm Tree of Devorah*. Translated by Moshe Miller. Spring Valley, N.Y.: Targum/Feldheim, 1993.

Dalai Lama XIV, Tenzin Gyatso. *Freedom in Exile: The Autobiography of the Dalai Lama*. New York: HarperCollins, 1990.

De Bary, William Theodore, ed. *Sources of Indian Tradition*. New York: Columbia University Press, 1958.

Dempsey, Corinne. "Rivalry, Reliance and Resemblance: Siblings as Metaphor for Hindu-Christian Relations in Kerala State." Unpublished paper delivered at the American Academy of Religion, 1996.

Dorff, Elliot, and Louis Newman, eds. *Contemporary Jewish Ethics and Morality*. New York: Oxford University Press, 1995.

Driedger, Leo, and Donald B. Kraybill. *Mennonite Peacemaking: From Quietism to Activism*. Scottdale, Pa.: Herald, 1993.

Dueck, Kenneth, and Donald Froese. "Attitudes towards Jews Encountered among Selected Segments of Mennonites in Canada." Student essay (1972) available in the libraries of Canadian Mennonite Bible College and Associated Mennonite Biblical Seminary.

Duncan, Ronald, ed. *Gandhi: Selected Writings*. New York: Harper Colophon, 1971.

Eck, Diana. *Encountering God*. Boston: Beacon, 1993.

Eckhardt, Meister. "About Activities of the Inner Life and Outer Life." In *Meister Eckhardt*. Translated by Raymond B. Blakney. New York: Harper, 1941.

Epp, Frank Henry. "An Analysis of Germanism and National Socialism in the Immigrant Newspaper of a Canadian Minority Group, the Mennonites, in the 1930s." Ph.D. diss., Univ. of Minnesota, 1965.

———. "National Socialism among the Canadian Mennonites in the 1930s." Paper for the Fifteenth Conference on Mennonite Educational and Cultural Problems. Bluffton College, Ohio, 1965.

———. *Mennonite Exodus: The Rescue and Resettlement of the Russian Mennonites since the Communist Revolution*. Altona, Manitoba: D. W. Friesen and Sons, 1966.

———. "Facing the World." In his *Mennonites in Canada, 1920–1940*. Toronto: Macmillan of Canada, 1974.

Erny, Pierre. *Rwanda 1994: cles pour comprendre le calvaire d'un peuple*. Paris: L'Harmattan, 1994.

Esack, Farid. *The Qur'an, Liberation and Pluralism*. London: One World, 1996.

Fakhry, Majid. *Ethical Theories in Islam*. Leiden and New York: E. J. Brill, 1994.

Ferguson, John. *War and Peace in the World's Religions*. New York: Oxford University Press, 1978.

Fisher, Eugene. "Evolution of a Tradition." In *Fifteen Years of Catholic-Jewish Dialogue, 1970–1985*, edited by the International Catholic-Jewish Liaison Committee. Rome: Vatican Library, 1988.

———. *Faith without Prejudice*. New York: Crossroads, 1993.

Fisher, Eugene, and Leon Klenicki. *In Our Time: The Flowering of Jewish-Catholic Dialogue*. Mahwah, N.J. Paulist Press, 1990.

Fisher, Roger, and Scott Brown. *Getting Together: Building Relationships as We Negotiate*. New York: Penguin, 1988.

Fisher, Roger, and William Ury. *Getting to Yes*. New York, N.Y.: Penguin, 1991.

Folger, J., M. Poole, and R. Stutman, eds. *Working through Conflict*. New York: Longman, 1997.

Fox, Marvin, ed. *Modern Jewish Ethics*. Columbus, Ohio: Ohio State University Press, 1975.

Francis, E. K. "The Russian Mennonites: From Religious to Ethnic Group." *American Journal of Sociology* 54 (Sept. 1948): 101–7.

Friedman, Menachem. "The *Haredim* and the Holocaust." *Jerusalem Quarterly* 53 (1990): 87–144.

Friedman, Robert I. *The False Prophet, Meir Kahane: From FBI Informant to Knesset Member*. Brooklyn, N.Y.: Lawrence Hill, 1990.

Friedman, Yohanan. *Prophecy Continuous: Aspects of Ahmadi Religious Thought and Its Medieval Background.* Berkeley: University of California Press, 1989.

Fry, Douglas P., and Kaj Bjorkqvist, eds. *Cultural Variation in Conflict Resolution: Alternatives to Violence.* Mahwah, N.J.: Lawrence Erlbaum, 1997.

Gadamer, Hans. *Truth and Method,* 2d rev. ed. Translated by Joel Weinsheimer and Donald G. Marshall. New York: Crossroad, 1989.

Galtung, Johan. "Peace, Violence, and Peace Research." *Journal of Peace Research* 6 (1969): 167–91.

————. *Peace by Peaceful Means: Peace and Conflict, Development and Civilization.* Oslo and London: International Peace Research Institute and Sage, 1996.

Gandhi, Mohandas. *All Men Are Brothers.* Edited by Krishna Kripalani. New York: Continuum, 1980.

Geertz, Clifford. *The Interpretation of Cultures.* New York: Basic, 1973.

Gendler, Everett. "War and the Jewish Tradition." In *Contemporary Jewish Ethics,* edited by Menachem Kellner. New York: Hebrew Publishing, 1978.

Gioberti, Vincenzo. *Introduzione allo studio della filosofia.* Brussels: M. Hayez, 1840.

————. *Del primato moral e civile degli Italiani.* Brussels: Meline, Cans, 1843.

Girard, René. *Violence and the Sacred.* Translated by Patrick Gregory. Baltimore: Johns Hopkins University Press, 1979.

Glatzer, Nahum. "The Concept of Peace in Classical Judaism." In *Der Freide: Idee un Werwirklichug.* [Leschnitzer Festschrift], edited by Erich Fromm et al. Heidelberg: L. Schneider, 1961.

————. *Hillel the Elder: The Emergence of Classical Judaism.* c. 1956. Reprint. New York: Schocken, 1970.

Glazer, June. "A Transformed Orthodoxy Explored at Harvard." *Yeshiva University Review* (Winter 1998): 27–28.

Gopin, Marc. "The Religious Ethics of Samuel David Luzzatto." Ph.D. diss., Brandeis Univ., 1993.

————. "Is There a Jewish God of Peace?" In *The Challenge of Shalom,* edited by Murray Polner and Naomi Goodman. Philadelphia: New Society, 1994.

————. "Religion, Violence and Conflict Resolution." *Peace and Change* 22, no. 1 (Jan. 1997): 1–31.

————. "The Heart of the Stranger and the Transformation of Sectarianism." Unpublished paper delivered in Belfast, June 1997, at the Bonds and Boundaries Conference on Religious Sectarianism.

————. "Confronting the Secular/Religious Conflict in Israel: Suggested Solutions." In *Religious Secular Relations in Israel: Social and Political Implications,* edited by Ephraim Ya'ar and Tamar Herman. Tel Aviv: Steinmetz Center for Peace Research, Tel Aviv University, and the Konrad Adenauer Foundation, 1998.

————. "Forgiveness as an Element of Conflict Resolution in Religious Cultures: Walking the Tightrope of Reconciliation and Justice." Unpublished paper, delivered Feb. 19, 1999, at American University.

————. "Conflict Resolution and International Development: Conflict or Cooperation?" In *Conflict Resolution and Social Injustice,* edited by R. Rubenstein and F. Blechman. Forthcoming.

Gosananda, Maha. *A Report from the Inter-Religious Mission for Peace in Cambodia.* Providence, R.I.: Cambodian Mission for Peace, 1988.

————. *Step by Step: Meditations on Wisdom and Compassion.* Berkeley, Calif.: Parallax, 1988.

Greenberg, Gershon. "Ontic Division and Religious Survival: Wartime Orthodoxy and the Holocaust (Hurban)." *Modern Judaism* 14, no. 1 (1994): 21–61.

————. "Consoling Truth: Eliezer Schweid's *Ben Hurban Le'Yeshua:* A Review Essay." *Modern Judaism* 17, no. 3 (1997): 297–311.

Greenspan, Stanley. *The Growth of the Mind and the Endangered Origins of Intelligence.* Reading, Mass.: Addison-Wesley, 1997.

Guetta, Alessandro. "Elia Benamozegh: Bibliografia." *Rassegna mensile di Israèl* 53, nos. 1–2 (1987): 67–81.

Guttmann, Julius. *Philosophies of Judaism.* New York: Holt, Rinehart, & Winston, 1964.

Hallie, Phillip. *Lest Innocent Blood Be Shed.* New York: Harper and Row, 1979.

Hand, Sean, ed. *The Levinas Reader.* Cambridge, Mass.: Basil Blackwell, 1989.

Henderson, Michael. *The Forgiveness Factor.* Salem, Oreg., and London: Grosvenor, 1996.

Herford, R. Travers, ed. and trans. *The Ethics of the Talmud: Sayings of the Fathers.* New York: Schocken, 1962.

Heschel, Susannah. "Transforming Jesus from Jew to Aryan: Protestant Theologians in Nazi Germany." The Albert Bilgray Lecture Presented at the University of Arizona, Apr. 1995.

Horowitz, David. *Ethnic Groups in Conflict.* Berkeley and Los Angeles: University of California Press, 1985.

Hull, Robert. *A Chronology of Christian Peacemaker Teams 1984–1992.* Newton, Kans.: CPT Steering Committee, 1991.

Hutcheson, Francis. *An Essay on the Nature and Conduct of the Passions and Affections with Illustrations upon the Moral Sense.* London: Sold by J. Osborn & T. Longman, 1728.

————. "Concerning Good and Evil." In *The Classical Moralists,* compiled by Benjamin Rand. Boston: Houghton Mifflin, 1937.

Ibn Paquda, Bachya ben Joseph. *Duties of the Heart.* Translated by Moses Hyamson. Jerusalem and New York: Feldheim, 1970.

Jack, Homer, ed. *World Religions and World Peace: The International Inter-Religious Symposium on Peace.* Boston: Beacon, 1968.

James, William. *The Varieties of Religious Experience.* New York: Modern Library, 1936.

Johnson, James Turner, and John Kelsay, eds. *Cross, Crescent and Sword: The Justification and Limitation of War in Western and Islamic Tradition.* New York: Greenwood, 1990.

Johnston, Douglas. "The Churches and Apartheid in South Africa." In *Religion: The Missing Dimension of Statecraft,* edited by Cynthia Sampson and Douglas Johnston. New York: Oxford University Press, 1994.

Johnston, Douglas, and Cynthia Sampson, eds. *Religion: The Missing Dimension of Statecraft.* New York: Oxford University Press, 1994.

Juhnke, James. *A People of Two Kingdoms: The Political Acculturation of the Kansas Mennonites.* Newton, Kans.: Faith and Life Press, 1975.

Kahane, Meir. *Uncomfortable Questions for Comfortable Jews.* Secaucus, N.J.: L. Stuart, 1987.

Kakar, Sudhir. *The Colors of Violence: Cultural Identities, Religion, and Conflict.* Chicago: University of Chicago Press, 1996.

Kamenetz, Rodger. *The Jew in the Lotus.* San Francisco: HarperSanFrancisco, 1994.

Kant, Immanuel. "The Metaphysical Foundations of Morals." In *The Philosophy of Kant: Immanuel Kant's Moral and Political Writings,* edited by Carl Friedrich. New York: Modern Library, 1977.

Karo, Joseph. *Shulhan Arukh.* n.d. Reprint. New York: M. P. Press, 1976.

Kasimow, Harold, and Byron Sherwin, eds. *No Religion Is an Island: Abraham Joshua Heschel and Interreligious Dialogue.* Maryknoll, N.Y.: Orbis, 1991.

Kellner, Menachem, ed. *Contemporary Jewish Ethics*. New York: Hebrew Publishing, 1978.

Kelsay, John. *Islam and War*. Westminster: John Knox, 1993.

Kelsay, John, and Sumner Twiss, eds. *Religion and Human Rights*. New York: Project on Religion and Human Rights, 1994.

Khadduri, Majid. *War and Peace in the Law of Islam*. Baltimore: Johns Hopkins Press, 1955.

Kimelman, Reuven. "Non-Violence in the Talmud." *Judaism* 17 (1968): 316–34.

———. "War." In *Frontiers of Jewish Thought*, edited by Steven Katz. Washington, D.C. B'nai B'rith Books, 1992.

Kishtainy, Khalid. "Violent and Nonviolent Struggle in Arab History." In *Arab Nonviolent Political Struggle in the Middle East*, edited by R. Crow, P. Grant, and S. Ibrahim. Boulder and London: Lynne Rienner, 1990.

Klenicki, Leon. "The New Catholic Catechism and the Jews." In *Service International De Documentation Judéo-Chrétienne* 27, no. 2 (1994).

Kohn, Alfie. *The Brighter Side of Human Nature*. New York: Basic, 1990.

Kook, Abraham Isaac. *Abraham Isaac Kook: The Lights of Penitence, the Moral Principles, Lights of Holiness, Essays, Letters and Poems*. Compiled and translated by Ben Zion Bokser. New York: Paulist Press, 1978.

Kraemer, David. *The Mind of the Talmud*. New York and Oxford: Oxford University Press, 1990.

Kraft, Kenneth, ed. *Inner Peace, World Peace: Essays on Buddhism*. Albany: State University of New York Press, 1992.

Kraybill, Ron. "Peacebuilders in Zimbabwe." Ph.D. diss., Univ. of Cape Town, 1996.

Kriesberg, Louis, Terrell A. Northrop, and Stuart J. Thorson, eds. *Intractable Conflicts and Their Transformation*. Syracuse, N.Y.: Syracuse University Press, 1989.

———. *Constructive Conflicts*. Lanham, Md.: Rowman & Littlefield, 1998.

Lamm, Maurice. *The Jewish Way in Death and Mourning*. New York: Jonathon David, 1969.

Lao-tzu. *The Tao of the Tao Te Ching: A Translation and Commentary*. Edited and translated by Michael LaFargue. Albany: State University of New York Press, 1992.

Lederach, John Paul. "Pacifism in Contemporary Conflict: A Christian Perspective." Paper commissioned by the U.S. Institute of Peace, Washington, D.C. (July 20, 1993).

———. *Building Peace: Sustainable Reconciliation in Divided Societies*. Tokyo: United Nations University, 1994.

———. *Preparing for Peace: Conflict Transformation across Cultures*. Syracuse, N.Y.: Syracuse University Press, 1995.

Lederach, Paul M. *The Third Way*. Scottdale, Pa.: Herald, 1980.

Levinas, Emmanuel. *Ethics and Infinity*. Translated by Richard A. Cohen. Pittsburgh, Pa.: Duquesne University Press, 1985.

———. *Time and the Other*. Translated by Richard A. Cohen. Pittsburgh, Pa.: Duquesne University Press, 1987.

Little, David. *Ukraine: The Legacy of Intolerance*. Washington, D.C.: U.S. Institute of Peace, 1991.

———. *Sri Lanka: The Invention of Enmity*. Washington, D.C.: U.S. Institute of Peace, 1994.

Luz, Ehud. "The Moral Price of Sovereignty: The Dispute about the Use of Military Power within Zionism." *Modern Judaism* 7 (Fall 1987): 51–98.

Luzzatto, Moshe Hayyim. *Sefer Mesilat Yesharim*. n.d. Reprint. Jerusalem and New York: Feldheim, 1969.

Luzzatto, Samuel David. *Ha-Mishtadel.* Vienna: I. I. Busch, 1847.
————. *Il Giudaismo Illustrato.* Padua: A. Bianci, 1848.
————. *Lezioni di teologia morale israelitica.* Padua: A. Bianci, 1862.
————. *Il Pentateuco.* Padova: Sacchetto, 1874.
————. *Autobiografia di S. D. Luzzatto.* Padua: Crescini, 1878.
————. *Ketavim.* Edited and translated by M. E. Artom. Jerusalem: Bialik Institute, 1976.
Mack, John. "The Enemy System." In *The Psychodynamics of International Relationships,* vol. 1, edited by Vamik Volkan, Demetrios Julius, and Joseph J. Montville. Lexington, Mass.: Lexington Books, 1990.
Magasa, Laurenti. *African Religion: The Moral Traditions of Abundant Life.* Maryknoll, N.Y.: Orbis, 1997.
Manuel, Frank. *Utopian Thought in the Western World.* Oxford: Blackwell, 1979.
Marty, Martin, and F. Scott Appleby, eds. *Fundamentalisms and the State: Remaking Polities, Economies, Militance.* Chicago: University of Chicago Press, 1993.
————, eds. *Accounting for Fundamentalisms.* Chicago: University of Chicago Press, 1994.
Mayer, Peter, ed. *The Pacifist Conscience.* New York: Holt, Rinehart and Winston, 1966.
McKinney, Bruce. "A Critical Analysis of Transformative Mediation." *Peace Research* 29, no. 1 (Feb. 1997): 41–52.
Meklenburg, Yaacov Tzvi. *Ha-Ketav v'ha-Kabbalah.* Leipzig: 1839.
Mendelssohn, Moses. *Jerusalem, or, Religious Power and Judaism.* Translated by Allan Arkush. Hanover: Brandeis University Press, 1983.
Merton, Thomas. "The Climate of Mercy." In his *Love and Living,* edited by Naomi Stone and Patrick Hart. San Diego: Harcourt Brace Jovanovich, 1979.
————. *The Nonviolent Alternative.* New York: Farrar, Straus, Giroux, 1980.
Meyer, Michael. *Response to Modernity.* Detroit: Wayne State University Press, 1995.
Miller, Alice. *For Your Own Good: Hidden Cruelty in Child-Rearing and the Roots of Violence.* New York: Farrar, Straus, Giroux, 1983.
Mitchell, C. R. *The Structure of International Conflict.* New York: St. Martin's, 1981.
————. *Handbook of Conflict Resolution: The Analytical Problem Solving Approach.* New York: Pinter, 1996.
Montville, Joseph. "Psychology, War, and Integrity," *Psychologist/Psychoanalyst* 11, special supp. (Summer 1991): 11–17.
————. "The Healing Function in Political Conflict Resolution." In *Conflict Resolution Theory and Practice,* edited by Dennis Sandole and Hugo van der Merwe. Manchester, N.Y.: Manchester University Press, 1993.
————. "Reconciliation in America." *American Civilization* (May–June 1995): 14ff.
Moses, Rafael. "The Leader and the Led: A Dyadic Relationship." In *The Psychodynamics of International Relationships,* vol. 1, edited by Vamik Volkan, Demetrios Julius, and Joseph Montville. Lexington, Mass.: Lexington Books, 1990.
————. "Self, Self-view, and Identity." In *The Psychodynamics of International Relationships,* vol. 1, edited by Vamik Volkan, Demetrios Julius, and Joseph Montville. Lexington Mass.: Lexington Books, 1990.
Nader, Laura. "Harmony Models and the Construction of Law." In *Conflict Resolution: Cross-Cultural Perspectives,* edited by Kevin Avruch, Peter Black, and Joseph Scimecca. Westport, Conn.: Greenwood, 1991.
Nardin, Terry, ed. *The Ethics of War and Peace.* Princeton, N.J.: Princeton University Press, 1996.
Nhat Hanh, Thich. *Being Peace.* Berkeley, Calif.: Parallax, 1987.
Novak, David. *Law and Theology in Judaism.* New York: Ktav, 1974.

———. *Jewish-Christian Dialogue: A Jewish Justification*. New York: Oxford University Press, 1989.

———. "Jews and Catholics: Beyond Apologies." *First Things* 89 (Jan. 1999): 20–25.

Nyamiti, C. *The Scope of African Theology*. Kampala: Gaba, 1973.

Oliner, Pearl, et al., eds. *Embracing the Other: Philosophical, Psychological and Historical Perspectives on Altruism*. New York: New York University Press, 1992.

Otto, Rudolf. *The Idea of the Holy*. London: Oxford University Press, 1923.

Oz Ve-Shalom. English Bulletin Series. Jerusalem, Israel. Nos. 1–8 (1982–1999).

Pagels, Elaine. *The Gnostic Gospels*. New York: Vintage, 1981.

Paige, Glenn et al., eds. *Islam and Nonviolence*. Honolulu: Center for Global Nonviolence Planning Project, Matsunaga Institute for Peace, University of Hawaii, 1993.

Pallière, Aimé. *Le Sanctuaire inconnu; ma "conversion" au Judaisme*. Paris: Rieder, 1926.

———. *The Unknown Sanctuary: A Pilgrimage from Rome to Israel*, translated by Louise Wise. New York: Bloch, 1928.

Palmer, Richard. *Hermeneutics: Interpretation Theory in Schleiermacher, Dilthey, Heidegger, and Gadamer*. Evanston, Ill.: Northwestern University Press, 1969.

Peck, M. Scott. *The Different Drum: Community Making and Peace*. New York: Simon and Schuster, 1987.

Polner, Murray, and Naomi Goodman, eds. *The Challenge of Shalom*. Philadelphia: New Society, 1994.

Prunier, Gerard. *Rwanda Crisis: History of a Genocide*. New York: Columbia University Press, 1995.

Pyarelal. *A Pilgrimage of Peace: Gandhi and the Frontier, Gandhi among N.W.F. Pathans*. Ahmedabad, India: Navajivan, 1950.

Quiring, Ken. "Anti-Semitism and North American Mennonites in the Twentieth Century." Student essay (1998) available in the libraries of Canadian Mennonite Bible College and Associated Mennonite Biblical Seminary.

Rabten, Geshe, and Geshe Dhargyey. *Advice from a Spiritual Friend: Buddhist Thought Transformation*. Translated by Brian Beresford. London: Wisdom, 1984.

Raphael, D. Daiches. *The Moral Sense*. London: Oxford University Press, 1947.

Ravitsky, Avi. "Peace." In *Contemporary Jewish Religious Thought*, edited by Arthur A. Cohen and Paul Mendes-Flohr. New York: Free Press, 1988.

Redekop, John. "The Roots of Nazi Support among Mennonites, 1930–1939." *Journal of Mennonite Studies* 14 (1996): 81–95.

Rorty, Richard. "Method, Social Science and Social Hope." In *The Postmodern Turn*, edited by Steven Seidman. Cambridge: Cambridge University Press, 1994.

Ross, Marc. *The Culture of Conflict*. New Haven: Yale University Press, 1993.

Rothman, Jay. *Resolving Identity-Based Conflict in Nations, Organizations, and Communities*. San Francisco: Jossey-Bass, 1997.

Rubenstein, Richard E. *Alchemists of Revolution: Terrorism in the Modern World*. New York: Basic, 1987.

———. "Unanticipated Conflict and the Crisis of Social Theory." In *Conflict: Readings in Management and Resolution*, edited by John Burton and Frank Dukes. New York: St. Martin's, 1990.

———. "The Analyzing and Resolving of Class Conflict." In *Conflict Resolution Theory and Practice*, edited by Dennis Sandole and Hugo van der Merwe. Manchester, N.Y.: Manchester University Press, 1993.

Sachedina, Abdulaziz A. "The Development of *Jihad* in Islamic Revelation and History." In *Cross, Crescent and Sword: The Justification and Limitation of War in*

Western and Islamic Tradition, edited by James Turner Johnson and John Kelsay. New York: Greenwood, 1990.

————. "Is There a Tradition of Pacifism and Nonviolence in Islam?" Paper presented at the U.S. Institute of Peace workshop on Religious Perspectives on Pacifism and Nonviolence in Washington, D.C., July 28, 1993.

Sampson, Cynthia. "Religion and Peacebuilding." In *Peacemaking in International Conflict*, edited by I. William Zartman and Lewis Rasmussen. Washington, D.C.: U.S. Institute of Peace, 1997.

Sampson, Cynthia, and John Paul Lederach, eds. *From the Ground Up: Mennonite Contributions to International Peacebuilding*. New York: Oxford University Press, 2000.

Sandole, Dennis. "Paradigms, Theories and Metaphors in Conflict and Conflict Resolution." In *Conflict Resolution Theory and Practice*, edited by Dennis Sandole and Hugo van der Merwe. Manchester, N.Y.: Manchester University Press, 1993.

Sandole, Dennis, and Hugo van der Merwe, eds. *Conflict Resolution Theory and Practice*. Manchester, N.Y.: Manchester University Press, 1993.

Satha-Anand, Chaiwat. "The Nonviolent Crescent: Eight Theses on Muslim Nonviolent Action." In *Arab Nonviolent Political Struggle in the Middle East*, edited by Ralph Crow, Philip Grant, and Ibrahim E. Saad. Boulder and London: Lynne Rienner, 1990.

Satha-Anand, Chaiwat, Glenn D. Paige, and Sarah Gilliat, eds. *Islam and Nonviolence*. Honolulu, Hawaii: University of Hawaii and Spark M. Matsunaga Institute for Peace, 1993.

Schechter, S., ed. *The Fathers According to Rabbi Nathan*. Vienna: Ch. D. Lippe, 1887.

Scholem, Gershom. *Major Trends in Jewish Mysticism*. 1941. Reprint. New York: Schocken, 1977.

Schrag, James F. "The Jewish 'Protocols': An Assessment of Their Origins, Content, and Influence on American Mennonites." Student essay (1971) available from the Associated Mennonite Biblical Seminary library.

Schwarzschild, Steven. "Shalom." In *The Challenge of Shalom*, edited by Murray Polner and Naomi Goodman. Philadelphia: New Society, 1994.

Schweid, Eliezer. "Land of Israel." In *Contemporary Jewish Religious Thought*, edited by Arthur A. Cohen and Paul Mendes-Flohr. New York: Free Press, 1988.

Sefer Orhot Tsaddikim. Prague: 1581. Reprint. Jerusalem: Eshkol, n.d.

Sells, Michael. *The Bridge Betrayed: Religion and Genocide in Bosnia*. Berkeley: University of California Press, 1998.

Seltzer, Robert M. *Jewish People, Jewish Thought*. New York: Macmillan, 1980.

Shapiro, David S. "The Jewish Attitude towards Peace and War." In *Studies in Jewish Thought*, vol. 1, edited by David S. Shapiro. New York: Yeshiva University Press, 1975.

————. "The Doctrine of the Image of God and *Imitatio Dei*." In *Contemporary Jewish Ethics*, edited by Menachem Kellner. New York: Hebrew Publishing, 1978.

Sharoni, Simona. *Gender and the Israeli-Palestinian Conflict: The Politics of Women's Resistance*. Syracuse, N.Y.: Syracuse University Press, 1995.

Silberstein, Laurence J., ed. *Jewish Fundamentalism in Comparative Perspective: Religion, Ideology and the Crisis of Modernity*. New York: New York University Press, 1993.

————, ed. *The Other in Jewish Thought and History*. New York: New York University Press, 1994.

Simon, Ernst. "The Neighbor (*re'a*) Whom We Shall Love." In *Modern Jewish Ethics*, edited by Marvin Fox. Columbus, Ohio: Ohio State University Press, 1975.

Smock, David, ed. *Religious Perspectives on War: Christian, Muslim, and Jewish Attitudes to Force after the Gulf War*. Washington, D.C.: U.S. Institute of Peace, 1992.

Soloveitchik, Haym. "Migration, Acculturation, and the New Role of Texts in the Haredi World." In *Accounting for Fundamentalisms*, edited by Martin Marty and F. Scott Appleby. Chicago: University of Chicago Press, 1994.

————. "Rupture and Reconstruction: The Transformation of Contemporary Orthodoxy." *Tradition* 28, no. 4 (1994): 64–106.

Soloway, Arnold, and Edwin Weiss. *Truth and Peace in the Middle East: A Critical Analysis of the Quaker Report*. New York: Friendly House, 1971.

"Soul Wars: The Problem of Proselytism in Russia." *Emory International Law Review* 12, no. 1 (Winter 1998).

Sperber, Daniel, ed. *Masekhet Derekh Eretz*. Jerusalem: Tzur-Ot, 1979.

Sprinzak, Ehud. *Brother against Brother: Violence and Extremism in Israeli Politics from Altalena to the Rabin Assassination*. New York: Free Press. 1999.

Staub, Ervin. *The Roots of Evil: The Origins of Evil and Other Group Violence*. Cambridge: Cambridge University Press, 1989.

Stecker, Robert. "Moral Sense Theory." Ph.D. diss., M.I.T., 1975.

Stewart, M. A. *Studies in the Philosophy of the Scottish Enlightenment*. Oxford: Clarendon, 1990–1991.

Stoll, David. " 'Jesus Is Lord of Guatemala': Evangelical Reform in a Death Squad State." In *Accounting for Fundamentalisms*, edited by Martin Marty and F. Scott Appleby. Chicago: University of Chicago Press, 1994.

Stoner, John. *Interventions of Truth: Christian Peacemaker Teams*. Chicago: Christian Peacemaker Teams, 1993.

Tambiah, Stanley. *Buddhism Betrayed? Religion, Politics, and Violence in Sri Lanka*. Chicago: University of Chicago Press, 1992.

Thangaraj, M. Thomas. *The Common Task: A Theology of Mission*. Nashville: Abingdon, 1998.

Thompson, Henry O. *World Religions in War and Peace*. Jefferson, N.C.: McFarland, 1988.

Thompson, W. Scott, et al., eds. *Approaches to Peace: An Intellectual Map*. Washington, D.C.: U.S. Institute of Peace, 1992.

Toews, James. *Czars, Soviets and Mennonites*. Newton, Kans.: Faith and Life Press, 1982.

Trachtenberg, Joshua. *The Devil and the Jews: The Medieval Conception of the Jew and Its Relation to Modern Anti-Semitism*. Philadelphia: Jewish Publication Society, 1993.

Tsong-kha-pa. *Lam rim chen mo*. In *Ethics of Tibet*, translated by Alex Wayman. Albany: State University of New York Press, 1991.

Urbach, Ephraim. "Jewish Doctrines and Practices in Halakhic and Aggadic Literature." In *Violence and Defense in Jewish Experience*, edited by Salo Baron, George Wise, and Lenn Goodman. Philadelphia: Jewish Publication Society of America, 1977.

————. *The Sages*. Translated by I. Abrahams. Cambridge, Mass.: Harvard University Press, 1987.

Urry, James. *None but Saints: The Transformation of Mennonite Life in Russia, 1789–1889*. Winnipeg, Manitoba: Christian Press, 1978.

Vendley, William. "Religious Differences and Shared Care: The Need for Primary and Secondary Language." *Church and Society* (Sept.–Oct. 1992): 16–29.

Vendley, William, and David Little. "Implications for Communities: Buddhism, Islam, Hinduism, and Christianity." In *Religion: The Missing Dimension of Statecraft*, edited by Douglas Johnston and Cynthia Sampson. New York: Oxford University Press, 1994.

Volkan, Vamik. "The Need to Have Enemies and Allies: A Developmental Approach." *Political Psychology* 6, no. 2 (1985): 219–47.

——. "An Overview of Psychological Concepts Pertinent to Interethnic and/or International Relationships." In *The Psychodynamics of International Relationships*, vol. 1, edited by Varmik Volkan, Demetrios Julius, and Joseph Montville. Lexington, Mass.: Lexington Books, 1990.

——. *The Need to Have Enemies and Allies*. Northvale, N.J.: J. Aronson, 1994.

——. *Bloodlines: From Ethnic Pride to Ethnic Terrorism*. New York: Farrar, Straus, Giroux, 1997.

Volkan, Vamik, Demetrios Julius, and Joseph Montville, eds. *The Psychodynamics of International Relationships*, vol. 2. Lexington, Mass.: Lexington Books, 1991.

Von Rad, Gerhard. *Holy War in Ancient Israel*. 1958. Reprint. Grand Rapids, Mich.: William B. Eerdmans, 1991.

Walli, Koshelya. *The Conception of Ahimsa in Indian Thought according to Sanskrit Sources*. Varanasi, India: Bharata Manisha, 1974.

Walzer, Michael. *Just and Unjust Wars*. New York: Basic, 1977.

Wedge, Bryant. "Psychology of the Self in Social Conflict." In *International Conflict Resolution: Theory and Practice*, edited by Edward Azar and John Burton. Boulder, Colo.: Lynne Rienner, 1986.

Wolfe, Alvin W., and Honggang Yang, eds. *Anthropological Contributions to Conflict Resolution*. Athens: University of Georgia Press, 1996.

Yang-Ming, Wang. "Inquiry on the Great Learning." In *A Source Book in Chinese Philosophy*, edited by Wing-Tsit Chan. Princeton, N.J.: Princeton University Press, 1963.

Yoder, John. *The Politics of Jesus*. Grand Rapids, Mich.: William B. Eerdmans, 1972.

——. *Nevertheless: Varieties of Religious Pacifism*. Scottdale, Pa.: Herald, 1992.

Zenner, Walter. *Minorities in the Middle*. Albany: State University of New York Press, 1991.

Zertal, Idith. *From Catastrophe to Power: The Holocaust and Israel, 1944–1948*. Berkeley, University of California Press, 1998.

Zunz, Leopold. *Die vierundzwanzig Bücher der Heiligen Schrift*. Basel, Germany: Goldschmidt Verlag, 1980.

Index

Aaron as a model peacemaker, 80, 136, 137, 182–186

Abimelekh and Biblical inter-faith relations, 93

Abortion
and the conflict over the sanctity of life, 21
as obligatory when the mother is threatened, 71, 254n23
and terrorism, 213

Abraham ben David of Posquières, 188

Abraham, and a covenant of justice, 16, 257n50
in a constructive relationship with idolaters, 93, 94, 102
identity of, 229
as a path of reconciliation for the monotheisms, 255n30

Abrahamic faiths, 9, 11, 57, 229

Abu-Nimer, Mohammed, 250n22

abuse and conflict generation
and *haredi* memories, 122
mollified by opportunities to heal, 140, 269n18
mollified by prosocial forms of othering, 204
and terrorism, 59
as a trait of abused groups, 6
undermined by specially designed moral constructs, 277n75

academics and conflict resolution, 266

'Adi, Yahya ibn, 83

Africa, 13, 83, 123, 205, 236
and biblically based rationalizations of conquest, 259n29
and Christian peacemakers, 261n52
and Israeli humanitarian intervention, 123
and the relationship of drama and violence, 263n36
and the use of symbol in reconciliation, 190

African religions, 50
and confrontation with the Devil, 220, 221, 244n39. *See also* devil, the

Afrikaaners, 215
and their religion, 88, 259n18

agape, 7

agnosticism, 124

ahikha (your brother), 95

ahimsa (nonviolence), 229, 283n28

Ahmadi sect of Islam, 247n56

aid agencies and conflict, 272n30, 279n93

aid to victims as conflict resolution, 136

Akiva, Rabbi, 277n75

al-'adl (justice), 83

Algeria, 53

al-haqq (truth and right), 83

Ali, 282

al-iqsat (equity), 83

Allah, 37

altruism and the peacemaker, 4, 18, 55, 268n12

Amalekites as the embodiment of evil, 69, 119, 262n3

American Civil War, the, 58, 215

Amish, the, 143, 144, 269n14

Amos, 93

Anabaptist tradition, 142, 144, 243n24, 268n8

angelology, 100, 229

anomie, 56

anti-Semitism
and changes in the Catholic Catechism, 61
directed by Jews at other Jews, 176
healing from through mourning rituals, 170, 171
and Israeli perceptions of progressive Christians, 160
and its impact on Orthodox Jewish hermeneutics, 89
and Jewish paths of reconciliation 210
and Mennonites, 141
as a progenitor of Jewish patterns of self-abuse, 121–122
and the psycho-cultural impulse of scapegoating, 283n35
and its psychological impact on Jews and Jewish culture, 116–118, 125, 170
and the radicalization of the American Christian Right, 25

Breinigsville, PA USA
17 December 2009
229343BV00001B/6/A